PERSUASION AND HEALING

Revised Edition

PERSUASION AND HEALING

A Comparative Study of Psychotherapy

Jerome D. Frank

The Johns Hopkins University Press
Baltimore and London

The Johns Hopkins University Press, Baltimore, Maryland 21218
The Johns Hopkins University Press Ltd., London

Library of Congress Catalog Card Number 72-4015
ISBN 0-8018-1443-X

Originally published, 1961
Second printing, 1963
Revised edition, 1973

Library of Congress Cataloging in Publication data will be found on the last
printed page of this book.

To the memory of
Lester H. Gliedman and
Earl H. Nash,
friends and colleagues

CONTENTS

FOREWORD

There are many persons, disturbed by unanswerable doubts, who need the reassuring hand of a wise and trusted guide. Others, jumping from the frying pan of doubt into the fire of urgent, but poorly chosen action, need both a helping hand and a pointing finger to see the situation as it is and as it may be remedied. For all persons, coping with life situations is inherently a co-operating enterprise, in which everyone, at some time or other, needs help and guidance from another.

For man is a domestic creature, with infinite social and cultural involvements. He is continually and crucially influencing others and being influenced by others. Without the others he would be next to nothing; with them he has created the family, civilization, culture, morals, law, industry, religion, war—in short, heaven and hell. There is therefore nothing more important for man to understand and to master than the processes of person-to-person influence. Yet, in this influence business, knowledge lags behind action; we perform better than we understand.

We who are physicians and who work as psychiatrists have reason to be strongly aware of the disparity between our fairly good results and our very poor understanding. We are so much aided by the healing power of nature and by the numerous self-righting and resocializing propensities with which biology and culture have endowed our patients, that we may perhaps take undue credit when our patients do well.

Ambroise Paré is credited with the comment: "Je le pansay; Dieu le guarit" ("I dress him; God cures him"). We care for the patient; there is much evidence that good care provides a favorable influence; we would like very much to know more surely how this influence works, and how to use it better through better understanding.

Jerome Frank has devoted himself, shrewdly, to the task of observing and understanding psychotherapy. He has devised methods of research in this field that have served as models to a new generation of investigators. He has shown wisdom in his conceptualization of goals and measures of therapy. And he has kept within his range of vision much more than the minutiae of method or of doctrine.

In the constructing of this book, Dr. Frank devotes particularly searching attention to what is common to many ways of exerting psychotherapeutic influence. In the reading of it, we can be thankful for the wide range of his knowledge, and for the charm and forcefulness of his style, which carries the reader, tirelessly, on far journeys and into strange places, but never into verbalistic jungles.

The emphasis in this book falls heavily upon what is common to many therapeutic methods. Such emphasis invites a risk—the risk that, in tracking down a least common denominator, discernible in all psychotherapy, even the poorest, one may be missing those differences that may characterize psychotherapy at its best. The thoughtful reader will not condemn Dr. Frank for taking this risk. It is a good rule to ask questions serially, not all at once; and a reasonable priority of goals calls for the identification of common factors as a step toward the identification of significant differences.

Before undertaking, too quickly, to expound hypotheses as to what makes a difference in psychotherapy, it is wise to find out what differences, if any, occur. Dr. Frank's methods of evaluation, and other methods developed in the Henry Phipps Psychiatric Clinic of The John Hopkins Hospital, are crucially important for determining observable differences, and thereby establishing a sound foundation for judging what makes a difference.

In his work, Dr. Frank has been effectively reducing the fogs of misunderstanding and ignorance that shroud the art of psychotherapy; in this book, he elucidates the general character of professional psychotherapeutic processes and examines more broadly the nature of person-to-person influence as used for promoting health.

JOHN C. WHITEHORN
September, 1960

PREFACE TO THE REVISED EDITION

The modest but continuing demand for this book has afforded a welcome opportunity to consider the implications of developments in the field of psychotherapy since the appearance of the first edition, especially those in the areas of psychological research pertinent to psychotherapy, behavior therapy, and the newer group approaches.

As one who has devoted his professional life to the practice and study of psychotherapy, I have been disturbed to discover that many view this book as nihilistic—as promulgating the view that psychotherapy is ineffective—so it may be well to state my position as succinctly as possible. That persons can powerfully influence and help one another by strictly psychological means is obvious. The question this book attempts to explore is not whether psychotherapy works—this goes without saying—but what are the ingredients that account for the effectiveness of its many different forms.

Each school of psychotherapy is characterized by a conceptual scheme and procedure that distinguish it from others. Since the trained psychotherapist's claim to status and recognition depends on his mastery of a special theory and technique, all therapists naturally stress these features of their work. The presentation of evidence that much of the effectiveness of psychotherapy depends on attributes possessed by all its forms is a threat to the psychological security of those who have been trained in specific approaches; this may partly account for the widespread misunderstanding of the thesis of this book. To say that much of the healing and persuasive power of psychotherapy depends on features shared by all schools, however, is by no means to assert that psychotherapy is ineffective.

The hypothesis of this book is that features common to all types of psychotherapy combat a major source of the distress and disability of persons who seek psychotherapeutic help. The source of this distress may be termed demoralization—a sense of failure or of powerlessness to affect oneself and one's environment. Psychotherapies may combat the patient's demoralization not only by alleviating his specific symptoms of subjective distress and disordered behavior but also, and more importantly, by employing measures to restore his self-confidence and to help him to find more effective ways of mastering his problems. Features that combat demoralization and facilitate helpful changes in attitude and behavior are shared not only by all forms of secular psychotherapy and religious healing in the West, but also by healing methods of other cultures.

These shared attributes include certain features of the therapeutic relationship and the setting, and a particular conceptual framework linked to certain activities. In conjunction, these features intrinsic to all psychotherapies help the patient to clarify his symptoms and problems, inspire his hopes, provide him with experiences of success or mastery, and stir him emotionally. Although the achievement of these aims requires a conceptual framework and certain activities linked to it, the specific content of these may be largely irrelevant.

This view does not exclude the possibility that for some forms of distress or disturbed behavior or with certain types of patients, one technique may indeed have more powerful healing effects than another. Except for relatively rare conditions such as circumscribed phobias, however, no compelling evidence for the superiority of one method has yet been produced. Moreover, when therapies have a differential effect, it may depend on the differential ability of the technique to mobilize certain features common to all. For example, structured behavior therapies may more readily engender success experiences than unstructured interview ther-

[e. g. success experiences]

apies in certain patients, while for others, unstructured therapies may be more effective.

The thesis of this book is that it is worthwhile to explore features shared by all psychotherapies, because evaluation of the differential effectiveness of different techniques, if any, will depend to a large extent on one's ability to determine the effects of those features common to all.

With respect to terminology, in recognition of the fact that most psychotherapy is carried out by nonmedical persons, I have used the term "psychotherapist" or "therapist" to refer to all psychological healers and reserved "psychiatrist" for the medically trained, when their training is relevant. For the recipient of psychotherapy, I have used the term "sufferer" or "patient," since everyone who undergoes therapy is experiencing some sort of distress or disability and I wish to emphasize that psychotherapy is a healing art.

It is a pleasure to acknowledge the valuable critique of the manuscript made by my colleague, Dr. Shashi Pande. His transcultural insights illuminated many issues. Members of the Johns Hopkins Psychotherapy Research Unit, Drs. Rudolf Hoehn-Saric, Stanley D. Imber, Bernard Liberman, Anthony R. Stone, and Mr. Frederick Ribich, undertook the chore of reading parts or all of the manuscript, and it has benefited greatly from their comments and suggestions. During the past decade the Unit suffered a second grievous loss through the death of Dr. Earl Nash.

The assistance of my secretary, Miss Frances Partlow, has again been invaluable, and the readability of the text owes much to the copy-editing of my daughter, Julia. Both have my gratitude.

JEROME D. FRANK
May, 1972

PREFACE TO THE
FIRST EDITION

The American psychotherapeutic scene is characterized by a multitude of conflicting theories and methods. Despite their apparent diversity, however, all are attempts to heal through persuasion. That is, they try to induce changes in patients' attitudes and behavior which, it is believed, will diminish their suffering. As such they share features not only with each other but with many other forms of persuasion and healing. This book attempts to identify and describe these common features by exploring healing in primitive societies, miracle cures, religious revivalism, Communist thought reform, the so-called placebo effect in medical practice, and experimental studies of persuasion. Some types of contemporary psychotherapy are then considered from the perspective thus gained. The choice of these is not intended to be exhaustive but to reflect my own interests. To those readers who find that their favorite form of psychotherapy has been passed over, I can only offer apologies. I believe, however, that the features shared by the methods that are described are also important in those that have been neglected.

The writing of this book was made possible by a fellowship at the center for Advanced Study in the Behavioral Sciences, for 1958–59. I am deeply grateful to Ralph Tyler, the Director of the Center, and to its staff, for giving me this opportunity and affording ideal conditions for its fulfillment. It is impossible to acknowledge all the informal help received from other Fellows via casual conversations over the coffee cups, but I wish to express special gratitude for the comments and criticisms of Michael Argyle and Cora Dubois, who struggled through all of the preliminary draft, and Kaspar Naegele and Melford Spiro, who read parts of it. I am grateful also to Otto Kernberg, who gave the manuscript a careful reading and made many helpful suggestions, and to my research colleagues at The Johns Hopkins Hospital, Stanley Imber, Earl Nash, and Anthony Stone, who contributed to all stages of this enterprise from its first stirrings to the finished product. My thinking has been greatly influenced by the late Lester H. Gliedman, whose dynamic personality and creative intelligence are greatly missed.

My greatest debt is to John Whitehorn for his guidance and encouragement over many years. His wisdom and insight have been a constant source of illumination, and much of this book reflects his thinking, however imperfectly.

The research studies reported in Chapters 6 and 9 have been supported in part by grants from the Ford Foundation and the National Institute of Mental Health, which are herewith gratefully acknowledged.

These acknowledgements would be incomplete without an expression of gratitude to Miss Frances Partlow for her invaluable help with all technical aspects of the manuscript. My wife, Elizabeth K. Frank, deserves a special word of appreciation for translating the passages from Lévi-Strauss, tidying up my style, and supplying patient, loving support during the prolonged birth pangs of this volume.

JEROME D. FRANK
September, 1960

PERSUASION AND HEALING

PSYCHOTHERAPY IN AMERICA TODAY

I

They all crowded round, panting, and asking, "But who has won?"
This question the Dodo could not answer without a great deal
of thought. . . .
At last the Dodo said
"*Everybody* has won, and *all* must have prizes."

Lewis Carroll, *Alice's Adventures in Wonderland*

Throughout his life every person is influenced by the
behavior of others toward him. His relationships with
his fellows shape his own behavior, attitudes, values,
self-image, and world view and also affect his sense of
well-being. It is customary to classify different forms of
personal influence in accordance with their settings and
the role of the influencing figure. Thus we say that a
person is brought up by his parents in the family, educated by his teachers in school, and led by his officers in
battle.

Attempts to combat suffering and disability are usually labeled treatment, and every society trains some of
its members to apply this form of influence. Treatment
always involves a personal relationship between healer
and sufferer. Certain types of therapy rely primarily on
the healer's ability to mobilize healing forces in the sufferer by psychological means. These forms of treatment
may be generically termed psychotherapy.

Although psychotherapeutic methods have existed
since time immemorial and a vast amount of accumu-

1

lated experience supports a belief in their value, some of the most elementary questions about them remain unanswered. Research has not yet yielded sufficient information to permit description of the different methods in uniform terms, specification of the conditions for which different methods are most suitable, or comparison of their results. These difficulties spring largely from a persisting lack of precise knowledge concerning the nature of psychotherapeutic principles.

Despite decades of effort, it has been impossible to show convincingly that one therapeutic method is more effective than any other for the majority of psychological illnesses. This suggests that any specific healing effects of different methods would be overshadowed by therapeutically potent ingredients shared by all. The purpose of this book is to identify and clarify the features common to various forms of psychotherapy, in other cultures as well as in our own, on the assumption that their appearance in so many different guises is persuasive evidence for their therapeutic power. Thus it seems appropriate to begin this undertaking with a definition of psychotherapy, followed by a brief consideration of its historical roots and its place in America today, and of the problems involved in the evaluation of the relative efficacy of its different forms.

WHAT IS PSYCHOTHERAPY?

Since practically all forms of personal influence may affect a person's sense of well-being, the definition of psychotherapy must of necessity be somewhat arbitrary. We shall consider as psychotherapy only those types of influence characterized by:

1. a trained, socially sanctioned healer, whose healing powers are accepted by the sufferer and by his social group or an important segment of it

2. a sufferer who seeks relief from the healer

3. a circumscribed, more or less structured series of contacts between the healer and the sufferer, through which the healer, often with the aid of a group, tries to produce certain changes in the sufferer's emotional state, attitudes, and behavior. All concerned believe these changes will help him. Although physical and

chemical adjuncts may be used, the healing influence is primarily exercised by words, acts, and rituals in which sufferer, healer, and—if there is one—group, participate jointly.

These three features are common not only to all forms of psychotherapy as the term is generally used, but also to methods of primitive healing, religious conversion, and even so-called brainwashing, all of which involve systematic, time-limited contacts between a person in distress and someone who tries to reduce the distress by producing changes in the sufferer's feelings, attitudes, and behavior. By this definition, the administration of an inert medicine by a doctor to a patient is also a form of psychotherapy, since its effectiveness depends on its symbolization of the physician's healing function, which produces favorable changes in the patient's feelings and attitudes. Our search for the active ingredients of psychotherapy, then, will require exploration of these activities, as well as a consideration of experimental studies of the transmission of influence.

HISTORICAL ROOTS OF PSYCHOTHERAPY

Since at least part of the efficacy of psychotherapeutic methods lies in the shared belief of the participants that these methods will work, the predominant method would be expected to differ in different societies and in different historical epochs. This is, in fact, the case. Modern psychotherapies are rooted in two historical traditions of healing—the religio-magical and the naturalistic, or scientific. The former, originating before recorded history, regards certain forms of suffering or of alienation from one's fellows as caused by some sort of supernatural or magical intervention, such as loss of one's soul, possession by an evil spirit, or a sorcerer's curse. Treatment consists in suitable rites conducted by a healer who combines the roles of priest and physician. These rites typically require the active participation of the sufferer and members of his family or social group and are highly charged emotionally. If successful, they undo the supernaturally or magically caused damage, thereby restoring the victim's health and reestablishing or strengthening his ties with his group. As we shall see, the religio-magical tradition is still influential, even in secularized Western society, and many of its principles have been incorporated into naturalistic forms of psychotherapy.

The earliest surviving account of naturalistic principles dates from writings of the fifth century B.C. attributed to the Greek physician Hippocrates. He viewed mental illness, like all other forms of illness, as a phenomenon that could be studied and treated scientifically. Though largely eclipsed in the Middle Ages, this view has come into increasing prominence since the early nineteenth century and is now the dominant one in the Western world.

Like the religio-magical view, the naturalistic one originally did not clearly distinguish mental illness from other forms of illness, and treatment for both was essentially similar. The emergence of psychotherapy as a distinctive form of healing probably began with the dramatic demonstration by Franz Anton Mesmer, in the late eighteenth century, that he could cause the symptoms of certain patients to disappear by putting them into a trance. Though his particular theories and methods were soon discredited, mesmerism was the precursor of hypnotism, which rapidly became recognized as a method of psychotherapy. Through the use of hypnosis, Sigmund Freud and Joseph Breuer discovered, toward the end of the nineteenth century, that many of their patients' symptoms seemed to be symbolic attempts to express and resolve chronic conflicts that had their roots in upsetting experiences of early life. This led Freud to develop a form of treatment based on detailed exploration of patients' personal histories, with emotional reliving of childhood experiences in the treatment setting. From the information thus gained he formed a theory of human nature and mental illness known as psychoanalysis, which supplied a rationale for his therapy. Freud's trail-breaking achievement opened a rich field for innovations, and many current psychotherapies have moved so far from their historical source that its influence is scarcely detectable. All rely, however, on repeated, emotionally charged interactions with a therapist aimed primarily at increasing the patient's awareness of his own feelings and attitudes.

Almost simultaneously with Freud, another giant, I. P. Pavlov, initiated his monumental researches on the laws governing the linking of autonomic responses to neutral environmental stimuli. He demonstrated that dogs could be made "neurotic" by exposing them to insoluble conflicts, and in his later years applied his theory and findings to mental illness. Pavlovian theory continues to dominate conceputalizations of mental illness and psychotherapy in the Soviet Union.[1]

In the United States his ideas were seized on by the psychologist J. B. Watson. Meanwhile a third strand in the web of modern American psychotherapy was being woven by E. L. Thorndike, whose ingenious experiments showed that the behavior of cats could be shaped by the consequences associated with certain actions. This principle, which he termed the "law of effect," came into full flower with the researches of B. F. Skinner. Reflecting their training, psychiatrists and psychiatric social workers have preferred Freudian and neo-Freudian conceptualizations, while psychologists have spearheaded the use of techniques of behavior modification.

Most current naturalistic theories of mental illness and its treatment represent various combinations, modifications, and extensions of concepts originating with Freud, Pavlov, and Skinner.[2] Fortunately these conceptual schemes are not incompatible, despite differences in terminology, and they supply a scientifically respectable rationale for contemporary methods of psychotherapy.

Contemporary Western psychotherapies include a third set of approaches which question the validity of scientific concepts and methods and instead appeal to direct experience. While psychoanalytic and behavioral therapies were devised by clinicians and experimentalists, existential therapies are based on the doctrines of European philosphers. Granting that a person's behavior and subjective life are in part determined by the interplay of present and past environmental influences with his genetically determined structure, they stress that his spiritual dimension gives him freedom of choice. Anxiety and despair are inevitable responses to the

---

1. Platonov (1959).
2. A good exposition of psychoanalytic theory is Brenner (1955); of behavioral theory, Skinner (1953); of behavior modification, Bandura (1969); of one form of existential psychotherapy, Frankl (1965). See also Binswanger (1956).

"existential predicament," but a person has the capacity to find a
purpose in life even in the midst of catastrophe. Man fashions his
world as well as being shaped by it. The therapeutic interview is a
free-flowing encounter in which the patient, through his experiences with the therapist, is enabled to achieve greater self-
realization. While psychoanalytically and existentially based therapies have much in common, the latter's more explicit emphasis on
a philosophy of existence brings it closer to religio-magical forms
of healing, and its stress on immediate experience is congenial to
the rationale underlying encounter groups.

Human beings are social creatures whose personalities, world
views, and behavior are molded by the standards of the groups to
which they belong. This has been implicitly recognized by all
forms of religio-magical healing, which incorporate group rituals.
From the days of Freud until recent years, however, dyadic forms
of naturalistic therapy have dominated the therapeutic scene. This
may be a historical accident, reflecting the absence of a theory of
group behavior comparable in power and scope to the conceptualizations mentioned above, and the fact that Freud, as a physician,
was trained to treat patients in privacy. In any case, after a slow
start, group approaches have mushroomed.[3]

At this historical juncture, then, group methods of therapy,
most of them time-limited, seem to be making increasing inroads
on the traditional two-person therapies conducted in privacy. Emphasis seems to be shifting from open-ended, long-term interview
treatment with rather ill-defined goals, for which psychoanalysis
was the initial model, to time-limited therapies aimed at crisis
management or relief of specific symptoms by techniques of behavior modification.

CULTURAL DEFINITIONS OF MENTAL ILLNESS AND PSYCHOTHERAPY

Before we proceed further, it is necessary to wrestle briefly with a
surprisingly thorny question: what is it that psychotherapy purports to treat? There are various paths into this conceptual briar

3. Yalom (1970).

patch and no entirely satisfactory one out of it. Perhaps because of my medical training, I find it convenient to start with the commonsense notion that treatment implies illness and psychotherapy treats a particular form of illness known as mental illness.

Like all illness, mental illness is a breakdown in the organism's adaptation to environment, creating subjective distress and objective disability. Longitudinal studies of life histories have revealed two facts about illness that are relevant to this discussion. The first is that illnesses occur in clusters during times of stress. Stress, however, is defined by the meaning of the events to the person, not the events in themselves. A divorce or a bankruptcy may mean disaster to one person and relief to another. The second pertinent fact is that there is no sharp line between so-called medical and psychiatric illnesses. Body and mind are inseparable.[4] Mental illnesses fall at the psychological end of a biological-psychological continuum and manifest themselves primarily by disturbances in thinking, feeling, and communicative behavior. The patient's suffering and disability are related to an inappropriate or distorted view of himself, faulty communications with others, sometimes even his views about the meaning of existence. While somatic deficits or vulnerabilities may contribute to some mental illnesses, damaging experiences of early life usually play a major role. These include both absence of opportunity to learn certain attitudes or behaviors, and traumatic interactions with others, either of which can warp or cripple personal development.

Because the resulting disturbances in personal functioning involve the person's social behavior, the attitudes and values of his society determine which manifestations of personal distress it classifies as mental illness.[5] For example, the same symptoms that in the Middle Ages were viewed as evidence of demoniacal possession to be treated by exorcism are now regarded as signs of mental

4. Data concerning the relation of illness to life stresses are provided by Hinkle (1961) and Wyler, Masuda, and Holmes (1971). Chapter 3 below considers the relation between pathological mental and bodily states in pre-industrialized societies.

5. For an excellent, concise statement of the interplay of social and personal factors in the causes, manifestations, and treatment of mental illness, see Clausen (1959). Freedman and Hollingshead (1957) show how the diagnosis of psychoneurosis is influenced by the interaction of patient, physician, and social group. See also Riessman, Cohen, and Pearl (1964).

illness to be treated by a psychiatrist. In World War II, Russian soldiers were never classified as having psychoneuroses, because, as far as one can see, the Russian army did not recognize this condition. Presumably soldiers with complaints that Americans would term psychoneurotic were regarded either as malingerers subject to disciplinary action or as medically ill and therefore treated by regular physicians. In the American army, by contrast, many commonplace reactions to the stresses of military life were initially regarded as signs of psychoneurotic illness, warranting discharge from the service. Today many of these same discharged soldiers would be promptly returned to duty.

In contemporary America, persons showing distress resulting from the normal vicissitudes of life are often classified as mentally ill and therefore eligible for treatment. Ironically, mental health education, which aims to teach people how to cope more effectively with life, has instead increased the demand for psychotherapeutic help. By calling people's attention to symptoms they might otherwise ignore and by labeling those symptoms as signs of neurosis, mental health education can create unwarranted anxieties, leading those to seek psychotherapy who do not need it. The demand for psychotherapy keeps pace with the supply, and at times one has the uneasy feeling that the supply may be creating the demand. The greater the number of treatment facilities and the more widely they are known, the larger the number of persons seeking their services. Psychotherapy is the only form of treatment which, at least to some extent, appears to create the illness it treats.[6] It can never suffer the unfortunate fate of the comedian Victor Borge's physician-uncle who became despondent on realizing that he had discovered a cure for which there was no disease.

Contemporary America has also advanced far in regarding certain forms of deviant behavior—such as alcoholism, drug addiction,

---

6. Karl Jaspers, the German psychiatrist, puts it succinctly: "Therapeutic schools unwittingly foster the phenomena which they cure." (Jaspers, 1964, p. 8.) Schofield, who is concerned with the discrepancy between the supply and demand for psychotherapy, is also worth quoting: ". . . case finding tends frequently to result in case making. . . . The individual who is dissatisfied in his work, unhappy in his social relationships, lacking in recreational skills . . . is not helped by sensitization to the notion that he is 'sick' . . . particularly . . . in a situation in which professional aid is not available to him." (Schofield, 1964, p. 27.)

and impulsive criminal behavior—as illnesses requiring treatment rather than as manifestations of wickedness. This humanitarian development is based partly on the recognition that many social deviants seem to be trying to deal with the same types of internal conflict and external stress as others regarded as mentally ill, but that their coping efforts take the form of socially destructive behavior.

While labeling such persons as ill rather than wicked in many ways represents an advance in understanding and treatment, it is not without disadvantages. One drawback is that it relieves the alcoholic or drug addict of responsibility for his plight. Calling him ill and putting him into a mental hospital is more humane and probably more helpful than putting him in jail, but it may also heighten his pathological dependency and reduce his incentive to assume any responsibility for his treatment. Without such a commitment, treatment cannot succeed.

Because the concept of mental illness includes deviant behaviors, it cannot be disentangled from moral judgments, and, as a result, it can be misused to take dissenters out of circulation by circumventing due process of law. Physicians can incarcerate a person in a mental hospital without a court trial on the grounds that he is insane. Dissenters have been handled in this way in the Soviet Union,[7] and some claim that compulsory hospitalization has been used as an instrument of social control in the United States.[8]

Whether or not a person is sent to a mental hospital also depends considerably on the culturally determined attitudes of his family and the community regarding his symptoms and behavior. Many actively hallucinating persons continue to function in the community because their families, friends, neighbors, and employers are willing to endure their eccentricities, while many senile persons are sent to hospitals or nursing homes largely because families find their care too burdensome.

Hospitalization is the final stage of what has been termed the "social breakdown syndrome." This, in essence, is a perceived dis-

7. Medvedev and Medvedev (1971).
8. Szasz (1963).

crepancy between a person's performance and what he and others expect of him, when, in addition, the discrepancy is blamed on him rather than on his environment.[9] As the person's failure to live up to expectations becomes more and more apparent, at some point the family decides that there is something wrong with him and seeks help through conventional channels. At this point he becomes labeled as mentally ill, and from then on his experiences with physicians and hospitals reinforce this appellation, which reaches its most powerful confirmation when the hospital door falls shut behind him. We shall consider this process in more detail later.

Psychotherapy, like psychiatric diagnoses, cannot be divorced from cultural influences and moral judgments. If mental illnesses are the causes and expressions of stress-producing interactions with others, then psychotherapy, in its broadest sense, is an effort to help the patient reduce these stresses. This creates few problems when the values of the patient and society coincide, because then the task is to help him to behave more effectively in accordance with these values. In periods such as the present one, however, when values are in flux and different groups within the society promulgate conflicting standards, the value orientations of a patient and groups important to him, such as his family, may diverge.

If the patient is mature and settled in his ways, the therapist's task should clearly be to help him live up to his own ideals and withstand the ensuing suffering, but with those whose personalities are still in formation the issue is less simple. Parents often bring an adolescent to a psychotherapist because the child's behavior deviates from their norms. If the adolescent finds the values of contemporary society abhorrent, drops out of college, and devotes himself to searching for better guides to living, perhaps with the help of mind-altering drugs, is he mentally ill? Is the psychotherapist's job to act as an agent of social control, whose task is to win the patient back into the fold, or should he encourage him "to do his own thing" and defy cultural forces he perceives as destructive?[10] As this example suggests, a therapist cannot avoid value

9. Gruenberg (1967).
10. Halleck (1971).

judgments, and these are bound to affect both his choice of patients and his therapeutic activities and goals.

For example, a perceptive Oriental student of Western psychotherapy has suggested that its underlying value system stresses interaction between the self and the outer world, in contrast with the Eastern emphasis on awareness as an end in itself. As a result, everything worthwhile involves some form of action. A Westerner feels guilty if he simply sits under a tree and savors the springtime; a parent and a child cannot enjoy being with each other without doing something together; and a helping relation such as psychotherapy must involve some sort of goal-directed task. Thus the measure of success of a therapeutic session is whether the patient has been productive, worked something through, advanced up a desensitization hierarchy, or the like, rather than whether the therapeutic encounter was an enriching one.[11]

There is no need to pursue these complex questions further at this time. It is sufficient to note that cultural norms and world views influence not only the definition of mental illness but also the nature of its treatment. Psychotherapies in societies or groups with a primarily religious world view are based on religio-magical theories, and healing rituals merge with religious rites. Western industrialized societies, consistent with their world view, see psychotherapy as the systematic application of the scientific understanding of human nature to the treatment of the mentally ill.[12]

Within a given society, however, the dominant type of treatment depends in part on the class position and group affiliation of the recipient. In America, religio-magical forms of healing are practiced by certain religious groups. Lower-class patients, who view treatment as something the doctor does to one, are more likely to receive directive treatment, often accompanied by medication.

11. London (1964) sees all psychotherapeutic systems as having three essential elements, of which the first two are a theory of the nature of man and a superordinate moral code. A body of therapeutic techniques is the third. Its function is to influence behavior in directions deemed desirable in the light of the first two. Pande (1968), in an exceptionally thought-provoking paper, identifies certain aspects of Western cosmology that create "deficits in the Western way of life and . . . negative psychological implications" and sees Western psychotherapy, especially the psychoanalytic model, as a "symbolic and substantive cultural undertaking" to correct them (p. 432).

12. See Chapter 8 below for a closer look at the relation between cultural attitudes and preferred forms of psychotherapy in the United States.

Middle- and upper-class patients, who put a high value on self-knowledge and self-direction, are more likely to receive permissive forms
of treatment stressing insight.[13]

In mid-twentieth-century America, mental illness has not fully
shaken off its demonological aura, as evidenced by the stigma still
attached to it. In the minds of many it implies moral weakness.
The insane still tend to elicit a kind of fascinated horror, reflected
in their being shunted off to isolated hospitals on the one hand
and being objects of morbid curiosity on the other (for example,
as popular subjects for novels, plays, and films). Nevertheless, all
forms of suffering or troublesome behavior that involve emotional
or psychological factors are viewed as treatable by psychotherapy.
This is reflected in the great variety of recipients and purveyors of
psychotherapy and its settings. To reduce this chaotic scene to
some sort of order, we shall describe it first from the standpoint of
those receiving psychotherapy and then from the standpoint of
those offering it.

WHO RECEIVES PSYCHOTHERAPY?

As implied in the previous section, the thousands of Americans
who undergo some form of psychotherapy cover an extraordin-
arily broad range. At one extreme are persons best characterized as
mental hypochondriacs, searching for someone to lift the normal
burdens of living from their shoulders. At the other, are persons
suffering from severe disturbances of thinking, feeling, and behavior. They constitute the populations of our mental hospitals. In
between are persons whose symptoms are a transient response to
life crises or attempts to cope with chronic stresses produced by
faulty life styles.

Psychotherapy is sought or offered when the person's suffering
or disability seems to have a significant emotional or psychological
component. Failure to recognize such a component, leading to the
misdefinition of the problem as primarily medical or surgical, can
lead to serious errors in choice of treatment. A striking example is
the case of a student nurse who, after her jaw had been dislocated
in the dentist's chair, suffered a severe spasm and was unable to

13. Hollingshead and Redlich (1958) thoroughly document this point.

close her mouth. For months she was subjected to drastic procedures, including surgical destruction of the hinge of the jaw and attempts to cut nerves to certain muscles which, fortunately, were unsuccessful. Finally her jaws were wired together—all to no avail. Only after the surgeons reached the end of their tether did they call in a psychiatrist. He discovered that her symptom was related to severe conflicts about her choice of career, whereupon her treatment shifted immediately from surgery to psychotherapy. This soon resolved the spasm so she could focus on the real problem of how to cope with many family problems and manage her relations with an autocratic father her opposed her career choice.

As the contributions of unhealthy emotional states to all forms of illness and disability become recognized, psychotherapeutic principles are having an increasing influence on all forms of medical healing. It is possible, however, to distinguish several classes of patients for whom psychotherapy, broadly defined, constitutes some portion of their treatment. The first class comprises patients who are hospitalized because they seem incapable of carrying out the ordinary tasks of life and therefore need protection. The bulk of these are seniles and schizophrenics. Next are neurotics, whose distress seems related to chronic emotional strain and often involves some disturbance of bodily function. Akin to these are patients with so-called "psychosomatic" illnesses such as asthma, peptic ulcer, and certain skin diseases, in whom definite disorders of bodily organs seem related to emotional tension. The fourth group of patients in whose treatment psychotherapy plays, or should play, a prominent part are the chronically ill. This category cuts across the other three and also includes those with chronic disease or disability initially unrelated to psychological causes— loss of a limb, epilepsy, rheumatic heart disease, and so on. Since the emotional stresses created by chronic disease usually contribute more to the distress and disability of these patients than their bodily damage,[14] rehabilitation methods are making increasing use of psychotherapeutic principles.

There is some question whether those who are not calssed as psychotics, psychoneurotics, psychosomatically ill, or chronically ill are suitable candidates for psychotherapy. One difficulty is that

14. For an example, see pp. 284-85 below.

many emotional stresses result in misbehavior, which, coming into conflict with the standards and values of society, has inseparable moral and medical aspects. Alcoholics, drug addicts, and some sexual deviates transgress certain social standards and come to the attention of legal authorities. Yet they are clearly sick in the sense that they are caught up in behavior patterns they cannot control. Their deviant behavior often seems the result of emotional difficulties rooted in disturbing childhood experiences, such as parental mistreatment or neglect, broken homes, and lack of adequate socialization, suggesting that these offenders might respond to psychotherapy. Modern criminology is increasingly emphasizing the use of psychotherapeutic principles in rehabilitation, but much work remains to be done to determine which approach is most suitable for different types of criminals.[15] Current views distinguish the socialized criminal, who represents the values of his own deviant group and is a well-integrated member of it, from the so-called sociopath or psychopath, who cannot get along with anyone and is always in trouble. The proper handling of offenders is a knotty problem requiring cooperation of the healing, legal, and corrective professions.

Another class of patients offered psychotherapy cuts across all the others—those reacting with an emotional crisis to life problems that temporarily overtax their adaptive capacities.[16] Many such persons seek help because of tensions on the job, at home or, in the younger age group, at school. They include married couples in difficulty, parents distraught over their unruly children, and the like. Persons differ greatly in the amount of stress they can tolerate; an event that constitutes a crisis for a schizophrenic, for example, might be shrugged off as a minor irritation by a business executive. Furthermore, as mentioned earlier, the severity of the stress depends on the meaning of the event to the person, which, in turn, is largely determined by his own life experience. To make matters more complicated, as we shall see in the next chapter, the environmental stress may be largely created by his own behavior. Whatever the main source of the decompensation, or the relative contribution of environmental and internal components, persons

15. See, for example, Boslow and Manne (1966).
16. Caplan (1964); Rusk (1971).

in a crisis display the whole gamut of psychotic and neurotic symptoms.[17]

Other persons who also have chronic difficulties in coping with life suffer from a host of malaises that are best summed up by the German word *Weltschmerz* (world pain). They seek help in their struggles with such problems as identity and alienation and look to psychotherapy to resolve their spiritual unrest or feelings that they are not getting all they should out of life. The number of these persons seems to be steadily increasing, reflecting the confusion of moral standards and disintegration of values in today's world, as well as the increasing proportion of the educated and affluent who have the leisure and inclination to brood about such issues.

For completeness, mention must be made of psychotherapists-in-training who are required to undergo psychotherapy as part of their training program. Although these are in no sense patients and represent a very small proportion of persons receiving psychotherapy, they are of some importance in the total scene because their own psychotherapy occupies a considerable portion of the time they would otherwise devote to patients.

WHO CONDUCTS PSYCHOTHERAPY?

The variety of practitioners of the many forms of psychotherapy is almost as great as the range of persons they seek to help. Psychotherapists in the naturalistic tradition include a relatively small group specifically trained for this art, a much larger number of professional healers who practice psychotherapy without labeling it as such in connection with their healing or advisory activities, and a growing army of nonprofessionals with various amounts of training. The largest group of professionals trained to conduct psychotherapy are psychiatrists, including psychoanalysts, numbering about twenty thousand. Their ranks are supplemented by over twelve thousand clinical psychologists and twenty-three thousand social workers.[18]

Psychologists enter the field of psychotherapy through the scientific study of human thinking and behavior, and they supply

17. Tyhurst (1957).
18. All figures are taken from *Health Resources Statistics* (1969).

most of the sophisticated research in this field. In clinical settings such as hospitals and psychiatric clinics they carry out diagnostic tests and do therapy under the more or less nominal supervision of psychiatrists. The major institutional settings in which they work independently are schools and universities. Increasing numbers, especially in the larger cities, are going into independent private practice as both diagnosticians and therapists.

Psychiatric social workers are specialists within the helping profession of social work. Like clinical psychologists in hospitals and clinics, they are members of treatment teams which, for legal reasons, are under psychiatric supervision. They also operate independently in social agencies, family agencies, marriage counseling centers, and so on, and as private practitioners.

Psychotherapy also forms part of the practice of many other professional groups. An indeterminate number of America's approximately 313,000 nonpsychiatric physicians and osteopaths use psychotherapy with many of their patients, often without recognizing it as such. To them must be added healers on the fringes of medicine such as chiropractors, naturopaths, and others, estimated to number about 18,000. Their effectiveness, especially with emotionally disturbed persons, probably rests primarily on their intuitive use of psychotherapeutic principles. In addition to the healers associated with medicine, a wide variety of counselors and guides may use psychotherapeutic principles with their clientele. These include marriage counselors, rehabilitation and vocational counselors, parole officers, group workers, and clergymen.

Members of these established disciplines, however, are ceasing to monopolize the field. The excess of demand for personal help over the supply, and the fact that many kinds of interventions can help people with a wide variety of psychic distress to feel better, coupled with the inability to evaluate the relative effectiveness of different approaches,[19] have combined to foster rapid proliferation of new training programs in psychotherapy for nonprofessionals, ranging from suburban housewives to slum-dwelling, ex-drug addicts. Many emphasize group and family therapy. Some of these programs are creating new professions with positions for

19. See pp. 19–22 below.

mental health counselors[20] or mental health technicians, and are awarding degrees or certificates of training.

In addition, persons trained in group dynamics, or without any training at all, are offering a wide variety of group experiences aimed at greater self-awareness, freedom of expression, heightened aesthetic awareness, more open and intimate communication with others, and the like. While not offered as therapeutic in the strict sense, the aims of these sensitivity or encounter groups obviously overlap with those of psychotherapy, and they are patronized by many persons indistinguishable from seekers of psychotherapy.

Moreover, patients have banded together to help themselves by group techniques. The oldest of these self-help organizations are Alcoholics Anonymous and Recovery Incorporated,[21] but new ones continue to emerge. Some, like Recovery Incorporated, have leadership-training programs and screen leaders for competence and reliability; others make no such efforts.

The settings in which psychotherapy or its equivalent are conducted have also multiplied. Community mental health centers financed by public funds have been added to the traditional locales of mental hospitals, outpatient clinics, community agencies, university counseling centers, and private offices. The encounter groups described above are conducted at "growth centers," such as Esalen, as well as in hotel rooms, meeting halls, and private homes.

Members of different disciplines tend to describe their activities in different terms. Medical and quasi-medical healers treat patients, psychiatric social workers do case work with clients, clergymen offer pastoral counseling, group workers do group work. For obvious reasons, each discipline tends to emphasize the special features of its approach, leading to a greater appearance of difference than may actually exist. In all likelihood, their similarities are far more important.

The distinction between different healers and advisers lies less in what they do than in the persons with whom they do it, and this, in turn, depends largely on the settings in which they work. Cer-

20. Rioch (1967).
21. See Alcoholics Anonymous (1953) and see Wechsler (1960) for Recovery Incorporated.

tain settings sharply limit the kinds of persons who seek or receive psychotherapeutic help. Thus the bulk of the population of mental hospitals consists of schizophrenics, alcoholics, and seniles; those using the services of social agencies tend to be persons struggling with economic, social, marital, or parental problems. The school psychologist inevitably deals with children with school problems, the prison psychologist or psychiatrist with offenders, and so on.

Other settings are open to all. These include community mental health centers, personal growth centers, and the offices of private practitioners. The referral channel a person happens to pick, or the way in which he defines his problems, partly determine whom he will finally consult for treatment. The same patient might be treated by a psychiatrist, a psychologist, a psychiatric social worker, a clergyman, or an untrained sensitivity group leader, depending on the size of his pocketbook and where his feet carry him.

The inability of different practitioners of psychotherapy clearly to define their aims, roles, therapeutic methods, or types of sufferers they treat, coupled with the lucrativeness of the private practice of psychotherapy, has resulted in unseemly jurisdictional disputes, especially in big cities. Just as those between psychiatrists, psychologists, and psychiatric social workers have been at least partly resolved, often with the aid of legislation, other mental health practitioners are joining the fray. In hospitals, psychiatric nurses, mental health counselors, and ward aides are jostling psychiatric social workers and clinical psychologists for the privilege of participating in the prestigious activity of psychotherapy, while psychiatrists labor to define the roles of these groups in such a way as to preserve their own prerogatives. In community mental health centers, contenders include the new sub-professionals, and "personal growth centers" draw patients away from all the established healing disciplines.

In short, the field of psychotherapy is undergoing a severe identity crisis involving practitioners, methods, settings, and persons for whom psychotherapy is believed suitable, and no satisfactory solution is in sight.

This review of psychotherapeutic practitioners would be incomplete without mentioning the thousands of religious healers who are members of established sects such as Christian Science and New Thought and, on their fringes, cultists of all sorts whose claim to healing powers rests solely on their own assertions. Though there is no way of counting religious healers, they must treat vast numbers of troubled people indistinguishable from those receiving secular forms of psychotherapy.[22]

WHAT ARE THE EFFECTS OF PSYCHOTHERAPY?

The ever-increasing investment of time, effort, and money in psychotherapy and its persistent popularity imply that both its recipients and its practitioners are convinced that it does some good. Patients must believe it to be helpful or they would not seek it in such numbers, and every psychotherapist has seen permanent and striking improvement in a patient following psychotherapy. To date, however, although proponents of every method offer persuasive reports of their successes, extensive and persistent research efforts have failed to produce conclusive evidence that any form of interview therapy with neurotics or schizophrenics is more effective than a simple helping relationship.

With schizophrenics, the introduction of anti-psychotic drugs has complicated the picture, but one detailed, critical review of all available outcome studies concludes that insight therapy with drug treatment is no more effective than drug treatment alone. The reviewer, however, stresses the importance of "psychotherapeutic management," including "application of understanding of psychopathology and psychodynamics to the remedial management of the individual patient,"[23] to help him learn to deal with his current life problems. This is consistent with a firmly established finding that various group treatments of schizophrenics produce a higher rate of improvement than simple institutional care.[24] That is, any systematic attention to these patients motivated by a desire

22. See Chapter 3 below.
23. May (1969), p. 715.
24. Meltzoff and Kornreich (1970).

to help them works better than lack of such attention—hardly a breath-taking discovery, but one that at least reassures psychotherapists that they are not wasting their time.

With neurotics, about two-thirds, on the average, are improved immediately after interview therapy. The same percentage of patients with neurotically based disabilities have returned to work after two years of treatment by insurance doctors.[25]

Simple comparison between average improvement rates in patients receiving interview therapy and in control groups receiving no treatment may obscure the effectiveness of therapy. For patients receiving therapy show a wider range of improvement than the controls. Some do better than the best of the controls and some do worse than the worst. In other words, it looks as if psychotherapy can make some people worse, and these may balance out the improvement scores of those who have been helped.[26] The fact that psychotherapy harms some people is, paradoxically, evidence of its power. All effective remedies can do harm if misused. If interview psychotherapy appeared only to do good, it would be suspect for that reason alone.

Studies of behavior modification techniques suggest that they relieve circumscribed, irrational fears—so-called phobias—more effectively than brief interview therapies.[27] Most of these studies, however, have been done with student volunteers whose phobias were unearthed by surveys—that is, how closely they resembled neurotic patients is unclear. Of persons who define themselves as needing psychotherapy, no more than 3 percent[28] have circumscribed phobias, so this finding hardly represents a major breakthrough in the psychotherapy of neuroses.

Nevertheless, one should not hastily conclude from the dearth of convincing demonstrations of the effectiveness of psychotherapy that it does not work. Failure to find differences in improvement rates following different forms of or amounts of psychotherapy is a sign of ignorance, not knowledge. The only justified conclusion is that the specific effectiveness of most forms

25. Eysenck (1965).
26. Bergin (1971). Like almost every finding in the field of psychotherapy, Bergin's results have been challenged (May, 1971), but the weight of evidence supports them.
27. Paul (1966); Marks (1969).
28. Marks (1969), p. 77.

of psychotherapy for most forms of mental illness has not been proven. This may well be due to the inadequacy of current research conceptualizations and designs.[29] For example, we lack both a scheme for classifying patients and criteria of improvement that would permit comparison of different forms of treatment for different types of patients.[30] In many reports, improvement is left undefined; thus, there is no way of knowing precisely what the therapist had in mind or whether or not he shifted his criterion from one patient to another. When improvement is defined, criteria used in different studies usually are not comparable. Criteria determining the discharge of patients from state hospitals, the resumption of work by patients receiving disability payments, and the diagnosis of "recovered" by a psychoanalyst obviously have little in common.

It is probably no accident that behavior modification therapies yield the clearest findings, since these are well-defined, short-term interventions with precise goals. Circumscribed phobias are especially attractive for study because students, a captive research population, reveal them in sufficient numbers to yield adequate statistical samples. This is not true for most patients and most therapies. Psychoanalytic techniques, for example, have been particularly resistant to research because of their long duration, open-ended goals, and the impossibility of obtaining samples large enough for statistical analysis without pooling the data from many therapists. Sensitivity groups, which would yield adequately large samples, are difficult to study because most are not conducted in settings that lend themselves to research and because their members and leaders are hopelessly heterogeneous. Yet many people claim to have been mightily helped by psychoanalytic therapies and sensitivity groups; this would suggest that they may have considerable therapeutic power.

29. For a discussion of conceptual and methodological problems in research on outcomes of psychotherapy, see Frank (1959, 1968); Meehl (1965); Group for the Advancement of Psychiatry (1966); Kiesler (1971); and many others.

30. Actually, raters of improvement, regardless of theoretical orientation, agree with respect to patients who are greatly improved or apparently cured. Agreement drops sharply, however, with respect to lesser degrees of improvement; this suggests that the criteria underlying these judgments are affected by theoretical preconceptions and need greater explication than has yet been achieved.

Finally, the possibility must be recognized that some of the most powerful healing components of psychotherapy may lie in qualities of the therapist—such as, perhaps, innate healing power—that elude any current scientific methods of investigation.

In short, the inability to prove that a phenomenon exists is quite different from proving that it does *not* exist. The difficulty in demonstrating by statistical or experimental methods that therapy works or that one form is superior to another may lie in our inability to define adequately any of the variables involved.

In the present state of ignorance, the most reasonable assumption is that all forms of psychotherapy that persist must do some good; otherwise they would disappear. Furthermore, it is likely that the lack of clear differences in improvement rate from different forms of psychotherapy results from features common to them all. The improvement rate for each form, then, would be composed of patients who responded to the features it shares with other forms and therefore would have improved with any type of psychotherapy, plus, perhaps, some patients who would have responded favorably only to the particular type of psychotherapy under consideration. If this were so, it would be hard to tease out the unique contributions of different forms of treatment until the features they share—and the attributes of patients that cause them to respond favorably to these features—were better understood.

We shall try to identify these shared active ingredients by looking for features common to many different forms of interpersonal healing, and then seeing if these features are also present in American psychotherapies. This exploration will lead quite far afield and into some largely uncharted areas. Therefore, before setting out, it seems desirable to identify home base more clearly. To this end, the next chapter outlines a theoretical framework for psychotherapy.

SUMMARY

This chapter has attempted a general definition of psychotherapy, briefly reviewed its historical roots, and described the types of patients, therapists, and settings characteristic of psychotherapy in America today. It appears that many thousands of troubled people of all sorts seek psychotherapy or have it thrust upon them, and its practitioners are almost as varied as its recipients. The enduring popularity of psychotherapies is strong evidence that they do some good; yet extensive research efforts have produced little conclusive knowledge about the relative efficacy of different forms. Although this may be partly due to formidable methodological problems, it also suggests that features common to all types of psychotherapy probably contribute as much, if not more, to their effectiveness than the characteristics that differentiate them.

A CONCEPTUAL FRAMEWORK FOR
II   PSYCHOTHERAPY

Alice knew it was the Rabbit coming to look for her, and
she trembled till she shook the house, quite forgetting
that she was now about a thousand times as large as the
Rabbit and had no reason to be afraid of it.

Alice's Adventures in Wonderland

The attempt to describe features common to all forms
of psychotherapy requires consideration of a wide variety of patterned personal and social interactions. To
keep our bearings in this exploration, a general conceptual framework is needed. Such a scheme should be able
to relate a person's inner life to his interactions with
other persons and to his group allegiances. It should
suggest how certain kinds of distress might arise from
and contribute to disturbed relationships with others,
and how particular types of interpersonal experience
might help to ameliorate both. This is obviously a very
big order, and to handle it adequately would require a
complete theory of personality development and structure as related to social and cultural influences, which is
beyond the scope of this book.[1] The following presentation attempts only to sketch a few useful concepts in
sufficient detail for orientation purposes. It makes no
claim to completeness. Although the exposition is primarily in terms of psychiatric patients and psychotherapy as they exist in America, with slight modifica-

1. For example, see Kardiner *et al.* (1945) and Kluckhohn *et al.* (1953).

24

tions it also applies to the other forms of influence and healing to be considered.

PSYCHIATRIC ILLNESS, PSYCHOTHERAPY, AND INTERPERSONAL STRESS

Although the conditions for which psychotherapy may be sought or offered are protean, all of them can be viewed as temporary or persistent unsuccessful adaptations to stress. Everyone repeatedly must deal with experiences that temporarily disturb his equanimity and bring him into conflict with others. The healthy person is able to handle most of them promptly and effectively, without excessive expenditure of energy. Thus he can push forward and may even seek stress to enjoy the triumph of mastering it (like Sir Edmund Hillary, who was impelled to climb Mt. Everest simply because it was there).

It is useful to think of all illnesses as "non-adapted" states[2] characterized by disability and distress. These states become regarded as illnesses when the person or his family feels that he cannot cure himself and he turns to someone whom he knows to be an expert in the theory and treatment of his illness, as he defines it. By and large, persons who attribute their distress and disability to bodily causes turn to physicians; those whose illnesses are seen as related primarily to disturbed relations with others or internal psychological conflicts gravitate toward psychotherapists.

As we shall see, such persons have much in common with other victims of interpersonal stress, notably the ill savage, the person on the verge of religious conversion, and the prisoner subjected to Communist thought reform. Failures of adaptation are determined by an imbalance between the environmental stress and the person's susceptibility to it. Sometimes the stress is so great that it exceeds the adaptive capacity of almost everyone. Examples are the prisoner who finally yields to the prolonged tortures and deprivations of thought reform, the soldier who collapses after overwhelming battle stress,[3] or the housewife with no income, six

2. Stunkard (1961).
3. Glass (1957) reports that both the intensity and the duration of combat are related to the rate of neuropsychiatric breakdown.

young children, and an alcoholic husband who mistreats her. That persons show emotional strain under such circumstances is hardly surprising, but their treatment obviously must focus on alleviating the environmental pressures.

Failures of adaptation caused by personal inadequacies arising from important early life experiences are our primary concern. For completeness, however, brief mention may be made of constitutional handicaps limiting adaptive capacity. The term "constitutional" refers to defects or vulnerabilities caused by inborn defects, physical illnesses, or life experiences that cause permanent structural damage to the organism. It is now well established that the adaptive capacity of many schizophrenics is reduced by congenital factors, probably involving defective enzyme systems in the brain. This may also be true of certain depressive reactions and behavior disorders. Mishaps during pregnancy—such as rubella in the mother—can result in poor health and behavioral disturbances in the child.[4] After birth, noxious experiences in infancy and childhood—such as the lack of adequate mothering[5] or of opportunities to interact with other infants—can produce damage to the developing nervous system which cannot be later rectified by psychological means. The same holds true for illnesses that limit adjustive capacity through nonprogressive handicaps such as residual paralysis from poliomyelitis or, more seriously, progressive deterioration as in Huntington's chorea. Aging, finally, is characterized by generalized reduction of ability to cope with stress.

Many handicapped persons are discouraged and demoralized, and this further reduces their ability to function. Psychotherapy may therefore help them considerably by enabling them to make stress-reducing changes in their lives and to take a more optimistic view of the future.

Since constitutional defects and vulnerabilities account for only a small portion of the distress for which people come to psychotherapists, however, and their relevance to psychotherapy is largely indirect, they may be passed over with this brief mention.

4. Rogers, Lilienfeld, and Pasamanick (1955), for example, report a statistically significant association between mental retardation and behavioral disorders in childhood and damaging prenatal experiences.
5. Harlow and Harlow (1965); Spitz (1954).

Let us now turn to the task of characterizing defects in adaptive mechanisms that arise from early interpersonal experiences and result in more or less persistent maladaptations, reflected in both a person's relationships with others and in his inner life.

THE ASSUMPTIVE WORLD

In order to be able to function, everyone must impose an order and regularity on the welter of experiences impinging upon him. To do this, he develops out of his personal experiences a set of more or less implicit assumptions about himself and the nature of the world in which he lives, enabling him to predict the behavior of others and the outcome of his own actions. The totality of each person's assumptions may be conveniently termed his "assumptive world."[6]

This is a short-hand expression for a highly structured, complex, interacting set of values, expectations, and images of oneself and others, which guide and in turn are guided by a person's perceptions and behavior and which are closely related to his emotional states and his feelings of well-being.

The more enduring assumptions become organized into attitudes with cognitive, affective, and behavioral components.[7] Every attitude may potentially result in some form of behavior—that is, interaction with the environment—although it can, of course, express itself only in silent thoughts. The cognitive aspect of the attitude can be considered the pilot who guides the behavior, and the affective part the engine or fuel which drives it. To take a simple example, my attitude toward hats when it is activated will lead me to think about them, go and buy one, or avoid hat stores. What I do (the behavioral aspect) will depend in part on

6. This term has been borrowed from Cantril, but it is given a much wider meaning here. He confines it to the sphere of perceptions only, but his discussion of the "assumptive form world" seems to justify the broader use. For example, he says: "The net result of our purposive actions is that we create for ourselves a set of assumptions which serve as guides and bases for future actions." (Cantril, 1950, p. 87.)

Kelly (1955, p. 561) has developed an elaborate theory of psychological functioning and a psychotherapeutic method based on the "fundamental postulate" that a "person's processes are psychologically channelized by the ways in which he anticipates events."

7. The conceptualization of attitudes follows Rokeach (1968) with a slight difference in terminology.

what I know about hats and where they are to be found (the cognitive aspect), but also on my feelings abouts hats—pleasure, distaste, and the like—and how strong they are. These three components of attitudes are usually inseparable, and efforts to influence attitudes involve all three, although, as we shall see, different methods stress different ones.

One aspect of the cognitive component of an attitude especially pertinent to our purpose is the attribution of causality.[8] The cause to which we attribute an event strongly determines our feelings and behavior toward it. If I get sick after eating fish, it makes a difference if I attribute my nausea to the market's having sold me spoiled fish or to my wife's trying to poison me. Attribution of cause can create some amusing paradoxes—for example, when persons with insomnia were given a sugar pill and told it was a stimulant, they fell asleep more rapidly than if told it was a sedative.[9] A plausible explanation is that the former group, feeling no more tense than usual in spite of being given a supposed stimulant, concluded that they were improving and consequently fell asleep more easily. Those receiving the supposed sedative may have thought that they were unusually tense that evening because the pill failed to calm them and so lay awake longer.

The emotional components of attitudes also deserve a special word. Attitudes that are connected with a sense of uncertainty or confusion or with the prediction of an unfavorable outcome of a course of action tend to generate unpleasant emotions such as anxiety, panic, and despair. Those that give the person a sense of security and promise a better future are related to feelings of hope, faith, and the like. As will be seen, these emotional states not only have direct bearing on a person's ability to modify his perceptions and behavior, but also largely determine his state of well-being.

Attitudes range widely in scope. An example of one extreme would be those connected with brushing one's teeth; of the other, those concerning the nature of God. They also vary in their time orientation—some being primarily concerned with the past, some

8. Kelley (1967).
9. Storms and Nisbett (1970).

with the present, and some with the future. In addition, attitudes may be enduring or transient. Attitudes about the attractiveness of a hat can usually be changed as easily as the hat itself; but this is not true for attitudes about the nature of God. Some attitudes are held only tentatively, others with firm conviction. The degree of subjective conviction accompanying them need not parallel their persistence—a lady may be absolutely convinced that a hat becomes her one day and that it is hideous the next—but generally conviction and tenacity vary together.

Different parts of the assumptive world exist at different levels of consciousness. Only a minute part of it is in awareness at any one time, and the relative accessibility to awareness of different aspects of it may differ greatly. A person may be clearly aware of his attitudes toward the nuclear arms race, let us say, but be oblivious of his unverbalized belief that he must be perfect in order to gain his mother's love. Yet the latter conviction may have considerably more effect on his behavior than the former. Unconscious assumptive systems are especially pertinent to psychotherapy, not only because they are of profound importance to personal functioning but because, for reasons to be considered shortly, they are especially resistant to change.

Attitudes vary in their degree of internal consistency. Disharmonies can exist between the cognitive, affective, and behavioral components of an attitude, and certain symptoms can be thought of as expressing such conflicts—for example, if a person cannot resist washing his hands excessively, even though he knows that it is absurd, his affect toward the act may be one of repulsion. Conflicts also exist between attitudes at both conscious and unconscious levels. For example, conscious hatred of an enemy may arouse urges to fight that conflict with pacifistic convictions, and both sides of the conflict may gain strength from unconscious fears of violence and impulses toward it derived from frightening and frustrating experiences of early life. Since internal conflicts are major sources of feelings of insecurity and other types of distress, humans devote much intellectual energy to maintaining the internal consistency of their assumptive worlds, as we shall see, and much of psychotherapy can be viewed as an effor to help them to resolve such conflicts.

FORMATION OF THE ASSUMPTIVE WORLD

For a person to be able to function successfully and enjoy life, his assumptive world must correspond to conditions as they actually are. For it is only to the extent that a person can successfully predict the results of his acts that he can behave in such a way as to maximize chances for success and minimize those for failure. Thus everyone is strongly motivated constantly to check the validity of his assumptions, and every act is both a consequence of a more or less explicit expectation and a test of its validity. If the consequences of the act fail to confirm the prediction, the person is in trouble. He must either modify his expectations and the corresponding behavior or resort to maneuvers to conceal their incorrectness and evade their unfortuante consequences. This process for the most part goes on automatically and outside of awareness.

The validity of some aspects of the assumptive world can be checked against experiences unmediated by other persons. For example, the test of the assumption that a glowing poker is hot is to touch it. But since man is a social creature, his most significant experiences are with other persons, and those aspects of his assumptive world most essential to his functioning—his attitudes and values—can only be validated through his interactions with others, individually or in groups. An example of an interaction chain between two persons, which is guided by, and helps to form, the attitudes of each, is the following:

A man comes home late for supper after a hard day at the office and greets his wife with a warm kiss. She responds in kind and makes a sympathetic remark about his work load as they go in to supper. This encourages him to tell her about the events of the day. She shows interest, so he continues until he has gotten everything off his chest. Then he is prepared to listen to his wife's account of her doings, which he encourages with appropriate signs of interest, and so they have a pleasant chatty meal. Such an interactional chain is based on mutual expectations of affection and understanding and, in turn, stregthens these expectations, increasing the likelihood of similar mutually gratifying behavior on subsequent occasions. Thus the favorable behavior and assumptive systems of each member of the couple with respect to their relationship continually reinforce each other.

Starting the same way, the interaction might run quite a different course. The wife does not return her husband's kiss, but says coldly that he is late for supper again. As they go in to dinner he makes an angry rejoinder to which she responds in kind. He picks up the paper and buries himself in it while he eats. She does the same with a book. Here the husband's initial favorable expectations, which he expressed by a warm kiss, are disappointed by his wife's coolness. This leads him to alter his assumption about his wife's attitude and to change his behavior correspondingly. The subsequent interactions lead to a progressive breakdown of communication, confirming the unfavorable mutual expectancies of each spouse and increasing the likelihood that future interactional chains will run the same unsatisfactory course. This example illustrates how interactions between two persons form a mutually regulative system in which the behavior of each infuences the other and simultaneously helps each to form his own psychic life.

The development of the assumptive world starts as soon as the infant enters into transactions with his environment. These generate experiences leading him to form assumptions about the world in which he finds himself. These coalesce into generalizations, whose validity depends on two factors: the representativeness of the sample on which they are based, and the accuracy of the information it gives him.[10]

The infant, of course, has only very small samples to go on. This does not matter too much with respect to the inanimate world because its features are relatively homogeneous and supply clear, unambiguous information. One does not have to experience many chairs or shoes to reach valid generalizations about chairs and shoes, and a single experience with a lighted match suffices to reach a valid conclusion about the properties of fire.

This does not hold true in the world of people. Their messages are often ambiguous and complex, and the child's sample—his own family in the first instance—may be far from typical. If the family group provides a rich repertory of adaptive skills, and if his parents make him feel loved and wanted and treat him as if he is capable and good, then he comes to see himself as a well-equipped, com-

10. Imboden (1957).

petent, lovable person in a friendly, secure universe. The world is his oyster. He welcomes new experiences, tackles them with confidence, and easily modifies his behavior and assumptive world according to the outcome. Thus he readily learns and develops.

The family environment may fall short of this ideal in many ways. It may be lacking in opportunities for certain experiences. For example, there may be no adequate father figure or inadequate opportunity to play with other children. Thus the child may grow up lacking certain important assumptive systems simply for want of a chance to develop them. More serious difficulties occur if the child is unfortunate enough to have unloving or inconsistent parents. If they are profoundly inconsistent, he may become so confused that he loses all confidence in his ability to interpret experience. This may contribute to a schizophrenic breakdown in later life.[11] Parental rejection may lead him to see himself as unlovable, in a hostile world: "I a stranger and afraid. In a world I never made."[12] If he has been constantly belittled, he may grow up feeling inadequate to deal with many situations. Assumptive systems like these obviously tend to cause a person to avoid new experiences since he fears the worst from them.

Persons often try to resolve stresses initially created by their families by means that bring temporary relief but lay the ground for future trouble. The following example of a miniature neurosis illustrates how a person resorted to such a solution in childhood and was able to correct it years later through a lucky combination of circumstances. A scientist walking with some professional colleagues on the boardwalk at Atlantic City suddenly launched into an angry diatribe against the worthlessness of the merchandise in the curio shops. Although his remarks had some justification, the disportionate intensity of his feelings aroused quizzical looks. Noting this, he became uncomfortable and began to wonder about it himself. He then suddenly remembered a long-forgotten childhood experience. At the age of seven he spent a few days at Atlantic City with his mother and grandmother. To give his grandmother a birthday present he emptied his piggy bank and bought

11. This is the "double-bind" hypothesis of the etiology of schizophrenia (Bateson et al., 1956).
12. Housman (1922).

her a cuckoo clock. Instead of being pleased, the grandmother angrily criticized his mother for letting him be so extravagant. As he told of this, he laughed and seemed relieved.

Let us describe this little episode in theoretical terms. In giving a birthday present to his grandmother, the boy was acting on the assumption that she would be pleased. The unexpected failure of his prediction must have been most unpleasant for him. He probably felt resentment and anger at his grandmother as well as guilt for upsetting her and especially for the pain that he had inadvertently caused his mother. He might even have been angry at his mother for letting him get into such a fix.

A young child obviously cannot resolve such feelings by "having it out" with the adults who caused them, but must resort to more oblique solutions. Our patient, if he may be so termed for the moment, resorted to two common neurotic "mechanisms of defense"[13]—repression and displacement. He blotted the unpleasant episode from awareness, and displaced the object of his angry feelings from his grandmother to the curio shops. This solution had two advantages. It afforded a less dangerous object for his anger than his grandmother, and it allowed him to relieve his guilt by blaming the shops instead of himself. Like all neurotic solutions, however, it also had drawbacks. It left him with an overly negative evaluation of curio shops, and prevented him from correcting it through subsequent experience, because he thereafter avoided them. It also left him with a definite, if trivial, psychic scar in that curio shops continued to arouse an unpleasant feeling when circumstances again brought him in contact with them. By sharing it with his peers, he was implicitly trying to validate it. Their quizzical looks, indicating they did not share his feeling, led him to examine himself for its source, and he discovered a past situation for which the feeling had been appropriate. By the same act he realized that this situation no longer existed. That is, he gained insight into the inappropriateness of his attitude, enabling him to bring it into line with that of his colleagues.

13. This psychoanalytic term refers to more-or-less automatic and unconscious ways of protecting the self against unpleasant emotions, especially anxiety. See Brenner (1955).

It may be noted for future reference that his emotions were aroused when his grandmother initially failed to confirm his assumption that curio shops were sources of pleasure, leading him to change it, and when he again changed it years later on the basis of a different interaction, as shown by his discomfiture and laugh. It is worth noting, too, that the supportive, relaxed attitude of his colleagues made it relatively easy for him first to express his feelings, then to search himself for their source, and finally to offer a bit of self-revelation that explained and resolved them.

The family is only the first, although the most influential, of the many reference groups—groups to which he belongs or aspires to belong—that shape a person's assumptive world. In the above example, the scientist's colleagues represented one of his reference groups. In the aggregate, these groups form a person's culture, which supplies many ready-made categories by which to label and evaluate the experiences generated by his encounters with the world about him. Each reference group transmits to him its own idiosyncratic assumptions and values as well as those of the larger society. The relative power of the cultural assumptions depends on how well knit the culture is and on the extent to which its world view permeates the lives of its members. The assumptive worlds of, let us say, the members of an isolated tribe on a small Pacific atoll probably have more in common than those of twentieth-century Americans.

That members of a culture selectively perceive those stimuli that accord best with the culture's assumptive world was demonstrated by a simple experiment with a stereopticon, a device permitting the presentation of two different pictures simultaneously, one to each eye. When a picture of a baseball player was shown to one eye and that of a bullfighter to the other, Americans tended to see the baseball player, Mexicans the bullfighter.[14]

Societies, like families, often contain built-in conflicts, or sources of stress, which create disharmonies in the assumptive worlds of their members. Often a society also contains institutionalized ways of resolving the stresses it creates. As we shall see, societies that believe in witchcraft, for example, also have ways of

14. The example is from Cantril (1957).

counteracting witches' spells. Too often, however, no readily available institutionalized way exists to handle a conflict engendered by discrepancies in the assumptive world of a society. Americans, for example, are taught to be aggressive, yet at the same time to be affable and considerate. Violence is glorified in the entertainment and mass media, yet condemned in personal relationships or in the encounters of daily life. American society offers no institutionally sanctioned way of resolving the confusion and guilt engendered by these conflicting social values. As a result, just as neurotic conflicts in Freud's day centered on sex, today, although sexual conflicts have by no means disappeared, neuroses often derive from conflicts related to aggression.

THE CONFLICT-RIDDEN ASSUMPTIVE WORLD
OF A MINIATURE CULTURE

An assumptive world of a culture that contains insoluble conflicts can be stressful for its members, and their attempts to resolve the conflicts may make matters worse. This was graphically demonstrated by the experiences of some American soldiers hospitalized in the Philippines during World War II with schistosomiasis—a fluke infestation.[15] Many of them continued to ail after obvious signs of infestation had disappeared, suggesting that emotional reactions might be contributing importantly to their persistent invalidism. Accordingly, fifty patients who had been hospitalized for two to four months were selected at random and interviewed about their attitudes. Only two seemed completely well. Of the remaining forty-eight, only seven had objective signs of schistosomiasis and most of these were questionable, so forty-one, or four-fifths, of these patients had complaints with nothing physical to show for them. The complaints were mainly weakness, shakiness, headaches, and upper abdominal cramps. Review of the attitudes of all fifty patients showed that all but seven were anxious, resentful, or confused, or showed some combination of these feelings.

The assumptive world of the little society in which these men lived confronted them with a vague menace against which there

15. The example is from Frank (1946).

was no clearly indicated course of action. It should be emphasized that this threat arose solely from the meaning of the situation to them. They were well fed and housed, did not feel very ill, and most had never been very uncomfortable at any time. Nor, as their subsequent recovery showed, were they in any actual danger from the disease. Yet they were badly demoralized as a result of their attitudes toward the disease itself, the doctors, and the army. First, they believed the disease to be a threat to their survival since prognosis was considered uncertain and the efficacy of treatment questionable. Only two of the fifty were convinced that they had been cured, while thirty-two expected either to die of the disease or to become invalids. Second, doctors could not avoid conveying their own uncertainties to the patients. They might say different things at different times, or different doctors might contradict each other. As one man put it, "[The doctors] tell you one thing one day and kind of contradict themselves. Like they say the sickness is all in your head and then they want to give you more shots." Moreover, at the same moment that the doctors were trying to be reassuring, the radio on the wards carried alarmist reports of the disastrous nature of the disease to discourage bathing in infected streams. The soldiers did not know whom to believe: "Either the radio or the doctors are screwed up about something. I suppose the doctors are right, but then I suppose the doctors write the radio programs."

Finally, the soldiers felt that nobody really cared about them. This feeling seemed to have been created by fluctuations in disposition policies, reflecting the lack of knowledge about the disease, so that the decisions to return some soldiers to duty, hold others in the hospital, and promptly send others home appeared to the men to be purely capricious. The feeling of abandonment was accentuated by the attitudes of the harassed doctors, who, burdened with huge caseloads and not knowing what to make of the patients' endless complaints, inevitably tended to become somewhat aloof: "I tell them something and they pass it off as though it didn't exist. I feel I might as well be talking to myself."

The healthy way of coping with an ambiguous, threatening assumptive world is to clear up the uncertainty by getting more information, and the soldiers went at this with a vengeance. They read every scrap of literature on schistosomiasis they could find, wrote friends to look up the disease in medical texts, pestered the treatment staff for information, and compared notes with each other. Of course, this only made matters worse. The lack of authoritative information, the inability to comprehend the information that was available, and the general level of anxiety conspired to create a mass of rumors that enhanced the general confusion and intensified the morbid atmosphere.

Concomitantly with unsuccessful efforts to deal with the threat in appropriate fashion, the patients inevitably fell back on patterns of behavior that they had developed in early life to cope with similar predicaments. They "regressed" in that, like children, their complaints became a way of trying to elicit signs of interest and caring from the doctors, who were, in a sense, parent surrogates. Their symptoms, furthermore, afforded an indirect and acceptable way of expressing their resentment toward the treatment staff. A patient can legitimately complain that his headache has not been relieved, but it is considerably harder to complain of the doctor's incompetence.

This regressive way of dealing with the stressful assumptive world tended to confirm and heighten its threatening quality. By constantly dwelling on their symptoms, patients heightened their fears and forebodings. The variety and vagueness of their complaints added to the doctors' confusion and increased their uneasiness. They reacted by becoming impatient, intensifying the patients' anxiety and resentment.

It must be added that despite the self-aggravating nature of the threat and its apparent insolubility, individual reactions to it varied greatly. At one extreme, as already mentioned, two soldiers in the sample interviewed were apparently completely unscathed, while at the other, two were so disturbed emotionally as to require hospitalization on this basis alone. Even when an assumptive world is widely shared, people show widely differing abilities to cope with it successfully.

THE STABILITY OF THE ASSUMPTIVE WORLD IN RELATION TO PSYCHOTHERAPY

According to the formulation offered here, the aim of psychotherapy is to help a person to feel and function better by enabling him to make appropriate modifications in his assumptive world. What helps or hinders such changes? Assumptive systems, once established, tend to resist change for a variety of reasons. One is that with increasing age new experiences lose their power to produce changes in established patterns. This may be partly because of physiological changes concomitant with maturation and also because, as life goes on, new experiences are increasingly outweighed by the accumulation of previous ones.

Thus most reference groups against which a person tests the validity of his assumptions are not actually present, but exist as residues of past experiences that he has internalized. Internalized groups range from single individuals such as "my father" to groups that exist only as concepts such as "patriotic Americans" or "the scientific community." These internalized standards of reference are necessary for a stable personality organization and help the person to withstand the temporary pressures of groups he may be in at different times. At the same time they are a source of resistance to changes in his attitudes that might be beneficial.

Since a person relies on his assumptive world to create a predictable universe, anything that casts doubt on any part of it is a threat to his personal security. An experience that is inconsistent with a person's expectations arouses a feeling of surprise. This may be tinged with fear or other unpleasant feelings if the person doubts his ability to make the necessary adjustment, or exhilaration if he is confident he can cope with the situation. That is, the emotional impact of an experience seems related to the extent to which it implies the necessity of a change in the assumptive world. It seems as if the emotional upheaval is greater the more crucial to the person's security the attitude is and the greater the change required. Contrast the emotions accompanying the discovery that what one took to be a robin is really a bluebird with those accompanying a religious conversion involving far-reaching changes in the convert's values.

Although it seems likely that no change in a person's assumptive world takes place without a concomitant emotional reaction, an emotional upheaval in itself is not sufficient to produce major change. Even when a person is much upset by being compelled to recognize an error in his attitudes, no correction occurs automatically. He may, however, be strongly motivated by the experience to reexamine his assumptions and seek more reliable guides to expectation.

Of the many ways in which attitudes maintain themselves in the face of new experiences that challenge them, two are especially relevant to mental patients—avoidance and pseudoconfirmation. All attitudes filter incoming information, emphasizing those aspects that are confirmatory and minimizing those that are not. Contradictory information is either not attended to or quickly forgotten. A conscientious scientist such as Charles Darwin, recognizing this, made a special effort to note down instances that did not fit his hypothesis.

Information that threatens a person's psychic equilibrium may arise from internal sources (such as memories) or from the external world. Active avoidance of input from the internal world, called "repression" in Freudian terminology, is exemplified by the man who repressed memories of his painful childhood experience with curio shops. Banishing an experience from consciousness prevents the erroneous conclusions that were initally drawn from it from being modified by subsequent experiences, in part because the patient cannot link them to the original one. Moreover, repressed emotions or thoughts reduce both a person's adaptive capacity and his sense of security. He must expend some effort to keep them out of awareness, thus decreasing energy available for meeting current stresses. Since repression is seldom perfect, repressed emotions or thoughts are apt to erupt into consciousness attached to obviously inappropriate objects or at inappropriate times, so that they are mysterious to the patient. In the example, the scientist was startled at the inappropriate intensity of his dislike of the shops. The sense of not being able to account for one's feelings or thoughts may be partly responsible for the common fear of psychiatric patients that they are going crazy.

Persons also seek to avoid disturbing stimuli emanating from the external world, thereby depriving themselves of the chance to discover that these situations may no longer hold any terrors. Someone who has been frightened by a snake in early life, for example, will continue to avoid them. As a result, he cannot gain new experiences with snakes that might overcome his fear. As we shall see, psychotherapy, by persuading patients to face what they fear, enables corrective learning to take place.

Pseudoconfirmation, a second way in which inappropriate attitudes perpetuate themselves, is made possible because each participant in a social interaction tends to elicit behavior from the other that reinforces his preconceptions. Friendliness tends to beget friendly responses, and anger, angry ones, thus strengthening the assumptions on which the initial act was based. Furthermore, a person's own behavior, guided by his expectations, influences his interpretation of the other's response. Thus in the example cited earlier, the husband would interpret the same response of the wife quite differently, depending on how he perceived his own initial greeting. If he saw it as friendly, this would predispose him to interpret her response as such; if he meant it to be cool, he would be inclined to interpret her response as being similar. In either case, he would guide his next action accordingly, predisposing the wife to respond in accord with his expectations. Thus a continuing relationship tends to lead each participant to develop an enduring, structured set of expectations about himself and the other person, with corresponding behaviors, which become ever harder to modify by new experience.

Pseudoconfirmation seems to play an especially important part in maintaining the assumptive worlds of persons whose repertory of social behavior is limited. Since they do the same thing repeatedly and with many different people, they effectively "train" many persons to respond in such a way as to confirm their expectations.[16] A paranoid patient, for example, who is convinced that everyone hates him, will react to most persons in a surly, suspicious manner, therby antagonizing even those who initially bear him no ill will. This, in turn, intensifies his dislike-creating behavior. In the schistosomiasis example, patients came to expect the doctors to confuse them and show a lack of interest in them. By their vague but constant complaining, they tended to elicit from the doctors precisely such behavior. This, in turn, aggravated their complaints. Thus patients tend to get caught in self-fulfilling prophecies,[17] and their behavior is both self-perpetuating and self-

16. See discussion by Leary (1957, pp. 91-131), on the interpersonal reflex.
17. See Merton (1957), pp. 421-36.

defeating. Breaking these vicious circles, by confronting patients with discrepancies between their preconceptions and reality, is another important goal of psychotherapy.

Since the assumptive worlds of mental patients deviate from the general consensus of a society and therefore create more distress, one might think that they would be easier to change than those of well-adjusted persons. The reverse is true. An inaccurate or unrealistic assumptive world leads the person to experience frustrations and failures, resulting in feelings of impotence and bewilderment. A person in the grip of such feelings, whose sense of "self-potency"[18] is weak, loses confidence in his ability to control either external events or his own feelings, so he fears new experiences. Like Hamlet, he prefers to bear the ills he has than fly to others he knows not of.

Chronic frustrations, furthermore, elicit anger, resentment, and other unattractive emotions, and the patient's awareness of these may increase his sense of unworthiness. He may be further demoralized by the recognition that he is not living up to his capabilities. His self-image as being different from others and inferior to them, which may be reinforced by the attitudes of those about him, results in a sense of alienation. This makes him less accessible to others, especially when he feels that they do not understand, thus depriving him of a major means of correcting his misperceptions. To such a person, the act of seeking psychotherapy may represent public admission of his inadequacies, a further source of resistance.

In short, whereas the healthy person seeks new experiences in order to display his competence, the mental patient, being preoccupied with merely surviving, fearfully avoids them. As a result, he may be more inaccessible to help than the person whose assumptive world is less out of joint.

Applying this analysis to psychotherapy, the aims of all its forms are to help the patient correct the attitudes causing him trouble. These may be quite circumscribed and specific, such as a fear of snakes, or very general, such as a sense of alienation or despair; but in all cases success in psychotherapy depends, in the

18. McClelland (1951).

first instance, on combating the more general attitudes that hamper the patient's ability to change. Thus success in therapy depends in large part on its ability to combat the patient's demoralization and heighten his hopes of relief. All forms of psychotherapy do this implicitly, regardless of their explicit aims. Progress in therapy, in turn, further shifts the balance toward the "welfare emotions,"[19] such as love, joy, and pride, so that, with luck, the process becomes self-enhancing.

Major assumptive systems, especially unhealthy ones, are resistant to change, and in most cases the changes produced by psychotherapy are minor. Fortunately, this often suffices. Many maladaptive patterns can be improved without extensive changes in the patient's assumptive world. Much psychotherapy consists of supporting patients through crises until they can regain their previous state of equilibrium. Small changes produced by psychotherapy in one assumptive system may initiate a train of events that eventually produce changes in many others. By enabling a patient to gain a more favorable perception of his boss, for example, psychotherapy may lead him to treat the boss differently. This may evoke changes in the boss' behavior that heighten the patient's self-confidence, initiating a widening circle of beneficial changes in his assumptions about himself and other people.

This is not to deny that the aim of many forms of psychotherapy—to promote personal growth—can be achieved to some extent. This concept, of course, is rather nebulous, and what it means depends on the conceptualizations underlying the therapy in question. In terms of the schema offered here, "growth" would involve movement toward more accurate and realistic perceptions of oneself and others, including greater accessibility to one's own inner life, and behavior better suited to achieving one's goals. To the extent that psychotherapy has promoted a patient's personal growth, he should have gained a heightened sense of self-acceptance and emotional security, enabling him to be flexible and spontaneous in his dealings with others and to experience a fuller measure of welfare emotions.

Psychotherapies differ in their emphasis, notably on whether they focus primarily on influencing emotions, cognitions, or be-

19. Rado (1956).

havior. Since all attitudes involve all three components, however, it is inconsequential which component a therapy emphasizes, for it affects all three. Thus behavior therapies, by definition, concentrate on modifying behavior, but in doing so rely heavily on manipulating imagery and sometimes on stressing emotional arousal. Interview therapies stress to varying degress interchanges of feelings with the therapist and cognitive reorganization, but all assume that these will be reflected in behavioral change. Recently there has been a revival of interest in methods of eliciting intense emotional reactions, on the assumption that this is the preferred route to new insights and changed behavior.

Whatever the specific nature of the psychotherapeutic enterprise, its success depends on the ability of one person to influence another, so this chapter may close with a brief mention of the sources of this influence. To oversimplify vastly, these can be grouped into two categories: power and similarity. Powerful figures, first represented by parents and later by teachers, bosses, and so on, gain their ascendancy through their control of the person's well-being. They exert this power through control of the means he needs to achieve his goals and by their ability to determine the consequences of his behavior. The ability of one person to influence another also depends on similarities of manner and outlook. These largely determine the influencer's credibility and also how easily the recipient of influence can accept him as a model or identify with him.[20]

Members of groups to which a person feels he belongs or aspires to belong—his reference groups—affect his attitudes and behavior through both power and similarity. Their ability to determine his acceptability as a member leads him to conform to their expectations in order to retain his membership, or to gain admission if he does not have it. Members of such groups, because of their many resemblances to one another, afford ready objects for emulation or identification. Both factors play a large part in the effectiveness of group therapies.[21]

20. Festinger (1954) regards the need to evaluate one's own opinions and abilities as a major determinant of human behavior. This leads a person to compare himself with others, whose influence depends on the perceived similarity between their opinions and abilities and his own.
21. See pp. 276–83 below.

The psychotherapist's influence on his patient springs primarily from the fact that the latter looks to him for relief, an expectation heightened by the therapist's cultural role and special training. On the other hand, as has long been recognized, dissimilarities between the therapist with respect to class an education can create obstacles to treatment.[22] These are often counterbalanced, however, by the fact that the therapist is a representative of a group to which the patient aspires. Much of the psychotherapist's persuasive ability may derive from the fact that he represents attitudes and values held by the patient's family, peers, or the larger society, while at the same time he accepts the patient's views. Thus he can act as a bridge between society and the patient.

It must be added that matters are seldom this simple. For one thing, a patient's improvement may require that he oppose members of some of his reference groups, and for another his socially determined perceptions of the therapist as a powerful, potentially helpful person are often complicated by reactions arising from his unique life experience. These are encompassed by the term "transference," which implies that patients tend to transfer to the therapist attitudes about important figures in their lives, whether or not they are appropriate to him. Transference reactions may help or hamper the therapist's efforts, depending on whom he represents to the patient.

Consideration of the sources and nature of the psychotherapist's influence is a major object of this book. For the present, it suffices to indicate that although patients may present formidable resistance to change, the psychotherapist often has forces at his disposal that can overcome this, at least to some extent.

SUMMARY

Psychotherapy tries to relieve a person's distress and improve his functioning by helping him to correct errors and resolve conflicts in his attitudes about himself and others. These attitudes are organized into systems existing at varying levels of consciousness and in harmonious or conflicting relationships with one another.

22. See pp. 180–83 below.

They affect and are affected by emotional states, and changes in them are regularly accompanied by emotion. Healthy attitude systems are characterized by internal consistency and close correspondence with actual conditions. They thus lead to reliable, satisfactory social interactions, accompanied by a sense of competence, inner security, and well-being, which enables the person to modify them readily when necessary. Unhealthy attitude systems are internally full of conflict and do not accurately correspond to circumstances, leading to experiences of frustration, failure, and alienation. Efforts to cope with or evade these feelings tend to be both self-perpetuating and self-defeating, resulting in cumulative adaptational difficulties.

Despite the stubbornness of maladaptive attitudes, the psychotherapist, as a socially sanctioned expert and healer and a member of the patient's reference groups, may be able to mobilize forces sufficiently powerful to produce beneficial changes in them.

NONMEDICAL HEALING: RELIGIOUS
III   AND SECULAR

"I can't believe *that*," said Alice. "Can't you?" the Queen
said in a pitying tone. "Try again; draw a long breath,
and shut your eyes."

Lewis Carroll, *Through the Looking Glass*

Western industrial societies view illness essentially as a
malfunctioning of the body, to be corrected by appropriate medical and surgical interventions. Many believe,
not without reason, that the causes of even so-called
mental illnesses will be discovered to be subtle derange-
ments of the brain. In this view, which gains strong
support from the triumphs of scientific medicine, the
physician is a highly skilled scientist-technician, whose
job is to diagnose the bodily disturbance and correct it,
much as a good auto mechanic would deal with a poorly
running automobile.

While this approach to illness has scored notable successes and will undoubtedly score many more, it is
seriously deficient in a crucial respect. It fails to
acknowledge that psychological and bodily processes
can profoundly affect each other. High among the
former are the meanings of illness emerging from the
interplay of the sick person with his family and his culture. All illnesses, whatever their bodily components,
have implications that may give rise to noxious

46

emotions, raise difficult moral issues, damage the patient's self-esteem, and estrange him from his compatriots. Chronic illness, especially, causes demoralization. Constant misery, forced relinquishment of the activities and roles that supported the patient's self-esteem and gave his life significance, the threat of suffering and death—all may generate feelings of anxiety and despair, which, in turn, may be intensified by reactions of anxiety, impatience, and progressive withdrawal in those close to him, especially when his illness threatens their security as well as his own. Thus illness often creates a vicious circle by evoking emotions that aggravate it.

The insensitivity of scientific medicine to the noxious effects of these emotions probably accounts for many of its failures and also impels the ill to seek out forms of healing which operate on a different premise. "People do not visit a fringe practitioner because they are gullible, stupid or superstitious, though they may be; they go to him because they think, or hope, they can get something from him that their doctor no longer gives. They are right; often the doctor does not pretend to be able to give it."[1]

All practitioners of nonmedical healing, who, incidentally, minister to many more sufferers throughout the world than do physicians, see illness as a disorder of the total person, involving not only his body but his image of himself and his relations to his group; instead of emphasizing conquest of the disease, they focus on stimulating or strengthening the patient's natural healing powers. They believe that this can be done by the ministrations of a healer who, whatever his methods, enters into an intense relationship with the patient. In contrast with scientific medicine which, while paying copious lip service to the doctor-patient relationship, in actuality largely ignores it, all nonmedical healing methods attach great importance to it. Those operating in a religious context, which includes all forms of healing in primitive societies and faith healing in industrial ones, also see themselves as bringing supernatural forces to bear on the patient, with the healer acting primarily as a conduit for them.

1. Inglis (1965), pp. 53–54. He classifies nonmedical healing into three categories, progressively more distant from scientific medicine: those emphasizing the body, such as herbalism, homeopathy, chiropractic, and osteopathy; those emphasizing the mind, such as psychotherapy, hypnotherapy, and autosuggestion; and those stressing the spirit, such as Christian Science and spiritual healing.

This chapter focuses on healing in primitive societies, considers one Western healing shrine, and takes a brief glance at secular forms of nonmedical healing in the West.[2]

Examination of religious healing in so-called primitive societies and in Western society illuminates certain aspects of human functioning that are relevant to psychotherapy. Methods of supernatural healing highlight the close interplay of assumptive systems and emotional states and the intimate relation of both to health and illness. They also bring out the parallel between inner disorganization and disturbed relations with one's group, and indicate how patterned interaction of patient, healer, and group within the framework of a self-consistent assumptive world can promote healing. Certain properties of healing rituals in primitive societies, finally, show interesting resemblances to naturalistic psychotherapeutic methods that may serve to increase understanding of both.

The view that illness can be caused and cured by the intervention of supernatural forces stretches back to furthest antiquity and continues to be important, though often in attenuated form, in most modern cultures. Patients who come from ethnic groups that harbor beliefs in supernaturalism may attribute their illness to supernatural forces more often than they are willing to admit to the physician. Three patients recently seen in the psychiatric clinic of a teaching hospital, a veritable citadel of scientific medicine, come to mind. None was in any sense psychotic. One, born in Sicily, sheepishly confessed that he believed his nervousness and restlessness were caused by the evil eye, incurred because he had flirted with someone else's girl. Another, raised in Appalachia, attributed her severe anxiety to a fortuneteller's prophecy that her father was about to die. She believed firmly in vampires and was convinced that her grandmother was a witch. A third, a devout Catholic, was more than half convinced that her two miscarriages were God's punishment for having divorced her husband and married a Protestant.

Belief in supernatural forces, moreover, is not confined to the uneducated. A highly respected Negro physician once confided to me that, having failed to gain relief from foot pain from physi-

<hr>

2. For a comprehensive review of psychotherapy and religious healing, see Torrey (1972).

cians, she finally was cured by a Voodoo practitioner. The growing interest in astrology, tarot cards, I-Ching, and the like among the educated, as well as the widespread use of consciousness-altering drugs to produce transcendental experiences, all point to a resurgence of supernaturalism.

It is possible to make all kinds of distinctions in regard to the type of supernatural theories invoked, as to whether they dominate a society or are believed only by deviant groups, and in regard to the social acceptance and status of the healers. We shall consider primarily those theories that are integral parts of the religion of the total society or of a respectable and numerous portion of it, and in which the healing rituals are public and socially sanctioned. Thus the term "religious" seems applicable to them, even though few readers of this book would accept the validity of the religious beliefs on which most of these forms of healing are based.

Religious healing in primitive societies, as in the Western world, tends to exist side by side with naturalistic treatment by medicines, manipulations, and surgery. Its sphere of influence tends to shrink in the face of secularization and the introduction of scientific medicine.[3] In all cultures its chief realm is the treatment of illnesses with important emotional components—that is, the conditions for which naturalistically based psychotherapies are also used. It therefore is not surprising that, although their theoretical foundations differ profoundly, religious and naturalistic healing methods have much in common. Furthermore, both types of healing have persisted through the ages, suggesting that their efficacy may lie partly in their common features. In this chapter we shall search for these features in religious healing methods of primitive societies and note to what extent they are also found in a great contemporary shrine of miraculous healing.

To avoid the necessity of qualifying every statement, let it be said at the start that although the characteristics to be discussed are widespread, they are not universal. The diversity of healing

3. But religious healing still maintains a very strong hold, especially among members of a society not exposed to Western ideas (see, for example, Jahoda, 1961). In addition, as indicated on pp. 72–74 below, healing cults based on theories that are scientifically bizarre continue to flourish in the United States.

methods in primitive societies is very great and exceptions can be found to any generalization.[4] Moreover, the examples are not offered to prove a line of argument (which would require consideration of negative instances) but simply to support and illustrate it.

ILLNESSES IN PRIMITIVE SOCIETIES

Primitive societies regard illness as a misfortune involving the entire person, directly affecting his relationships with the spirit world and with other members of his group. Although they recognize different kinds of illness, their classifications often bear no relation to those of Western medicine. In particular, they may not distinguish sharply between mental and bodily illness, or between that due to natural and that due to supernatural causes.

Illnesses tend to be viewed as symbolic expressions of internal conflicts or of disturbed relationships to others, or both. Thus they may be attributed to soul loss, possession by an evil spirit, the magical insertion of a harmful body by a sorcerer, or the machinations of offended or malicious ancestral ghosts. It is usually assumed that the patient laid himself open to these calamities through some witting or unwitting transgression against the supernatural world, or through incurring the enmity of a sorcerer or someone who has employed a sorcerer to wreak revenge. The transgression need not have been committed by the patient himself. He may fall ill through the sin of a kinsman.

Although many societies recognize that certain illnesses have natural causes, this does not exclude the simultaneous role of supernatural ones. A broken leg may be recognized as caused by a fall from a tree, but the cause of the fall may have been an evil thought or a witch's curse.

Because of the high mortality rates among primitive peoples, many diseases represent a great threat to the patient, and the longer the illness lasts, the greater the threat becomes. In societies subsisting on a marginal level, illness is a threat to the group as well as to the invalid. It prevents the invalid from making his full

4. Kiev (1964) provides an excellent sampling.

contribution to the group's support and diverts the energies of those who must care for him from group purposes. Therefore, it seems likely that every illness has overtones of anxiety, despair and similar emotions, mounting as cure is delayed. That is, persons for whom healing rituals are performed probably are experiencing emotions that aggravate their distress and disability, whatever the underlying pathological condition. The invalid is in conflict within himself and out of harmony with his group. The group is faced with the choice of abandoning him to his fate by completing the process of extrusion, or of making strenuous efforts to heal him, thereby restoring him to useful membership in his community.

These considerations may be exemplified by a personal disaster that can befall members of certain groups and that may have a counterpart in civilized societies. This is the so-called taboo death, which apparently results from noxious emotional states related to certain individual and group assumptive systems about supernatural forces and which also involve the victim's relationships with his group.

Anthropological literature contains anecdotes of savages who, on learning that they have inadvertently broken a taboo, go into a state of panic and excitement leading to death in a few hours.[5] Unfortunately in none of these cases can more mundane causes of rapid death, such as overwhelming infection, be entirely excluded.[6] The evidence that members of certain tribes may pine away and die within a brief period after learning that they have been cursed is more fully documented and more convincing. The *post hoc* nature of the explanations must not be overlooked, especially since in groups where this type of death occurs, practically all illness and death is attributed to the invalid having been cursed. Nevertheless, the process has been observed in sufficient detail in different tribes to make the explanation highly plausible.

The most convincing examples are those in which a native at the point of death from a curse rapidly recovers when the spell is broken by a more powerful one, as in the following anecdote, which can be multiplied many times:

5. For examples see Webster (1942).
6. Since patients who believe themselves cursed also may refuse food and drink, dehydration and starvation may be contributory causes to taboo deaths (Barber, 1961b).

Some years ago my father, who lived in Kenya, employed a Kikuyu garden "boy," of whom we were all fond. Njombo was gay, cheerful and in the prime of life. He was paying goats to purchase a wife and looking forward to marriage and a bit of land of his own. One day we noticed he was beginning to lose weight and looked pinched and miserable. We dosed him with all the usual medicines to no avail. Then we persuaded him, much against his will, to go into a hospital. Three weeks later he was back with a note from the doctor: "There is nothing wrong with this man except that he has made up his mind to die."

After that Njombo took to his bed, a heap of skins, and refused all food and drink. He shrank to nothing and at last went into a coma. Nothing we could do or say would strike a spark, and all seemed to be up with him.

As a last resort, my father went to the local chief and threatened him with all sorts of dreadful penalties if he did not take action to save Njombo's life. This was largely bluff, but the chief fell for it. That evening we saw a man with a bag of stoppered gourds entering Njombo's hut. We did not interfere, and no doubt a goat was slaughtered. Next morning, Njombo allowed us to feed him a little beef tea. From that moment he started to rally—the will to live was restored. We asked no questions, but learned some time later that Njombo had had a serious quarrel over the girl and that his rival had cursed him. Only when the curse was removed could he hope to survive.[7]

In certain societies, the victim's expectation of death may be powerfully reinforced by the attitudes of his group. For example, in the Murngin, a North Australian tribe, when the theft of a man's soul becomes general knowledge, he and his tribe collaborate in hastening his demise.[8] Having lost his soul, he is already "half dead." Since his soul is in neither this world nor the next, he is a danger to himself as a spiritual entity and also to his tribe because his soul, not having been properly laid away, is likely to cause illness and death among his kin. All normal social activity with him therefore ceases and he is left alone. Then, shortly before he dies, the group returns to him under the guidance of a ceremonial leader to perform mourning rites, the purpose of which is "to cut him off entirely from the ordinary world and ultimately place him ... in ... the ... world ... of the dead." The victim, concomitantly, recognizes his change of status: ". . . the wounded feudist killed by magic dances his totem dance to ... insure his

7. Elspeth Huxley (1959), p. 19. Presumably Njombo was aware of the ministrations of the shaman, although he appeared comatose to his employers.
8. Warner (1941). The quotes are from pp. 241 and 242.

immediate passage to the totem well. . . . His effort is not to live but to die." The writer concludes: "If all a man's near kin . . . business associates, friends, and all other members of the society, should suddenly withdraw themselves because of some dramatic circumstance . . . looking at the man as one already dead, and then after some little time perform over him a sacred ceremony believed with certainty to guide him out of the land of the living . . . the enormous suggestive power of this twofold movement of the community . . . can be somewhat understood by ourselves."

Although this account stresses the role of group influences, the major source of the victim's decline is probably the emotional state induced by his conviction—grounded in his belief system—that he has lost his soul. In this example the group's withdrawal reinforces this conviction. It is conceivable, however, that the victim would have died even if surrounded by their loving care if his conviction that the situation was hopeless were sufficiently strong. Calling attention to the interpersonal forces involved in the process should not be taken as minimizing the importance of intrapersonal ones.

Plausible speculations based on work with animals have been offered to explain the physiological mechanism of death in these cases. One hypothesis is that it might be due to prolonged adrenal overexcitation caused by terror, leading to a state analogous to surgical shock.[9] Another, based on studies of physiological changes in wild rats who give up and die when placed in a stressful situation after their whiskers have been clipped, suggests that the emotional state is more one of despair than terror, and that the mechanism of death is stoppage of the heart resulting from overactivity of the vagus nerve.[10] This view is supported by fascinating and suggestive parallels between this phenomenon in wild rats and taboo deaths in primitive peoples—for example, prompt recovery even at the point of death if the stress is suddenly removed. Both hypotheses are plausible, and each may account for a particular variety of emotionally caused death—the first for the rapid form, if it occurs, and the second for the slower variety.

9. Cannon (1957).
10. Richter (1957).

In civilized as well as primitive societies a person's conviction
that his predicament is hopeless may cause or hasten his disintegration and death. For example, the death rate of the aged shortly
after admission to state mental hospitals is unduly high, and with
these and other age groups often no adequate cause of death is
found at autopsy, raising the possibility that some of these deaths
are caused by hopelessness, aggravated by abandonment by the
patient's group. Similarly, some young schizophrenics may go into
overactive panic states in which they exhaust themselves and die.
This fortunately rare reaction usually occurs in conjunction with
the patient's admission to the hospital—that is, at the moment
when his family withdraws and he feels abandoned. Sometimes it
can be successfully interrupted if a member of the treatment staff
succeeds in making contact with the patient and getting across to
him, by one means or another, that some still cares about him.[11]

Descriptions of the "give-up-itis" reaction of American prisoners of war of the Japanese and Koreans suggest a similar
interaction of hopelessness and group isolation to produce
death. A former prisoner of war well describes this reaction.[12] He
list the major factors that had to be dealt with in order to survive
as: "the initial shock and subsequent depression induced by being
taken prisoner by Oriental people; the feeling of being deserted
and abandoned by one's own people; the severe deprivation of
food, warmth, clothes, living comforts, and sense of respectability;
the constant intimidation and physical beatings from the captors;
loss of self-respect and the respect of others; the day-to-day uncertainty of livelihood and the vague indeterminable unknown future
date of deliverance." It will be noted that physical and psychological threats are placed on the same footing. Under these circumstances: "Occasionally an individual would . . . lose interest in

11. Will (1959) cites two examples of deaths of schizophrenics possibly precipitated
by their sense of "unrelatedness." Adland (1947) reviews the literature on "acute exhaustive psychoses" up to that time and cites a case in which the process was successfully interrupted when the psychiatrist succeeded in making contact with the patient.
Rosen (1946) describes his successful interruption of three acute catatonic excitements
by playing the role of the patient's protector, in terms of the patient's delusional system.
The less dramatic but careful studies of Lesse (1958) demonstrate that anxiety is a
forerunner of many psychopathological symptoms and parallels them in severity.
12. Nardini (1952). The quotes are from pp. 244 and 245.

himself and his future, which was reflected in quiet or sullen withdrawal from the group, filth of body and clothes, trading of food for cigarettes, slowing of work late . . . and an expressed attitude of not giving a damn. . . . If this attitude were not met with firm resistance . . . death inevitably resulted."

This is clearly a description of hopelessness. It could be successfully combatted by "forced hot soap-and-water bathing, shaving and delousing, special appetizing food, obtaining a few days rest in camp . . . a mixture of kindly sympathetic interest and anger-inducing attitudes. Victory was assured with the first sign of a smile or evidence of pique." It is of interest that successful measures may include anger-arousing as well as nurturant behavior. As another observer reports: "One of the best ways to get a man on his feet initially was to make him so mad, by goading, prodding, or blows, that he tried to get up and beat you. If you could manage this, the man invariably got well."[13] Thus it may be that any kind of emotional stimulus, whether pleasant or not, may successfully counteract lethal despair if it succeeds in breaking through the victim's isolation, demonstrates that others care about him, and implies that there are things he can do to help himself.

To descend to less spectacular examples of the harmful effects of emotional states, a study of forty-two patients hospitalized with medical illnesses concluded that "psychic states of helplessness or hopelessness may be related to increased biological vulnerability."[14] The findings of a study described earlier[15] suggested that emotions such as anxiety, depression, and resentment were associated with delayed convalescence from a fluke infestation. A series of elegantly designed investigations has produced convincing evidence that depression, which could not be attributed to the illness itself, is associated with delayed convalescence from both undulant fever and influenza.[16]

13. Major Clarence L. Anderson, quoted in Kinkead (1959), p. 149. Strassman *et al.* (1956) present an interesting discussion of apathy as a reaction to severe stress in war prisoners.
14. Schmale (1958), p. 271. Although methodologically flawed, the study gains plausibility from accounts of a similar relationship of illness to noxious emotional states in primitives and prisoners.
15. See pp. 35–37 above.
16. Imboden *et al.* (1959, 1961).

THE ROLE OF THE SHAMAN
IN PRIMITIVE SOCIETIES

Having considered how certain emotional states activated by personal assumptive systems interacting with group forces may contribute to disintegration and death, let us turn now to the role of these factors in healing, as illustrated by religious healing rituals in primitive societies.[17] These rituals, which grow directly out of the tribe's world view, are usually conducted by a shaman[18] and involve participation of the patient and usually members of his family and tribe.

The powers of the shaman are explained in terms of the society's assumptive world and are unquestioningly accepted as genuine by it. The routes for acquiring shamanistic powers vary greatly. In some societies the shaman acquires them, sometimes against his will, through personal and private mystical experiences, and he is regarded as a deviant person with little status except when his powers are invoked. In others, shamans are drawn from the ranks of cured patients.[19] And in others, as in the Kwakiutl, they undergo an elaborate training course, analogous to medical training in our culture, and enjoy a high prestige.

Shamans usually are adept at distinguishing illnesses they can treat successfully from those that are beyond their powers, and they manage to reject patients with whom they are likely to fail. This enables them to maintain a reputation for success which, by arousing favorable expectancies in the patient and the group, undoubtedly enhances their healing power.

17. The discussion of primitive healing is based primarily on the following sources: Deren (1953); Gillin (1948); Leighton (1968); Lévi-Strauss (1958); Opler (1936); Sachs (1947); and Spiro (1967).
18. Although anthropologists draw distinctions between terms such as "shaman," "witch doctor," and "medicine man," "shaman" seems to be gaining acceptance as the generic designation for primitive healers of all types and is so used in the text.
19. See Field (1955). According to Spiro (1967), Burmese healers may be shamans, recruited from those with pathogenic symptoms, who can only propitiate harmful supernatural spirits, and exorcists or members of magico-religious sects who can control them. The Burmese example points to at least two sources of a healer's ability to inspire a patient's confidence: having successfully overcome similar problems (which should also strengthen rapport) and being a member of a culturally-valued healing sect. The analysed psychoanalyst partakes of both. See Prince (1968). Henry (1966) considers parallels between life histories of shamans and American psychotherapists. Another way of acquiring shamanistic powers is through inheritance, calling to mind the frequency of physician dynasties in all societies (Sachs, 1947).

The importance of the group's attitudes in determining not only the shaman's effectiveness but also his self-evaluation is well illustrated by the remarkable autobiography of Quesalid, a Kwakiutl shaman.[20] He entered training motivated by skepticism concerning the shaman's powers and by the desire to expose them. (Perhaps, like many converts, he exaggerated his former skepticism.) The training included learning to master various arts of deception, and especially how to spit out of one's mouth at the right moment a bit of down covered with blood, representing the foreign body that had made the patient ill and had been magically extracted from him.

Knowing that he was in training, a family called him in to treat a patient, and he was brilliantly successful. He attributed the cure to psychological factors: ". . . because the patient believed strongly in his dream about me." What shook his skepticism was a visit to a neighboring Koskimo tribe, in which the shamans simply spit a little saliva into their hands and dared to pretend that this was the illness. In order to find out "what is the power of these shamans, if it is real or if they only pretend to be shamans," he asked and received permission to try his method since theirs had failed. Again the patient said she was cured. Apparently some forms of healing were more fraudulent than others. This presented Quesalid with a problem "not without parallel in the development of modern science: two systems, both known to be inadequate, nevertheless, compared with each other appear to differ in value both logically and experimentally. In what frame of reference should they be judged?"

The Koskimo shamans, "covered with shame" because they had been discredited in the eyes of their countrymen, and thrown into self-doubts, tried very hard to ferret out his secrets, but to no avail. Finally one of the most eminent challenged him to a healing duel, and Quesalid again succeeded where the other failed. Two interesting consequences followed. The old shaman, fearing to die of shame and unable to get Quesalid to reveal his secret, vanished the same night with all his relatives "sick at heart," returned after a year insane, and died three years later. Quesalid, although he

20. Lévi-Strauss (1958). Quotes are from pp. 193, 194, and 196. Translation is by Elizabeth K. Frank.

continues to expose imposters and is full of scorn for the profession, remains uncertain about whether there are real shamans or
not: "only once have I seen a shaman who treated patients by
suction and I was never able to find out if he was a real shaman or
a faker. For this reason only, I believe that he was a shaman. He
did not allow those he had cured to pay him. And truly I never
once saw him laugh." At the end it is unclear whether he considers
himself to be a real shaman: ". . . he pursues his calling with con-
science . . . is proud of his successes and . . . defends heatedly against
all rival schools the technique of the bloodstained down whose
deceptive nature he seems completely to have lost sight of, and
which he had scoffed at so much in the beginning." Quesalid's
skepticism is not able to withstand his own successes and the
belief of his group in his powers.

THE HEALING CEREMONY
IN PRIMITIVE SOCIETIES

Healing in primitive societies utilizes both individual and group
methods. It may be conducted by the shaman with the patient
alone, analogous to the pattern of Western medicine. The shaman
makes a diagnosis by performing certain acts and then offers a
remedy, which may be a medication or the performance of suitable incantations as in the example cited above.[21] The healing
power of these procedures probably lies in the patient's expectation of help, based on his perception of the shaman as possessing
special healing powers, derived from his ability to communicate
with the spirit world.

Other forms of primitive healing involve a long-term two-person
relationship between shaman and patient, which seems analogous
in some ways to long-term psychotherapy.[22] The only available
descriptions, however, are too sketchy to warrant consideration
here.

This section considers a third type of primitive healing which
has been adequately described by anthropologists and which bears

21. See also Sachs (1947).
22. Field (1955) gives sketchy examples of long-term individual therapy in the
African Gold Coast, and Lederer (1959) adds a consideration of exorcism in the Middle
Ages and in Zen Buddhism. Both writers discuss parallels with Western psychotherapy.

on psychotherapy—the group healing ceremonial. These rituals may involve ancestral or other spirits, for example, and are intensive, time-limited efforts aimed at curing specific illness and involving members of the patient's family. As a result, they cast little, if any, light on certain features that may be of central importance in long-term individual psychotherapy, such as the development and examination of transference reactions between patient and therapist. On the other hand, they throw certain aspects of long-term therapy into relief, as it were, by compressing them into a brief time span, and highlight the healing role of group and cultural forces, which may be underestimated in individual therapy because they are present only implicitly. With these considerations in mind, it may be instructive to consider a healing ceremony in some detail—the treatment of "espanto" in a sixty-three-year-old Guatemalan Indian woman.[23] This was her eighth attack. Her symptoms seem similar to those that would lead an American psychiatrist to diagnose an agitated depression. The Indians attribute it to soul loss.

The treatment began with a diagnostic session attended not only by the patient but by her husband, a male friend, and two anthropologists. The healer felt her pulse for a while, while looking her in the eye, then confirmed that she was suffering from "espanto." He then told her in a calm, authoritative manner that it had happened near the river when she saw her husband foolishly lose her money to a loose woman, and he urged her to tell the whole story. After a brief period of reluctance, the patient "loosed a flood of words telling of her life frustrations and anxieties.... During the recital ... the curer ... nodded noncommitally, but permissively, keeping his eyes fixed on her face. Then he said that it was good that she should tell him of her life." Finally they went over the precipitating incident of the present attack in detail. In essence, she and her husband were passing near the spot where he had been deceived by the loose woman. She upbraided him, and he struck her with a rock.

The curer then told her he was confident she could be cured and outlined in detail the preparations that she would have to make for the curing session four days later. She was responsible

23. Gillin (1948). Quotes are from pp. 389, 391, and 394.

for these preparations, which involved procuring and preparing certain medications, preparing a feast, persuading a woman friend or kinsman to be her "servant" during the preparatory period and healing session, and persuading one of the six chiefs of the village to participate with the medicine man in the ceremony.

The ceremony itself began at four in the afternoon and lasted until five the next morning. Before the healer arrived, the house and the house altar[24] had been decorated with pine boughs, and numerous invited guests and participants had assembled. After they were all present, the healer made his entrance, shook hands all around, and checked the preparations carefully. Then there was a period of light refreshment and social chitchat, which apparently helped to organize a social group around the patient and to relax tension.

After dusk the healer, chief, and others of the group went off to church, apparently to appease the Christian deities in advance, since "recovery of a soul involves dealing with renegade saints and familiar spirits certainly not approved of by God Almighty." When they returned, a large meal was served. The patient did not eat, but was complimented by all present on her food. Then the healer carried out a long series of rituals involving such activities as making wax dolls of the chief of evil spirits and his wife, to whom the healer appealed for return of the patient's soul, and elaborate massage of the patient with whole eggs, which were believed to absorb some of the sickness from the patient's body.[25] The curer, the chief, two male helpers, and the ever-present anthropologists next took the eggs and a variety of paraphernalia, including gifts for the evil spirits, to the place where the patient had lost her soul,

24. The altars are Christian. In Christianized societies embarrassing problems may be created by incompatibilities between the assumptive systems underlying healing rituals and Christian beliefs. As a result, a considerable part of the healing rite may be devoted to arranging a truce between them, as in the example.

25. With a few notable exceptions, such as Wilhelm Reich and J. L. Moreno, Western psychotherapists have eschewed bodily contact, relying solely on words as means of communication. This probably reflects a culturally induced suspicion that all bodily contacts are erotic. As a result, psychotherapists have deprived themselves of a powerful means of relieving tension and strengthening rapport, widely used in other cultures (Torrey, 1972). The appeal of chiropractors and osteopaths may lie partly in their free use of massage and manipulation. The encouragement of members to indulge in a wide variety of bodily contacts may also help to account for the attraction of sensitivity training and encounter groups (see Chapter 10 below).

and the healer pleaded with various spirits to restore her soul to her.

On their return they were met at the door by the patient, who showed an intense desire to know whether the mission had been successful. The curer spoke noncommittal but comforting words. This was followed by much praying by the healer and the chief before the house altar and a special ground altar set up outside, and by rites to purify and sanctify the house. Some of these activities were devoted to explaining to the household patron saint why it was necessary to deal with evil spirits. About 2 A.M., the ceremony came to a climax. The patient, naked except for a small loin cloth, went outside. Before the audience, the healer sprayed her entire body with a magic fluid that had been prepared during the ritual and that had a high alcoholic content. Then she had to sit, naked and shivering, in the cold air for about ten minutes. Finally she drank about a pint of the fluid. Then they returned indoors, the patient lay down in front of the altar, and the healer massaged her vigorously and systematically with the eggs, then with one of his sandals. She then arose, put on her clothes, lay down on the rustic platform bed, and was covered with blankets. By this time she was thoroughly relaxed.

Finally, the healer broke the six eggs used in the massage into a bowl of water one by one, and as he watched their swirling whites he reviewed the history of the patient's eight "espantos," pointing out the "proofs" in the eggs. The sinking of the eggs to the bottom of the bowl showed that all the previous "espantos" had been cured and that the present symptoms would shortly disappear. The healer "pronounced the cure finished. The patient roused herself briefly on the bed and shouted hoarsely, 'That is right.' Then she sank back into a deep snoring sleep." This ended the ceremony and everyone left but the patient's immediate family.

The patient had a high fever for the following few days. This did not concern the healer, whose position was that everyone died sooner or later anyway, and if the patient died, it was better for her to die with her soul than without it. He refused to see her again, as his work was done. The anthropologist treated her with antibiotics, and she made a good recovery from the fever and the depression. The author notes that for the four weeks he was able to observe her "she seemed to have developed a new personality. . . . The hypochondriacal complaints, nagging of her husband and relatives, withdrawal from her social contacts, and anxiety symptoms all disappeared."

This example illustrates certain generalizations about religious healing which, if not universal, are at least widely applicable. It should be noted that healing rituals are not undertaken lightly. Usually they are resorted to only after simpler healing methods have failed. The analogy springs to mind that in America patients are often referred for psychiatric treatment only after all other forms of treatment have failed to relieve their suffering. In any case, this suggests that the state of mind of a patient receiving a healing ritual and that one receiving psychotherapy often resemble each other in some respects. Both types of patient are apt to be discouraged and apprehensive about their condition, while at the same time hopeful for relief from the treatment.

The theory of illness and healing, and the healing method itself, are integral parts of the culture's assumptive world. They supply the patient with a conceptual framework for making sense out of his chaotic and mysterious feelings, and suggest a plan of action, thus helping him to gain a sense of direction and mastery and to resolve his inner conflicts. As has been said about another magical cure:

> That the mythology of the shaman does not correspond to objective reality does not matter. The patient believes in it and belongs to a society that believes in it. The protecting spirits, the evil spirits, the supernatural monsters and magical monsters are elements of a coherent system which are the basis of the natives' concept of the universe. The patient accepts them, or rather she has never doubted them. What she does not accept are the incomprehensible and arbitrary pains which represent an element foreign to her system but which the shaman, by invoking the myth, will replace in a whole in which everything has its proper place.[26]

The shaman's activities validate his supernatural powers. In this example his manner in the diagnostic interview and especially his

---

26. Lévi-Strauss (1958), p. 217. See also Leighton (1968) on the functions of the "dramatic myth" underlying all primitive healing rituals.

revelation to the patient of an event that she did not know he knew, and that he therefore presumably learned about through magic, must have had this effect. In other rituals the shaman may start by reciting how he got his "call" or citing examples of the previous cures, to which others present may add confirmation. He may resort to legerdemain, as in the Kwakiutl, but most authorities agree that this is not regarded as trickery, even when the audience knows how it is done. They seem to give emotional assent to the proposition that the bloody bit of cotton is the patient's illness and has been extracted from his body, while at another level they know perfectly well that it is only a piece of cotton. Perhaps their state of mind is analogous to that of partakers of communion, for whom in one sense the bread and wine are the body and blood of Christ while in another they are just bread and wine. In any case, the healing ritual reinforces the image of the shaman as a powerful ally in the patient's struggle with the malign forces that have made him ill.

In his struggle with the forces of evil, the shaman may risk his own soul.[27] Heightening the emotional intensity of the ritual may increase its therapeutic power in several ways. It implies that the shaman has sufficient confidence in his own powers to risk the danger; this not only increases the patient's confidence in him, but conveys the message that the shaman cares enough about the patient and considers him important enough to risk his own safety on his behalf.

The conceptual scheme is validated and reinforced by the rituals that it prescribes. In the above example, this reinforcement occurred especially when the healer examined the eggs swirling in the water and pointed out to the assembled group the "proofs" of the patient's previous illnesses. The scheme, moreover, cannot be shaken by failure of the ritual to cure the patient. If this one had died, the ceremony would still have been regarded as successful in restoring her soul.[28]

27. Fox (1964, p. 185) describes titantic battles between doctors and evil spirits in Cochiti therapy, during which, according to a doctor, "we are more scared than [the lay participants] are. The witches are out to get us." See also Spiro (1967), p. 200.

28. As in Western medicine, the criterion of the success of a healing procedure is not always the patient's recovery. The old surgical quip comes to mind: "The operation was successful but the patient died."

Rituals often involve a preparatory period, which represents a dramatic break in the usual routine of daily activities. In the case of "espanto," the preparation for the ritual served to jolt the patient out of her usual routines, heighten her sense of personal importance by letting her have a "servant," and start the process of rallying family and group forces to her aid. In addition, like the rest of the ritual, it gave her something to do to combat her illness, in it itself a powerful allayer of anxiety and a boost to hopes of cure. The patient's family, as well as respected representatives of the tribe, convey their concern for him by their participation. Since they represent a healthy group, the patient's associates are not likely to reinforce his pathological trends, as may occur, for example, in a mental hospital.[29]

Aspects of the healing ritual heighten the patient's sense of self-worth, and, in fact, increase the merit of all participants. The patient is the focus of the group's attention and, by implication, worthy of the invocation of supernatural forces on his behalf. Important, also, is the altruistic quality of the activities. The group tries to help the patient by performing parts of the ritual, interceding for him with the powers he has presumably offended, or defending the patient to them. Sometimes the patient also performs services for the group. In our example, the patient was responsible for preparing the feast. Mutual performance of services cements the tie between patient and group. The patient's activities may also help to counteract his morbid self-absorption and enhance his sense of self-worth by demonstrating that he can still be of use to others.

In those ceremonies that involve confession, atonement, and forgiveness, the gaining of merit is especially apparent.[30] The fact that confession is required for cure implies a close link between illness and transgression, as discussed earlier. Impersonal forms of confession and repentance, as in some Christian liturgies, serve the purpose of general purification.

Some healing rituals elicit confessions of specific personal transgressions based on detailed review of the patient's past history

29. Cf. "network therapy" in Speck and Rueveni (1969).
30. See LaBarre (1964) for many examples of confessional rituals in North and South American Indian tribes. Rasmussen (1929) offers an excellent account of a confessional ritual.

with special emphasis on the events surrounding his illness. These events are expressed or interpreted in terms of the tribe's assumptive world. In addition to its confessional aspect, this procedure brings the patient's vague, chaotic, conflicting, and mysterious feelings to the center of his attention and places them in a self-consistent conceptual system. Thus they are "realized in an order and on a level which permits them to unfold freely and leads to their resolution."[31]

Naming something is the first step toward controlling it, for "naming a sin is to recall it, to give it form and substance, so that the officiating medicine man can deal with it in the prescribed manner. No vague announcement of sinfulness suffices; each sin that has been committed must be specified. Sometimes when the patient can think of nothing serious done by him he will confess imaginary sins."[32]

As in the example cited, the shaman's technique of eliciting this type of confession may be a way of demonstrating his powers. That is, he warns the patient that the spirits have already told him what the true facts are and that they cannot be hidden. As the patient confesses, the shaman confirms that this is what he already knew and urges the patient to confess further. Often the other participants jog the patient's memory or bring up episodes with the patient in which they too transgressed, or even crimes ostensibly unrelated to the patient's illness. Thus the process further cements the group, and participants other than the patient may gain virtue from it. The confession may be followed by intercession with the spirit world on behalf of the patient by the whole group as well as by the shaman, heightening the patient's hope that forgiveness will be forthcoming.

Thus confession may have many implications. It helps the patient to make sense of his condition, counteracts his consciousness of sin, brings him into closer relationship with his group, impresses him with the shaman's powers, and improves the relationship of all concerned with the spirit world. In these ways it counteracts his

31. Lévi-Strauss (1958), p. 219.
32. Webster (1942), p. 311. Labeling is common to all forms of psychotherapy, as we shall see. The confessions of prisoners undergoing thought reform frequently contained fabrications (p. 100 below) as did the "memories" of Freud's early patients (p. 174 below).

anxiety, strengthens his self-estem, and helps him to resolve his conflicts.

Healing ceremonies are highly charged emotionally.[33] As mentioned above, shaman may act out a life-and-death struggle between his spirit and the evil spirit that has possessed the patient. The patient may vividly reenact past experiences or act out the struggles of spirit forces within himself. The emotional excitement may be intensified by rhythmic music, chanting, and dancing. It frequently mounts to the point of exhausting the patient and not infrequently is enhanced by some strong physical shock. In our example, it will be recalled, the patient was sprayed by an alcoholic liquid, which gave her a bad chill.

Finally, many rituals make a strong aesthetic appeal. The setting may be especially decorated for the occasion, and participants may costume themselves elaborately, perform stylized dances, draw sand paintings, and the like. Since these trappings and activities have symbolic meanings, they not only are soothing and inspiring aesthetically but also represent tangible reinforcements of the conceptual organization that the ritual endeavors to impose on the patient's inchoate sufferings. Participation of the whole group either actively or as attentive spectators fosters group solidarity.

In short, methods of primitive healing involve an interplay between patient, healer, group, and the world of the supernatural; this serves to raise the patient's expectancy of cure, help him to harmonize his inner conflicts, reintegrate him with his group and the spirit world, supply a conceptual framework to aid this, and stir him emotionally. The total process combats his demoralization and strengthens his sense of self-worth.

LOURDES AND RELIGIOUS HEALING IN THE WESTERN WORLD

From its inception, Christianity has included the notion of healing through divine intervention. Starting with the healing miracles of Christ, this form of curing has persisted through the centuries. Today healing sects (like Christian Science) and shrines of miracu-

33. Deren (1953) gives a fascinating account of the emotional exaltation of a Haitian voodoo ceremony that she experienced.

lous healing have millions of devotees. Since the rituals of these groups and places parallel religious healing in primitive societies in many ways, it may be of interest to take a look at one of them. The great modern shrine of Lourdes is particularly suitable because it has been well described and because the cures of severe illness that have occurred there are exceptionally well documented and have received careful critical scrutiny.[34]

The history of Lourdes, starting with the visions of Bernadette Soubirous in 1858, is too well known to require retelling here. It is perhaps odd, in view of subsequent developments, that the apparition that appeared to Bernadette and told her where to dig for the spring said nothing about its healing powers. Be that as it may, miraculous cures following immersion in the spring were soon reported, and today over two million pilgrims visit Lourdes every year, including over thirty thousand sick.

The world view supporting Lourdes, like those on which religious healing in primitive tribes is based, is all-inclusive and is shared by almost all the pilgrims to the shrine. While cures are regarded as validating it, failures cannot shake it. Those who seek help at Lourdes have usually been sick a long time and have failed to respond to medical remedies. Like the primitives who undergo a healing ritual, most are close to despair. Being chronic invalids, they have had to withdraw from most or all of their community activities and have become burdens to their families. Their activities have become routinized and constricted, their lives bleak and monotonous, and they have nothing to anticipate but further suffering and death.

The decision to make the pilgrimage to Lourdes changes all this. The preparatory period is a dramatic break in routine. Collecting funds for the journey, arranging for medical examinations, and making the travel plans requires the cooperative effort of members of the patient's family and the wider community. Often the congregation contributes financial aid. Prayers and masses are offered for the invalid. Member of the family, and often the patient's physician or a priest, accompany him to Lourdes and serve

---

34. The account of Lourdes is drawn mainly from Cranston (1955). The quotes are from pp. 31, 36–37, and 127, respectively. See also Janet (1925), vol. 1, chap. 1.

as tangible evidence of the interest of the family and larger group in his welfare. Often pilgrims from many communities travel together, and there are religious ceremonies while the train is en route and at every stop. In short, the preparatory period is emotionally stirring, brings the patient from the periphery of his group to its center, and enhances his expectation of help. It is interesting in this connection that, except for the original cures, Lourdes has failed to heal those who live in its vicinity. This suggests that the emotional excitement connected with the preparatory period and journey to the shrine may be essential for healing to occur.

On arrival at Lourdes after an exhausting, even life-endangering journey, the sufferer's expectation of help is further strengthened. He is plunged into "a city of pilgrims, and they are everywhere; people who have come from the four corners of the earth with but one purpose: prayer, and healing for themselves or for their loved ones. . . . One is surrounded by them, and steeped in their atmosphere every moment of existence in Lourdes." Everyone hopes to witness or experience a miraculous cure. Accounts of previous cures are on every tongue, and the pilgrim sees the votive offerings and the piles of discarded crutches of those who have been healed. Thus the ritual may be said to begin with a validation of the shrine's power, analogous to the shaman's review of his cures in primitive healing rites.

The pilgrims' days are filled with religious services and trips to the Grotto, where they are immersed in the ice-cold spring. Every afternoon all the pilgrims and invalids who are at Lourdes at the time—usually forty or fifty thousand—gather at the Esplanade in front of the shrine for the procession that is the climax of each day's activities. The bedridden are placed nearest the shrine, those who can sit up are behind them, the ambulatory invalids behind them, while the hordes of visitors fill the rest of the space. The enormous emotional and aesthetic impact of the procession is well conveyed by the following quotation:

At four the bells begin to peal—the Procession begins to form. The priests in their varied robes assemble at the Grotto. . . . The bishop appears with the monstrance under the sacred canopy. The loud-speakers open up. A great hymn rolls out, the huge crowd joining in unison, magnificently. The Procession begins its long, impressive way down one side and up the other of the sunny Esplanade. First the Children of Mary, young girls in blue capes, white veils . . . then forty or fifty priests in black cassocks . . . other priests in white surplices . . . then come the Bishops in purple . . . and finally the officiating Archbishop in his white and gold robes under the golden canopy. Bringing up the rear large numbers of men and women of the different pilgrimages, Sisters, Nurses, members of various religious organizations; last of all the doctors. . . . Hymns, prayers, fervent, unceasing. In the Square the sick line up in two rows. . . . Every few feet, in front of them, kneeling priests with arms outstretched praying earnestly, leading the responses. Nurses and orderlies on their knees, praying too. . . . Ardor mounts as the Blessed Sacrament approaches. Prayers gather intensity. . . .The Bishop leaves the shelter of the canopy, carrying the monstrance. The Sacred Host is raised above each sick one. The great crowd falls to its knees. All arms are outstretched in one vast cry to Heaven. As far as one can see in any direction, people are on their knees, praying. . . .

What are the results of the tremendous outpouring of emotion and faith? The great majority of the sick do not experience a cure. However, most of the pilgrims seem to derive som psychological benefit from the experience. Like participation in healing rituals in primitive societies, the pilgrimage is regarded as conferring merit in itself and the whole atmosphere of Lourdes is spiritually uplifting. In this connection, the altruism of all involved is espcially worthy of note. Physicians, brancardiers (who serve the sick), and helpers of all sorts give their time and effort freely, and throughout the ceremonies the emphasis is on self-forgetfulness and devotion to the welfare of others. The pilgrims pray for the sick and the sick for each other, not themselves. Therefore, the words attributed to an old pilgrim may well be largely true: "Of the uncured none despair. All go away filled with hope and a new feeling of strength. The trip to Lourdes is never made in vain."

The evidence that an occasional cure of advanced organic disease does occur at Lourdes is as strong as that for any other phenomenon accepted as true. The reported frequency of such cures varies widely depending on the criteria used. The piles of crutches attest to the fact that many achieve improved functioning, at least temporarily. In many of these cases, however, improvement is probably attributable to heightened morale, enabling the patient to function better in the face of an unchanged organic handicap. Fully documented cures of unquestionable and gross organic disease are extremely infrequent—probably no more frequent than similar ones occurring in secular settings.

In the century of the shrine's existence, less than a hundred cures have passed the stringent test leading the Church to declare them miraculous. This figure may be much too low, as many convincing cases fail to qualify because they lack the extensive documentary support required. But even several thousand cures of organic dieases would represent only a small fraction of 1 percent of those who have made the pilgrimage. As a sympathetic student of spiritual healing writes: "... there is probably no stream in Britain which could not boast of as high a proportion of cures as the stream at Lourdes if patients came in the same numbers and in the same psychological state of expectant excitement."[35]

The processes by which cures at Lourdes occur do not seem to differ in kind from those involved in normal healing, although they are remarkably strengthened and accelerated. Careful reading of the reports reveals that healing is not instantaneous, as is often claimed, but that, like normal healing, it requires time. It is true that the consciousness of cure is often (not always) sudden and may be accompanied by immediate improvement in function—the paralyzed walk, the blind see, and those who had been unable to retain food suddenly regain their appetites. But actual tissue healing takes hours, days, or weeks, and persons who have lost much weight require the usual period of time to regain it, as would be expected if healing occurred by the usual processes. Moreover, gaps of specialized tissues such as skin are not restored but are filled by scar formation as in normal healing. No one has regrown an amputated limb at Lourdes.

It should be added that cures at Lourdes involve the person's total personality, not merely his body. The healed, whatever they were like before their recovery, all are said to be possessed of a remarkable serenity and a desire to be of service to others.

Rivers of ink have been spilled in controversy over whether or not the cures at Lourdes are genuine, based on the erroneous assumption that one's acceptance or rejection of them is necessarily linked to belief or disbelief in miracles or in the Catholic

35. Weatherhead (1951), p. 153.

faith. Actually, it is perfectly possible to accept some Lourdes cures as genuine while maintaining skepticism about miraculous causation, or to be a devout Catholic while rejecting modern miracles. The world is full of phenomena that cannot be explained by our present cosmologies.

Inexplicable cures of serious organic disease occur in everyday medical practice. Every physician has either personally treated or heard about patients who mysteriously recovered from a seemingly fatal illness. Two surgeons have assembled from the literature 176 cases of unquestionable cancer that regressed without adequate treatment.[36] Had these remissions occured after a visit to Lourdes, many would have regarded them as miraculous. Since no physician sees enough of these phenomena to acquire sufficient sample for scientific study, and since they cannot be explained by current medical theories, the fascinating questions they raise have been neglected. Depending on one's theoretical predilections, one may choose to believe that all, none, or a certain class of spontaneous recoveries from what appear to be fatal illnesses are miraculous. The mere fact of their occurence leaves the question of their cause completely open.

A not implausible assumption, in the light of our review of primitive healing, is that Lourdes cures are in some way related to the sufferer's emotional state. This view is supported by the conditions under which the cures occur, and the type of person who seems most apt to experience them. Although they may occur en route to Lourdes, on the return journey, or even months later, most cures occur at the shrine and at the moments of greatest emotional intensity and spiritual fervor—while taking communion, or during immersion in the spring or when the host is raised over the sick at the passing of the sacrament during the procession. The persons who have been cured include the deserving and the sinful, believers and apparent skeptics, but they tend to have one common characteristic: they are "almost invariably simple people—the

36. Everson and Cole (1966). The authors stress that regression does not necessarily imply cure, but about half their cases were well two years or more after cancer was diagnosed, and about one-eighth had been followed ten years or more without recurrence. Unfortunately, the possible role of psychological factors is not even mentioned, much less considered.

poor and the humble; people who do not interpose a strong intellect between themselves and the Higher Power."[37] That is, they are not detached or critical. It is generally agreed that persons who remain entirely unmoved by the ceremonies do not experience cures.

The cured skeptics typically have a devout parent or spouse, suggesting either that their skepticism was a reaction-formation against an underlying desire to believe, or at least that the pilgrimage involved emotional conflict. In this connection, all cured skeptics have become ardent believers.

A point of considerable theoretical interest, to be discussed again, is that the emotions aroused by Lourdes or by the healing ritual described earlier, may be not only intense, but as unpleasant as those created by the illness itself. The sufferings of a debilitated invalid in a prolonged healing ritual or on the long trip to Lourdes must often be severe; yet their effect is usually beneficial. This suggests that the effects of strong emotions on one's well-being depend on their meaning or context—that is, on how the person interprets them. Intense emotional arousal, for example, if it occurs in a setting of hopelessness and progressive isolation of the patient from his usual sources of support, may contribute to his death. If he experiences the same arousal in a setting of massive human and supernatural encouragement so that it carries a context of hope, it can be healing.[38]

In short, the healing ceremonials at Lourdes, like those of primitive tribes, involve a climactic union of the patient, his family, the larger group, and the supernatural world by means of a dramatic, emotionally charged, aesthetically rich ritual that expresses and reinforces a shared ideology.

OTHER FORMS OF NONMEDICAL HEALING

Lourdes may serve as one example of institutionalized religious healing in the West. An adequate survey of Western forms of nonmedical healing would have to include other institutionalized reli-

37. Cranston (1957), p. 125.
38. See pp. 51–53 above and pp. 108–10 below.

gious healing such as Christian Science, and secular therapies ranging from homeopathy, which considers itself a form of medicine, through medicine-related methods such as osteopathy and chiropractic, to healers who function as individuals with idiosyncratic theories. Together these practitioners probably treat many more persons than do physicians,[39] but they do not warrant extended attention for our purposes because of the lack of dispassionate, objective information about most of them. In general, they do not seem to involve any healing principles beyond those already considered.

One feature they all share that is worth emphasizing because, as we shall see, it is highly relevant to psychotherapy, is the ability to evoke the patient's expectancy of help, a factor also involved in religious healing. Two sources of this expectancy are discernible. The first is the personal magnetism of the healer, often strengthened by his own faith in what he does. As an investigator who interviewed many such healers writes: "The vast majority of the sectarians sincerely believe in the efficacy of their practices . . . the writer has talked to [chiropractors] whose faith was . . . nothing short of evangelistic, whose sincerity could no more be questioned than that of Persia's 'whirling dervishes.' "[40] However, the success of peddlers of obviously worthless nostrums and gadgets attests to the fact that the healer need not necessarily believe in the efficacy of his methods to be able to convince his patients of their power.

Another source of the patient's faith is the ideology of the healer or sect, which offers him a rationale, however absurd, for making sense of his illness and the treatment procedure, and places the healer in the position of transmitter or controller of impressive healing forces. In this he is analogous to the shaman. Often these forces are called supernatural, but the healer[41] may pose as a

39. Healing cults are astonishingly popular. A survey (Reed, 1932) found some 36,000 sectarian medical practitioners, exclusive of esoteric and local cults, which equaled almost one-fourth of the total number of medical practitioners at that time, to whom people paid at least $125,000,000 annually. One physician found that 43 percent of his private patients and 26 percent of his clinic patients had patronized a cult during the three months preceding their visits to him. Inglis (1965) cites an estimate of 35 million patients of chiropractors in the United States. See also Steiner (1945).

40. Reed (1932), pp. 109-10.

41. Oursler (1957) provides readable, anecdotal surveys of faith healing groups and individuals in the United States.

scientist who has discovered new and potent scientific principles of healing, thus surrounding himself with the aura that anything labeled scientific inspires in members of modern Western societies. These healers characteristically back up their pretensions with an elaborate scientific-sounding patter and often add an imposing array of equipment complete with dials, flashing lights, and sound effects.

The apparent success of healing methods based on various ideologies and methods compels the conclusion that the healing power of faith resides in the patient's state of mind, not in the validity of its object. At the risk of laboring this point, an experimental demonstration of it with three severely ill, bedridden women may be reported.[42] One had chronic inflammation of the gall bladder with stones, the second had failed to recuperate from a major abdominal operation and was practically a skeleton, and the third was dying of widespread cancer. The physician first permitted a prominent local faith healer to try to cure them by absent treatment without the patients' knowledge. Nothing happened. Then he told the patients about the faith healer, built up their expectations over several days, and finally assured them that he would be treating them from a distance at a certain time the next day. This was a time in which he was sure that the healer did *not* work. At the suggested time all three patients improved quickly and dramatically. The second was permanently cured. The other two were not, but showed striking temporary responses. The cancer patient, who was severely anemic and whose tissues had become waterlogged, promptly excreted all the accumulated fluid, recovered from her anemia, and regained sufficient strength to go home and resume her household duties. She remained virtually symptom-free until her death. The gall bladder patient lost her symptoms, went home, and had no recurrence for several years. These three patients were greatly helped by a belief that was false—that the faith healer was treating them from a distance— suggesting that "expectant trust"[43] in itself can be a powerful healing force.

42. Rehder (1955).
43. The phrase is from Weatherhead (1951), p. 26, and is his characterization of religious faith as it refers to healing.

If, as pointed out earlier, depression and certain other emotional states seem to retard healing, it seems reasonable to assume that hope could enhance it, and this is strongly suggested by miracle cures and the example just cited. A final bit of evidence is worth reporting because scientifically it is virtually impeccable. Patients about to undergo an operation for detached retina were interviewed before the operation and rated on a scale of "acceptance," including such items as trust in the surgeon, optimism about the result, and confidence in ability to cope. Scores on this scale correlated very highly with speed of healing after the operation, rated independently by the surgeon.[44]

One cannot conclude this review of nonmedical healing without mentioning the possibility that some individuals, like Quasalid, may have a gift of healing that defies scientific explanation. In this it resembles the charisma of certain political leaders. Nor can one rule out the possibility—indeed the evidence for it is quite persuasive—that some healers serve as a kind of conduit for a healing force in the universe, often called the life force, that, for want of a better term, must be called supernatural.[45] That is, it cannot be conceptually incorporated into the secular cosmology that dominates Western scientific thinking. Many will reject the notion out-of-hand on this account. Others, of whom I am one, are ever mindful of Hamlet's admonition to Horatio and prefer to keep an open mind.

A fitting conclusion for this chapter is supplied by two quotations which highlight the striking similarity between religious healing in primitive groups and in the Christian world, with respect to the interaction of patient, healer, group, and supernatural forces. The first sums up primitive healing, the second Christian spiritual healing:

> The medicine man is a soul doctor. . . . He gives peace by confessing his patient. His rigid system, which ignores doubt, dispels fear, restores confidence, and inspires hope . . . the primitive psychotherapist works not only with the strength of his own personality. His rite is part of the common faith of the whole community which not seldom assists *in corpore* at his healing

44. Mason *et al.* (1969).
45. See Oursler (1957), Inglis (1965).

act. . . . The whole weight of the tribe's religion, myths, and community spirit enters into the treatment.[46]

The intercession of people united in love for Christ . . . and the laying on of hands . . . by a priest or minister or other person who is the *contact-point . . . of a beloved, believing and united community standing behind him and supporting his ministration to a patient who has been taught to understand the true nature of Christian faith* . . . is the true ministry of the Church.[47]

SUMMARY

This review of nonmedical healing of bodily illness highlights the profound influence of emotions on health and suggests that anxiety and despair can be lethal; confidence and hope, life-giving. The current assumptive world of Western society, which includes mind-body dualism, incorporates this obvious fact with difficulty and, therefore, tends to underestimate its importance.

The core of the techniques of healing reviewed in this chapter seems to lie in their ability to arouse the patient's hope, bolster his self-esteem, stir him emotionally, and strengthen his ties with a supportive group, through several features that most methods share. All involve a healer on whom the patient depends for help and who holds out hope of relief. The patient's expectations are aroused by the healer's personal attributes, by his culturally determined healing role, or, typically, by both. The role of the healer may be diffused, as at Lourdes, where it resides in participating priests.

All forms of healing are based on a conceptual scheme consistent with the patient's assumptive world that prescribes a set of activities. The scheme helps him to make sense out of his inchoate feelings, thereby heightening his sense of mastery over them. Nonmedical healing rituals are believed to mobilize natural or supernatural healing forces on the patient's behalf. Often they include detailed confessions followed by atonement and reacceptance into the group. Many rituals also stress mutual service, which counteracts the patient's morbid self-preoccupation, strengthens his self-

46. Ackerknecht (1942), p. 514.
47. Weatherhead (1951), p. 486. Author's italics.

esteem by demonstrating that he can do something for others, and, like confession, cements the bonds between patient and group. Confession and mutual service contribute to the feeling that performance of the healing ritual confers merit in itself. If the patient is not cured, he nevertheless often feels more virtuous. If he is cured, this may be taken as a mark of divine favor, permanently enhancing his value in his own and the group's eyes. This may also help maintain the cure, for if he relapses he is letting the group down. Finally, in religious healing, relief of suffering is accompanied not only by a profound change in the patient's feelings about himself and others, but by a strengthening of previous assumptive systems or, sometimes, conversion to new ones.

RELIGIOUS REVIVALISM AND THOUGHT
IV   REFORM

"Please your majesty," said the knave, "I didn't write it
and they can't prove I did; there's no name signed at the
end." "If you didn't sign it," said the King, "that only makes
the matter worse. You *must* have meant some mischief,
or else you'd have signed your name like an honest man."

Alice's Adventures in Wonderland

So far we have reviewed phenomena that may be related
to one aspect of psychotherapy—the relief of suffering
through mobilization of healing emotional states. The
goal of many forms of psychotherapy, however, usually
is more ambitious than this. They seek to bring about
enduring modifications in the patient's assumptive
world that will enable him to function more effectively.
In more conventional terms, their goal is to facilitate
development or maturation of the patient's personality,
to help him become less conflicted or better integrated,
to help him become, in some sense, a better person.[1] As
already indicated, faith healing is said to promote such a
change even when the patient's suffering is unrelieved.
This chapter shifts attention to religious revivals and
Communist thought reform, direct attempts to produce
personality change that may cast light on the influencing processes of psychotherapy. In the former, the

1. Wolberg (1967) cites the goal of "reconstructive therapies," which
include all analytical forms, as "extensive alterations of character structure" and "expansion of personality growth." He classes other psychotherapies as either supportive or reeducative (p. 14).

change is viewed as beneficial by both the convert and the revivalist; in the latter, only the interrogator considers it meritorious.

These procedures are difficult to consider dispassionately because they raise issues involving our deepest convictions. It should therefore be stressed that this chapter considers thought reform and revivalism only from the standpoint of their bearing on psychotherapy. We are interested only in their means of attempting to produce attitude changes and the determinants of their effectiveness. Questions about the desirability of the attitude changes, the moral implications of the methods, or the validity of the world views underlying them are ignored as irrelevant to our present purposes.

Thought reform will receive considerably more attention than religious revivalism because the issues it raises are not complicated by the question of supernatural intervention and because it has been intensively studied and reported upon by social scientists. But certain aspects of religious revivalism are similar enough to psychotherapeutic processes to warrant brief consideration.

RELIGIOUS REVIVALISM AND CONVERSION

The suffering of many persons who seek psychotherapy includes some degree of spiritual malaise or existential anxiety, so psychotherapy cannot avoid issues concerning the meaning of life and other questions usually considered the exclusive province of philosophy or religion.[2] Successful psychotherapy, along with other changes in the patient's values, often includes development of a more optimistic view concerning the meaning of existence. In this sense its results resemble those of a religious conversion. This may be characterized as a change in the person's attitudes toward God or the Universe, with concomitant changes in his attitudes toward himself and the people significant to him.

Conversion may be an undramatic reawakening and reaffirmation of previously held but dormant religious beliefs, an end result of a slow maturational process such as might occur in long-term psychoanalysis, or a result of an abrupt shift in assumptive systems

2. See Pattison (1965); London (1964).

such as might be produced by an encounter group.[3] Conversions can vary in scope, depth, and permanence—from the libertine who becomes a monk to the person who "makes a decision for Christ" at a revival meeting but is quite himself again the next morning. Our interest will be confined to sudden conversions characterized by drastic and far-reaching psychic upheavals, usually accompanied by strong emotion, sometimes leading to permanent changes in attitude and behavior.[4]

A sudden religious conversion is typically preceded by a period of severe demoralization sometimes so intense that the person becomes confused[5] —often to the degree that he attributes inner experiences to the outer world, as in schizophrenic psychoses. A sense of isolation and estrangement from others characterizes the pre-conversion state. The dominant affects include despair, hatred, resentment, and helpless fury, often directed toward a parent or parent-substitute. The candidate for conversion is tormented by self-doubts and guilt. He feels unable to find God, or abandoned by him. In such a state he longs to submit himself to an all-powerful, benevolent figure who can give him absolution and restore order to his world. At the moment of conversion he feels closer to God and confident of his favor. As with miracle cures, this experience is intensely emotional and may be followed by a sense of inner joy and peace.[6]

3. See pp. 264–68 below.
4. James (1936) offers a classic account of these experiences. Argyle (1958) estimates that between 10 percent and 30 percent of religious people have undergone a more or less evident conversion experience.
Viewed in a broader context, these states represent examples of *kairos*, the moment at which a person becomes ripe for profound changes in values and attitudes (Kelman, 1969). *Kairos* can take a wide variety of forms. In addition to religious conversions, it can include the experience of a faith cure, ecstatic experiences of other types, responses to life crises, and sometimes states of black despair, as in thought reform. With luck, the patient may experience it in almost all forms of psychotherapy, especially those that are deliberately emotionally arousing, and certain drugs like LSD seem able, under proper circumstances, to increase the likelihood of its occurrence. Much too little is known about it, however, to be able to command it at will.
5. Christensen (1963), Linn and Schwarz (1958), and Salzman (1953) offer essentially similar accounts, based on patients in psychoanalysis (chiefly adolescents), so they may overemphasize psychopathological aspects of states preceding sudden conversion. Salzman regards these as disintegrating experiences, the others as reintegrating ones. All conceptualize them as regression to an infantile state characterized by dependence on an all-powerful parent.
6. Clark (1929) found that 57 percent of a group of sudden converts experienced subsequent joy. Quoted by Argyle (1958), p. 160.

The change in the convert's perception of himself in relation to the deity implies certain changes in his picture of himself and of others, and changes in his patterns of social participation. The invocation of supernatural forces to support certain attitudes may resolve certain intrapersonal conflicts and so promote personality integration. It also enhances the convert's sense of self-worth at the same time that he paradoxically feels a new sense of humility. The paradox is only apparent, however, for it is hard to conceive of a greater source of inner strength and personal security than the conviction that one is God's chosen instrument. Some persons for whom the convert previously had felt contempt or anger, such as a long-suffering spouse or parent, become objects of love and admiration. Others whom he had admired and emulated become persons to be shunned as evil, or targets for proselytizing. He forsakes his previous haunts and cronies and characteristically joins the group that converted him.

Conversion typically involves a spiritual leader with whom the convert is having, or has had, an intense relationship. Previous contact with such a figure can usually be found in the lives of persons whose conversion experiences occur in isolation.[7] In any case, there are no recorded instances of persons being converted to a religious belief antithetical to that of the revivalist. No one has been converted to Buddhism while listening to Billy Graham.

The revivalist and his congregation, furthermore, show deep concern for the penitent's welfare. General William Booth, the founder of the Salvation Army, is quoted as saying: "The first vital step in saving outcasts consists in making them feel that some decent human being cares enough for them to take an interest in the question whether they are to rise or to sink."[8]

In the modern Western world, evangelistic revivals are important means of producing conversions. These events are characterized by high emotional intensity.[9] Before the evangelist comes to town, there may be a preliminary build-up through publicity and ser-

7. Weininger (1955).
8. James (1936), p. 34.
9. Sargant (1957) discusses the part played by excessive emotional excitation in facilitating attitude change in religious revivals, brain-washing, and similar phenomena. The material on John Wesley's methods is taken from this source. See also Sargant (1968).

mons, which creates some anticipatory excitement, arouses latent feelings of guilt, and holds out the hope of relief through salvation. The meetings themselves are highly emotional. The impact of the dramatic pleas, threats, and exhortations of the evangelist may be intensified through the singing of highly emotional gospel hymns by the entire audience, led by a choir and soloists. Billy Graham's revivals sometimes have a choir of fifteen hundred.[10] In susceptible persons the emotional excitation may be sufficient to produce manifestations of dissociation such as "speaking in tongues," shaking, and convulsions, similar to signs of "possession" in non-Christian religions such as voodoo.

The revivalist tries to arouse feelings of sin, guilt, and fear in his hearers by harping on their wickedness and the dire punishments that await those who do not repent. At the same time he dwells on the bliss that awaits them if they confess their sins, ask God's forgiveness, and mend their ways. The relative emphasis on these two contrapuntal themes seems to vary considerably with different evangelists and at different periods of history. Great evangelists of previous eras, like Jonathan Edwards and John Wesley, dwelt on the horrors of damnation, while some modern evangelistic movements, such as the Salvation Army, stress the joys of salvation.[11]

The effectiveness of revivalistic services varies in different epochs. At Billy Graham's revivals an average of only 2 to 5 percent of the attenders "make a decision for Christ" and only about half of these converts are active a year later. About 15 percent remain permanently converted.[12] Though no precise figures are available, Wesley's percentage of conversions must have been much higher. God's wrath was much more vivid to man in the eighteenth than in the twentieth century, and emotionally Graham's revivals must be but a pale shadow of Wesley's. Moreover, Wesley recognized the importance of a like-minded group in sustaining the

10. The source of the material on Billy Graham's revivals is Argyle (1958).

11. "It is the rejoicing, singing, irrepressible happiness of the Salvationist which often makes him such a powerful savior of other men." (Begbie, 1909, p. 19.) This book contains nine vivid vignettes of London slum dwellers who were converted by the Salvation Army.

12. Argyle (1958), pp. 54–55. Over a decade later, the proportion is still the same. See *Newsweek*, July 20, 1970, p. 53.

assumptive world of its members.[13] Hence he placed great stress on continuing class meetings to consolidate and strengthen the new world view. He divided his converts into groups of not more than twelve, who met weekly under an appointed leader. Problems relating to their conversion and their future mode of life were discussed in agreed secrecy. The leader kept close watch for evidences of backsliding, and members who "grew cold and gave way to the sins which had long easily beset them"[14] were expelled from both the classes and the Methodist Society.

Little can be said with assurance about the personal qualities that make for a successful evangelist. Some highly successful ones have led disorderly lives or been financially unscrupulous. Some great historical religious leaders might be considered psychotic by today's standards. Their delusions and hallucinations, however, must have been couched in terms that gained them wide cultural acceptance as veridical. Probably all successful evangelists have a deep religious conviction, a capacity for vivid, intense emotional experiences, which they can successfully communicate to others, sensitivity to audience response, and great organizing ability. Personal prestige may also contribute to an evangelist's success. Billy Graham, for example, gained a higher percentage of conversions during his English tour than did his assistants.

There is equally little firm knowledge concerning social and personal factors that might heighten susceptibility to conversions. Personal attributes related to general susceptibility to influence seem to predispose one to conversion experiences. Thus hysterics, persons with low self-esteem, and those with undue fear of social disapproval seem to be good candidates.

Similarly, adolescents are the age group most prone to sudden conversions. This age, at least in the West, is characterized by internal and external conflicts, the former caused by the upwelling of sexual and aggressive feelings, the latter by efforts to establish an independent identity by resisting or attacking authorities. The

13. The importance of continuing group reinforcement in sustaining new attitudes is implicitly or explicitly recognized by many current schools of psychotherapy, including the various schools of psychoanalysis whose members continue attendance at their institutes indefinitely—programs for alcoholics, addicts (Deissler, 1970); "primal therapy" (Janov, 1970); and reevaluation counseling (Jackins, 1965).

14. Sargant (1957), p. 220.

result may be feelings of anger, guilt, and isolation characteristic of the pre-conversion state, and the relatively fluid state of adolescent personalities facilitates marked shifts of attitude.

Many converts have had a religious upbringing, so that for them conversion is more a resurgence of dormant attitudes than a shift to totally new ones. As with miracle cures, however, the passionate skeptic may be as susceptible to conversion as the believer. Many persons have become suddenly converted at revival meetings while they are in a state of high indignation at the proceedings.[15] Only the emotionally detached are immune.

From the social standpoint, the resurgence of religious revivalism in the Western world today may be one consequence of the confusion and anxiety created by the conditions of modern life. Among its many unsettling features are the threat of annihilation posed by nuclear weapons and environmental pollution, as well as the decline of value systems and institutions that provided a sense of hope and conviction that life has meaning. Traditional religions are losing their hold and no substitutes have emerged. Science, on which so many placed great hopes, appears to be a false god luring mankind to its destruction. Not only has it failed to satisfy the needs met by religion; it cannot even tame the monsters it has created. Democracy appears incapable of solving the problems of our society, and the suspicion is growing that progress is an illusion.

Under these circumstances, increasing numbers turn to the supernatural world for reassurance. Some look inward seeking mystical experiences through meditation or mind-altering drugs. Others turn to astrology and similar cults for guidance, while still others seek to regain their psychic security through revivalist religions.

Revivalistic or messianic religions, whose adherents have dramatic, emotionally charged conversion experiences, flourish especially under social conditions of misery and frustration. For example, voodoo, which is extremely emotional and involves possession by deities, is the dominant religion of a people the majority of whom "are doomed to a life without one moment's

15. Sargant (1957), p. 99. He comments (p. 109): "The best way to avoid possession, conversion, and all similar conditions is to avoid getting emotionally involved in the proceedings."

relief from the most desperate, nerve-wracking struggle to eke out daily subsistence."[16]

In affluent societies, though the evidence is inconclusive, there seems to be some tendency for evangelistic sects to flourish more among the economically or socially underprivileged. As adherents of these sects rise in the economic and social scale and have increased opportunities for worldly satisfactions, they tend to leave the sects, or the religious observances of the sects themselves become less dramatically emotional, as demonstrated for example by the evolution of Quakerism and Methodism in Western society.

It seems plausible that the ecstasies of evangelical religions provide outlets for pent-up emotional tensions, relief from the impoverishment and monotony of daily life, and a gratification of important psychological needs. This gratification includes a glimpse of an after-world in which the roles of oppressed and oppressor will be reversed. The ecstatic experience of union with God is a sign that the convert is "saved," and thus evidence of the intercession of infinitely powerful forces on his behalf. In these ways revivalistic religions probably help their adherents to maintain their personal integration in the face of widespread and enduring frustrations.

In short, confusion, guilt, or frustration springing from personal characteristics or social conditions seems to heighten the attractiveness of revivalistic religions and enhance their effectiveness. This suggests that these feelings may increase a person's susceptibility to emotionally charged methods of influence that offer detailed guides to behavior, based on an inclusive, infallible assumptive world, which also strongly arouses hope.[17]

THOUGHT REFORM

It may seem odd that attempts by Communist governments to produce confessions could aid understanding of either religious revivalism or psychotherapy. Certainly, thought reform or brain-

16. Deren (1953), p. 165. A. Huxley (1959) speculates interestingly on how the physiological disorders created by starvation and disease might predispose one to hallucinatory religious experiences.

17. Hoffer (1958) offers a brilliant, if somewhat uneven, discussion of mass movements, much of which is directly pertinent to religious revivalism.

washing differs strikingly from each of them in many respects. Yet certain similarities of aims and methods are also marked and have considerable theoretical interest. The relevance for psychotherapy of both evangelical Christianity and communism lies in their heroic efforts to win converts, since these activities cast light on ways of inducing attitude changes. Proselytizing in both is motivated and guided by a systematic, comprehensive world view, which purports to govern every aspect of the thinking and behavior of its disciples. Though the Communist assumptive world has no place for supernatural powers, it incorporates a suprapersonal one that has many of the attributes Christianity invests in God. This is the Party, to which all Communists are expected to submit themselves willingly, absolutely, and unquestioningly. Through being the obedient instrument of this power, the individual gains a feeling of value in his own eyes and in those of his compatriots.

Thought reform resembles both religious healing and revivalism in utilizing emotional arousal and group pressures to achieve its goals. It differs from them in that its subjects are incarcerated, so all aspects of their lives can be controlled. In addition, it is a prolonged process with open-ended goals rather than a brief one with a circumscribed goal.[18] These properties lead to considerable differences in the means of emotional arousal and application of group pressures, and to a great emphasis on the confession, which becomes a detailed life history, obtained in the setting of a prolonged intense relationship between subject and interrogator.

At first glance it seems hard to imagine more dissimilar activities than psychotherapy and thought reform. Psychotherapy is a form of treatment; thought reform is a method of indoctrination. Psychotherapy characteristically attempts to help persons in distress; thought reform creates distress in its objects as a way of facilitating the indoctrination process. Psychotherapists usually ad-

18. This statement may require qualification on two counts. Members of some primitive societies may have just as little individual freedom of action and live in as completely determined a social environment as Communist prisoners, though the forms of restriction differ. To speak of the goal of revivalist religion as circumscribed is only partly true, for the assumption is that being saved will bring far-reaching changes in its train. Nevertheless, the immediate goal is to bring about a clearly defined inner experience signalized by a particular act. Thought reform lacks such a definite end point.

here to the same world view as their patients, and the success of psychotherapy may depend in part on the extent to which this is true. The assumptive worlds of the person undergoing thought reform and his interrogator are opposed in essential respects. Outpatient psychotherapy exerts only the mildest overt pressures, if any. Practitioners of thought reform do not hesitate to apply the most extreme forms of pressure.

Although the differences between psychotherapy of outpatients who voluntarily seek help and thought reform are relatively clearcut, they are less distinct with regard to the treatment of patients hospitalized against their will[19] or of sociopaths. The latter group, especially, give one pause. Like persons subjected to thought reform, they are not in distress, and the goal of treatment is to modify their assumptive world in the direction of the psychotherapist's, who represents the larger society. It is also likely that such individuals can only be successfully treated—that is, reeducated—if they are incarcerated and subjected to firm discipline, which characteristically creates considerable emotional distress in them. What they perceive as coercion is seen by the treatment staff as therapy, just as the Chinese Communists view thought reform as a "morally uplifting, harmonizing and scientifically therapeutic experience."[20] And this is a reminder that all psychotherapy tries to modify certain assumptive systems of its patients, along lines which, the therapist believes, will help them to function better, and that this process inevitably creates distress.

Finally the very respect in which thought reform differs sharply from revivalism is the one in which it most closely resembles psychotherapy—the detailed, open-ended review of past history in a setting of a prolonged, intense relationship between a distressed person and a person whom he perceives as having some control over his welfare. In this connection, the typical interrogator, as a convinced Communist, probably regards himself, in a sense, as a therapist. In his own eyes he is trying to help the prisoner become a better, more effective person by helping him to see the error of his ways and accept his penance, after which he is ready to be-

19. See pp. 292–95 below.
20. Lifton (1961), p. 15.

come a full-fledged member of the new society. Moreover, like the psychotherapist, he may have considerable emotional investment in the prisoner's progress not only because his success strengthens his own self-image and his confidence in his world view, but also because his own position depends on getting results. If he is unsuccessful, he may become the next victim. In this he bears a faint resemblance to the psychiatrist-in-training whose standing with his teachers and colleagues depends on his therapeutic success.

The interrogator's zeal is enhanced by his wish to believe in the genuineness of the patient's confession. According to his ideology, the prisoner would not have been arrested if he had not been guilty. Therefore, the prisoner's admission tends to confirm and support the interrogator's world view. It also helps him justify to himself the suffering he had inflicted on the prisoner and relieves his own anxiety about not having obtained a confession. Thus both prisoner and interrogator may collaborate in erecting a shared delusional system, each confirming the other in the false belief.

To digress a bit, the collaboration of interrogators and accused to produce a confession that confirms the assumptive world of a society is fascinatingly portrayed in the following example from the Zuni of New Mexico.[21] An adolescent was accused of witchcraft, a capital crime, because a girl had a convulsion just after he touched her. Brought before the priests, he first tried vainly to deny his guilt. He then changed his tactics and made up a long account of his initiation into witchcraft, including how he had been taught the use of two drugs, one of which made girls mad and the other cured them. Ordered to produce the drugs, he got two roots, ate one, feigned a trance, and brought himself out of it with the other. He then gave the second to the girl and declared her cured. This still did not satisfy the family of the girl, so he invented a more dramatic story, telling how all his ancestors were sorcerers and how he could change into a cat and do other wonderful things by means of magic feathers. Then he was ordered to produce one of the feathers. After tearing down several walls in his home he finally found an old feather in the mud, which he presented to his prosecutors with a long explanation of how it was

21. Lévi-Strauss (1958). The quotes are from pp. 191 and 192.

used. Then he had to repeat the whole story in the public square, adding new embellishments all the time and ending with a touching lamentation over the loss of his supernatural powers. After this he was freed.

Thus the boy acquits himself not by proving his innocence, but by producing evidence confirming his guilt. It seems obvious that the judges want to believe that he is a sorcerer, for they do not suggest tests that would be impossible for him to pass, such as changing himself into a cat, but ask him only to find a feather. "The judges require [the accused] to corroborate a system to which they hold only a fragmentary clue and which they want him to reconstitute in an appropriate way. . . . The confession, strengthened by the participation, even the complicity of the judges, turns the accused from culprit into a collaborator in the charge . . . the youth succeeded in transforming himself from a menace to the physical security of the group into proof of its mental coherence." The boy, too, became convinced: "Since [sorcerers] exist, he may well be one. And how was he to know in advance the signs that would reveal his vocation to him? Perhaps they are to be found in this ordeal. . . . For him too, the coherence of the system and the role assigned to him to prove it have a value no less essential than the personal safety he risks in the exploit."

To what extent the effort to confirm their world view may have contributed to the enormous effort made by the Chinese Communists to obtain confessions is an open question, but unless something like this was at work it is hard to explain why they went to such lengths to convert not only influential persons such as intellectuals and foreigners who would serve propaganda purposes, but even lowly merchants and artisans, whom they could just as easily have summarily shot. In any case, one would expect those groups who are least sure of their world view to be the most fervent proselytizers, other things being equal. Thus it has been shown that if a religious sect makes a prophecy, it starts to proselytize only after the prophecy fails.[22] These considerations may have some pertinence for some current American psychotherapeutic training programs.[23]

22. Festinger et al. (1956).
23. See p. 176 below.

To return to thought reform, in the course of the interrogation, an intense relationship might develop between interrogator and prisoner, similar in some respects to that between patient and therapist in long-term psychotherapy. The prisoner may become very dependent on the interrogator as his sole potential source of help, and the interrogator may be genuinely concerned at the prisoner's recalcitrance. There are even reports of prisoners confessing in order to help the interrogator out of a difficult situation. In addition, as in psychotherapy, each may come to project onto the other personal attitudes toward important persons in his own life—so-called transference and countertransference reactions.

These parallels suggest that scrutiny of thought reform may increase our understanding of certain aspects of psychotherapy. The account of thought reform which follows considers primarily the Chinese form, which reached its peak shortly after the Communists came to power. It was more closely related to psychotherapy than its Russian counterpart. In particular, it relies less on physical torture than on psychological pressures, especially the manipulation of group forces, and its goal seems to be to secure a genuine conversion rather than to obtain a mere confession.

The exposition is based on first-hand accounts and interviews with American military prisoners in the Korean war, Chinese civilian military prisoners, and Chinese intellectuals who underwent indoctrination in a "revolutionary college." The last-named are especially interesting because they were not subjected to the physical hardships that tend to obscure the psychological features of the process with prisoners. Material from first-hand descriptions by Russian prisoners is mentioned where it seems pertinent. Reports from all these sources confirm each other to such a degree that they create considerable confidence in the general picture that emerges from them.[24]

24. Hinkle and Wolff (1956) present an excellent description of both Chinese and Russian procedures and a consideration of their relevance for psychotherapy. Kinkead (1959) and Biderman (1963) are the chief sources for Korean prisoners, and Lifton (1957) for the revolutionary colleges and (1956) for American civilian prisoners. Rickett and Rickett (1957) and Rigney (1956) offer contrasting first-hand accounts of thought reform—the former through the eyes of a convert, the latter through those of an implacable foe. Beck and Godin (1951) are the source of first-hand material on Russian techniques.

The account includes aspects of thought reform that appear very different from most forms of psychotherapy, especially the use of harassment and mobilization of strong group pressures. As will appear in due course,[25] however, they have counterparts, albeit in less blatant form, in certain features of mental institutions.

The processes of thought reform can be conveniently grouped according to three interrelated aspects—extreme emotional arousal, total milieu control, and the interrogation. Methods of thought reform attempted to produce an intense, disorganizing emotional state in their subjects, to cut them off as completely as possible from all social supports of their previous world view, and to immerse them in a social milieu that consistently and uniformly represented the Communist one. The actual influencing effort came to a focus in the interrogation and confession, which have both individual and group aspects.

The emotional build-up started some time before the arrest when the marked person began to sense from his progressive isolation that something was in the wind. As one man described it:

As time went on, I was more and more avoided by those I knew, until finally, I was practically deserted by all.

No one visited me.

Hardly anyone recognized me on the street.

Usually, if a Chinese who knew me, saw me coming, he or she turned and went in the opposite direction, or simply refused to look at me, in passing.

Friends and acquaintances destroyed all their photographs that featured me—destroyed all evidences, as letters, recommendations, books, indications of ever having known me, spoken to me or received any benefit from me.

I was abandoned.

Staff members and students of Fu Jen, many of whom I had helped, now turned against me, accused me to the police, requesting my arrest, in order to save themselves.[26]

The tension aroused by the premonitory period was heightened by the method of arrest, which was calculated to intensify the prisoner's apprehensiveness and demoralization. Russians characteristically arrested persons secretly in the early morning hours,

25. See Chapter 11 below.
26. Rigney (1956), p. 23.

when one is apt to feel most solitary and helpless. Chinese went to the opposite extreme, making arrests in broad daylight with maximum public humiliation. A principal of a Jesuit college, for example, had to confront groups of jeering school children and pass through a denunciatory mob of his students.

American prisoners of war also underwent devastating emotional experiences before the actual indoctrination program began. These were precipitated by their capture, which led to a calamitous fall in their standard of living and an abrupt and drastic withdrawal of sustaining group forces. By the time they reached the prison camp, many had lost all sense of discipline or of responsibility to their fellow soldiers: "They refused to obey orders. . . . At first the badly wounded suffered most. . . . the able-bodied refused to carry them, even when their officers commanded them to do so. . . . the strong regularly took food from the weak. There was no discipline to prevent it."[27]

Once in prison, men found that emotional tension was increased by both physical and psychological means. The degree of physical maltreatment varied considerably and sometimes, as with the Chinese intellectuals, was nonexistent, so it cannot be regarded as a necessary ingredient of thought reform. In addition, much of it may have been inadvertent, a simple reflection of the generally less comfortable living conditions of the Chinese. Nevertheless, for many prisoners even the unplanned stresses were severe. They could not sleep on boards or stomach the food. But deliberate tortures were also used, especially with recalcitrant prisoners, such as depriving them of sleep,[28] beating them, manacling their hands behind their backs for long periods, and forcing them to stand until their feet were badly swollen and then applying pressure to them, which was excruciatingly painful.

Psychological harassment might be very severe. Its three major forms were the creation of uncertainty and anxiety about the future, personal humiliation, and manipulation of privacy. A distressing aspect of both military and civilian prison life was uncertainty about what would happen next. Lenient and harsh treat-

27. Kinkead (1959), p. 155.
28. See Rigney (1956, p. 36) and Beck and Godin (1951, p. 185) for vivid accounts of the disorganizing effects of sleep deprivation.

ment alternated unpredictably. Civilian prisoners never knew when their confession was adequate, when they would be tried and sentenced, when they would be transferred to another prison, or even if they were going to be taken out and summarily shot. War prisoners feared that they might die, that they might never be repatriated, and that no one even knew they were alive. Thus present miseries were compounded by fear that the worst was yet to come, with death ever lurking in the background.

Personal humiliation took many forms. On admission to prison, civilians had to surrender their clothes and personal belongings, including all status identifications, and the treatment they received was determined solely by their "progress." Military prisoners were similarly deprived of all insignia of rank and the personal recognition accorded them was guided solely by the degree to which they collaborated or resisted. The details of prison life could be made occasions for severe humiliation. For example, when a person's hands are manacled behind his back, he has to eat like an animal and to depend on others to help him perform his excretory functions. Sometimes such a prisoner would be forced to stand for hours over the bucket used for excreta.

A powerful form of harassment was manipulation of privacy. Consistent with the differences in their methods of arrest, Russians and Chinese seemed to go to opposite extremes in this regard. Russian prisoners often had to undergo prolonged isolation.[29] The prisoners of the Chinese, on the other hand, were placed in crowded cells, in which it was impossible to escape from one's fellows, even for an instant.

The emotion-arousing psychological pressures on the students in the revolutionary college were for the most part more subtle than those applied to prisoners, but, after an initial "honeymoon" period, apprehension about the future played some part, and group pressures might be extreme. In any case, some of the students, at least among those who defected (the only ones available for interviews) underwent considerable emotional turmoil and some felt deeply resentful.

29. Morita therapy in Japan starts by isolating the patient for a week (Kora, 1965). Primal therapy in the United States does it for twenty-four hours (Janov, 1970).

Prolonged misery, frustration, and uncertainty tended to dull prisoners' critical faculties and weaken their capacity to withstand the continual and ubiquitous pressures to adopt the Communist world view. The Chinese immersed the prisoner or student completely in an "airtight communication system" characterized by "a highly charged morality and an absolute doctrinal authority for the 'correctness' of any solution or point of view,"[30] and permitted him to receive or send communications only in terms of this system. "Input" from the outer world was severely reduced and systematically manipulated to weaken his ties with his former groups. Communist literature was the only available reading matter. Prisoners learned only of Communist "victories" and American "atrocities." All incoming and outgoing mail was read, and only those communications allowed to pass in either direction that would estrange the prisoner from his loved ones or worry him about them.

The Communists also attempted to make all the prisoners' and students' "output" conform to their world view. Communications that indicated acceptance of the Communist position were rewarded, while all others were rejected. Prolonged, severe conflict between inner beliefs and outer behavior is hard to stand, so the enforcement of behavioral conformity tends eventually to bring about changes in one's belief system to harmonize with it.[31]

Measures were designed to prevent the formation of ties among prisoners that would strengthen their ability to resist. In Russian prisons, "No prisoner was ever allowed to see any prisoner confined in any cell but his own. . . . Prisoners were conducted along the corridors by warders . . . [who by tapping metal parts of their uniforms] gave audible warning that they had a prisoner with them and thus avoided meeting others. If an encounter occurred, however, the prisoner had to face the wall. . . ."[32]

The Chinese fostered the breakdown of group cohesiveness in American prisoners of war. They watched for the emergence of structured groups and promptly transferred their leaders. They

---

30. Lifton (1957), p. 14.
31. Bettelheim's discussion of his concentration camp experiences (1943) and of the effects of having to say "Heil Hitler" in Nazi Germany (1952) is pertinent in this connection, as is Festinger's (1957) theory of cognitive dissonance.
32. Beck and Godin (1951), pp. 61–62.

fomented mutual distrust by encouraging and rewarding informers. They would, for example, interrogate a prisoner about some aspect of his activities, no matter how trivial, obtained from an informer, show him a signed statement from another prisoner revealing information he had withheld, or bestow special favors upon noncollaborators as if they were collaborators. The encouragement of self-criticism and group confessions, considered below, inevitably led persons to reveal more than they had intended, however innocuously they might begin, and this would increase their motivation to get others to produce self-damaging material as well.

The contrast between the way ex-prisoners behaved in a hospital ward, as compared with other American soldiers, bore striking witness to the effectiveness of the Communist isolation procedures. Most of the ex-prisoners stayed on the wards—less than 5 percent asked for passes to go to town, and those who did go went alone. They formed no groups, did not play cards, and stayed as much by themselves as they could. But they talked compulsively and incessantly to the treatment personnel and seemed unable to evaluate whether the things they said about each other might be harmful or not.[33]

The clinical impression of apathy and personal isolation in most of the prisoners was borne out by their performance on psychological tests. The outstanding characteristic of the stories they made up to explain neutral pictures that they were shown was the rarity of interaction and feeling. Their interpretations of ink blots, which often reveal hidden attitudes and feelings, were described as showing varying degrees of apathy coupled with strong pent-up aggressive-destructive feelings.[34] In short, the Chinese "evolved a means of isolating every person emotionally from every other person, permitting each to turn only to the system for guidance and friendship.[35]

33. Mayer (1956).
34. Singer and Schein (1958).
35. Kinkead (1959), p. 137. Asch (1952) in a classic experiment demonstrated that a single person had great difficulty in maintaining a perceptual judgment when opposed by a unanimous group and that the support of even one person who agreed with him greatly increased his ability to withstand the group pressure. Hardy (1957) has duplicated this finding with respect to statements of attitudes about divorce.

Furthermore, the Communists tried to present their society as more congenial to the prisoner's values than his own society. With American prisoners of war they harped on the injustices and inequalities of American life and portrayed themselves as fighting for justice, decency, racial equality, and the like. Their manner and words were usually solicitous and sympathetic, and they played the role of "benevolent but handicapped captor."[36] They reminded the Americans that they were being treated just as well as the average Chinese. At the same time they never ceased to point out that American Air Force bombings were responsible for their inadequate supplies. Thus in a sense they tried to make the prisoners feel responsible for their own plight.

The focal point of the indoctrination process was the interrogation, which had individual and group forms. The general strategy of both was to obtain as much information from the prisoner as possible, including the apparently innocuous and irrelevant, and use it to undermine his own assumptive world and prevail upon him to adopt the Communist one. The preparation of a "confession" was the chief means to this end, as well as a way of gauging the prisoner's "progress." In its full-blown form, as required of civilian prisoners and the intellectuals at the revolutionary colleges, the confession was a detailed life history. Since wrong thoughts as well as wrong deeds were crimes, the confession included not only the account of alleged crimes and the events that led up to them, but also of attitudes and motives and their sources in the prisoner's early life. All of this had to be expressed in such a way as to demonstrate his complete and unqualified acceptance of the Communist world view.

Confessions were produced partly by group pressures, of which the most severe form was the "tou-cheng," or accusation process. In this, each group member had to criticize himself before the others, going into all his supposed misdeeds and his motives, while they hammered away at him to confess still more. Since the whole group was held responsible for the progress of each member, a recalcitrant one often was subjected to the severest pressure: "a 'tou-cheng' consisted of many gathering around a prisoner,

36. Schein (1957), p. 23.

shouting at him, insulting him, pointing fingers at him, while he usually stood with head down. Often a 'tou-cheng' lasted for hours. Few could stand it very long."[37] Mutual criticism, by keeping all the members angry at each other, incidentally helped to forestall development of resistance-strengthening bonds between members.

At the revolutionary college, the preparation of each student's confession was primarily a group process. With prisoners the confession was largely obtained through the interrogation, in which each prisoner was seen singly, although more than one interrogator might be present and usually there was a secretary taking notes.

The interrogator's attitudes combined complete rigidity in some respects with equally complete ambiguity in others. He maintained an absolutely dogmatic and inflexible conviction of the prisoner's guilt, but gave no clues about what the content of his confession should be: "Just confess your crimes and all will be forgiven! No one is clearly told what crimes he is charged with . . . but he must confess the crimes he is charged with."[38] Although never told what to confess, the prisoner might undergo any degree of punishment from mild disapproval to torture if the confession was not what the interrogator wanted. No matter what he confessed, it was never enough, but he was continually offered the hope that once he made a proper and complete confession he would be repatriated, if a war prisoner, or be permitted to start serving his sentence, if a political one.

The flavor of the interrogation process with a cooperative prisoner is conveyed in the following brief excerpt from the account of an American woman who, incidentally, was largely converted to the Communist viewpoint. The interchange is not too dissimilar from what might go on in long-term psychotherapy. Ostensibly the procedure is completely permissive—responsibility for producing pertinent material rests entirely with the prisoner. But there is an implicit threat of unfortunate consequences if she does not make a full and correct confession, perhaps analogous to

37. Rigney (1956), p. 31. Group attacks on members are integral parts of treatment programs for drug addicts (Deissler, 1970) and also characterize some encounter groups (Sohl, 1967; Stoller, 1968).

38. Rigney (1956), p. 51.

the psychiatric patient's fear of not getting relief if he does not cooperate fully. In the end, the prisoner "voluntarily" comes to think of her past life in the conceptual framework of the Chinese and her conversion is well underway: "[The assistant interrogator] asked: 'Do you feel that you have finished, Li-Yu-An [the prisoner's Chinese name]?' "

"Yes," I replied, "I can think of nothing more."

"Well, we feel there are some points you have missed, and we would like you to go on thinking a bit more . . . it is to the interest of both of you [the prisoner and her husband, also a prisoner but separated from her] that you get all possible details cleared up. We will not force you in any way, but we would like you to think about your history and your activities some more. Is there anything in your history that you have failed to make a clean breast of?"

I stared at him hopelessly for a moment. "But I have thought and thought these past few weeks and there just isn't any more. Can't you give me a hint, or some line toward which to direct my thoughts?"

"That would be no help. You just think if there is anything at all that should be cleared up. . . . "

For the next six weeks I sat and thought. . . .

[I] began to look at our actions from the standpoint of the Chinese. . . . I tackled the problem from the standpoint of what I felt they wanted about us and not from what I considered wrong myself.[39]

Since everyone has thought or done things of which he is ashamed, a detailed review of his past acts and thoughts is bound to reveal some sources of guilt, and the interrogator played upon these. In addition, under the pressures of thought reform the prisoner almost inevitably committed acts in conflict with his ideals and his self-image, such as false denunciation of former associates, friends, and family members. "Everyone was required to denounce at least one other person who had 'recruited' him . . . and as many other people as possible whom he had himself . . . induced to commit political crimes. . . . [This] necessarily incriminated others and to the conscientious [it] presented a terrible moral problem."[40]

39. Rickett and Rickett (1957), p. 114.
40. Beck and Godin (1951), pp. 45–46.

The interrogator harped on guilt from these and other sources, thereby mobilizing the prisoner's inner conflicts[41] and demonstrating to him that his own ideology could not protect him. His confusion was further intensified by physical and emotional exhaustion. In this condition he might be expected to seize on any of the interrogator's hints or suggestions that seemed to offer a means of resolving his conflicts, achieving some cognitive clarity, and absolving his guilt.[42] At first the prisoner might be uncertain about whether the idea was his or the interrogator's, especially since his mental alertness was reduced. The interrogator, however, by pointing out that the prisoner had said it first, could progressively persuade him to accept it as true.

Two related aspects of thought reform deserve special mention because of their pertinence to psychotherapy—participation and repetition. Thought reform forces the person to participate actively in bringing about his own change of attitude. In the Russian form "the method of interrogation . . . consisted of making it the arrested man's primary task to build up the whole case against himself. . . . [He] . . . not only had to invent his own 'legend' but . . . to do his utmost to make it plausible in every detail. . . ."[43] In the Chinese revolutionary college "each group member had to demonstrate the genuiness of his reform through continuous personal enthusiasm and active participation in the criticism of his fellow students,"[44] and in the prisoner of war camps "some kind of verbal or written response was always demanded. . . . The Chinese apparently believed that if they could once get a man to participate . . . eventually he would accept the attitudes which the participation expressed."[45]

---

41. The free-association technique of psychoanalysis has a similar effect, partly also attributable to the mobilization of guilt. Cf. p. 221 below.

42. That producing a state of distressing confusion in a person is an effective means of increasing his susceptibility to influence is suggested by the fact that giving a patient contradictory commands may be an effective way of rapidly inducing a hypnotic trance. The technique of Zen Buddhism that involves forcing a novitiate to meditate endlessly on insoluble problems, such as "clapping with one hand," also comes to mind in this connection (Stunkard, 1951).

43. Beck and Godin (1951), p. 44.

44. Lifton (1957), p. 9.

45. Schein (1956), p. 163.

The repetitive quality of thought reform is apparent from the above descriptions. The same material was gone over again and again, and the interrogators never tired of repeating their demands or expressing the Communist viewpoint. Many prisoners of war stated that "most of the techniques used gained their effectiveness by being used in this repetitive way until the prisoner could no longer sustain his resistance."[46]

The cumulative effects of the influencing procedure in thought reform might be sufficiently intense to cause prisoners to confess sincerely to "crimes" that they could not possibly have committed. One, for example, described in circumstantial detail and with full conviction how he had tried to attract the attention of an official representative of his country who passed by the door of his cell, only to discover that no such person had been anywhere near his prison at the time.[47]

Completion of the confession to the interrogator's satisfaction meant surcease from torment and the reintegration of the prisoner's world view along lines that would enable him to become a valued member of the group. It was therefore often accompanied by a feeling of relief and even joy, analogous to that following a religious conversion.

Regarding overall effectiveness, almost all Americans and Chinese subjected to the intense, prolonged pressures of thought reform eventually signed confessions, since this was required for survival. Even the most stout-hearted might sign and then repudiate several confessions. As one of these signers writes: "Almost every prisoner embarked on a program of confessing every possible crime he ever committed or could have committed."[48]

The program with American prisoners of war in Korea was much less successful, probably because it was shorter. Only about 15 percent became collaborators, and these tended to be the less intelligent and to occupy a low status in American society. This suggests that they had reasons to be dissatisfied with it and would

46. Schein (1956), p. 163.
47. Lifton (1961), p. 46. Similar confabulations are known to occur in intensive long-term psychotherapy. See p. 174 below.
48. Rigney (1956), p. 51.

be more accessible to a philosophy apparently devoted to the welfare of the underdog.

As to qualities that strengthened the prisoners' capacity to resist, one was simple resentment at being coerced. Anger at being bullied, rather than ideological conviction, is believed to be the strongest motive for resistance in American prisoners.[49] For the rest, personal qualities and attitudes that enabled the person to maintain a sense of personal identity and group solidarity and to detach himself emotionally from the proceedings seemed related to ability to resist. Thus the greater the prisoner's conviction of the correctness of his world view and the more firmly it was anchored in his group identifications, the less likely he would be to convert. In fact, the harsh measures used against him might serve mainly to harden his resistance by mobilizing his resentment. Four years of extreme pressure served only to confirm a Jesuit more firmly in his rejection of the Communist viewpoint.

Another source of resistance was the ability to construct a theory of what was going on. Making sense out of the proceedings, which gave the person a sense of being able to predict what would happen next, helped dispel the terrifying fear of the unknown and the sense of complete helplessness. In addition, intellectualization can serve as a means of avoiding emotional involvement. The ability to maintain detachment aided resistance. It was the dominant quality in 80 percent of prisoners on whom the army compiled no convincing derogatory information. They "withdrew from the prison environment . . . [and] . . . 'blended with the scenery' . . . and . . . came out of internment as see-ers, hearers, and speakers of less 'evil' or 'good' than their fellows."[50] Performance on various psychological tests tended to support the impression that the middle group was less emotionally involved than either the collaborators or the resisters.[51]

While thought reform succeeded well in producing false confessions, its ability to produce sustained attitudinal change seemed to be very small unless the new attitude was constantly reinforced by

49. Biderman (1963).
50. Segal (1957), p. 37.
51. Singer and Schein (1958).

the group the prisoner joined after his release. That it occasionally led to genuine internalization of the new outlook, especially in Chinese prisoners, is suggested by the following passage:

> My cell mates were fired with the desire to be a part of the new China, and the feeling that they were criminals outside of it all weighed heavily on them. . . . No longer was it just a question of reforming simply to avoid punishment. Now there was a positive hope for a vital and fruitful future in helping the new country.[52]

Presumably some Chinese remained loyal disciples of Chinese communism. Available data on repatriated military and civilian Americans, on the other hand, indicate that very few were fully converted to communism, and many who were partly shaken returned to their former value system after being reimmersed in American culture. Even the extreme pressures of thought reform seem unable in themselves to produce long-lasting changes unless they are sustained by subsequent group support.

Thus the main lesson to be drawn from thought reform is not its success in generating false confessions but its failures to produce permanent changes in attitude. In this it resembles religious revivals. Adult assumptive systems, especially those on which a sense of identity and personal security depends, are very resistant to change, and changes such as those produced by extreme environmental pressures tend to snap back once these are removed.

These findings raise some doubts about the claims of certain schools of psychotherapy to produce fundamental personality change. From this perspective, such changes may be analogous to false confessions. That is, the person has not changed fundamentally, but rather has learned to couch his problems and to report improvement in the therapist's terms.

On the other hand, revivalism, while resembling psychotherapy in that both revivalist and penitent typically operate within the same assumptive world and desire to produce the same types of change, differs from many psychotherapies in being sharply time-limited. Presumably long-term, gradual pressure would be more

52. Rickett and Rickett (1957), p. 207.

effective in producing personality change than a crash program. Thought reform with Westerners, while long-term, is handicapped by the fact that prisoner and interrogator have different goals and value systems. With Chinese, where this does not obtain to the same extent, it may be more effective. In any case, both methods occasionally produce extensive, permanent shifts in assumptive systems, suggesting that they can also occur in psychotherapy, but they are rare. Fortunately, as we shall see, considerable improvement in well-being and social functioning can occur without extensive personality change.

SUMMARY

Since thought reform, revivalist religion, miracle cures, and religious healing in primitive societies have important common features that will be found to bear on psychotherapy, a brief recapitulation of these characteristics may be in order at this point. Since the English language lacks a common word for invalid, penitent, and prisoner on the one hand and shaman, evangelist, and interrogator on the other, the first categories will be referred to as sufferers and the second as persuaders. The sufferer's distress has a large emotional component, produced by environmental or bodily stresses, internal conflicts and confusion, and a sense of estrangement or isolation from his usual sources of group support. He is demoralized, despairing, and hungry for supportive human contacts.

The persuader and his group represent a comprehensive and pervasive world view, which incorporates supremely powerful suprapersonal forces. That communism identifies these forces with the Party, while religions regard them as supernatural is relatively unimportant for the purpose of this discussion. The world view is infallible and cannot be shaken by the sufferer's failure to change or improve. The suprapersonal powers are contingently benevolent; the sufferer may succeed in obtaining their favor if he shows the right attitude. In return for complete self-submission he is offered the hope of surcease from suffering, resolution of conflicts, absolution of guilt, and warm acceptance, or reacceptance, by the group. The persuader is the point of interaction between the sufferer, his immediate group, and the suprapersonal powers. He guides the group's activities and embodies, transmits, interprets, and to some extent controls the suprapersonal forces. As a result the sufferer perceives him as possessing power over his own welfare.

The means by which changes in the sufferer are brought about include a particular type of relationship and some sort of systematic activity or ritual. The essence of the relationship is that the persuader invests great effort to change the sufferer's bodily state or attitudes in ways he regards as beneficial. The systematic activity characteristically involves means of emotional arousal, often to the point of exhaustion, leading to an altered state of consciousness that increases susceptibility to outside influences. This may be highly unpleasant, but it occurs in a context of hope and potential support from the persuader and group.

The activity requires the participation of the sufferer, persuader, and group and frequently is highly repetitive. The sufferer may be required to review his past life in more or less detail, with emphasis on occasions when he may have fallen short of the behavior required by his world view, thus mobilizing guilt, which can only be expiated by confession and penance. This serves to detach him from his former patterns of behavior and social intercourse and facilitates his acceptance by the group representing the ideology to which he becomes converted.

If the process succeeds, the sufferer experiences a sense of relief, peace, and often joy. His sense of identity is restored and his feeling of self-worth enhanced. His confusion and conflicts have diminished or been resolved. He is clear about himself and his world view and feels himself to be in harmony with his old group, or with a new one representing the new world view, and with the universe. Life regains its meaning or becomes more meaningful. He is able to function effectively again as a significant member of a group which, by its acceptance, helps to consolidate the changes he has undergone.

From the standpoint of psychotherapy, religious healing, revivalism, and thought reform all highlight the importance of emotions in facilitating or producing attitude change and in affecting one's state of health. Some degree of emotional involvement seems to be a prerequisite for susceptibility to any of these procedures. Maintenance of emotional detachment is the most effective form of resistance to them. Religious healing underscores the inseparability of mental and physical states. Thought reform and revivalism highlight the importance of a person's immediate social milieu in sustaining or shaking his self-image and world view. Thought reform, in addition, illustrates the use of detailed review of the sufferer's past history, with special emphasis on guilt-arousing episodes, followed by opportunity for confession and atonement, as a means of producing attitude modification.

EXPERIMENTAL
STUDIES
OF
V # PERSUASION

"That's very important," the King said. . . . "*Un*important your majesty means, of course," the White Rabbit said in a very respectful tone, but frowning and making faces at him as he spoke. "*Un*important, of course, I mean," the King hastily said.

Alice's Adventures in Wonderland

Far from the hurly-burly of the scenes described in the last two chapters, psychologists in laboratories are patiently teasing out the essential ingredients of the processes whereby one person influences another.[1] Since the psychotherapist tries to influence the attitudes of his patients, these experimental findings are pertinent to our interest. In the evaluation of the significance of psychological experiments for psychotherapy, however, certain important differences between the two situations should be kept in mind.

Psychotherapy tries to produce enduring changes in persons who seek relief from some form of distress or disability. Treatment lasts several sessions at least, and considerable effort is expected of the patient. By contrast, the subjects of most of the psychological experiments to be reported are college sophomores who volunteer or are commandeered for very brief experiments to elicit inconsequential responses without relevance to the

1. For a thorough review and discussion of nonclinical research relevant to psychotherapy, see Goldstein, Heller, and Sechrest (1966).

rest of their lives. Furthermore, while psychotherapy tries to induce enduring changes, most experiments seek only immediate results. Change has to be produced, however, before it can be maintained, and to this extent the experiments to be reviewed are relevant to our concerns.

A further limitation on generalizing from psychological experiments to psychotherapy is that problems are selected by entirely different criteria. The therapist is guided by the needs of patients, while the experimenter seeks problems amenable to the experimental method—that is, those on which the variables can be controlled. This limitation accounts for the mountains of experimental findings that seem trivial, obvious, or both.

On the other hand, the purpose of the experimental method is to guard against the great danger of empirical research—the acceptance as true of discoveries that are actually false. One of the great virtues of the experimental method is that it permits the precise statement of the probability that a relationship it has unearthed is not a chance finding or based on inaccurate observations by a biased observer. What experimental findings lose in general applicability they gain in certainty. Confidence in the validity of a clinical finding is greatly enhanced if something similar to it can be produced in a controlled experiment.

Furthermore, just as clinical observation sets questions for experimental investigation, so the experimental method helps to guide clinical investigations by leading to clearer concepts. For example, experimental analyses have made clear the importance of distinguishing between forces that produce attitude change and those that maintain it.

Since it is manifestly impossible to evaluate, much less review, all potentially relevant contributions from the laboratory, the sampling that follows is necessarily somewhat arbitrary, and the acceptance of the validity of the findings rests on my confidence in the researchers rather than on first-hand evaluation.

Although the experiments reviewed may seem to have little in common, all are relevant to one or more aspects of psychotherapy. The first casts light on the nature of emotions—a topic relevant to all forms of psychotherapy. Since the patient's active participation in the therapeutic process is always necessary, studies illuminating the importance of a person's participation in events designed to affect his attitudes are next reviewed, followed by brief consideration of findings concerning personal attributes related to persuasibility. Because of their potential relevance to the psychotherapist's influence on his patients, experiments on factors affecting transmission of the experimenter's influence to his subjects are reviewed in some detail. These factors include the demand characteristics of the situation, the experimenter's unspoken expectations, the subject's state of mind, and the experimenter's ability to mold the subject's verbal behavior by minimal cues. An experiment supporting the possibility of telepathic communication in therapy is next considered. Finally, since to the patient the therapist is an anticipated audience, experiments concerning the effect of such an audience on memory are briefly described.

COGNITIONS AND EMOTION

Most persons seeking psychotherapy are gripped by disturbing emotions. They may be depressed, anxious, or furious, apparently without any adequate cause. This, in turn, may lead to fears of insanity, heightening their distress. Successful psychotherapy diminishes such feelings or causes them to disappear, primarily by helping patients resolve the problems and frustrations to which they are responding. Indeed, merely naming the feelings and offering interpretations of their cause may ameliorate them.

An ingenious series of experiments provides a clue to the explanation. They showed that persons who are physiologically aroused are impelled to search for a reason and that the emotion they actually experience seems to be a fusion of the state of arousal with the person's attribution of its source.[2] The basic experiment consisted of arousing subjects physiologically with a small injection of adrenalin, then exposing different groups to different cues for the explanation of their feelings. The subjects, male college students, were told that the purpose of the experiment was to test the effects of a new drug, "suproxin," on vision. All were reassured regarding its harmlessness. One group was told the actual effects of adrenalin—that it might make them feel tense

2. Schachter (1965).

with rapid pulse, slight tremor, and the like. Let us call these the "informed" subjects. A second group—the "uninformed"—were told nothing about how the injection would make them feel or were misled about its effects. Thus they were unlikely to attribute their feelings of tension to the injection.

After receiving the injection, each subject was asked to wait a few minutes for the drug to take effect. While they waited, another apparent subject, who was actually an accomplice, entered the room and tried to create either a jovial or an angry atmosphere, through acting out a carefully planned scenario. Joviality was created by his clowning; anger by his increasing irritation at an insulting questionnaire that both groups were asked to fill out. Half of those in both the informed and uninformed groups were subjected to the "anger" and half to the "amusement" condition. During this period, their behavior was observed through a one-way screen and, after it, the subjects made self-ratings on scales of happiness and anger. The informed subjects neither showed nor reported any emotion in either condition. They knew that their aroused state was caused by the injection. The uninformed subjects, who had no explanation for their feelings, acted happy and reported feelings of happiness in the amusing situation and acted angry in the annoying one. (In accordance with the demand character of the situation, discussed below, subjects in the annoying situation did not *report* anger—it is hard to tell the experimenter, who may influence your course grade, that his experiment angers you.)

In short, the identical physiological state is felt as anger, happiness, or no emotion at all, depending on how the person explains it. In the experiment, explanations were suggested by cues in the immediate situation. In addition to these, in real life one would have memories of similar circumstances in which one felt the same way. The implication for psychotherapy is that one way in which interpretations relieve patients may be by relabeling their emotions to make them less upsetting. An undefined feeling of uneasiness at work, for example, may be interpreted as anger at the employer, who is a stand-in for the patient's father, whereupon it loses its terrors.[3] This finding also helps to explain why pilgrims to

3. See pp. 226-29 below for a clinical example.

healing shrines seem so ready to bear the sufferings of the pilgrim-age. Part of the reason may be that their distress has come to signify hope instead of despair.

PARTICIPATION, ROLE-PLAYING, AND ATTITUDE CHANGE

All methods of promoting healing or attitude change through personal influence seem to require their object to participate actively in the proceedings. He must do much of the work himself. Moreover, characteristically the nature of his activities is not com-pletely prescribed, so that he must take some intiative. The con-tents of his confession, for example, in religious healing, revival meetings, and thought reform are always up to him. The persuader merely keeps urging him to confess more, sometimes backing this up by stating that he already knows what the sins or crimes are, but without telling what he knows. The universality of this pro-cedure suggests that an individual may be more likely to change his attitude if he can be brought to participate in the process himself and especially if he assumes some of the initiative. Some experimental studies of the induction of opinion change support this hypothesis.

In one experiment[4] students were first asked to fill out a ques-tionnaire asking when they thought they would be drafted and how long they expected to be required to serve. Several months later they were randomly divided into three equivalent groups. All received the same persuasive and personally meaningful written statement, which presented arguments in support of two main conclusions: that over 90 percent of college students would be drafted within a year after graduation and that the majority of these would be required to serve a year longer than current draftees. Subjects in the first group were asked to study the script, put it aside, and then play the role of a sincere advocate of the viewpoint it expressed. Members of the second group were asked to read it aloud as effectively as they could. They were told that their talk would be tape recorded and presented later to a group of

4. King and Janis (1956).

judges. The purpose was to give them as much incentive to do a good job as the first group, but to give them no opportunity to improvise. The third group simply read the statement to themselves. Immediately afterward each student filled out the questionnaire he had received several months before. Opinion change was measured by changes in replies to the questions.

Only the first group, which had to improvise, showed a significant opinion change in the direction of the communication. By suitable analyses of the data the experimenters showed that this could not be attributed to either greater attention to the material or greater satisfaction with their performance than was experienced by the two control groups. They concluded that the crucial factor is improvisation. When a person has to improvise, he thinks up "exactly the kinds of arguments, illustrations and motivating appeals that he regards as most convincing . . . [he] . . . is induced to 'hand-tailor' the content so as to take account of the unique motives and predispositions of one particular person—namely himself."[5] In improvising, the person not only emphasizes the arguments most convincing to him, but pays less attention to conflicting thoughts such as opposing arguments, doubts about the persuader's trustworthiness, and anticipations of unfavorable consequences that might follow from adopting the persuader's position.

Another experiment, similarly designed but including a six-week follow-up, found that the students who had composed persuasive appeals showed a greater persistence of the induced opinion change than those who had merely read the appeal.[6] Furthermore, the active participants indulged in more subsequent discussion and reading about the topic and showed superior recall of the topic and the side they supported. Thus active participation not only facilitates attitude change but contributes to its persistence.

5. Hovland *et al.* (1953), p. 237. Festinger (1957) can account for these and many other findings by his ingenious theory of "cognitive dissonance." According to this theory, there is a strong drive to resolve internal conflict. These results would be explained by the assumption that improvising arguments in favor of a view with which one disagrees creates internal dissonance, whereas reading someone else's arguments aloud does not, because the goal is simply to read convincingly. Only in the first condition, therefore, would there be the incentive to reduce dissonance by changing one's opinion to conform with one's statements.

6. Watts (1967).

In these experiments, participation was limited to speaking or writing. Role-playing, which requires improvisation of behavior as well as words might be expected to have strong power to produce both immediate and persistent changes in attitude.[7] It is used for this purpose in many types of psychotherapy, especially its group forms, and is the cornerstone of psychodrama.

Role-playing has endless forms. One involves acting the part of someone else, who represents a position different from one's own. The role-player knows in general how the person whose role he takes should behave and what he stands for, but is not told precisely what to do or say. For example, two persons might be asked to play the respective roles of an employer opposed to a closed shop and a union leader who wants to unionize the employer's business, as they try to reach an agreement. Since the behavior of each participant depends in part on the other's response to his previous act, the course of such an interaction is not fully predictable and role-players must do considerable improvising.

In another form of role-playing, the person plays himself in a situation in which he is exposed to pressures to change. That this may produce not only verbal but also behavioral changes is shown by an experiment on smoking. The subjects were young women who smoked at least fifteen cigarettes a day. Half participated in a twenty-five-minute role-play with five scenes. In the first the subject soliloquized while waiting in the physician's waiting room to learn the results of a diagnostic examination. In the second she heard the news that she had lung cancer; in the third, soliloquized while the doctor was phoning for a bed; in the fourth, discussed hospital arrangements with him; and in the fifth, discussed the causes of lung cancer with him and was urged to stop smoking at once. The control group simply heard the role-play on tape. Compared with a pre-experiment questionnaire, the experimental group showed a significantly greater shift in attitudes against smoking than the controls. More impressively, role-playing also resulted in a greater change in behavior a week later. At that time the role-players had cut their smoking on the average by 10.5 cigarettes a day, whereas average reduction for the controls was

7. Sarbin (1964) offers a well-organized exposition of role theory as related to psychological change.

only 4.8. Fear, which was much more strongly aroused in the role-playing subjects, seems to have been the main incentive.[8] Eighteen months later the role-players still smoked significantly fewer cigarettes than the controls.[9]

Although participation and role-playing cause attitude or behavioral changes that persist for a short while, the fact that even such drastic measures as thought reform do not succeed in producing enduring change in the absence of a supporting group suggests that, as already mentioned, determinants of the persistence of an attitude change may not be identical with determinants of its cause. Some light is thrown on this question by a follow-up study, twenty to twenty-five years after graduation, of graduates of a girls' college known for its liberal attitudes. When freshmen entered the college, their political attitudes did not differ on the average from those at other colleges, but at graduation they were much more liberal. Despite the fact that their attitudes were considerably less conservative than those of most members of similar socio-economic groups, these changes were still present at the time of the follow-up. The author was able to show that an important reason for this was that the girls married like-minded husbands. He concludes that "an existing attitude may be maintained by creating environments in which *either* new information can be avoided *or* in which other persons support one's own information."[10]

This observation is consistent with the high relapse rates in persons converted by thought reform or revival meetings when they return to their usual environments. The presence or absence of a supporting group seems especially relevant to those forms of group therapy which produce marked shifts in attitudes that are not supported by the participant's ordinary life situation. This can create a serious "reentry" problem.

PERSONAL CHARACTERISTICS AND PERSUASIBILITY

The psychotherapist would like to know not only what conditions facilitate attitude change, but also what kinds of persons are most

8. Janis and Mann (1965).
9. Mann and Janis (1968).
10. Newcomb (1963), p. 13.

susceptible to these conditions. Everyone knows that some people are more suggestible or malleable than others, but it has proved difficult to define these characteristics precisely and relate them to the person's tendency to yield to various forms of pressure. In fact, there is some question about whether a general trait of persuasibility exists independently of the particular characteristics of the influencing situation.[11]

One study found that opinion changes following one persuasive written communication were positively related to opinion changes on other communications dealing with unrelated topics, and that subjects most readily influenced in a particular direction were also most readily influenced in the reverse direction by communications taking the opposite stand on the same issue. This finding suggests that a personal factor may be involved in persuasibility. The subjects were all high-school students, however, and the communications were given in a classroom in the form of booklets that resembled tests, so the generalizability of these findings to other populations and settings remains in doubt.

With this caution, two studies that attempted to relate persuasibility to other personality attributes may be briefly reviewed. One was a group pressure experiment in which each subject heard other members of a group unanimously make a particular judgment before he was called upon to do so. Unknown to him, the other members were simply recorded voices. (This technique permits precise manipulation of group pressures.) Subjects who had been given a paper and pencil test for submissiveness were asked to judge the number of clicks of a metronome. The most marked yielding to the uniformly incorrect answers given by the simulated group occurred in subjects rated as submissive on the test, when disclosure of personal identity was required. They showed significantly less yielding when allowed to remain anonymous. Rate of yielding for subjects rated as ascendant on the test was unrelated to disclosure of personal identity. The experimenters conclude that an important source of the susceptibility to group pressures of submissive persons is the possibility of being criticized or held accountable for deviations from the group.[12]

11. Janis and Field (1956).
12. Mouton et al. (1955–56). See also Helson et al. (1956).

This finding seems consistent with the results of another study in which the entire process of persuasion was public. The design was similar to that of the improvisation experiment described earlier in this chapter, except that three different communications and two different conditions of persuasion were used—passive reading and listening to the communication or active advocacy of the viewpoint.[13] The students were divided into three groups in accordance with their persuasibility. The most persuasible were influenced by all three statements, the moderately persuasible by two, and the least persuasible by one or none. Personality attributes related to persuasibility were sought in the clinic records of sixteen who had voluntarily sought psychological counseling and by statistical analysis of the scores of the entire group on a personality inventory that they had filled out.

The sixteen who had sought psychotherapy did not differ as a group from the sixty-six who had not. That is, coming to psychotherapy was not in itself related to persuasibility. Among the treated, however, those who were most persuasible had sought help "primarily because of social inhibitions and feelings of personal inadequacy," while the least persuasible had symptoms that the experimenter termed more circumscribed and fixed, such as hypochondriacal complaints, insomnia, and work inhibitions. Scores of the whole sample on the personality inventory showed a similar trend. Students who scored high in social inadequacy tended to be persuasible, those with fixed neurotic symptoms tended not to be.[14] Apparently persons in a public situation who feel generally unsure of themselves are more open to persuasion than those whose conflicts have jelled into clearly defined symptoms.

In general, researches on personal characteristics that seem to go with susceptibility to influence have unearthed only those that would be expected on the basis of common experience. These include low threshold for anxiety, lack of self-confidence, low self-esteem, and submissiveness. They are characteristics of many persons seeking psychotherapy, as will be seen.[15]

13. Janis and King (1954).
14. Hovland *et al.* (1953), pp. 174-214; Janis (1953-54).
15. See pp. 190-92 below.

EXPERIMENTS ON THE TRANSMISSION OF INFLUENCE

Up to this point we have taken for granted that the behavior of
the experimental subject was a direct response to the experimenter's manipulations or instructions—that is, that the subjects
were analogous to the materials of a physical or chemical experiment being acted upon by the experimenter. This is, of course, a
grossly inaccurate picture. The subject is an active agent, and how
he behaves in an experiment depends on a host of factors besides
the experimenter's activities. These include not only his own
motivations and personality attributes and those of the experimenter, but also what the context of the experiment leads him to
think is expected of him. Psychological experimentation is a
two-way street in which the subject may be trying to influence the
experimenter as well as vice versa, and much of the process can go
on out of the awareness of both participants.

The same holds for psychotherapy. Just as an experimental
subject may be motivated to produce the results the experimenter
wants or to foul up the experiment, so the patient may try to get
help by pleasing the therapist or by defying him, and what he does
and how he goes about it depend on how he sizes up the total
situation.

Demand Characteristics of the Experimental Situation

One set of experimental studies bearing on this problem concerns
the effect of the "demand characteristics" of the experimental
situation on the subjects' behavior. "Demand characteristics" are
defined as "the cues . . . which communicate what is expected of
[the subject] and what the experimenter hopes to find."[16] Experimental psychologists study the demand characteristics of an
experiment chiefly to make sure that their possible effects on the
subjects' behavior have been adequately taken into account. Our
interest is to relate them to understanding the patient's behavior
and evaluating his statements of improvement. It must be stressed
at this point that to demonstrate that a particular behavior or
verbal report could be in response to the demand character of the

16. Orne (1969), p. 146.

situation does not necessarily mean that it was. It serves only as a caution to keep the possibility in mind when interpreting findings.

A striking demonstration of the power of the demand character of a situation is the behavior of hypnotized subjects. It has been shown that much of their "spontaneous" behaviors are not direct manifestations of the hypnotic state, but rather expressions of the subject's concept of how a hypnotized person should behave.[17] This was convincingly demonstrated by an experiment in which half of a class of naïve students were shown a demonstration in which the subject "spontaneously" (as the result of an earlier post-hypnotic suggestion) showed "catalepsy of the dominant hand." The hypnotized subject did not show this sign for the other half of the class. All subjects were then hypnotized by a hypnotist who was ignorant of the experiment. Most of the subjects who had witnessed catalepsy of the dominant hand spontaneously displayed it in trance; none of the others did. Along the same lines, it was found that, if sufficiently motivated, non-hypnotizable subjects could fake most of the traditional signs of hypnosis such as catalepsy and insensitivity so sucessfully that experienced hypnotists could not tell them from the genuinely hypnotized.

The simulation studies also yielded another observation germane to psychotherapy—hypnosis proved to be a kind of *folie à deux* in which the hypnotist plays a role complementary to the subject's. The subject acts as though he were unable to resist, and the hypnotist as if he were all-powerful. Unless each plays his reciprocal role, the situation breaks down, as was neatly illustrated by the inability of a hypnotist to hypnotize an excellent hypnotic subject whom he was convinced was a simulator. Apparently while giving suggestions as usual, he failed to play his role convincingly, with the result that the subject failed to enter a deep trance and finally became angry at the hypnotist.

An important demand characteristic of both experimentation and therapy is that if a person is given a test and then undergoes any sort of procedure after which the test is repeated, the implica-

---

17. Orne (1970) offers an excellent summary of his extensive studies on aspects of the situation affecting motivation and behavior of hypnotized subjects.

tion is that his scores on the second test will differ from those on the first. In therapy his scores on the second administration should show "improvement." This may account for an indeterminate amount of the improvement in test scores after psychotherapy.

A final implication of this line of thinking for psychotherapy is that the main function of a therapeutic maneuver may sometimes be to enable the patient to give up a symptom to which he has become committed. To abandon it without a good reason would then entail considerable loss of face; therapy, by providing the reason, enables him to escape this consequence. It legitimizes a change that he is already prepared to make.

Experimenter's Expectations and Subject's Performance

Another line of research that has illuminated conditions determining how the experimenter influences the experimental subject, and by implication how the therapist influences his patient, consists of studies concerning the effect of the experimenter's expectations on the subject's performance.

The basic experiment involved two kinds of subjects: those who acted as experimenters and those who served as subjects in the experiment.[18] Let us call the former "experimenters" and the latter "subjects" and the person conducting the experiment the "principal investigator." In one procedure the experimenter showed the subject a series of ten photographs of people's faces and asked him to rate the degree of success or failure shown in the face, using a scale of +10 for extreme success and -10 for extreme failure. The photos had been selected so that on the average they were neutral with respect to this characteristic—that is, they had an average numerical score of zero.

The principal investigator gave the experimenters identical instructions for administering the test and identical instructions to read to their subjects. They were cautioned not to deviate from these instructions. Now comes the crucial point. The experimenters were told that the purpose of the experiment was to see how well they could duplicate results that were already well established. Half were told that their subjects should rate the photos as

18. Rosenthal (1969).

being of successful people (average rating +5) and half that their subjects should rate the photos as being of unsuccessful people (average rating -5).

It was found repeatedly that experimenters given the "success" expectation obtained consistently higher ratings from their subjects than those given the "failure" expectation. The effect was far from trivial: overall about two-thirds of the experimenters biased subjects in the direction of their expectations, and the same proportion of subjects made judgments confirming the experimenters' expectations.

A particularly intriguing question is: how are these expectations transmitted to the subject? One thing is clear—the experimenter did not know that he was signaling them. It was found that either visual or auditory cues alone sufficed to transmit the experimenter's expectations. With respect to the auditory ones, tape recordings of instructions read by experimenters with different expectations were shown to have a biasing effect. When the matter was further pursued, it was found that deliberate, slight shadings of emphasis toward positive or negative biasing in reading the instructions were sufficient to affect the responses of subjects with high evaluation apprehension,[19] a state of mind described in the next section. The most startling finding was that the experimenter transmitted his expectations very rapidly. They affected the subject's first response, indicating that the experimenter must transmit them while he greets, seats, and reads the instructions to the subject.

The transmission of expectations proved to be a widespread phenomenon. Other studies showed that an experimenter's expectancies could influence the performance of rats and other animals, and that teachers' expectations were related to the gain in scores pupils made on an intelligence test.[20] That transmission of expectations also plays a part in psychotherapy would seem probable, since it, too, is a situation in which the therapist has certain expectations. Moreover, the relationship between student experimenter and principal investigator is in some ways analogous to that between psychotherapist-in-training and his supervisor.

19. Duncan *et al.* (1969).
20. Rosenthal (1969) is the source of all the findings reported in the rest of this section as well as those cited on pp. 122-23 below.

Certain findings of the experiments seem particularly relevant to psychotherapy. One was that the greater the power, prestige, or status of the experimenter, the greater his biasing effect. With college students, if the experimenter's status was higher than the subject's, his biasing effect was almost four times greater than if they were of the same level. In psychotherapy the therapist is in a superior power position because the patient seeks his help; in addition, the therapist usually possesses higher status by virtue of his professional training. With lower-class patients, this is reinforced by his higher education and socioeconomic level. Furthermore, the supervisor of the therapist-in-training has considerable power to determine his rate of academic progress. Thus it seems reasonable to expect that therapists could easily bias patients and that supervisors would have the same effect on trainees.

Another set of findings that seems pertinent to psychotherapy concerns the reciprocal relationship between a therapist's expectations and his subject's performance over a series of trials. It appears that subjects' performances in early trials influence the experimenter's expectations, which in turn affect how subjects perform later in the experiment. This finding was established by the use of accomplices as the first few subjects of a series. If they confirmed the experimenter's hypothesis, his behavior toward subsequent naïve subjects was affected in such a way that they confirmed it further. If the accomplices deliberately disconfirmed the experimenter's hypothesis, his behavior changed so that later genuine subjects also disconfirmed it. When naïve subjects were used throughout, expectancy effects were greater with those contacted later in the series than with those seen earlier, as if the subjects progressively shaped the experimenter's behavior, leading him to emit increasingly effective cues.

These findings would support the assumption that the longer a person receives treatment, the more he may be influenced by his therapist. Moreover, the patient's behavior in the first interviews may cause the therapist to reinforce it by his subsequent behavior. This works in the patient's favor if his early behavior arouses the therapist's positive expectations but could well work against him should it lead his therapist to make a pessimistic prognosis. The disquieting possibility exists that a patient who makes an unfavorable first impression might induce anti-therapeutic behavior in the therapist, which, in turn, would elicit further discouraging behavior from the patient. This would be analogous to the *folie à deux* between hypnotist and subject described above and both are examples of self-fulfilling prophecies.

Evaluation Apprehension and Susceptibility to Influence

One powerful determinant of susceptibility to influence that is particularly pertinent to psychotherapy has been termed "evaluation apprehension."[21] The typical human subject approaches psychological experiments with the expectation that the experimenter will draw some conclusion about his emotional adequacy, mental health, or the like from his performance. If this suspicion is confirmed in the initial contacts with the experimenter, it may significantly affect the experimental results. Patients approach their therapists with considerably more evaluation apprehension than the average subject approaching an experiment, an apprehension that is reinforced by the therapist's taking his history and performing psychological examinations. The patient wonders what the therapist will find wrong with him, how serious it is, whether he is going insane, whether the therapist will form a poor opinion of him, and the like. Hence findings concerning the effects of evaluation apprehension on subjects' performance in psychological experiments should be especially relevant to psychotherapy.

One way of exploring this question is to heighten or counteract evaluation apprehension by the instructions of the experiment. In a modified replication of the experiment on judgments of success from photographed faces, described above, high evaluation apprehension was aroused in half the subjects by preliminary instructions stating that prior research had found that poor social perception is usually associated with psychopathology; that, in fact, on the basis of performance on the social perception task it was possible to determine from a colllege population those who would be judged clinically to be maladjusted. The purpose of the experiment was to replicate the previous results.

21. Rosenberg (1969).

Evaluation apprehension was weakened in another group of subjects by instructions that this was an effort to collect preliminary data on social perception for use in a later study. The purpose was to establish a baseline against which could be judged the effects of the manipulations in the later experiments. To this end, data from all subjects would be averaged to obtain a measure of how subjects typically perform.

The subjects were then put through the experiment by graduate-student experimenters who were informed that their subjects had been classified either as "success perceivers" or "failure perceivers" on the basis of personality test data collected earlier in the year. The results confirmed other studies in that, overall, the expectations of the experimenters biased the judgments of the subjects in the direction of their expectations. The crucial finding, however, was that the expectancy effect was confined entirely to the subjects with high evaluation apprehension—it was nonexistent in those whose evaluation apprehension had been reduced.

Characteristics of both subjects and experimenters that would be expected to make them susceptible to evaluation apprehension seem related to the transmission of influence. Thus one experiment using ratings of photos found that the higher the subjects' scores on a post-experimental test of anxiety, the more susceptible they were to directional cuing. Furthermore, the biasing effect of the experimenters was positively related to their own scores on a test of need for social approval and test anxiety—that is, their own evaluation apprehension.

These findings are consistent with those of a photo-rating experiment in which hospitalized mental patients served as both experimenters and subjects. Subject-experimenter pairs that were more anxious than hostile showed more biasing effect than those who were more hostile than anxious.

With college students, a strange and interesting finding was that the experimenter's biasing effect was related not only to his own anxiety level but also to that of the principal investigator. For example, in one elaborate study, several principal investigators were each given two assistants who carried out a standard photo-rating study with a group of subjects. Not only was the anxiety level of the principal investigators positively correlated with the biasing effect of their assistants, but, astonishingly, the correlation was higher than that between the anxiety levels of the research assistants themselves and their biasing effect. In other words, the anxiety level of the assistants was not as good a predictor of the subjects' responses as was the anxiety level of their principal investigator. Since the principal investigators never came into contact with the subjects, the effect of their anxiety must have been transmitted through their assistants.

The potential relevance of these findings to psychotherapists-in-training is apparent. They inevitably have evaluation apprehension, which should heighten their susceptibility to the influence of their supervisors (who are analogous to principal investigators) and also increase their biasing effect on patients. Moreover, the findings raise the possibility that the supervisor's own feelings could affect the trainee's therapeutic results. We have already seen how a patient's behavior early in therapy could lead to behavior by the therapist creating a self-fulfilling prophecy. Now we must add the possibility that the supervisor's prognosis, transmitted through the therapist-in-training, could have a similar effect.

OPERANT CONDITIONING OF VERBAL BEHAVIOR

The type of behavior influenced in the experiments just described is very different from that shown by patients in psychotherapy, who are not asked to judge photographs and the like, but simply to talk. Therefore, experiments showing how one person can influence the speech of another may be more pertinent to our interest. Many of these have used operant conditioning,[22] a technique initially developed with animals. It consists in shaping the animal's behavior by promptly rewarding or punishing selected spontaneous acts. For example, a hungry pigeon placed in a box will peck about at random. If he immediately gets a grain of corn on pecking at a certain spot, he quickly learns to peck at that spot only, and his rate of pecking can be manipulated in all sorts of ways by varying the schedule of reward. A few years ago a psychologist had the bright idea that human speech, being a form of

22. Skinner (1953), pp. 59–141.

spontaneous behavior, might be conditionable in an analogous manner. That is, a person might be able to influence what another person said by giving signs of approval after he made statements in certain categories. If human speech were subject to operant conditioning, as time went on an increasing proportion of the speaker's statements should fall into the approved categories.

That a person's speech can be influenced by minimal signals of approval or disapproval was first demonstrated by the following experiment.[23] Some graduate students were told to say any words that came into their minds, and say as many as they could, for about an hour. The experimenter sat behind the subject, writing down what he said, but exerting no ostensible control over him. In accordance with a preconceived plan, however, every time the subject named a plural noun he grunted, with either an affirmative or negative inflection. Although the subjects were apparently unaware of what he was doing, he was able to show by statistical analyses that affirmative grunts caused them to name more plural nouns, and negative grunts had the opposite effect.

This experiment inspired an increasing series of studies that are gradually tracing out the conditions under which verbal behavior can be affected, using a variety of communication situations, categories of statements, and signals of approval.[24] Since many of the studies have used an interview-type situation with psychiatric patients as subjects, some of their findings are worth a brief review for what they may indicate about aspects of psychotherapy.

As with other forms of influence already described, the effectiveness of operant conditioning depends on characteristics of the subjects and the experimenter. In general, the findings are consistent with those obtained by other methods. Thus the higher the status of the experimenter, the greater his influence on the subjects' productions. Graduate students were less consistently influenced by one another than by their instructors, and patients in hospitals were quite responsive to members of the treatment staff.

Personal attributes of the experimenter may also affect his influencing power. For example, a slight, soft-spoken woman was

23. Greenspoon (1955).
24. Bandura (1969, pp. 564–79) summarizes this massive literature.

more effective than a big, athletic man in conditioning male students to express moderately hostile words.[25] A related finding from an experiment too complex to be described here was that college students to whom the experimenter had previously behaved in a hostile fashion showed less conditioning effect than those to whom he had been sympathetic.[26] Similarly, an experiment using neurotics as subjects found that they showed verbal conditioning if the procedure had been preceded by a brief interview in which the experimenter showed interest and concern, but none when the preliminary interview was omitted.[27] If you feel that someone is unsympathetic, you are less apt to try to do what he wants.

Regarding characteristics of the subjects that affect their susceptibility to operant conditioning of their verbal behavior, findings are consistent with studies using judgments of photos. Thus college students with a high need for approval, as measured by a paper-and-pencil test, produced more positive self-reference than those with a low need for approval in response to the experimenter's approving grunts.[28] Analogously, highly anxious, hospitalized mental patients proved more conditionable than those with low anxiety.[29] In other words, with both students and patients, high evaluation apprehension, whether its source is need for approval or high anxiety level, increases susceptibility to the experimenter.

Turning once again to the question of how influence is transmitted, the reader will recall that in the photo-judging studies the experimenters were unaware that they were exerting influence. In operant conditioning of verbal behavior, the experimenter knows that he is trying to influence the subject's responses. The question

25. Binder et al. (1957).
26. Krasner et al. (1959).
27. Gelder (1968).
28. Marlowe (1962).
29. Taffel (1955); Sarason (1958). This result was not confirmed in one study of graduate students (J. M. Rogers, 1960). A possible explanation of the discrepancy may be that a patient with high anxiety, interviewed by a member of the hospital staff, would be hoping that the staff member could provide relief, whereas a graduate student in a laboratory would be unlikely to expect this from another student. That is, the difference in findings is consistent with the view that a major determinant of the success of operant conditioning is evaluation apprehension, in this case arising from the subject's feeling of dependency on the interviewer.

is, does the subject know it too? The great interest initially aroused by these studies was based on the supposition that the conditioning occurred outside the subject's awareness. Otherwise they would simply be an elaborate way of demonstrating that subjects in psychological experiments or patients in hospitals tried to comply with what they perceived to be the experimenter's or therapist's wishes.

One thing became clear very quickly—for cues to influence a subject's verbal behavior they must have some connotation that enables the subject to associate them with the correctness or incorrectness of his response. A few examples may clarify this statement. A flashing light will condition graduate students to say more plural words.[30] Confronted with an essentially meaningless task, they are probably especially sensitive for clues of what the experimenter really wants, and the light could be interpreted as such a clue. A flashing light, however, does not affect productions of patients being interviewed by a hospital staff member. When asked what they thought it meant, patients said that it was either some sort of timing device or an effort to distract them.[31] Similarly, affirmative grunts tend to be effective conditioners in an interview situation, but were ineffective when uttered in the course of a telephonic interview.[32] "Mm-hm" in a face-to-face interview tends to signify approval; at the other end of a telphone it probably conveys little more than that the interviewer is still there.

Although findings of this type strongly suggest that for conditioning of his verbal behavior to occur, the subject must have some awareness of the response contingencies, they do not specify how much. The problem of determining this bristles with complexities. For one thing, in accord with the demand character of the situation, subjects might tend to deny awareness so the experiment would not be spoiled. For another, questions arise about how aware the subject has to be—whether he must detect the exact category of responses being reinforced by the experimenter, or only the general type. To make matters more complex, if he re-

30. Greenspoon (1954).
31. Taffel (1955).
32. Hildum and Brown (1956).

ports awareness after the experiment, does this mean that he became aware before or after he began to give the correct responses? That is, the awareness might have been produced by hearing himself shift his responses rather than the other way around.

In the same connection, the degree of awareness elicited by the post-experimental interview depends on how it was conducted. One study found that even when subjects were fully informed in the middle of the experiment, only half revealed complete awareness in a typical post-experimental interview.[33]

In short, the upshort of years of work is that "learning can take place without awareness, albeit at a slow rate, but . . . symbolic representation of response-reinforcement contingencies can markedly accelerate appropriate responsiveness."[34]

TRANSMISSION OF THE THERAPIST'S INFLUENCE IN PSYCHOTHERAPY

As already suggested, the experiments on transmission of influence just reviewed cast light on the question of the extent of the influence of the therapist's expectations on the productions of his patients. To recapitulate the chief findings, an experimenter's expectations can strongly bias the performance of his subjects by means of cues so subtle that neither experimenter nor subject need be aware of them. Furthermore, the subject's performance in the early runs of a series may shape the experimenter's expectations so that he influences the subject more strongly in the later ones. Several factors were found to heighten the experimenter's influencing effect, among them a friendly attitude, higher status than the subject, and evaluation apprehension in either of them, as measured by need for approval or anxiety level. Finally, if the experimenter worked for a principal investigator, he might transmit the latter's expectations to the subject.

If these findings were applied to psychotherapy, it would appear that a therapist cannot avoid biasing his patient's performance in accordance with his own expectations, based on his eval-

33. Weinstein and Lawson (1963).
34. Bandura (1969), p. 577.

uation of the patient and his theory of therapy. His influence is enhanced by his role and status, his attitude of concern, and his patient's evaluation apprehension. If the therapist is in training, his own evaluation apprehension would increase the likelihood that the supervisor's expectations would affect the patient's productions. Finally, in long-term therapy, patient and therapist could progressively shape each other's behavior so that the patient comes increasingly to fulfill the therapist's expectations, as these have been determined by the patient's behavior in the early interviews.

Therapists of psychoanalytic and other nondirective types of therapy have claimed that they do not influence the patient and that, in fact, the purpose of the therapeutic method is to guard against such influence. They believe that they create a situation in which the patient can freely explore himself so that his statements about himself are true reflections of his internal state. Freud's disconcerting discovery that some analysands fabricated infantile memories to fit his theories, as well as the widespread finding that patients dream in accord with their therapists' theories,[35] had already shaken this view, and the experiments just reviewed would seem to make it even more untenable.

The clinching evidence, however, that therapists bias their patients' productions—even unintentionally—is supplied by several studies of psychotherapy itself. One found that psychotherapists tend to approve or discourage statements by patients that are related to their own personality characteristics. Twelve psychotherapists of parents in a child guidance clinic were rated by the research staff, on the basis of prolonged social and personal contacts, with respect to their ability to express hostility directly and their need for approval. Those who could express their hostility directly were more likely to make an encouraging response after a hostile statement by a patient, than those who could not give vent to their hostility or those who sought approval. The patients responded to the therapists' leads. Encouraging responses were followed by a continuation of hostile responses 92 percent of the time, discouraging ones only 43 percent of the time. In this study, most of the therapist's encouraging or discouraging responses were fairly obvious, but, consistent with the findings on studies of

35. See p. 212 below.

operant conditioning, there was no relation between their obviousness and their effectiveness. A subtle sign of approval such as reflecting the patient's feeling was just as encouraging as open expression of approval, and simply ignoring the hostile content of a patient's remark discouraged him as effectively as suggesting a change in topic.[36]

That psychotherapists influence patients' productions by operant conditioning even when they are unaware of this is strongly suggested by an analysis of a treatment record, published as an example of "nondirective therapy," in which the therapist supposedly simply encouraged the patient to speak by his supportive attitude without influencing his productions in any way. Two startling findings emerged. The therapist's responses could be reliably categorized without difficulty as approving or disapproving— that is, he was conveying his attitudes in spite of himself. Furthermore, the patient's productions were strongly influenced by this implicit approval or disapproval. Statements in categories disapproved by the therapist fell from 45 percent of the total number of statements in the second hour to 5 percent in the eighth, while over approximately the same period statements in approved categories rose from 1 percent to 45 percent.[37]

This finding was confirmed by a detailed analysis of the statements of Carl Rogers, the initial promulgator of nondirective therapy, and a patient of his in long-term therapy.[38] Nine classes of patients' verbal behavior were selected. It was found that, despite his theoretical position that the therapist must offer warmth and empathy nonselectively to whatever the client says, Dr. Rogers responded selectively by increased empathy, warmth, or directiveness to five of the categories, but not to the other four. Of the five systematically reinforced, four showed changes in the predicted direction over time; of the four others, three neither increased nor decreased. Since this was a correlational study, it leaves unclear who was influencing whom and how much; that is, each might be causing the other to give responses that reinforced his own.

36. Bandura et al. (1960).
37. Murray and Jacobson (1971), p. 728. The protocol is in C. R. Rogers (1942), pp. 261-437.
38. Truax and Carkhuff (1967), pp. 158-59.

To clarify this issue, in a later study a therapist deliberately tried to maintain high levels of warmth and empathy during the first and last thirds of an initial interview with three schizophrenic patients and to lower these levels during the middle third. He used as a criterion of his influence the patient's level of self-exploration, a form of verbal behavior he viewed as desirable. Each patient showed a drop in level of self-exploration during the middle third—that is, when the therapist was least warm and empathic.[39]

These findings, although fragmentary, support the assumption that patients in therapy do respond to cues from the therapist in a fashion similar to the way college students in experiments respond to the experimenters. Left open is the question of what, if anything, this process contributes to effecting the enduring changes in personality and behavior that are the goals of psychotherapy. In particular, the findings concern changes in only the patient's conscious verbal responses. To what extent they correspond to what he actually feels remains unknown. Moreover, nothing is known about how long the changes endure. That is, the studies show only that patients comply with therapists' expectations. As with thought reform, the important question is whether they become internalized,[40] and the conditions determining whether this occurs are not to be found in the experiments reviewed. It should be added, however, that one's attitudes are probably affected by one's own words. As pointed out earlier, most persons cannot indefinitely tolerate a discrepancy between their words and their underlying attitudes, especially when they must improvise what they say, and under some circumstances the attitudes may yield. Furthermore, a technique of influence of which the person is not fully aware may be especially effective because he has no incentive to mobilize his resistance against it.

TRANSMISSION OF INFLUENCE THROUGH TELEPATHY

One cannot conclude consideration of ways in which expectations may be transmitted from experimenter to subject or from psycho-

---

39. *Ibid.*, pp. 105–6.
40. Kelman, H. C. (1958) offers an illuminating discussion of the distinction between what he terms compliance, identification, and internalization.

therapist to patient without mentioning telepathy. Actually, none of the research reviewed considers this possibility, nor is it even mentioned. Western scientists are made uncomfortable by telepathy because it seems to defy physical laws of the transmission of energy and creates conceptual difficulties for the Cartesian worldview, which regards mental and physical phenomena as totally distinct and which still dominates Western thought. Furthermore, the phenomenon is elusive. Telepathic sensitivity fluctuates capriciously in the same person and may be influenced by the immediate state of the relationship between sender and receiver. The degree of correspondence between the message sent and the one received also varies widely and often may be only approximate. As a result, telepathy presents great obstacles to investigation by the usual scientific methods and results can seldom be reliably replicated, so grounds for rejecting any particular report can always be found.

An additional reason for skepticism of published reports is that many investigators of parapsychological phenomena are so eager to prove its existence on philosophical grounds that they are subject to witting or unwitting bias. An impartial review of the enormous amount of supportive data, however, forces the conclusion that evidence for telepathy is at least as good as that for most phenomena accepted as true. One category of evidence consists of statistical analyses of results of experiments involving repeated trials of guessing a card someone else is thinking of and the like—procedures so far removed from psychotherapy that they can be ignored for our purposes. At the other extreme, the literature of psychoanalysis abounds with anecdotes of apparent telepathic communication between analysts and patients, usually discovered through analysis of a patient's dreams that suggests he had picked up an unspoken preoccupation of the analyst.[41] Although these occurrences bear the imprimatur of Freud himself, such reports never convince the skeptic because anecdotes contain too many sources of contamination. Mere multiplication of erroneous observations does not make them true.

There is at least one study of telepathic influence on dreams, however, that is methodologically so strict that it should convince

41. Eisenbud (1970); Ehrenwald (1966).

the most skeptical.[42] Sender and dreamer were in separate rooms
and had no communication with each other or with the experimenter. The experimenter monitored the dreamer's sleep and,
when eye movements showed that he was dreaming, signaled the
sender to select one of eight pictures by a randomized procedure
and study it. The sleeper was then awakened and asked to report
his dream. The next morning he reported the dreams of the entire
night. He was then shown the eight pictures and rated the correspondence of his dreams with each of them. Dream protocols and
pictures were mailed to an independent judge who did the same.
The experiment was repeated on several nights, and the most rigorous controls were instituted against any possibility of collusion.

Although some nights were more successful than others, overall
the rated correspondence between one of the dreams on each
night and the picture the sender was viewing, as determined by
both dreamer and independent judge, was well above the chance
level. The dreams incorporated some details of the pictures accurately; others, although recognizable, were transformed, indicating, as would be expected, that the subject's dreams modified
the telepathic communications in accordance with his own
dynamics.

Added to all the anecdotal evidence, this study places a heavy
burden of proof on those who reject the possibility that telepathy
may be one way in which some therapists can influence some
patients in therapy.

INFLUENCE OF AN ANTICIPATED
AUDIENCE ON RECALL

In conclusion, two experimental studies exploring the effect on
one's recall of anticipation that one will have to present material
to a biased audience deserve mention. They are pertinent to
psychotherapy because the therapist is an "anticiapted audience"
between sessions. His patients are likely to think of him from time
to time, wondering how he would handle a problem they have
encountered, how he would react to certain of their thoughts, or
what they will tell him at the next session. Some even consciously

42. Krippner and Ullman (1970). See also Ullman and Krippner (1970).

rehearse what they will say, despite the therapist's efforts to discourage this. The studies reviewed to this point suggest that the therapist may exert considerable influence on his patients' productions when they are in direct contact. The two to be described accord with the clinical impression that his influence continues to operate when they are apart.

In the first study[43] the experimenter told groups of students that she was seeking persons to speak before an organization on the subject of teachers' pay, and that the following week they would be asked to write sample speeches on this topic. She told half the groups that she represented the "Taxpayers' Economy League," which wanted to save the taxpayers' money, and the other half that her organization was the "National Council of Teachers," which was interested in improving the teachers' lot. She then read a short passage of information and arguments they could use in their speeches. Half the students in each group heard a passage that supported a rise in pay; half heard one opposing it. Immediately afterward the students were asked to write the passage from memory. A week later they were asked to write it again, as literally as they could. There was no difference in the amount of material recalled from the two passages by the different groups immediately after hearing them. After a week, however, students remembered significantly more of the passage that represented the same viewpoint as that of their anticipated audience than of the passage that expressed the opposing view.

A simpler experiment on a larger scale confirmed this finding.[44] College students were told that they would be asked to prepare speeches on voting age. The best speech was to receive a prize. Half of the students were told that the organization offering the prize opposed lowering the voting age, the other half that the organization advocated this. All students were given the same set of balanced arguments to read and told to remember them because they would be asked to write the speeches a week later. At that time they were given a memory test which revealed that they recalled significantly more arguments on the side represented by the organization they were to address.

43. Bauer (1958).
44. Schramm and Danielson (1958).

These studies suggest that images of future audiences affect the way in which a person organizes and retains new, incoming information. Since the psychotherapist is such an audience between sessions, the patient's image of him could well influence his recall of experiences happening between sessions. The experiments have no bearing on whether images of anticipated audiences similarly affect recall of earlier experiences, which form the bulk of many psychotherapeutic interviews, but the possibility is not excluded.

SUMMARY

Experiments have been reviewed that illuminate some of the processes of psychotherapy and factors influencing patients' reports. One set shows that a patient's interpretation of bodily feelings becomes incorporated into his experience of them, suggesting one way in which psychotherapeutic interpretations could affect a patient's subjective states. The others are concerned with aspects of the interpersonal influencing process. One series showed that a person's active participation increases his susceptibility to persuasive communications. Other studies found that expectations of both experimenter and subject can strongly influence the subject's behavior and speech. These expectations may be conveyed by the "demand character" of the total situation which leads the subject to surmise what is expected of him, as well as by cues emitted sometimes unconsciously by the experimenter which have been shown to influence the patient's productions in "nondirective" psychotherapy. One mode of transmission may be telepathy.

Influence is a two-way street. A subject's behavior early in an experimental series may create expectations in the experimenter which then influence the subject's subsequent behavior (or the behavior of later subjects), creating the possibility of a self-fulfilling prophecy. Expectations of persons he never sees may affect a person's behavior. Thus an experimental subject's behavior may be influenced by expectations of the experimenter's superior, and his memory of events by an anticipated audience.

A subject's influencibility is enhanced by such personality characteristics as lack of self-confidence, feelings of social inadequacy, and low threshold for anxiety; he is also affected by aspects of the situation that evoke apprehension that his personality is being evaluated.

Relevance of these findings to the influence process in psychotherapy is limited by differences between the roles of experimenter and therapist and between experimental subject and patient, by the nature of the behavior being influenced in the two situations, and by the lack of any simple correspondence between what a person says and what he really feels. The main importance of these experimental findings is to alert us to the many features of the therapeutic situation besides the therapist's technique that can influence patients. The results make clear that psychotherapists whose theory demands that they do not directly influence their patients may grossly underestimate the indirect influence of their own expectations on the patient's productions.

THE PLACEBO EFFECT AND THE ROLE OF EXPECTATIONS IN MEDICAL AND PSYCHOLOGICAL VI TREATMENT

> "I know *something* interesting is sure to happen," she said
> to herself, "whenever I eat or drink anything: so I'll just
> see what this bottle does."
>
> *Alice's Adventures in Wonderland*

Having roamed quite far afield in the search for information relevant to psychotherapy, our main concern, we
will now focus on some effects of patients' and
therapists' expectations on the course and outcome of
treatment.

In Chapter 2 we considered the importance of assumptions about oneself and the environment in determining perceptions, feelings, and behavior. Humans are
time-binding creatures, so assumptions about the future
have a powerful effect on one's present state. As we saw
in Chapter 3, hopelessness can retard recovery or even
hasten death, while mobilization of hope plays an important part in many forms of healing in both nonindus-
trialized societies and our own. Favorable expectations
generate feelings of optimism, energy, and well-being
and may actually promote healing, especially of those
illnesses with a large psychological or emotional component.

Hope has been defined as the perceived possibility of
achieving a goal.[1] It is aroused by cues in the immediate

1. Stotland (1969). See also Korner (1970).

situation associated with progress toward a goal in the past and is strengthened by evidence of progress toward the goal, regardless of how this progress is produced. Most patients seeking psychotherapy hope to obtain relief by taking the therapist's prescription, whether it is a medication or a course of action. In either case they look to him to heal them, and see their responsibility as limited to following his directions. To be sure, all forms of psychotherapy try, directly or indirectly, to enhance the patient's feeling of mastery over himself and his environment so that he becomes able to assume responsibility for achieving his goals. Obviously one's own activities form a sounder basis for hope than reliance on the good will and competence of someone else.

However, unless the patient hopes that the therapist can help him, he will not come to therapy in the first place or, if he does, will not stay long; and his faith in the therapist may be healing in itself. This chapter considers two bodies of observations concerning patients' hopes and the outcome of treatment: the effects of inert medications or placebos in both medical treatment and psychotherapy and the importance in psychotherapy of bringing the patient's expectations into line with what he will actually experience.

THE PLACEBO EFFECT

Physicians have always known that their ability to inspire expectant trust in a patient partially determines the success of treatment. As Freud put it: " . . . expectation colored by hope and faith is an effective force with which we have to reckon . . . in *all* our attempts at treatment and cure."[2] Until recently this knowledge, like that obtained from anthropological studies, rested on uncontrolled observations and clinical impressions, so that it was impossible to define in any systematic way the sources and limits of the effects of hope on different kinds of patients and their illnesses. The problem has been to domesticate the question, as it were, to lure it away from the bedside into the laboratory where the factors involved could be systematically manipulated and their effects sorted out.

2. Freud (1953), vol. 7, p. 289.

Fortunately, there is one form of medical treatment that makes this possible, since its effectiveness rests solely on its ability to mobilize the patient's expectancy of help. This is the use of a "placebo"—a pharmacologically inert substance that the doctor administers to a patient to relieve his distress when, for one reason or another, he does not wish to use an active medication. Thus he may use a placebo rather than a sedative in treating a patient's chronic insomnia to avoid the danger of addiction. Since a placebo is inert, its beneficial effects must lie in its symbolic power. The most likely supposition is that it gains its potency through being a tangible symbol of the physician's role as a healer. In our society, the physician validates his power by prescribing medication, just as a shaman in a primitive tribe may validate his by spitting out a bit of bloodstained down at the proper moment.

The symbolic power of a pill was neatly demonstrated by a rather complex study in which psychiatric outpatients were given capsules containing either a tranquilizer or a placebo, with or without psychotherapy. The most powerful symptom-relieving ingredient proved to be the capsule, whether or not it contained active medication. Patients receiving a capsule reported greater reduction in anxiety, depression, and tension; greater overall improvement; and more beneficial social changes. After the first four weeks, those receiving the placebo reported as much improvement as those receiving the drug.[3]

In this connection it may be worthwhile to recall that until the last few decades most medications prescribed by physicians were pharmacologically inert, if not actually harmful. As recently as 1860, Oliver Wendell Holmes wrote that if most of the drugs then in use "could be sent to the bottom of the sea, it would be all the better for mankind and all the worse for the fishes."[4] That is, physicians were prescribing placebos or worse without knowing it, so that, in a sense, the "history of medical treatment until relatively recently is the history of the placebo effect."[5] Despite their inadvertent reliance on placebos, physicians maintained an honored reputation as successful healers, implying that these reme-

3. Lorr et al. (1962a).
4. Quoted in Shapiro (1959), p. 301.
5. Shapiro (1959), p. 303.

dies were generally effective. Yet, when a physician today knowingly prescribes a placebo, he may feel a little guilty. For it seems to imply deception of the patient, which the physician finds hard to reconcile with his professional role. "Placebo" is Latin for "I shall please," and the dictionary defines a placebo as "a substance having no pharmacological effect but given merely to satisfy a patient who supposes it to be a medicine."[6] The word "merely" is the stumbling block, since it implies that a placebo does nothing but satisfy the patient. Perhaps because of this implication, the conditions determining the effects of placebo administration failed for a long while to receive the careful study they deserve.

In recent years the mounting flood of new pharmaceuticals requiring evaluation has given impetus to the study of placebo effects, for the pharmacological effects of any new drug must be disentangled from those due simply to the power of any new remedy to arouse hopes in physicians and patients. A common experimental approach to this problem has been the so-called "double-blind" method, in which neither physician nor patient knows whether a particular dose contains the medicine or a placebo. The patient's responses to each dose or course of treatment are recorded, and after the experiment is completed, responses to medication and placebo are compared. Any consistent differences can then be reliably attributed to the pharmacological action of the drug.

Study of the patients' reactions to pharmacologically inert medication is a means of investigating effects of their expectations, mediated by the doctor-patient relationship, on their physical and emotional states. A look at the present state of knowledge on this subject is therefore pertinent to our concerns.

In passing, it may be mentioned that a patient's expectations have been shown to affect his physiological responses so powerfully that they can reverse the pharmacological action of a drug. For example, the drug ipecac is an emetic, which normally causes cessation of normal stomach contractions shortly after ingestion. The patient experiences this as nausea. By having a patient swallow a balloon, which is inflated in the stomach and hooked to the

6. *Random House Dictionary of the English Language* (1966).

proper equipment, these changes in stomach motility can be directly observed. A pregnant patient suffering from excessive vomiting showed the normal response of cessation of stomach contractions with nausea and vomiting after receiving a dose of ipecac. When the same medication was given to her through a tube, so that she did not know what is was, with strong assurance that it would cure her vomiting, gastric contractions started up at the same interval after its administration that they would normally have stopped, and simultaneously the patient's nausea ceased.[7]

Evidence that placebos can have marked physiological effects has been afforded by demonstrations of their ability to heal certain kinds of tissue damage. The placebo treatment of warts, for example, by painting them with a brightly colored but inert dye and telling the patient that the wart will be gone when the color wears off, is as effective as any other form of treatment, including surgical excision, and works just as well on patients who have been unsuccessfully treated by other means as on untreated ones.[8] Apparently the emotional reaction to a placebo can change the physiology of the skin so that the virus which causes warts can no longer thrive.

Placebo treatment can also activate healing of more severely damaged tissues, especially when the damage seems related to physiological changes connected with unfavorable emotional states. In one study of patients hospitalized with bleeding peptic ulcers, for example, 70 percent showed "excellent results lasting over a period of one year," when the doctor gave them an injection of distilled water and assured them that it was a new medicine that would cure them. A control group who received the same injection from a nurse with the information that it was an experimental medication of undetermined effectiveness showed a remission rate of only 25 percent.[9]

The symbolic meaning of medication may not always be favorable. Some patients fear drugs and distrust doctors. In these patients a placebo may produce severe untoward physiological reactions including nausea, diarrhea, and skin eruptions.[10] Along

7. Wolf (1950).
8. Barber (1961*a*).
9. Volgyesi (1954).
10. Wolf and Pinsky (1954). See also Park and Imboden (1970).

the same lines, psychiatric outpatients with high levels of anxiety before treatment, as measured by a simple self-reporting scale, reported more untoward reactions from both placebos and tranquilizers than those with low pre-treatment anxiety, and the discrepancy was more marked for the placebos.[11] Anxiety implies lack of confidence in the physician, but the finding is also consistent with the possibility that anxious patients, failing to gain relief from a supposedly active drug, conclude that they are even worse off than they thought and become more anxious. Reacting thus, they resemble the patients with insomnia described earlier who lay awake longer after receiving a placebo they thought was a sedative.[12]

With psychiatric patients as with others, however, negative responses to placebos are the exception, not the rule. In five separate studies involving a total of fifty-six patients, an average of 55 percent showed significant symptomatic improvement from placebos.[13] This figure is about the same as that reported with medical patients whose disorders have an emotional component, suggesting that placebos produce their benefits by favorably affecting certain emotional states.

To explore this matter further, we conducted a study of reactions of psychiatric outpatients to placebos.[14] All patients received a routine evaluation interview on their first clinic visit. On their second visit they were given a symptom checklist and a subjective scale of mood, after which a psychologist administered some personality tests and tests of autonomic function, over a period lasting about one and a half hours. The symptom checklist and mood measures were then repeated, and the patient was given a placebo, described as a new pill, not yet on the market, known to be nontoxic but believed to help patients with complaints similar to his. The patient was then given more tests for about a half hour, after which he again filled out a symptom checklist and mood scale. He was asked to continue taking the medication, and to return after one and two weeks, at which times the measures of symptoms and mood were repeated.

11. Rickels and Downing (1967).
12. See p. 28 above.
13. Gliedman et al. (1958).
14. Frank et al. (1963).

We found that, whatever the interval between the initial and later measures, the overall decrease in symptoms and improvement in mood for the group as a whole was statistically significant, and more patients improved than became worse.

The temporal course of the mean discomfort score, derived from the symptom checklist, is graphically shown by the lower line in Figure 1, which contains the data from twenty-eight of the patients whom we were able to trace and persuade to return after three years. (Figure 1 also includes findings from a group of patients who received six months of psychotherapy, described presently.[15])

It will be noted that most of the drop in mean discomfort occurred very promptly, even before the administration of the

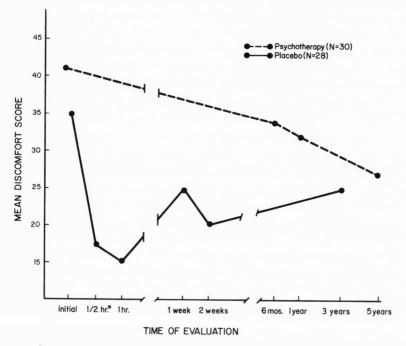

*Placebo administered.

Fig. 1   Change in Mean Discomfort Scores over Time in Psychotherapy and Placebo Patients

15. See pp. 152-55 below.

placebo, and was apparently related to the administration of personality tests and physiological measures of emotional tension. Discomfort increased slightly on the average over the two weeks during which patients continued to take the placebo, then apparently leveled off so that it was about at the same level three years later.

More detailed analysis of the data revealed two additional significant facts. For individual patients, drop in discomfort was greater the higher the initial score, and diminution of symptoms of anxiety and depression accounted for most of the symptomatic improvement. This is consistent with the observation that the ability of placebos to relieve pain in patients after surgical operations (they are temporarily effective in over one-third of these patients) lies in their success in combating the "processing" aspects of pain[16] —that is, the apprehensiveness and other emotions that aggravate the sensation of pain.

When the source of the pain is independent of the patient's emotional condition, like a surgical wound, the relief afforded by a placebo tends to be transient, although it may last as long as that produced by analgesics. When the improvement in emotional state produced by the placebo also diminishes the physiological disorder producing the pain, then the effect may be enduring, as in the peptic ulcer patients reported above. The placebo, by combating anxiety, probably diminished stomach motility and secretion, thereby facilitating healing of the ulcers.

In our patients the leveling-off of average discomfort score may be due in part to a statistical artifact known as regression to the mean; but, for reasons that would lead us too far afield to consider, we do not believe this is the main factor. Probably more significant is the fact that patients seek help when they are in a crisis situation; hence the average distress of any group of patients would be expected to dimish over time as they regain emotional equilibrium and the crisis recedes into the past. This is consistent with the fact that anxiety and depression, which, as already mentioned, are most likely to be diminished and to account for most of the improvement in average discomfort, are the most common emotional responses to crisis.

16. Beecher (1955).

Several mutually compatible explanations may be invoked to account for the remarkably prompt and extensive initial drop in reported discomfort. One is that some patients may exaggerate their complaints initially to dramatize their desire for help and minimize them later in response to the demand character of the therapeutic situation. Furthermore, if the same scale, in this case a symptom checklist, is administered before and after any intervention, the implicit expectation is that the score will change, and in a treatment setting the expected direction would be toward improvement.

Another explanation for the prompt improvement in reported discomfort is that the patient's initial symptoms may be aggravated by the evaluation apprehension induced by circumstances surrounding a first visit to a psychiatric clinic. At such a moment, patients are apprehensive about what the interview will be like, what will be found, whether they will be adjudged insane, and the like. The mere failure of these fears to be confirmed may produce considerable relief. The most significant factor, however, we believe to be the staff's attention and interest conveyed by the testing as well as the administration of the pill.

The great importance of staff attitudes in producing symptom relief has been demonstrated with both hospitalized and ambulatory psychiatric patients. When tranquilizing drugs were first introduced into mental hospitals, for example, it soon became clear that a large part of their effectiveness resulted from the hopes they inspired in the staff. Previously the staff had viewed their function as largely custodial. By producing symptomatic improvement in patients, tranquilizers probably set in motion a chain of therapeutic interactions. The rekindling of the staff's therapeutic interest would favorably affect the attitudes of all the patients on a ward, including those who, as a control, received placebos instead of active medication. The patients' improved attitudes, in addition to being beneficial in themselves, would increase their desire to please the staff by showing improvement, and this would further inspire the staff. As a result, for awhile in double-blind studies patients on placebos improved almost as much as those on tranquilizers. Behavior of delinquent boys in a training school improved equally on placebos and tranquilizers, presumably for the same reasons.[17] Similarly, the mere introduction of a research project into a mental hospital ward is followed by considerable improvement in patients, even when no medications are given. One reason may be that research introduces structure an order into a previously largely unstructured environment, which in itself relieves anxiety.[18] Probably as important, however, is that participation in a research project combats staff apathy and increases their interest in patients' progress.[19]

This supposition finds support from studies of psychiatric outpatients. In the investigation reported earlier, it will be recalled that patients filled out a symptom checklist at the beginning of the experimental session, then after having been administered a series of tests but before receiving the placebo, and again after receiving the placebo. Most of the improvement in symptom and mood occurred during the testing period *before* the administration of the pill (see Figure 1), as if the patients were responding to the interest and attention of the research staff.

This finding has received confirmation from a large-scale, double-blind study of the effects of various drugs on chronic psychiatric outpatients with a variety of diagnoses, all of whom complained of anxiety but were considered unsuitable for psychotherapy.[20] The first group of patients were rated initially on several scales, given the medication or placebo, and told to return in a month, when they would be retested. In an effort to get more data and increase the effectiveness of the drugs, a later series of patients were tested after two weeks, as well as after a month, and received double doses of the drug or placebo. The second group showed about twice as great a response to both active drugs and placebos as did the first.

As in our study, it appears likely that the greater response of the second group was largely due to the greater attention they received. Another possible determinant of the results—supported by a study reported below—was that the psychiatrists may have expected more improvement and paid more attention to the

17. Molling et al. (1962).
18. Rashkis (1960).
19. Frank (1952).
20. Lowinger and Dobie (1969).

patients (because of the greater likelihood of toxic effects) when patients received the double dose. Since all the patients sat in the same waiting room while awaiting their turn to see the psychiatrist, moreover, his expectations may have been transmitted indirectly through them to each other.

In any case, that the physician's expectations somehow get transmitted to the patient is supported by a study involving two psychiatrists who gave psychiatric outpatients complaining of anxiety meprobamate, phenobarbital, or placebo for two weeks each, the order being varied systematically, in a double-blind design.[21] At the start and at biweekly intervals—that is, at the time of change of medication—improvement was rated by the patient and his physician, and at the end of six weeks patient and physician ranked the capsules in order of their effectiveness. Although overall no difference in the effectiveness of the three agents was found, with one doctor's patients active medications were significantly superior to placebos, while with the other's they were not. The first doctor expected to find such a difference; the second did not. The first was also older, more fatherly in his manner, and was checked significantly more often as "helpful" and "dependable" on an adjectival checklist on which patients were asked to characterize their physician at the end of the study.

Taken together, these studies suggest that among the situational factors affecting patients' responses to medication are the physician's expectations. These may sharpen his and the patient's perceptions of differences in reactions to medicine and placebos and increase the patient's responsiveness to both by raising his hopes.

There is considerable evidence, which we shall now sample, that aspects of the immediate situation play a larger part in placebo responsiveness than enduring personality traits. For one thing, the same person may respond differently to a placebo at different times or under different conditions of discomfort-producing stress. This was demonstrated when we again administered placebos for one week to some patients who had responded favorably to the first administration but had suffered some relapse at the time of their return three years later. Figure 2 shows what happened. Again ignoring the psychotherapy study for the moment, we see

21. Uhlenhuth *et al.* (1959).

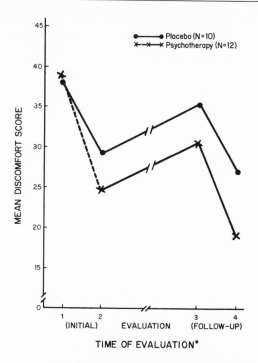

*Interval between 1 and 2 is one week in the placebo study, 6 months
in the psychotherapy study. Interval between 2 and 3 is 3 years
in both studies. Interval between 3 and 4 is one week in the placebo study, 2 weeks in the psychotherapy study.

*Fig. 2   Average Discomfort Scores of Psychiatric Outpatients Re-
ceiving Psychotherapy and Placebos*

that the group as a whole showed an *average* drop in discomfort of
almost exactly the same degree as they had three years previously.
To our astonishment, however, there was no correlation between
the responsiveness of individual patients on the two occasions;
some who showed a strong response the first time failed to respond the second time and vice versa. Nor were we able to find
any strong relations between patients' scores on our measures of
personality and autonomic functions and their responses to
placebos. This suggests that the extent of response to a placebo
depends primarily on the interaction of the patient's state at a
particular time with certain properties of the situation, a conclusion consistent with the finding that only a small percentage of

medical and surgical patients showed a consistent positive response to placebo.[22]

The situation-bound nature of placebo reponsiveness was also demonstrated by a study in which obstetric patients were given a placebo to reduce pain created by three different causes—labor pains, after-pains, and self-induced pain caused by contracting muscles whose blood supply had been cut off by a tourniquet.[23] In all three situations the placebo produced more relief of pain than occurred in a control group not receiving placebos, but the number of patients who showed the same reaction in all three situations was no greater than would be expected by chance. That is, although the placebo relieved pain on the average, whether it did so for a given patient on a particular occasion seemed to depend on an interaction between the momentary state of the patient and the specific source of the pain, rather than on enduring personality attributes.

Despite the importance of the immediate situation, however, certain personality characteristics of placebo responders have been consistently found in different studies. In general, they are people who can let themselves depend on others for help and who can readily accept others in their socially defined roles. In the study of patients with surgical pain, placebo responders tended to be more dependent, emotionally reactive, and conventional, while the non-reactors were more likely to be isolated and mistrustful.[24]

Occasionally, however, a patient who expresses strong distrust of doctors reacts positively to a placebo. A diabetic who was a trained nurse, for example, was the desapir of her physicians because of her refusal to take her medicines and her constant diatribes against them. Yet in the very midst of her rebelliousness she showed a striking relief of abdominal pain following an injection of distilled water by a physician. This suggested that her attitude might have been an overcompensation for strong feelings of dependency, as if she were longing to accept help but could not admit it. The analogy to "skeptics" who benefit from a pilgrimage to Lourdes is obvious.

22. Lasagna et al. (1954).
23. Liberman (1964).
24. Lasagna et al. (1954).

Psychiatric outpatients who showed strong responses to placebos, as compared with a group who showed no response, were more apt to take vitamins and aspirins regularly, were more outgoing, participated more in organizations, and were less cautious. These findings suggest that they expected medicines to help them, were better integrated socially, and were less mistrustful than nonreactors.

This supposition is confirmed by the relation of placebo responsiveness of a group of schizophrenic patients to their subsequent clinical course.[25] Thirty-three who appeared at a follow-up clinic for a routine check-up shortly after their discharge from a state hospital were given placebos for three weeks. Their response was a remarkably good prognosticator of whether they would have to go back to the hospital or not. Of those who had to return within thirty days not one responded favorably, while of those who remained well enough to stay out of the hospital, four-fifths had felt better after receiving the placebo. Apparently placebo responsiveness was an indicator of the ability of these patients to trust their fellow man as represented by the clinic physicians, and this had something to do with their capacity to adjust to the world outside the hospital.

Along the same lines, the investigators in a later study were able to differentiate two groups of patients with delusions of persecution. One group seemed to try to guard themselves against external threat by seeking shelter and support; the other, by maintaining sharp boundaries between the fantasied attacker and themselves— that is, they were more oppositional. In response to placebos, the former group showed a significant decrease in paranoid symptomatology, the latter a slight increase.[26]

A final bit of evidence that a propensity to have faith in the physician is related to placebo responsiveness emerged from a study in which psychoneurotic adult outpatients were given a placebo and told precisely what it was.[27] The exact instructions were: "Many people with your kind of condition have also been helped by what are sometimes called sugar pills, and we feel that a

25. Hankoff et al. (1958).
26. Freedman et al. (1967).
27. Park and Covi (1965).

so-called sugar pill may help you, too. Do you know what a sugar pill is? A sugar pill is a pill with no medicine in it at all. I think this pill will help you as it has helped so many others. Are you willing to try this pill?"

Patients were told to take it three times a day for a week, after which a final recommendation for treatment would be made. The criteria of improvement were the patient's global rating of improvement, a symptom checklist, and target symptoms, defined as those selected by both patient and therapist on the symptom checklist.

Of the fourteen patients who returned (the fifteenth was dissuaded by her husband's ridicule for taking an inactive pill), all reported improvement on target symptoms and thirteen improved on all measures. This astonishingly high success rate may have been partly a reflection of the promise of definite help after a week of placebos. Of more interest for our purpose was that patients who were sure in their own minds that the pill was a placebo or, conversely, that it was an active medication, reported significantly more relief of distress than those who had doubts. Those who were certain either way linked their certainty to their conviction that the doctor was doing it to help them. Thus one patient who was sure the pill was inactive feared becoming addicted to medication and thought the doctor had given her an inactive pill to protect her. Another connected active medication with her mother's suicidal gestures and felt the doctor gave her an inert pill for moral support.

In concluding our review of placebo effects, a word of caution is needed. The ability of placebos to produce symptomatic relief under some circumstances should not be regarded as justification for their widespread use. In addition to the obvious consideration that this would cause them to lose their effectiveness and damage patients' faith in the medical profession, they have several serious drawbacks. Insofar as the doctor feels that he is deceiving a patient by giving him a placebo, this may undermine the doctor-patient relationship. For if the patient showed a good response, the doctor might consider him gullible and lose respect for him; and if the patient failed to respond, he would have lost some faith in the doctor. The very power of the placebo makes it dangerous, for it may relieve distress caused by serious disease. This may cause neglect of diagnostic studies that would have revealed the condition and result in failure to give adequate treatment.

From the standpoint of psychotherapy, the psychiatrist by prescribing a placebo implicitly conveys that he considers medication the best treatment for the patient's condition. This decreases the patient's motivation to solve the personal problems that are the real source of his distress.

There are three conditions in which the use of a placebo may be indicated. Sometimes it can be helpful when an active agent for the patient's illness cannot be used or does not exist. It also may have a proper use with patients whose anxiety over their condition aggravates or prolongs it. To the extent that a placebo will relieve this anxiety, it is a genuine healing agent. Finally, for some patients treatment means receiving a medicine or an injection, and if they do not get it, they will not return. It may sometimes be advisable to meet the expectations of such a patient by giving him a placebo in order to hold him in treatment long enough to establish a therapeutic relationship with him.

In most circumstances the physician can best arouse the expectant trust of his patients by his serious interest and competence and, where indicated, by the use of treatment measures that combat the pathological condition underlying the patient's symptoms. The chief value of placebo will continue to be as a research tool to study some of the determinants and effects of expectancy of help, and to test the pharmacological action of new drugs.

In any case, the major conclusion to be drawn from studies of the placebo effect is that its simplicity is only apparent. One investigator[28] has listed fourteen aspects of patients and eight of physicians that may affect it, and many of these are fleeting, difficult to define, and differ from one clinic and its patients to another. As a method of studying effects of psychiatric patients' expectations on outcome of treatment, placebo response has proved more confusing than helpful. A more promising approach has been the direct study of patients' expectations in psychotherapy and their experimental manipulation, to which we now turn.[29]

28. Rickels (1967).
29. For an extensive review of expectations and psychotherapy, see Goldstein (1962).

PSYCHOTHERAPY AND THE EXPECTATION OF HELP

If part of the success of all forms of psychotherapy may be attributed to the therapist's ability to mobilize the patient's expectation of help, then some of the effects of psychotherapy should be similar to those produced by a placebo.[30] This possibility was first drawn to our attention by an exploratory study of three forms of psychotherapy with psychiatric outpatients, which revealed that degree of symptom relief was independent of the type of therapy and followed a different temporal course than improvement in social effectiveness.[31] The experiment involved a comparison of individual therapy in which patients were seen one hour once a week; group therapy in which groups of five to seven patients were seen one and a half hours a week; and minimal contact therapy, in which they were seen not more than a half hour once every two weeks. The first two therapies differed from the third in amount of treatment contact. They differed from each other in that patients were treated singly in one therapy and in a group in the other.

The patients were all outpatients in the Phipps Clinic of The Johns Hopkins Hospital, diagnosed as having a psychoneurosis or personality disorder. They were all white, from eighteen to fifty-five years old, and about two-thirds were women. They were assigned at random to the three types of treatment, conducted by three psychiatrists in the second year of residency training. Each had six patients in each form of treatment. The design called for each patient to receive six months of treatment. Although this goal was not quite achieved, it was reasonably approximated.

The patients were evaluated at the end of the experimental period of treatment and six months, eighteen months, and five years later. It was possible to examine thirty of the fifty-four treated patients at all three reevaluations. No effort was made to control patients' treatment experiences during the follow-up period, but they were watched carefully. In line with our thinking about the effects of psychotherapy, we chose as measures of improvement criteria that are used by all the healing arts—in-

30. Rosenthal and Frank (1956).
31. Frank *et al.* (1959). The study is considered from a methodological standpoint in Frank (1959).

creased comfort and increased efficiency.[32] Changes in discomfort were measured by a symptom checklist on which the patient indicated which symptoms he had and how much they distressed him. Changes in efficiency were measured by a social ineffectiveness scale, consisting of items such as overdependence, overindependence, officiousness, isolation, impulsiveness, and caution.

The results with respect to discomfort are summarized graphically by the upper line in Figure 1 (see p. 142). In this figure, as in Figure 2 (see p. 147), decreases in score indicate improvement. Since initial discomfort scores and changes in discomfort did not differ significantly with the type of treatment, results for all three forms of treatment are combined. It will be seen from Figure 1 that average improvement is marked by the first evaluation at six months.[33] Although the average score is somewhat lower at five years than at six months, it does not show a progressive trend during the intervening time. Of considerable interest, in view of the widely held belief that symptom relief is transient, is the finding that the average discomfort score remains low throughout the follow-up period. This means that for many of the patients the relief of discomfort produced during the first six months was persistent.

The findings with regard to improvement in social effectiveness, graphically summarized in Figure 3, show some interesting differences from changes in discomfort. First, while patients in all three therapies had the same initial discomfort scores, those who stayed in group therapy for six months were most socially effective initially (that is, had lower ineffectiveness scores) than those who stayed in individual or minimal treatment. The experimental design made group therapy more stressful than the usual group therapy program by assigning patients to groups without selection and without opportunity to meet their group therapists in advance. This may have caused the more socially inept patients to drop out.

32. The thinking leading to this decision is described by Parloff et al. (1954).

33. Figures 1 and 2 include only the thirty patients who were evaluated at every follow-up visit. That they are a representative sample is indicated by the fact that the averages of their discomfort and ineffectiveness scores initially and at six months do not differ significantly from the averages of the total sample. This also holds true for patients receiving group, individual, and minimal contact therapy considered separately.

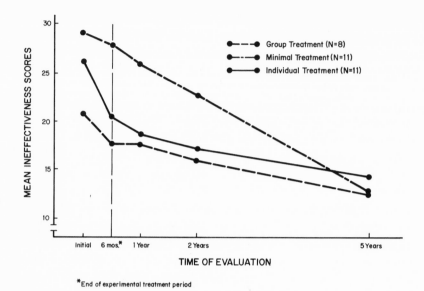

Fig. 3   Mean Scores on Social Ineffectiveness Scale

Second, amount of improvement in social ineffectiveness during the six months of the experiment seems related to the type of treatment, in that those receiving group or individual treatment improved about the same amount, while those receiving minimal treatment did not improve. That is, improvement on this measure seemed related to amount of treatment contact, which was not true of discomfort relief.

Finally, during the follow-up period, patients continued to improve progressively in social effectiveness, so that the average improvement between six months and five years is about twice as great as during the initial six-month period. By the end of five years, however, the difference in favor of individual and group therapies as opposed to minimal therapy, which was pronounced at six months, has disappeared.

These findings suggest that improvement in discomfort and in social ineffectiveness depends to some extent on different processes, a supposition that gains support from the statistically insignificant correlations between changes in them at different evaluations. Improvement in social effectiveness seems to be related to the amount of contact with a helping person, suggesting that some sort of influencing or learning process is involved. Relief of discomfort, on the other hand, occurs promptly and to the same degree, on the average, regardless of the form of therapy or amount of therapeutic contact, suggesting that it is produced by mobilization of the patient's expectations. In this connection, as indicated in Figure 1 (see p. 142), after three to five years, average relief of discomfort was the same following psychotherapy as following the administration of placebos.

Further evidence that the same factors may be involved in prompt relief of discomfort produced by psychotherapy and placebos is given in Figure 2 (see p. 147), which shows the average response to a two-weeks' trial on placebos of twelve patients in the psychotherapy study who had shown some recurrence of symptoms two to three years after the initial study. As can be seen, the drop in average discomfort score in response to placebos closely resembles the drop after six months of psychotherapy. It also parallels the decline in average discomfort in patients receiving placebos at follow-up.

The fact that the drop in average discomfort after six months of psychotherapy, the first time it was measured, is almost identical with that seen after two weeks of placebos suggests that it might have reached the six-months' level much earlier. Support for this is the finding that the same decline was found at six months for patients who had dropped out of treatment within the first month.

That a procedure which merely convinces a person that the therapist is interested in him and doing something for him can cause prolonged relief even of specific symptoms has been shown by an unusually well-conceived and executed study of treatment by different methods of college students with interpersonal performance anxiety.[34] Not only did the same proportion of students receiving only "attention-placebo" treatment improve as those receiving insight-oriented therapy, but all had maintained or increased their improvement when reexamined two years later.[35] The investigator was able to show that the attention-placebo com-

34. Paul (1966).
35. Paul (1967).

ponent accounted for about half the maximal improvement, which was achieved by desensitization therapy.

The intensity of the hope that can be elicited by psychotherapy must be but a pale shadow of that evoked by religious healing, so it is the more surprising that symptomatic relief following even minimal psychotherapy proved to be so enduring. Some possible reasons for this have been considered with reference to the placebo response. An additional possibility is that relief of symptoms by whatever means frees the patient to make better use of the healthy parts of his personality, so that he functions more effectively in general. As one writer puts it: "If the patient believes strongly in a cure . . . by his very belief he at once obtains sufficient moral support to *face all his problems* with some degree of equanimity."[36] Greater success in solving his problems, in turn, results in increased satisfaction and diminished frustration, further ameliorating his distress.

Several studies have suggested that prompt symptom relief following initial psychotherapeutic contact is related to the strength of the patient's expectancy of help. Thus, a group of psychiatric outpatients who showed marked symptomatic improvement after two one-hour sessions were distinguishable from those who failed to improve in only one respect—the proportion who reported disappearance of an initial feeling of desperation was about four times greater in the improved group.[37] Another study of a similar group of patients showed that initial, expressed optimism about the results of treatment was a major determinant of symptomatic improvement after six weeks of therapy.[38] Finally, outpatients in both the United States and England showed a correlation between their estimate of how well they expected to feel after six months of treatment and the degree of reported symptom relief after an initial interview that the interviewer perceived as purely evaluative.[39] Although the findings of the last two studies could be explained by the desire of patients to appear consistent, that they may reflect a genuine relationship between expectation and im-

36. Kraines (1943), p. 135. Author's italics.
37. Jacobson (1968).
38. Uhlenhuth and Duncan (1968*b*).
39. Friedman (1963).

provement is suggested by their consistency with the evidence reported earlier that "acceptance" is associated with rapidity of healing following an operation for retinal detachment.[40]

The expectations that patients bring to therapy are often quite vague and at variance with what they actually experience in therapy. A patient will probably not remain in therapy or profit from it unless his expectations are soon brought into line with what actually transpires. Since psychotherapy is such a powerful influencing situation, the patient usually accepts the parameters implicitly or explicitly set by the therapist. With respect to frequency of therapeutic contact, for example, an eminent psychoanalyst has pointed out that when psychoanalysis was transplanted from Europe to America, the frequency of sessions soon dropped from six times a week to five, then to three times a week or even less. There is no reason to think that this reduction depended on differences in the severity of illness between European and American patients, and the writer suggests that it was probably a reflection of the increasing demands on the therapists' time created by the growing number of patients seeking help. Yet "in actual duration of treatment, in terms of months or years, the patient going five times a week takes about as long to be cured as the patient going three times."[41]

A massive study of "moderately disturbed" veterans undergoing "intensive psychotherapy" in several Veterans Administration outpatient clinics found no differences in a variety of improvement measures after four to eight months of therapy, whether patients were seen twice a week, weekly, or biweekly.[42] Of course, treatment contact cannot be attenuated indefinitely without reducing its effectiveness. For example, as indicated earlier, in our own study patients who received minimal therapy, which consisted of not more than half an hour every two weeks, reported less improvement in social effectiveness than patients who were seen once a week in group or individual therapy.[43] However, optimal frequency of contact has yet to be determined.

40. See p. 75 above.
41. Thompson (1950), p. 235.
42. Lorr et al. (1962b).
43. Imber et al. (1957).

As with frequency of sessions, total duration of therapeutic contact seems to depend heavily on the expectations of the therapist, often strongly influenced by external circumstances. Practitioners of long-term therapy such as psychoanalysis find that their patients take months or years to respond; behavior therapists, hypnotherapists, and others who believe they can produce good results in a few sessions report that their patients respond promptly.[44]

In the absence of external constraints, psychotherapy seems to take longer and longer with the passage of years. Psychoanalysis that originally took one or, at most, two years now often lasts five or six years. At the University of Chicago's counseling center the average number of sessions increased from six in 1949 to forty-five in 1970.[45] Practitioners of various forms of behavior therapy are also taking longer to obtain results.[46] It is hard to believe that the lengthening of treatment reflects changes in the severity of patients' problems or symptoms. More probably it reflects a decrease in therapists' zeal with the disappearance of the novelty effect, and reduction of the need to proselytize as therapy gains recognition.

On the other hand, external constraints such as patient load and ability to pay seem to have a remarkably accelerating effect on duration of treatment. For example, as the number of patients with insurance covering only one month of stay in a mental hospital gradually increased over a five-year period, the median duration of stay in one such hospital showed a concomitant drop from sixty-five to thirty days.

These uncontrolled observations suggest that patients will comply with the therapists' expectations of how long therapy should take, a supposition that gains support from comparison of time-limited with open-ended therapy. Two studies of group therapy of patients with peptic ulcers, for example, one limited to six weeks and the other without a time limit, obtained essentially similar improvement rates.[47] In a well-controlled test of time-limited therapy, one of two matched groups of clients at a university

44. For example, Aldrich (1968); Conn (1953); Ellis (1957); Paul (1967).
45. Personal communication from B. Allen.
46. Klein et al. (1969).
47. Chappell et al. (1936); Fortin and Abse (1956).

counseling center was offered treatment without a time limit. The control group was told they could have twenty interviews over a ten-week period. The patients given a time limit started to improve after the seventh interview (the control group showed no change at this point) and reported as much gain at the end of twenty interviews as the controls reported after an average of thirty-seven interviews. Moreover, both groups maintained their improvement equally well during a follow-up period averaging twelve months. These findings, obtained with client-centered therapy, were replicated at another clinic using an Adlerian approach.[48]

While these scattered findings do not rule out the possibility that some patients may benefit from long-term more than short-term therapy, there is no evidence that a larger proportion of patients in long-term treatment improve or that improvement resulting from long-term therapy is more enduring than that produced by briefer methods.

If expectations of patient and therapist seem to affect duration and outcome of treatment, it follows that the more congruent these are, the better the outcome of treatment should be; this leads us to a consideration of the preparation of patients for therapy. University students going to the counseling center and well-educated persons seeking psychoanalysis and related treatments are usually so well informed about psychotherapy that they respond almost automatically to the demand character of the therapeutic situation, and the therapist can take it for granted that they know the rules of the game.

This is not true with lower-class patients and those referred through medical channels. Psychiatrists have long been concerned with the failure of referring physicians to prepare their patients adequately for psychiatric treatment. Too often the patient experiences this as a "brush-off," an indication that the physician believes that his complaints are imaginary, is tired of hearing them, or has despaired of being helpful. This attitude is epitomized by one note on a patient's chart: "Refer to the psychiatric service as a last resort."

Patients prepared, or rather not prepared, in this fashion arrive at the psychiatrist's office humiliated, confused, and apprehensive.

48. Shlien *et al.* (1962).

The psychiatrist is, therefore, implicitly or explicitly concerned about what happens to the patient before they meet. Private practitioners urge their referring sources to prepare the patient properly for the psychiatric consultation by carefully informing him of its purpose and what it will be like. Clinics usually put the patient through some sort of intake procedure.[49] Traditionally this consists of one or more interviews with a social worker, the purpose of which is to determine the patient's suitability for psychotherapy and prepare him for it. Implicitly it may also heighten the importance of the psychiatrist and psychotherapy in the patient's eyes by appearing like a probationary period to determine his worthiness to receive this form of treatment. In this sense it may not be too far-fetched to liken the intake procedure to the preparatory rites undergone by suppliants at faith-healing shrines, with the intake interviewer in the role of acolyte and the psychiatrist as high priest.

In the early days of psychoanalysis, before the setting and procedures had achieved their culturally induced symbolic power, the analyst might find it necessary to impress the patient by other means. This is illustrated by Freud's example of the patient who fails to shut the door to the waiting room when the waiting room is empty. He points out that this omission

throws light upon the relation of this patient to the physician. He is one of the great number of those who seek authority, who want to be dazzled, intimidated. Perhaps he had inquired by telephone as to what time he had best call, he had prepared himself to come on a crowd of suppliants. . . . He now enters an empty waiting room which is, moreover, most modestly furnished, and he is disappointed. He must demand reparation from the physician for the wasted respect that he has tendered him, and so he omits to close the door between the reception room and the office. . . . He would also be quite unmannerly and supercilious during the consultation if his presumption were not at once restrained by a sharp reminder.

In terms of this discussion, Freud interprets the patient's behavior as expressing a lack of confidence in him as a successful healer and seeks to restore this confidence by a brusque command.[50]

49. Krause (1966) offers an excellent conceptual framework concerning motivation for treatment, with implications for clinic intake procedure.
50. Freud (1920), pp. 212 ff.

When the patient is in the presence of the psychiatrist, his image of the psychiatrist as a help-giver and authority figure is reinforced by certain culturally established symbols. The clinic or hospital office automatically is identified with the healing activities of the institution.[51] The private office of the psychiatrist who keeps his identity as a physician contains all the trappings with which the patient is familiar: the framed diploma and license, examining table, stethescope, ophthalmoscope, reflex hammer, doctor's white coat, and so on. Psychoanalysts, whose medical identification has been weakened, have developed special symbols of their healing art. These include heavily laden bookcases, couch with easy chair, and usually a large photograph of the leader of their particular school gazing benignly but impressively on the proceedings.

Psychologists may establish their expertise and strengthen the patient's expectation of help by putting him through an elaborate battery of personality tests. While psychiatric social workers seem to lack specific symbols of professional competence, they partake of the healing aura of the institutions or agencies in which they work (this is also true of nonprofessional therapists). In any case, once therapy has started, personal qualities of the therapist and the way he behaves soon outweigh symbols of his therapeutic role in mobilizing favorable expectations.

In the first therapeutic sessions, the experienced therapist usually reviews with the patient how he expects the patient to behave, what the patient can expect of him, and what the goals of treatment are. One detailed study of psychotherapy as a social system, based on content analyses of recorded interviews with neurotics consulting therapists in office practice, determined that from 20 to 50 percent of both patients' and therapists' remarks in the first three sessions were concerned with clarifying "the primary role system," as the authors term it. As the patients learned their roles, communication by both patient and therapist about the primary role system dropped off to 8 percent.[52]

51. Reider (1953); Wilmer (1962).
52. Lennard and Bernstein (1960). Hospitalized schizophrenics in psychotherapy and their therapists showed much less asking or offering of primary role information (Lennard and Bernstein, 1967). The authors speculate that this reflects a general inabil-

As these findings suggest, therapists in all schools indulge in considerable role induction at the beginning of the therapeutic contact, coupled with implicit or explicit communications aimed at enhancing the patient's positive expectations from treatment. Analysts, for example, go to some pains to explain the "basic rule" of free association. Although some analysts explicitly avoid any promise of therapeutic benefit, this expectation is implicit in the analyst's accepting the patient for treatment. It is not credible that he would be willing to devote so much time and effort to the patient, or that he would let the patient undertake such an expensive and wearisome task, unless he believed some good would result.

Behavior therapists go to greater lengths than psychoanalysts to orient patients at the beginning of treatment. This is in accord with their conceptualization. It may also reflect recognition that they cannot rely on the patient's knowing what to expect, since information about behavior therapy is not widespread in the educated community. A group of mental health experts who were permitted to observe two prominent behavior therapists at work for five days report that during the orientation period:

The therapist tells the patient at length about the power of the treatment method, pointing out that it has been successful with comparable patients and all but promising similar results for him too. The patient . . . is given a straightforward rationale for the way in which the specific treatment procedures will "remove" his symptoms. . . . The explicit positive and authoritarian manner in which the therapist approaches the patients seems destined, if not designed, to establish the therapist as a powerful figure and turn the patient's hopes for success into concrete expectations.[53]

Patients who come to a psychiatric clinic characteristically expect that, as in medical treatment, they will tell the psychotherapist their symptoms and he will give them medicine or advice.[54] That is, their expectations from psychotherapy are likely to be highly discrepant from what actually occurs.

---

ity of schizophrenics to learn social roles, which may be related to their poor response to psychotherapy (May, 1969).
53. Klein *et al.* (1969), p. 262.
54. Riessman *et al.* (1964).

Therapists who work in a clinic setting share the impression that a major reason why patients drop out of treatment is that they do not know what is supposed to be going on or how it can help them. Because they are in awe of the therapist, they politely answer all his questions and he thinks everything is going well; but all the time the patients are wondering what it is all about, until suddenly they quit without warning.

These observations led us to devise an "anticipatory socialization interview"[55] or "role induction interview"[56] to socialize clinic patients into the role of psychotherapy patients. We tested its effectiveness in a controlled experiment with forty psychiatric outpatients, judged suitable for psychotherapy, but who had not had extensive previous treatment. They were offered psychotherapy by four second- or third-year psychiatric residents, each of whom had ten patients. The residents were told to treat the patients as they usually would, except that they were not required to commit themselves for more than four months. As far as they were concerned, the patients were like any other outpatients, except that they had had one preliminary contact with the research staff.

A senior psychiatrist, who did not participate in the patient's therapy, conducted the initial evaluation interview and gave half the patients a role induction interview at its close. To the patient, this was simply part of his initial evaluation. It was conducted informally and illustrated with examples from his own history and psychopathology. It sought to explain in simple terms the rationale of treatment, the importance of regular attendance, how the patient was expected to behave, and what he might expect of his therapist. The patient was led to expect a realistic degree of improvement in four months. In other words, the role induction interview attempted to tailor the patient's expectations to what would actually occur and also to help him to behave in accordance with the therapist's image of a good patient, thereby heightening the latter's interest and optimism. Elaborate precautions were taken to prevent the therapists from divining the purpose of the

55. Orne and Wender (1968).
56. Hoehn-Saric et al. (1964).

experiment and to assure that the initial interviewer's knowledge of which patients had received a role induction interview was not transmitted to the therapists. As a group, patients receiving the role induction interview showed more appropriate behavior in therapy and had a better outcome than those who failed to receive this interview. These findings have been replicated in other settings.[57]

In conclusion, it should be emphasized that mobilization of the patient's hopes, including tailoring his expectations to what actually occurs, accounts for only some therapeutic effects, mainly relief of the psychic and somatic manifestations of anxiety and depression. Although it is doubtful that any form of therapy can succeed unless it eventually mobilizes the patient's hopes, other factors are also involved, especially in relieving specific symptoms and improving general social effectiveness.

SUMMARY

Experimental studies of the effects of the administration of inert medications by physicians demonstrate that the alleviation of anxiety and arousal of hope through this means commonly produce considerable symptomatic relief and may promote healing of some types of tissue damage. The relief may be enduring. Although persons predisposed to trust others and to accept socially defined symbols of healing are most likely to respond favorably, the response seems to depend primarily on interactions between the patient's momentary state and aspects of the immediate situation. Important among these are the attention and interest of the healer.

Relief of anxiety and depression by psychotherapy closely resembles the placebo effect, suggesting that the same factors may be involved. Psychotherapeutic success depends in part on congruence between the expectations a patient brings to treatment and what actually occurs; hence shaping these expectations through instructions or a preliminary role induction interview enhances the effectiveness of short-term psychotherapy.

57. Sloane *et al.* (1970); Yalom *et al.* (1967).

THE
PSYCHOTHERAPIST
AND THE
VII   PATIENT

"You're thinking about something, my dear, and that
makes you forget to talk. I can't tell you just now what the
moral of that is, but I shall remember it in a bit."
"Perhaps it hasn't one," Alice ventured to remark.
"Tut, tut child!" said the Duchess. "Everything's got a
moral, if only you can find it."

Alice's Adventures in Wonderland

Psychotherapy will now be examined in the light of the
observational and experimental data reviewed in the preceding chapters. As we have defined it, psychotherapy is
a form of help-giving in which a trained, socially sanctioned healer tries to relieve a sufferer's distress by facilitating certain changes in his feelings, attitudes, and behavior, through the performance of certain activities
with him, often with the participation of a group. It is
convenient to separate the therapeutic process into two
parts—the relationship between psychotherapist and
patient, and the therapeutic activities they jointly perform—even though these obviously affect each other.

The success of all methods and schools of psychotherapy depends in the first instance on the patient's
conviction that the therapist cares about him and is
competent to help him. This chapter reviews determinants of this state of mind, including the therapist's
training, the socioeconomic positions of therapist and
patient, and personal qualities of both. With this survey
as a background, we will be in a better position to re-

165

view and evaluate features distinguishing different methods of psychotherapy from one another.

The material that follows comes from naturalistic forms of psychotherapy as practiced by professionally trained persons in offices, clinics, and hospitals. Reflecting my own background and experience, interest will center on treatment by professionals, especially psychiatrists, and their patients; but some data from related fields such as student counseling will also be considered. Although psychotherapy by nonprofessionals and subprofessionals is becoming more widely practiced, it falls largely beyond our purview. It should be noted, however, that since nonprofessionals ordinarily are not highly trained in specific techniques, their growing use is further evidence of the importance of the relationship aspects of therapy.

PSYCHOTHERAPEUTIC AND PSYCHOANALYTIC TRAINING

The patient's belief that the therapist can help him is based in large part on his recognition that the therapist is an expert who has received special training for his job. Recent trends, however, suggest that therapists with little training can also inspire the patient's confidence.

The demand for psychotherapy is so great that psychotherapists trained in the traditional disciplines—psychiatry, psychology, and social work—cannot begin to meet it. Filling the gap are nonprofessionals of all sorts, from those with minimal training or experience, such as many leaders of encounter groups, to highly trained mental health counselors.[1] Students, indigenous helpers, psychiatric aides, and fellow patients have been utilized with the chronically ill, hospitalized patients, the clientele of mental health community centers, and persons contemplating suicide.[2] All report good results. Nor is there any evidence that one type of professional training produces more effective therapists than another; psychiatrists, psychologists, and social workers seem to do equally well.

1. Rioch (1967).
2. Torrey (1972).

Some would argue that the reason is that much of the subject matter taught to professionals is irrelevant to psychotherapy. A more charitable hypothesis—and one probably nearer the truth—is that psychotherapeutic success with most patients depends primarily on the therapist's ability to establish a therapeutic relationship, and this ability is taught equally well by different disciplines.

An extensive interview and questionnaire survey of psychotherapists in three large American cities found that, regardless of whether they had been trained as psychiatrists, psychoanalysts, clinical psychologists or psychiatric social workers, they were remarkably similar in background and outlook. Compared with the population at large, children of Jewish immigrants from Eastern European cities were highly over-represented. They were more liberal politically than their parents, had abandoned their religion, and were socially mobile. Such persons would be expected to empathize easily with persons who have problems of personal adjustment.[3]

Anyone with a modicum of human warmth, common sense, some sensitivity to human problems, and a desire to help can benefit many candidates for psychotherapy. Among such candidates are the hospitalized, whose usual environment is so lacking in emotional support that they respond favorably to any display of interest, and persons in a crisis who simply need to be tided over until they regain their emotional balance. That is, many receivers of psychotherapy can be greatly helped by anyone who is able to combat their demoralization, mobilize their expectations of help, and shore up or restore their self-confidence.

In this connection, several studies have shown that medical students obtain about the same improvement rates in short-term therapy as do psychiatrists.[4] Operating within a teaching institution, they carry its sanction and embody its healing reputation. Moreover, they have not yet become blasé and, not yet disillusioned by experience, they are generally more optimistic than their seniors.[5] It seems as though their high level of emotional

3. Henry *et al.* (1971).
4. Heine (1962); Uhlenhuth and Duncan (1968a).
5. Strupp (1958).

involvement, eagerness to help, and favorable expectations compensate to a considerable extent for their inexperience.

Findings of this sort, however, are too fragmentary to permit the conclusion that lack of training can always be overcome by other factors. Indeed the weight of evidence is that experienced therapists, regardless of their special training, get better results than novices.[6] Conceivably this could simply be an indirect expression of a process of self-selection. Therapists who are personally poorly fitted to conduct psychotherapy would presumably discover this after a time and move on to other fields. Those who remain to become experienced would be the best suited for the task, which would explain their superior results. It seems more probable, however, that the relations of success to experience is evidence that psychotherapy is an art that improves with practice.

Whatever other components it may have, the essence of the art seems to be the ability to offer a certain type of relationship. A study of taped interviews revealed that experienced practitioners of different schools offered psychotherapeutic relationships that were more similar than those created by experts and novices of the same school. The relationships created by the expert therapists, furthermore, were more like the "ideal" therapeutic relationship than those created by non-experts. The ideal therapeutic relationship was determined simply by asking four experts of different schools to describe it. Among its most characteristic features were that the therapist was able to participate completely in patients' communication, understand that patients' feelings and convey his ability to share them. Apparently experience overcomes doctrinaire differences.[7] This finding was confirmed by the patients, insofar as those treated by therapists of different schools attributed their improvement to the different methods but described their relationships with their therapists in similar terms.[8] These descriptions were very similar to those of the ideal therapeutic relationship.

One training program has focused on the cultivation of a therapeutic relationship. It tries to enhance the trainee's ability to be

6. Meltzoff and Kornreich (1970), pp. 268-73.
7. Fiedler (1953).
8. Heine (1953).

empathic, genuine, and warm—the essential qualities of a healing attitude—through the study of tapes of interviews, role-playing with other trainees, and working with patients under close supervision, all of which are followed by group discussions.[9]

Most training programs, however, emphasize particular conceptual schemes and associated techniques. These include behavior therapies, group therapies, and a variety of interview approaches. In the process of teaching particular skills, all training programs indirectly enhance the trainee's ability to maintain a therapeutic attitude. In particular they strengthen his self-confidence by helping him to develop mastery of a procedure, by inducting him into a professional role and status, and by offering him the support of like-minded colleagues.

To illustrate these points we shall turn to a detailed examination of psychoanalytic training.[10] Features of psychoanalytic training that help a trainee to maintain a therapeutic attitude resemble those of training programs for healers in other cultures. Furthermore, in contrast with other American training programs that are changing so rapidly that any description would probably be outdated before the ink is dry, psychoanalytic programs change relatively slowly.

Most graduates of analytic institutes are psychiatrists. Medical training is the accepted route to the acquisition of healing powers and confers a high prestige in American society; the basic training of psychiatrists is the same as that of all specialized physicians and thus is one source of their self-confidence and the patients' faith in them. Although psychoanalysts may maintain their status as physicians by keeping membership in medical societies, their identification as physicians is often weak. In this connection, many analytic institutes train nonphysicians and accept them as members. Thus analysts' self-confidence rests heavily on the group-identification provided by the training program of the psychoanalytic institute.

9. Carkhuff (1969); Truax and Carkhuff (1967).
10. Since all training institutes referred to in the text teach Freudian psychoanalysis or one of its offshooots, for simplicity's sake they are referred to by the generic term "analytic institute," and the terms "psychoanalytic" and "analytic" are used interchangeably. This should not be taken to imply that doctrinal differences among different schools are unimportant, but only that they are not relevant for this discussion.

In its classical form, psychoanalysis involves frequent sessions over a period of months or years. The patient lies on a couch, with the analyst sitting outside his field of vision, and says whatever comes into his mind. This process leads him to review and relive important experiences, especially those in his early life, and to experience strong feelings to the analyst, who becomes a stand-in for parental and other family figures. The analyst facilitates the process by interpreting the meanings of the patient's feelings and behavior.

The aim of analytic training is to confer mastery of this technique and of the theory on which it is based. Training methods emphasize maximal participation of the trainee or "candidate"— the latter being a term not without significance, as will be seen. The core of the process is the detailed, continuous supervision by faculty members of his treatment of patients and a personal analysis through which he experiences the method at first hand. These activities are supplemented by lectures and seminars in which pertinent literature and theory are studied, and the treatment of certain cases is followed in detail.

The training program is prolonged, laborious, and expensive. It lasts at least four years and costs thousands of dollars. Since it does not replace the candidate's usual activities but competes with them, it reduces his mobility and seriously cuts into his free time. It usually requires that he go into debt, or that his wife work to supplement his income. Thus, in several ways it may require considerable sacrifices by both the trainee and his family.[11]

Although there is no evidence for the therapeutic superiority of psychoanalysis,[12] psychoanalysts enjoy a high prestige, and ana-

11. Potter et al. (1957).
12. Since this statement may be surprising to some readers, it may be supported by the following quotations from leading psychoanalysts: " . . . I once regarded it [psychoanalysis] . . . as also a therapeutic program par excellence. True, Freud warned us against the emphasis on the therapeutic effect. Now I know he was right; therapeutic effect it does have, but, in my opinion, were this its chief or only value, psychoanalysis would be doomed." (Menninger, 1958, p. xi.)
Dr. Harry I. Weinstock, when chairman of a fact-gathering committee of the American Psychoanalytic Association, stated: "No claims regarding the therapeutic usefulness of analytic treatment are made by the American Psychoanalytic Association." (Quoted in Eysenck, 1960, p. 40.)

lytic institutes attract many able, young psychiatrists, who are undeterred by the sacrifices involved. What are the reasons for this? Partly they lie in the appealing features of analytic theories. Other theories may explain certain aspects of human functioning more satisfactorily, or be more easily verifiable, but none approach analytic theories in scope or intellectual fascination. Moreover, many analytic concepts have been incorporated not only into theories of mental illness and treatment, but also into all aspects of America's intellectual and cultural life, so that mastery of these doctrines gives one the satisfaction of being thoroughly familiar with theories that others know only indirectly or partially.

Furthermore, completion of analytic training is marked by admission of the candidate to membership in the institute. This not only confers a high status but also assures a source of patient referrals, thereby yielding financial security. Whether such attractions are sufficient to explain the appeal of psychoanalysis is problematical. Probably more significant is the indoctrinating power of the training procedure, which in some respects resembles thought reform.[13] The analytic institute is a tight little island in which the candidate comes into continual, formal and informal contacts with other trainees and the teaching staff, all of whom represent a consistent viewpoint. This is conveyed most powerfully by the training analysis which is the core of the indoctrination process.

The avowed purposes of the training analysis are to familiarize the candidate with the method by having him experience it as an analysand and to foster those changes in his personality and attitudes believed to make him a better therapist. It is intended to enhance the candidate's self-knowledge, thereby freeing him of certain emotional conflicts and vulnerabilities and enabling him to guard against the effects of those he cannot eliminate. Through his training analysis, the candidate is believed to become more objective, more sensitive to and tolerant of the attitudes and feelings of his patients. This is essential because prolonged psychotherapy often creates a highly charged emotional relationship between

13. Winokur (1955); Wyatt (1956).

patient and therapist. Unless the latter is himself emotionally secure and clear about his own feelings and motives, his reactions may reduce his effectiveness or even harm his patients.

The personality changes fostered by the training analysis may improve the therapeutic ability of physicians whose medical training has taught them to protect themselves from the emotional impact of their patients by viewing them as specimens of disease rather than as persons. A training analysis may help a physician to become not only a better psychotherapist but also a better doctor, by helping him to dispense with this type of shield and to relate in a more personal way to his patients.

On the other hand, cultivation of objectivity and self-awareness may hamper the therapeutic efficacy of psychotherapists who are aloof, passive, or overly introspective. For there is only a fine line between objectivity and coldness, self-awareness and morbid introspection, tolerance and indifference. Thus psychoanalytic training may impede the ability of some therapists to enter fully into the therapeutic encounter, which seems so important for the success of therapy.

Regardless of its effects on the candidate's personality, the training analysis is a powerful method of indoctrination. It subjects the candidate to virtually the same technique as that used with patients. This technique will be considered more fully in the next chapter. It involves a detailed review of his current thoughts and feelings in relation to his life history, interpreted consistently by the training analyst in terms of the doctrines of the institute. Since the initiative in the production of material resides with the candidate, the method fosters improvisation and participation. Training analysis lasts for several years, with the same material being reviewed repeatedly. As we have seen, improvisation, participation, and repetition are important in producing attitude change. The training analysis, furthermore, is not complete until the candidate produces memories, thoughts, and feelings in a form that confirms the doctrines of the institute.

At this point the full significance of the term "candidate" becomes clear. Since the ultimate criterion for acceptance into membership in an analytic institute is completion of the training analysis, participation in the training program carries no guarantee of eventual membership, no matter how heavy a candidate's investment of time, effort, and money may be. One rejected candidate admitted to a sense of relief, because acceptance would have meant "being constantly involved in a trial situation in which they can sort of chop you off at any time for the next eight years or so of your professional life."[14] Such a predicament must provide a powerful incentive for a candidate to conform.

In short, there can be little doubt that the training analysis, regardless of its other effects, is a powerful method of indoctrination. As a leading psychoanalyst has written: "It is scarcely to be expected that a student who has spent years under the artificial . . . conditions of a training analysis and whose professional career depends on overcoming 'resistance' to the satisfaction of his training analyst, can be in a favorable position to defend his scientific integrity against the analyst's theory and practice. . . . for according to his analyst, the candidate's objections to interpretations rate as resistance. In short, there is a tendency in the training situation to perpetuate error."[15] The German psychiatrist-philosopher Karl Jaspers stated the issue well: "The founders of institutional psychotherapeutic training must ask themselves whether the demand for a training analysis does not sometimes hide something like a demand for a declaration of faith and the vindication of something that pertains more to the preservation of a sect than to a public form of therapy."[16]

The indoctrinating power of psychoanalytic theory is enhanced by the fact that it is all-inclusive and is not susceptible of disproof. Analytic theories do evolve and change in the light of accumulated experience, but the changes consist primarily of elaborations, accretions, and shifts in emphasis. Teaching seminars in institutes subject their theories to critical scrutiny, but the limitations of the critique are suggested by the fact that no training institute has yet disbanded because it concluded that its theory was inferior to that of another school.

One reason for the tenacity of all theories of psychotherapy, including psychoanalysis, is that practitioners elicit from patients

14. Quoted by Rogow (1970), p. 53.
15. Glover (1952), p. 403.
16. Jaspers (1964), p. 39.

material confirming their views. Operant conditioning may play some part in this process. Ordinarily the therapist accepts this material without question. Even if it proves to be false, this need not shake him. Freud nicely illustrated this point by his handling of the discovery that his patients confabulated infantile memories—in itself strong evidence for the influencing power of his techniques. As he was quick to see, "this discovery . . . serves either to discredit the analysis which led to such a result or to discredit the patients upon whose testimony the analysis, as well as the whole understanding of neurosis, is built up." This is a bleak predicament indeed, from which Freud extricates himself by a *tour de force*. He points out that "these phantasies possess *psychological* reality in contrast to *physical* reality" and *"in the realm of neurosis the psychological reality is the determining factor."*[17] That is, for Freud the fact that these infantile experiences were fantasies rather than actualities, far from refuting his theories, actually confirms them.

Analytic theories of human behavior rest on more solid evidence than real or fabricated infantile memories, of course, and Freud's point may well be correct. But the type of reasoning illustrates a characteristic not only of psychoanalysis but of many theories underlying psychotherapy which may be an important source of their power—that they cannot be refuted by the patient's productions.

In this connection, the analyst can protect his position against a patient's statements that are obviously incompatible with it by discrediting their validity. The patient's rejection of an interpretation becomes "resistance," and his criticisms of the therapist can be dismissed as based on "transference," implying that they are entirely the result of the patient's distorted perceptions. Faced with such behaviors, the young analyst is admonished not to become "defensive"—not to admit, even by implication, that his viewpoint requires defending.

The conceptual scheme is further protected by selection of only those patients suitable for analysis. The criteria of suitability are similar to those that would make the patient a good prospect for

17. Freud (1920), p. 321. Italics are Freud's.

any type of psychotherapy.[18] Like the shaman, the psychoanalyst maximizes the likelihood of success by his selection of cases for treatment.

Failure to improve can be readily attributed to the patient's unsuitability for analysis.[19] Since the length of treatment is indeterminate, the analyst may take refuge in the position that the patient broke off too soon. As long as a patient is undergoing treatment, the therapist need not admit failure. Occasionally he may entertain the possibility that he applied his technique incorrectly, but failures rarely lead him to question the technique itself or the premises underlying it. As one young psychoanalyst in training told the writer: "Even if the patient doesn't get better, you know you're doing the right thing." Thus, as in other forms of healing and influence, successful cases strengthen the underlying conceptual scheme while failures do not shake it.

The conceptual scheme is reinforced by the trainee's colleagues, who also are in the process of becoming indoctrinated. The more deeply they become immersed in their training, the more they tend to confine their professional and social contacts to each other. This may be partly because they learn a specialized vocabulary, the terms of which are fully grasped only by members of the same school, partly through the development of a common body of shared experience. The cohesiveness of each group is heightened by the lack of sympathy of rival groups and of large segments of the medical profession.

Like other specialists, analysts continue to associate primarily with their own group after their training is completed. This serves to preserve the conceptual scheme, in a fashion similar to Wesley's classes, especially since members who come to doubt the theory usually drift out of the group. Finally the magnitude of the sacrifices the trainee has made to master certain methods and doctrines, and his public adherence to them, create a strong incentive for belief. For if the analyst were to abandon his position, his

18. See pp. 188–93 below.
19. In a questionnaire study of a large number of psychiatrists treating patients in outpatient clinics (Board, 1959, p. 188), 82 percent thought the "outstanding difficulty" with unsuccessfully treated patients was "the patient's incapacity for treatment," indicating that this way of explaining failures is not confined to psychoanalysts.

sacrifices would have been in vain and he would be under the painful necessity of admitting that he had been wrong.

In this connection, that the method may not work well and that the doctrine is open to question may paradoxically strengthen the analyst's dogmatic adherence to them as a way of stifling his misgivings. It probably also contributes to the perpetuation of analytic institutes, irrespective of the actual merits of what they teach. For one of the best ways to allay self-doubts is to try to convert others to one's point of view, thereby gaining confirmation of its correctness from them. Conceivably this may be one factor in the energy devoted to the propagation of analytic doctrines.[20]

Responses of Freudian, Adlerian, and Jungian psychiatrists to a questionnaire afford some measure of the success of the training programs of analytic institutes as methods of indoctrination.[21] Seventy percent stated that they believed their form of therapy to be the best, a high figure in the absence of evidence that one therapy is more effective than another, especially since only 25 percent professed themselves satisfied with their theoretical orientation. It is interesting that these consisted mostly of adherents of Adler and Jung. Wolff comments: "The degree of identification of each member with the leader of the group is greater in minority groups, which defend their new system against the system of the majority group." A simple calculation reveals that 52 percent (75 percent of 70 percent) believed their therapy to be the best not only in the absence of objective evidence but also without being sure of the soundness of the theory on which it was based.

The relatively great reluctance of the questionnaire responders to express complete satisfaction with their conceptual schemes probably reflects the high value that psychiatrists, both as Americans and as physicians, attach to the scientific attitude, which is opposed to dogmatism.[22] Even if an analyst were completely satisfied with the conceptual framework, he might be inhibited from

20. Festinger (1954) offers an interesting theoretical exposition of this phenomenon in terms of the need to validate the correctness of one's own feelings and ideas against the experiences of other persons and shows how this is related to the tendency of prophetic religious sects to start proselytizing only after their prophecy has failed (Festinger et al., 1956).
21. Wolff (1954). The quote is from p. 470.
22. London (1964).

saying so publicly, because this would be incompatible with a scientific attitude.

The indoctrination aspect of analytic training has facilitated psychiatric progress in some ways. The support of analytic institutes has enabled analysts to persist in their trail-breaking explorations of the human psyche in the face of the widespread and often vehement opposition of influential segments of society, including many of their medical colleagues. Many physicians were made uneasy by aspects of human nature revealed by psychoanalysis, the strangeness of analytic terminology, and the content of its theories. As a result, for decades analysts had to pursue their studies and their teaching outside medical schools, with all that this meant in terms of absence of academic status, financial insecurity, and lack of access to students. They persisted, and psychoanalysis and its derivatives have had an invigorating and liberating influence that would be hard to overestimate, not only on psychiatry but on all scientific disciplines concerned with human beings, and on many forms of creative activity.

Nevertheless, at the present stage of psychiatric development, the influence of psychoanalytic institutes has certain potentially unfortunate implications, which must be considered in any attempt to evaluate their position in the current scene.

They exert a strong pressure on young psychiatrists to go into private practice, partly because they are run by private practitioners and are therefore oriented to it and partly because private practice is the easiest way for the psychiatrist to recoup the expenses of his training. This leads to a disproportionate expenditure of effort on a small segment of the patient population—those who can afford to pay for long-term therapy. Within this group those are favored who are considered to be most suitable for analytic therapy. These prove to be persons with good adaptive capacities who are intelligent and verbally skillful; that is, patients who might well benefit equally from simpler and briefer procedures. To the extent that able psychiatrists devote themselves to them, their energies are diverted from psychiatric patients who present a much greater social problem—the indigent and the hospitalized. The lure of private practice also tends to draw analytic psychiatrists from teaching and research, which cannot compete in financial rewards.

Psychoanalysis, both as an institution[23] and as a theory, has certain serious drawbacks from a research standpoint. Like all theories, it has fostered interest in certain areas at the expense of others that may be equally important. In particular, it has focused on psychological factors in mental illness to the relative neglect of biologically based assets and liabilities. It has also stressed the role of personal life experience, especially in childhood, in molding personality, to the relative neglect of sociocultural forces. Finally, it has emphasized early life experience rather than current faulty interaction patterns as sources of difficulty. Modern analytic theory has endeavored to encompass the factors it initially neglected, but not being constructed to explain them, it has not dealt with many of them adequately.

The most serious drawback of analytic concepts, however, lies not in their content but in their formal characteristics. As attempts at inclusive formulations of all human thinking, feeling, and behavior, they have to be able to explain everything that happens. The validity of analytic hypotheses cannot be tested by making predictions from them and determining whether the predictions are confirmed. For no matter how the test comes out, analytic theory can explain the results. Freud's handling of the discovery that traumatic experiences in infancy, which formed a cornerstone of psychoanalytic theory, were often fabrications, illustrates this point.

The type of imagination-catching, aesthetically appealing, all-inclusive conceptual scheme exemplified by psychoanalysis represents a necessary early step in the exploration of a new field. It directs attention to new data, shows their importance, and offers a framework for thinking about them. Its conceptual structure, however, becomes a handicap at a later stage, and psychiatry

23. Wheelis (1958) offers a discussion of the institutionalization of psychoanalysis as hampering its development as a science, and he describes the plight of the analyst when he becomes disillusioned about the efficacy of the technique (p. 231): "Of those courses open to him the least painful is a retreat into dogma. If he takes this path, the cancerous doubts which threaten his vested professional interest are abolished by fiat. . . . Henceforth the criterion of truth is not experience, but the book. The sanctity of psychoanalytic theory and technique is maintained, but at the cost of severing its connection with clinically observed events."

today may be ready to move ahead to the formulation of more rigorous, experimentally testable hypotheses.[24]

SOCIOCULTURAL STATUS OF PSYCHOTHERAPISTS AND PATIENTS

The psychotherapist's success depends in part on the patient's image of him as the possessor of healing knowledge and skills. In pre-literate societies the shaman's training is universally regarded as achieving this end, and this is generally true for training programs of therapists in industrialized societies despite their variety. The shaman, however, has an advantage over his western counterpart in one important respect. He represents and transmits the unified, all-encompassing world view of his society.

Reflecting the pluralism of industrialized societies, the trained psychotherapist cannot be sure of general acceptance. The psychiatrist, particularly, suffers from a mixed public image. Perhaps reflecting his dual heritage from religion and medicine, the psychiatrist may be invested with attributes of both witch doctor and physician, causing him to be overvalued in some respects and undervalued in others. Some persons regard him as the possessor of unusual wisdom and, at times, almost magical powers. At parties some guests may become uneasy in his presence and speak half-seriously of their fear that he will read their minds. Many of his patients expect him to resolve their lifelong problems in a few sessions. An important psychiatric skill is the ability gently to disabuse them of their exalted expectations without losing their confidence.

At the same time, hand in hand with overevaluation of the psychiatrist by patients and public goes derogation. He is the butt of endless jokes, the target of much irritation, and he is viewed by many, including quite a few of his medical colleagues, as something of a quack who promises more than he can perform. Thus with some patients his initial task may be to overcome their skepticism, rather than to find a way of climbing down gracefully from the pedestal on which he has been placed.

24. Bruner (1956).

While the pluralism of American society means that the psychotherapist cannot count on acceptance by all patients referred to
him, its tolerance of a considerable variety of assumptive systems
affords a multitude of routes to mental health. Certain psychotherapists can find group support for their own rejection of widely
held values such as conformity and social prestige, which may
contribute to their ability to help patients who share these views,
or who would gain improved mental health by moving in these
directions. Patients can achieve personal integration in terms of
values that are not widely shared and without having to achieve
harmonious relationships with any particular group. In this connection, although Americans place much emphasis on conformity,
one of their basic values is the worth of the individual, and obedi-
ence of the dictates of one's own best self is a highly regarded
virtue. So the therapist who helps his patient achieve greater inner
freedom and self-fulfillment, even at the expense of conformity,
may not be running counter to many important values of the
patient's group, and the patient may gain in respect and admiration from others what he loses in popularity.[25]

On the negative side, the complexity of American society makes
it possible for psychotherapists and patients to differ widely in
education and socioeconomic class, which creates certain problems. These have been brought to attention by community mental
health programs, which aim to reach all classes of society. It stands
to reason that, since interview therapies in all their forms were
developed for middle- and upper-class patients, they would fail to
meet the expectations and needs of lower-class ones. Currently
much thought and effort is being expended on the development of
therapeutic approaches more appropriate to them.

One would expect that the greater the class discrepancy between patient and therapist, the more their value systems would
differ and therefore the more difficulty they would have commu-

25. In emphasizing the close relationship between personal integration and group
integration, I do not exclude the possibility that an individual may sustain his integration
largely by adherence to the values of internalized reference groups. The socially isolated
scientist, for example, may maintain his self-esteem through his dedication to the pursuit
of truth, which enables him to view himself as a member of the "scientific community,"
a group existing only as an abstract embodiment of certain values.

nicating.[26] Furthermore, much of the meaning of verbal communications depends on the connotations and feeling tones attached to words rather than their dictionary definitions, and these nuances are determined by the usages of a person's group. Hence differences in group membership may impede the development of mutual understanding. In psychotherapy, this can be a serious obstacle to the development of the intimate, confiding relationship that is a prerequisite for successful psychotherapy.[27]

While lower-class patients, by and large, see life differently from those of higher status, one must not jump hastily to the conclusion that a middle-class therapist cannot help many of them. Most data suggesting the contrary conclusion deal only with patients' willingness to remain in treatment.[28] This information is useful to the planners of mental health services and is relatively easy to gather, especially by comparison with evaluation of therapeutic outcome, which bristles with conceptual and methodological problems. To be sure, a person cannot benefit from treatment unless he undergoes it, but factors determining whether or not persons accept treatment need not be the same as those determining whether it helps those who do accept it. Data on acceptance of psychotherapy are therfore only of indirect relevance to our primary concern, which is with factors determining therapeutic success. With this caveat in mind, let us now take a brief look at social class and psychotherapy.

The chief settings for psychotherapy are private offices, university counseling centers, and clinics conducted by public agencies or hospitals. Each to a large extent determines its own clientele. University health clinics, of course, see only university students. Private practice automatically excludes those with inability to pay private fees, so it is not surprising that it is limited to a relatively

26. The problem of divergencies in assumptive worlds between psychiatrist and patient is thrown into sharp relief when the psychiatrist tries to practice in a totally different culture. Thus Western-trained African psychiatrists such as Dr. Tigani El Mahi in the Sudan and Dr. Thomas A. Lambo in Nigeria found that they obtained much better results with their African patients by collaborating with local witch doctors than by ignoring them.
27. This point is well developed by Ruesch (1953).
28. Garfield (1971), pp. 274-78. Meltzoff and Kornreich (1970, pp. 240-46) summarize the extensive literature.

small group, mainly in large cities. For example, a survey of Boston some years ago found that over 70 percent of persons receiving private psychotherapy lived in an area containing about 7 percent of the population. Four-fifths were women, about two-thirds were between the ages of 20 and 34, and almost all were college-educated.[29]

Although clinics are available to less well-educated, lower-class persons, they are not accepted for psychotherapy as readily as patients of higher educational and socioeconomic status. Professionally trained psychotherapists are well educated by definition. Most have been born into or achieved middle-class status or better, and have the corresponding values and attitudes. As a result, they resist accepting lower-class patients. The higher a clinic patient's social class, the more likely he is to be accepted for treatment, to be treated by a senior staff member, and to be treated intensively over a longer period—for better or worse.[30]

Those lower-class patients who start therapy tend to terminate treatment prematurely. Their expectations are apt to differ widely from what is offered them, and their mode of problem-solving differs from that of psychotherapy.[31] As a group, with many individual exceptions, lower-class persons have a low frustration tolerance, think in concrete terms, and try to solve problems by action rather than by thought. Although, in response to the demand character of the clinic setting, they may say that their goal is increased self-understanding, in actuality they typically seek a direct solution to a specific problem.[32]

Since they are not accustomed to using language to describe their inner life, they do not derive any sense of accomplishment or progress from gaining "insights," that is, verbalizations of their feelings or conceptualizations of their problems.[33] In short, they do not share the belief in the healing power of self-knowledge which is basic to psychotherapies devised by educated, middle-class professionals who value it highly.

29. Ryan (1966).
30. Rogow (1970); Schofield (1964).
31. Overall and Aronson (1964).
32. Yamamoto and Goin (1965).
33. Bernstein (1964).

In addition to their failure to see psychotherapy as treatment, many lower-class patients face practical obstacles to repeated clinic visits. Clinic fees, transportation costs, and lost wages due to time missed at work may represent a significant portion of their income. A mother must impose on the good nature of family members or neighbors to mind the children, or she must pay someone to act as a baby sitter. With increasing duration of treatment, the financial drain becomes more burdensome, the patience of relatives thinner.

Despite practical and perceptual obstacles to staying in treatment, those lower-class patients who do remain respond at least as well as those of higher socioeconomic status.[34] Several possible reasons for this come to mind. The very fact that some patients overcome severe obstacles to make repeated clinic visits, is in itself a sign of strong motivation. Moreover, difference in class does not always imply a communications gap. Some lower-class patients have middle-class values and view the therapist as a member of a group to which they aspire to belong. For others, the handicap of class difference may be more than overcome by the therapist's prestige. By virtue of this, his mere willingness to take them seriously and see them repeatedly may have a powerful healing effect.

PERSONAL QUALITIES OF THE PSYCHOTHERAPIST

Although the therapist's training and his class position relative to that of his patient affect the therapeutic relationship, personal characteristics and attitudes of therapist and patient may well be more important. This section reviews data on personal qualities of the therapist related to his effectiveness.

It is generally agreed that the success of a psychotherapist depends in part on his genuine concern for the patient's welfare. One influential psychiatrist even says that the therapist should be willing to "risk his own existence in the struggle for the freedom of his partner's."[35] The odds are that he can invest more of him-

---

34. Frank et al. (1957).
35. Binswanger (1956), p. 148. This is reminiscent of the shaman's risking his soul in certain primitive healing rituals. See p. 63 above.

self, other things being equal, in patients he can like and respect, if not for what they are, then for what they can become. Freud expressed this clearly in his first publication on psychotherapy: "[Psychoanalysis] presupposes in [the physician] . . . a personal concern for the patients. . . . I cannot imagine bringing myself to delve into the psychical mechanism of a hysteria in anyone who struck me as low-minded and repellent, and who, on closer acquaintance, would not be capable of arousing human sympathy."[36] In short, the psychotherapist's personal predilections may influence his choice of patients and his relative success with different types.[37] Recognizing this, some psychiatrist will not attempt to treat alcoholics, while others avoid hysterics; some believe they do especially well with depressed patients, others regard their forte as schizophrenics.

In this connection, the choice of a career in psychotherapy may represent a way of solving the therapist's personal problems. For example, many mental health professionals have been found to have backgrounds that lead them to experience a special sense of isolation and to develop a heightened awareness of inner events. Their family and social relationships are often lacking in intimacy, which may be supplied by the psychotherapeutic relationship— "the psychic gains from intimacy are made in the office and not in the home."[38] Along the same lines, a study of psychiatric residents concluded that most are characterized by emotional conflict, and achieve personal integration through acquiring a professional and therapeutic role.[39]

The scanty objective studies of personal qualities of the good therapist are of three sorts. The first define a psychotherapist's competence in terms of the judgments of his colleagues or superiors; the second in terms of the opinions of his patients; the third in terms of his actual success.

The good therapist emerges from the first type of study as a good person in general—he is intelligent and responsible, has good judgment, and is creative.[40] He is also judged to be sincere, ener-

36. Breuer and Freud (1957), p. 265. See also Ginsburg (1950).
37. Rogow (1970), pp. 66–78.
38. Henry (1966), p. 53.
39. Ford (1963).
40. Holt and Luborsky (1958).

getic, and able to display controlled warmth to his patients, that is, to let himself become somewhat emotionally involved without losing his objectivity.[41] Moreover, the type of relationship he offers his patients probably is consistent with his general pattern of social behavior. One study that rated the attitudes of two group therapists toward the same patients—they took turns leading the same groups for a few sessions—found that the one whom colleagues and subordinates described as more tolerant, respectful, supportive of others, and self-confident offered his patients the better relationship.[42]

If qualities like self-confidence and energy are believed to contribute to a psychotherapist's success, then anxiety should militate against him, and one study found this to be true. Forty-two young psychotherapists in four clinics, all of whom were clinical psychology students, rated each other and themselves on a variety of personality traits and also received ratings of therapeutic competence from their supervisors. Those who were judged more anxious by their colleagues tended to be judged less competent by the supervisors. It is interesting that the degree of the therapist's insight into his own anxiety made no difference. His uneasiness militated against the patient developing confidence in him, whether he knew its cause or not.[43]

All studies relying on judgments of therapists' competence by their colleagues or supervisors are measuring what they think a good therapist should be, or how he should behave, not his actual therapeutic ability. Hence they must be viewed with caution. For example, one study found that supervisors judged residents' therapeutic competence in part by their ability to fit into an organization. The investigators conclude: "We wish to emphasize that *almost nothing is known about who gets the best results in psychotherapy* and that this question cannot be appropriately studied without studying the changes in patients. If we study supervisors' opinions . . . we are studying stereotypes of the Good Therapist, the Correct Therapy, and the Ideal Person."[44] That these studies may, nevertheless, have some validity is suggested by

41. Caudill (1957).
42. Parloff (1956).
43. Bandura (1956).
44. Knupfer *et al.* (1959), p. 384. (Authors' italics.)

the fact that judgments of therapists made by patients agree with those of colleagues as to the personal qualities associated with therapeutic success. Thus, responses to a questionnaire, filled out by 131 patients who had received at least 25 interviews of intensive psychotherapy in a university hospital outpatient clinic, yielded a composite image of the "good therapist" as a "keenly attentive, interested, benign and concerned listener—a friend who is warm and natural, is not averse to giving direct advice, who speaks one's language, makes sense and rarely arouses intense anger."[45]

Another study explored the problem by means of interviews with two college students who had made significant improvement following short-term psychiatric treatment. Each was asked to state what he believed had helped him, and these evaluations were compared with similar ones prepared by the psychiatrists. The discrepancies between the two evaluations are startling. Both psychiatrists stressed insight into the correlations of childhood experiences with current symptoms, and the bringing to awareness of unconscious feelings as the sources of therapeutic gain. Neither patient mentioned these. Instead, both stressed the psychiatrists' indirect reassurances (in one case by granting an emergency interview and in the other by offering factual information on the nondangerous nature of the patient's symptoms) and the encounter with an authority figure who was both firm and completely accepting. The therapists attributed the improvement to the method, the patients to the relationship.[46] These findings are highly tentative, being based on only two cases, but as far as they go they confirm that emotional support, acceptance, and kindly guidance—qualities related to the therapist's personality rather than to his technique—are therapeutically important.

The strongest evidence that personality attributes of the therapist may be related to his therapeutic success is supplied by a series of studies that related the actual results of treatment to aspects of the therapists' personalities. The therapists were psychiatric residents who were classified into two groups on the basis of

45. Strupp et al. (1969), p. 117.
46. Blaine and McArthur (1958).

their relative success with hospitalized schizophrenics before the introduction of tranquilizers. The more successful therapists offered a therapeutic relationship characterized by active, personal participation rather than passive, permissive interpretation and instruction or practical care.[47]

In an effort to place these findings on a more objective footing, the researchers compared the interest patterns of the more successful with the less successful therapists on the Strong Vocational Interest Inventory. It appeared that the more successful—labeled "A"—had interests similar to those of certified public accountants and lawyers. Like members of these professions, they enjoyed working with people, had a flexible approach to life, and were good persuaders. The less successful—labeled "B"— had interests resembling those of carpenters and high-school mathematics teachers. They enjoyed dealing precisely with objects, preferred to be alone, and saw life in terms of right and wrong. "A" and "B" physicians did equally well with patients hospitalized with other disorders.[48]

Efforts to replicate these findings in the treatment of schizophrenics with respect to therapists' interest patterns have not yielded consistent results, partly, perhaps, because the therapeutic effectiveness of tranquilizers masks any differential effectiveness of different psychotherapeutic tactics.[49]

Oddly, in contrast with the findings with hospitalized schizophrenics, "B" therapists were found to obtain significantly better results with outpatient neurotics than "A" therapists.[50] These apparently inconsistent findings can be reconciled by the assumption that "A" and "B" therapists offer different types of relationships to their patients and that hospitalized schizophrenics respond better to one type and outpatient neurotics to the other.

In concluding this brief section on the therapist's personal attributes we must add that probably the most important one has escaped systematic study. This attribute is healing power or charisma. While warmth, energy, persuasiveness, and similar quali-

47. Whitehorn and Betz (1954), p. 33.
48. Whitehorn and Betz (1960); Betz (1963).
49. Bowden, Endicott, and Spitzer (1972).
50. McNair et al. (1967).

ties are some of its ingredients, its essence has eluded scientific definition. Every age produces great healers who are typically dismissed as quacks by their conservatives brethren but who, nevertheless, are often astoundingly effective. Some proceed to create schools based on the doctrines they have devised to explain their healing ability—chiropractic being a notable example. The founder of such a method typically discovers his healing power before he evolves a theory to explain it. Many founders of schools of psychotherapy seem to be similarly gifted, and they obtained considerably better results than most of their disciples.

It may well be that healing ability, like musical talent, is widely but unevenly distributed in the population. If a person is unfortunate enough to be born tone deaf, no amount of training can turn him into a musician. Given a modicum of musical talent and sufficient determination, however, anyone can train himself to become a competent performer, even though he will never become a virtuoso. The same may hold for psychotherapeutic talent.

PERSONAL ATTRIBUTES OF PATIENTS

In the consideration of personal attributes of patients,[51] it is to be expected that traits related to susceptibility to personal influence on the one hand and to adaptive capacity on the other, would also be related to ability to profit from psychotherapy.

Patients who are persevering and dependable manifest these qualities by remaining in therapy, while impulsive ones are likely to drop out. That is, persons who stick to any task despite difficulties and disappointments also persist in psychotherapy. This trait, however, seems unrelated to improvement.

The ideal candidate for psychotherapy has been characterized by the acronym "yavis": young, attractive, verbal, intelligent, and successful,[52] traits that obviously equip one for coping with the problems of life and, in addition, would favorably predispose

---

51. Clinical impressions of personal attributes related to treatability are excellently summarized by Cameron (1950), pp. 50-62; Wolberg (1967), pp. 482-95. Strupp (1972) offers an illuminating theoretical discussion. Luborsky et al. (1971) critically survey the psychological literature.

52. Schofield (1964), p. 133.

persons to therapies that stress self-examination and conceptualization of feelings. These qualities also appeal to therapists and hence facilitate the development of a good therapeutic relationship.

Persons who become psychological casualties in the absence of obvious external pressures are believed to have a poorer prognosis than those whose symptoms seem to be responses to environmental stress.[53] One would expect the latter to have greater coping capacities. In actuality, the disturbance for which they seek psychiatric help may often be within the range of normal reactions to stress. In this connection, the manifestations of emotional turmoil seen in disaster victims include the entire gamut of neurotic and psychotic symptoms, and their absence may be a more ominous sign than their presence.[54]

Persons shaken by disaster, if tided over the immediate crisis by simple supportive measures, recover rapidly and completely. Analogously, of those patients whose distress is linked to environmental pressure, a considerable proportion may need only a little help to regain their emotional equilibrium, and whatever brand of psychotherapy the therapist uses receives credit for this outcome. The controlling factor in the recovery of these patients is the severity and modifiability of the environmental pressure under which they have broken down.

Patients who seek psychotherapy under situational stress tend to have two other characteristics probably related to responsiveness to psychotherapy. These are influencibility and emotional reactivity. That these patients are involved with other persons and respond to them is suggested by the fact that in civilian life most stresses involve interpersonal disturbances—marital, familial, or work conflicts or traumatic terminations of intimate relationships through death or separation. Emotional reactivity is implied by the fact that the stress upsets them sufficiently to cause them to seek treatment.

53. Barron (1953a, 1953b) presents psychological test data supporting the proposition that patients whose distress is related to environmental pressures have greater adaptive capacity or "ego-strength" and do better in treatment than those who show no such relationship.
54. Tyhurst (1957).

Evidence, so far fragmentary and inconclusive, suggests that correlates of accessibility to influence may also be related to responsiveness to psychotherapy. One is a willingness to enter into close relationships with others; this implies a willingness to trust them and also suggests that others have been helpful in the past, allowing such persons to enter psychotherapy with a hopeful attitude. Thus, persons who participate in group activities and generally get along well with others seem to do better than antagonistic, mistrustful ones who tend to be loners and nomads.[55] In a small, pilot study, we found that patients who had a close, confidential relationship with a family member or friend did better in brief psychotherapy.[56]

Another personality attribute measurable by paper-and-pencil tests that seems related to influencibility deserves mention. It is the extent to which a person sees his life as controlled by himself or by external forces.[57] Persons who see themselves as more externally controlled showed greater attitude change in response to a persuasive communication than those who feel they control their own destiny. The attitudes studied, however, were peripheral, so whether the finding would hold with respect to the more central attitudes that psychotherapy tries to change remains to be seen.[58]

Perhaps related to the dimension of internal vs. external control is that of repressers and sensitizers; the former being perceptually defensive toward threatening stimuli and the latter, perceptually vigilant against them. Sensitizers also score high on indices of anxiety and self-dissatisfaction and low on self-esteem, and therefore may be more willing to request help and accept a dependent role.[59] One study of students has found that, for any given degree of psychopathology, sensitizers are more likely to enter therapy than repressers and less likely to terminate it prematurely.[60]

The relevance of emotional reactivity to psychotherapy lies in the fact that emotional arousal seems to be a prerequisite and a

55. Rubinstein and Lorr (1956).
56. Stone *et al.* (1966).
57. Rotter (1966).
58. Hjelle and Clouser (1970).
59. Davis (1971).
60. Thelen (1969), cited in Davis (1971), p. 137.

concomitant of attitude change.[61] That emotional responsiveness is closely related to dependence on others is suggested by the somewhat complex relationship between the severity and nature of the patient's expressed misery and his response to therapy. Patients seeking psychotherapy show a great range of distress. Some are absolutely desperate, and most are sufficiently troubled so that they wish to change and are predisposed to look to a psychotherapist for help. But there are many reasons for coming to a psychotherapist, and some patients show little evidence of emotional tension.

The contribution of emotional disturbance to the establishment of a fruitful psychotherapeutic relationship is suggested by the facts that the greater the overall degree of expressed distress, as measured by a symptom checklist, the more likely the patient is to remain in treatment, while conversely two of the most difficult categories of patients to treat have nothing in common except lack of distress. One consists of certain so-called antisocial personalities, who seek or are forced into treatment to escape the consequences of their misbehavior and inwardly seem to be relatively content. The other category consists of intellectuals who look to psychotherapy to help them overcome vague self-dissatisfactions or to find more meaning in life. In the same group may be included many analysts in training, whose discomfort springs chiefly from having to submit to a time-consuming and expensive procedure. The psychotherapist's usefulness to these types of persons depends in part on his creating or unearthing some source of distress or otherwise convincing them that they are ill. As one writes: "Without a full-hearted acknowledgment of the sense of illness a patient can go through only the motions of treatment."[62] One is reminded of the effort to creat distress by primitive healers, revivalists, and interrogators as part of the endeavor to produce attitude change.

The specific nature of the patient's expressed distress also seems related to his responsiveness to psychotherapy. Patients who express their difficulties in interpersonal terms, thereby indicating

61. Hoehn-Saric *et al.* (1968). See also pp. 249–60 below.
62. Kubie (1936), p. 140.

an acceptance of psychotherapy, tend to stay in treatment longer than those who complain primarily of bodily symptoms. The latter also do less well in treatment than those who evince anxiety or other psychic symptoms. Anxiety heightens a person's dependency on others, as seen, for example, in the greatly increased susceptibility to hypnosis of soldiers with battle reactions.[63] Absorption with bodily complaints, on the other hand, is often understood as an attempt to retreat from involvement with others. Such patients would therefore be expected to find it difficult to relate closely to the therapist. In addition, bodily complaints are ordinarily treated by a physician, not a psychotherapist, so that the mere presentation of these as leading symptoms may be a sign that the patient does not expect to be helped by psychotherapy. And this illustrates another relevant point. A patient's willingness to admit distress, especially in conjunction with personal problems, implies a willingness to risk humiliating self-revelation, which in itself is evidence that he trusts the psychotherapist and expects to be helped by him. It also implies dissatisfaction with oneself, hence motivation to change.[64]

The close relationship between degree of expressed anxiety, dependency on others, and acceptance of psychotherapy has been beautifully demonstrated by some experimental and statistical studies, which have many thought-provoking implications.[65] Female college students were led to expect a painful shock after a ten-minute delay and were given the choice of waiting with other students in a similar predicament or staying by themselves. Their anxiety was simultaneously measured by asking them to rate how they felt about receiving a shock and by giving them a chance to withdraw from the experiment if they wished to do so. Those who were not willing to go through with it said they were more anxious than those who said they would see it through. Actually the experiment terminated before the shock was administered.

63. Kaufman and Beaton (1947).
64. Kirtner and Cartwright (1958) found that patients who succeeded in psychotherapy, among other attributes had a strong need for people to relate to in order to feel worthwhile and a tendency to berate or disvalue themselves.
65. Schachter (1959).

It was found that the desire to be with others was related to the expressed degree of anxiety produced by anticipation of a painful stimulus and that the level of anxiety was higher for subjects who were only or first-born children than for those who came later in the family. Moreover, first-born subjects with high anxiety had a stronger desire to be with others than later-born subjects with the same degree of anxiety.

The experimenter then analysed the statistics of a nearby Veterans Administration Mental Hygiene Clinic, and these indicated that patients who were first-born or only children accepted psychotherapy when it was offered, and stayed in it longer if they accepted it, than did those who were later-born. It should be added that the first group were no "sicker" than the second; that is, ordinal position in the family was unrelated to degree of psychological disturbance. In view of the experimental results, a plausible explanation of this finding is that first-born tend to be more dependent on others to relieve their distress than are later-born. There is considerable theoretical support for this along the lines that parents of first-born children are both more inexperienced and more anxious than they are when the subsequent children arrive, and they can give the first child undivided attention. Thus they may overprotect him and/or handle him inconsistently, both of which patterns would, on theoretical grounds, be expected to increase dependency.[66]

Parents have progressively less time for later-born children the farther down the line they are, and also, having become experienced, they handle them more consistently. Moreover, later-born children have to compete with their brothers and sisters for the parents' attention. On both counts one would expect them to be less likely to see others as a source of help when they are in distress. We may tentatively conclude that dependency is related both to acceptance of psychotherapy and susceptibility to anxiety. That all three of these turn out to be related to order of birth is a fascinating finding, which opens interesting vistas for further study.

66. Sears (1950), cited by Schachter (1959).

THE THERAPIST-PATIENT PAIR

Therapists and patients have so far been considered independently of each other. It is now time to recall that the therapy situation is a dynamic system whose properties are determined not only by what its members bring into it but by their interactions.[67] The literature of psychotherapy abounds with interactive concepts such as involvement, emotional investment, good working relationship, and therapeutic contract, which are powerful determinants of the therapist's and patient's evaluation of the success of their encounter.[68]

This section focuses on the therapist-patient encounter as a system whose properties are determined not only by the characteristics of the protagonists, but also by the context in which the encounter occurs. As the system develops, it, in turn, affects certain features of its members.

When therapy is viewed as a system, the relevance of personal attributes of patients to their responses to psychotherapy may lie primarily in the impression they make on the therapist, which, in turn, affects his behavior toward them. This has been implied by the relation of patients' demographic and personal characteristics to acceptance into psychotherapy and therapeutic outcome. We have already noted Freud's assertion that he could not imagine himself analysing patients who failed to arouse some human sympathy, a statement consistent with a quantitative study that revealed substantial correlations between clinic therapists' retrospective ratings of outcome and their feelings of warmth and liking for their patients.[69] Similarly, therapists' enthusiasm and comfort were found to correlate significantly with hospitalized patients' clinical states, as both varied in the course of therapy. Unfortunately, the design of the study permitted no conclusions about whether therapists were primarily affecting patients or vice versa.[70]

Since the characteristics of the "yavis" patient would appeal to most psychotherapists, this may be another reason why they are

67. Lennard and Bernstein (1960); Moos and MacIntosh (1970).
68. Strupp *et al.* (1963); Lorr and McNair (1964).
69. Strupp *et al.* (1963).
70. Rabiner *et al.* (1971).

regarded as good candidates for therapy. In confirmation of this impression was the finding in the study on preparation of patients for psychotherapy, described earlier, that "attractive" patients did better after four months of therapy than "unattractive" ones.[71] The rating of attractiveness was a global judgment made by the initial interviewer (not the patient's therapist) and turned out to be based primarily on youth, intelligence, education, and occupational level. Not all attractive patients, however, did well or all unattractive ones poorly, confirming the obvious fact that the favorableness of the impression made by the patient is not the only determinant of therapeutic outcome.

A suggestion that one source of patient-therapist compatibility is similarity of their interpersonal needs is afforded by a study of hospitalized patients, whose improvement was found to correlate with the degree of similarity between their scores and those of their therapists on relative strengths of needs for affection, inclusion, and control.[72]

Degree of compatibility between therapists' and patients' values might also be expected to affect the outcome of the therapeutic encounter. Thus clients at a university counseling center who shared the therapists' tolerant values were found to do better than those with a punitive morality or a religious orientation that was either fundamentalist or mystical.[73]

A confirmation of this finding is supplied by a study that measured certain values of psychoanalytic candidates and their patients. The values of each therapist resembled those of his own patients more than those of the patients seen by the other therapists, and each saw more improvement the more the patient's values resembled his own.

This study also brought out the interactive aspect of therapy in that the resemblance of patients' and therapists' values seemed to be at least partly a consequence of the therapeutic interaction. That is, since most patients were arbitrarily assigned to their therapists, the value similarity could not have been the result of selective bias. Moreover, there was a low but significantly positive

71. Nash et al. (1965).
72. Sapolsky (1965).
73. Rogers and Dymond (1954), chaps. 11 and 12.

correlation between length of treatment before the patients' values were tested and the degree of their similarity to those of the therapist—that is, similarity of values between patient and therapist tended to increase with length of treatment.[74]

Along similar lines, another study of outpatients compared ratings of therapists and their patients on the values of sex, aggression, and authority at the beginning and end of therapy, and found a positive correlation between ratings of improvement and change of the patient's moral values toward those of the therapists.[75]

These results depended solely on shift of the patients' values— that it, since the therapists' values were measured only once, whether or not their values also changed could not be determined. One ingenious investigation of intensive psychotherapy with outpatients repeatedly measured patients' and therapists' attitudes toward certain key persons in the patients' lives. It found that convergence of therapists' and patients' attitudes during therapy was due to movement of the therapists' attitudes as well as the patients'. Thus it confirmed that the therapeutic encounter involves reciprocal influence. As might have been expected, the patients shifted more than the therapists.[76]

A closer look at the therapist-patient system is afforded by efforts to describe the actual nature of the interaction. This problem has been approached primarily from the standpoint of the kind of relationship offered by the therapist. It will be recalled that, in their studies of "A" and "B" therapists, the investigators found that the "A" doctors offered "active personal participation," whereas the "B" doctors were more detached.[77] Using taped interviews of graduate students in clinical psychology treating neurotics, another investigator characterized the "A" therapists as assuming responsibility for the structure and direction of treatment, while the "B" therapists followed the clients' leads.[78] These descriptions are not incompatible. Since schizophrenics, because of their confused thinking and interpersonal perceptions,

74. Welkowitz et al. (1967).
75. Rosenthal (1955).
76. Pande and Gart (1968).
77. Whitehorn and Betz (1954).
78. Segal (1970).

need considerable structure, while a free situation fosters useful spontaneity in neurotics, both characterizations of "A" and "B" therapists are consistent with the finding that the former do better with schizophrenics, the latter with neurotics.

Extensive studies with a wide variety of patients in individual and group therapies using a client-centered approach have consistently shown that outcome is related to the therapist's ability to offer warmth, accurate empathy, and genuineness, as rated from excerpts of taped interviews.[79] In most reported studies, statistical analysis showed that these qualities emanated mainly from the therapist; others found that they depended mainly on the patient or on the interaction between the two. In any case, these characteristics describe a relationship which assures the patient of the therapist's interest and concern, improves his morale, and increases his susceptibility to the therapist's influence.

Finally, aspects of the therapeutic setting itself and the context in which therapy occurs seem to influence both the therapeutic relationship and the outcome. For example, an elaborate study of short-term psychoanalysis using eleven analysts and fifty patients found that the order in which the therapist treated his patients was the best predictor of improvement. Of the eight patients who received a maximal improvement score, four were the first cases seen, two the second cases, and only two the remainder. On the plausible assumption that his zeal was greatest with his first patient and diminished with each successive one, this finding suggests that the therapist's enthusiasm was the main therapeutic ingredient. It is consistent with the conclusion of the same study that "prognosis is best when there is a willingness on the part of both patient and therapist to become *deeply involved* and . . . to bear the tension that inevitably ensues."[80]

Two results of the study of a role induction interview described earlier[81] show the importance of contextual factors, even though

79. Truax and Carkhuff (1967). One study has succeeded in partly replicating these results with therapists using a non-client-centered approach (Truax *et al.*, 1966), but another completely failed to confirm them (Garfield and Bergin, 1971), so the generalizability of these findings to other forms of psychotherapy remains in doubt. Should they prove to be confined to client-centered therapy, they would represent one more manifestation of the effect of therapists' and patients' expectations on improvement.

80. Malan (1963), p. 274.

81. Nash *et al.* (1965).

the sources of their effects could not be conclusively established. It will be remembered that each patient had an initial evaluation by one of two interviewers who never saw him again, and that the patients were then assigned at random to four therapists. One of the initial interviewers was older and had a higher academic rank than the other and was the project director. The patients he interviewed did less well than those of the junior interviewer. At least two mutually compatible reasons for this come to mind. One is that when patients were transferred to a psychiatric resident, they felt more of a comedown if they had seen the senior rather than the junior interviewer. The other is that since only the senior interviewer had any control over the careers of the residents, they were more constrained with his patients.

This is consistent with the finding that the resident who obtained the best results was a foreigner with a career already established in his home country, while the one who did worst felt that he was being evaluated by his senior colleague. In addition, the most successful resident believed in short-term therapy and enjoyed participation in the study; the least successful one felt exploited and did not believe in short-term treatment.

In short, the therapists' feelings about the initial interviewers and the project itself seemed to affect their therapeutic ability, presumably by affecting their behavior in the therapeutic dyad.

SUMMARY

This chapter has examined influencing and healing features of the psychotherapeutic encounter from the standpoints of the therapists, the patient, and the therapeutic situation itself. The therapist's training affects his own self-image and the patient's attitudes toward him, and thereby his effectiveness as a healer. Psychoanalytic training is evaluated from the standpoint of its power as a method of indoctrination and form of group support, heightening the psychoanalyst's sense of personal worth and therapeutic competence.

With respect to sociocultural factors, the extent of social and educational distance between therapist and patient affects their acceptance of each other. Personal qualities of a therapist that contribute to his success inclue a capacity to convey concern for his patients' welfare, as well as healing qualities that elude precise definition. Patients' personal qualities predisposing to a favorable therapeutic response include good adaptive capacity and attributes similar to those heightening susceptibility to methods of healing in nonindustrial societies, religious revivals, thought reform, experimental manipulation of attitudes, and administration of a placebo. These include accessibility to other persons, self-dissatisfaction, and emotional distress.

When psychotherapy is viewed as a system, its success seems related not only to aspects of the patient-therapist interaction that affect the therapist's zeal and the patient's confidence in him, but also to a convergence of the therapist's and patient's values.

EVOCATIVE
FORMS OF
INDIVIDUAL
VIII PSYCHOTHERAPIES

"Would you tell me, please, which way I ought to go from
here?" "That depends a good deal on where you want
to get to," said the Cat.
"I don't much care where—so long as I get *somewhere*,"
Alice added as an explanation.
"Oh, you're sure to do that," said the Cat, "if you only
walk long enough."

Alice's Adventures in Wonderland

INTRODUCTION

We have completed the survey of methods of persuasion
and healing that have some kinship to Western psychotherapy, psychological experiments bearing on aspects
of the psychotherapeutic process, and features of the
patient-therapist relationship that influence outcome. It
is now time to examine current psychotherapeutic procedures in the United States in the light of this information.

To recapitulate briefly, I have suggested that the goals
of all forms of psychotherapy are to help the patient
reduce or overcome his distress, to function better in his
personal relationships and at work, and concomitantly
to increase his self-esteem and heighten his sense of control over himself and his surroundings. These changes
are typically accompanied by an increased sense of inner
freedom and satisfaction with his life. Psychotherapeutic procedures can be viewed as forms of personal influence that aim to provide the patient with morale-en-

hancing experiences that enable him to shed maladaptive patterns and adopt more successful ones.

At first glance, the task of trying to classify psychotherapies is distinctly daunting. It was not always thus. For many decades the field was dominated by dyadic interview therapies, differing to be sure in their conceptualizations, but all relying primarily on conversations between patient and therapist aimed at uncovering difficulties in adjustment, reexperiencing crippling emotions such as anger and fear in the therapeutic setting to thereby resolve them, and relieving the symptoms for which the patient sought help. Violent debates raged among adherents of Freud, Jung, Adler, Rank, and others, but these were concerned mainly with what the topics of the therapeutic conversation should be, not the method itself.

During the past thirty years or so, this relatively tidy state of affairs has been progressively disrupted by the introduction into individual psychotherapy of a whole panoply of techniques based on the discoveries of Pavlov and Skinner, initially made on animals but found to be transposable to humans. Almost simultaneously, group therapies, which for decades had been used only by a handful of pioneers such as Trigant Burrow and J. L. Moreno, began to undergo a wild, and still continuing, proliferation.

Founders of therapeutic methods continue to emerge, each with his band of disciples, his own rationale, and claims for therapeutic effectiveness ranging from reasonably modest ones to assertions of having at last discovered the royal road to mental health for everyone.[1]

This incredible profusion of psychotherapeutic procedures may be related to the thirst for novelty, which is perhaps stronger in the United States than in more traditional societies. For us, the new is always assumed to be better than the old until proved otherwise. It is a medical truism that all forms of treatment work best just after they are introduced, and the same is true of psychotherapies. In the light of material reviewed earlier, this probably results in part from the enthusiasm of the inventor and his emo-

---

1. A recent text (Wolberg, 1967) requires about 300 pages to summarize extant psychotherapies, and it is already out of date.

tional investment in the success of his invention, and in part from patients' pleasurable emotional anticipation at the prospect of a new remedy, especially when recommended by an authority. Thus all new remedies foster emotional states analogous to those aroused under favorable conditions by placebos. In addition, of course, the investment of both healer and patient may lead both of them to overestimate the effectiveness of a new treatment and make overoptimistic claims for it.

The wearing-off of novelty may also partly explain the increasing duration of well-established treatments such as psychoanalysis. Familiarity does not necessarily breed contempt but it does diminish enthusiasm.

Along with the flood of new therapies, the current psychotherapeutic scene has been complicated by the serious questioning of the scientific, empirical view on which all forms of psychotherapy have hitherto been based. According to this view, the troubles for which persons seek psychotherapeutic help are manifestations of disharmony between themselves and their environment, and the therapeutic task is to help the patient resolve this. One can debate, of course, whether in any particular case the main difficulty lay in the stresses created by the patient's environment or by his internal conflicts, and this could lead to differences of opinion concerning whether the focus of treatment should be on the communication network in which the patient was enmeshed or on the patient himself. In either case, however, the goal was to enable the patient to recognize and cope with "reality"—that is, the objective conditions of his life.

As it began to appear that science might be luring society to destruction, some psychotherapists raised the question of who was crazy, society or the patient. According to them, the inner world has as much, or perhaps more, claim to validity as the outer one, and much of what is termed mental illness is in large part a manifestation of a person's attempts to cope with the existential despair that is always latent but that the conditions of modern life have made acute. The goal of therapy, rather than helping the patient to adjust to a sick society, is to help him find his personal salvation through fully experiencing his own inner world. Therapy becomes a search for redemptive peak experiences that give meaning to existence. Some believe that this search can be aided by consciousness-altering drugs.

Proponents of these approaches view conventional diagnosis and treatment methods as "degradation ceremonials"[2] that deny the validity of the patient's inner experiences and are more or less subtle means of making him conform to the assumptive world of Western society. The fact remains, however, that the success of any form of psychotherapy depends in part on its compatibility with the norms and expectations of its surrounding culture. Since the pluralism of American society tolerates a wide range of values, it is hospitable to therapies based on widely differing assumptions. The fact that all flourish simultaneously is evidence that all have something to offer; the fact that none has yet succeeded in displacing any of the others is equally strong evidence that none has found the ultimate answer.

Turning at last to an attempt to classify Western psychotherapeutic procedures, we shall group them first in accordance with the size of the unit that is the therapeutic target and with the setting.

The target of treatment is, of course, the person seeking help, but he can be seen alone, with his customary associates (usually his immediate family, but sometimes also neighbors and friends), or with complete strangers. In group therapies the focus can be on the members as individuals, on their interactions in the group, or on the utilization of the emergent properties or the group itself to aid them.

Individual therapies regard the patient's problems as arising primarily from inner conflicts, which are reflected in his disturbed communications with others. Many group approaches reverse this perspective by considering inner conflicts to be created by the pathology of the communication system of which the patient is a part. They point out that so-called individual therapy is in reality a group of two, that analysis of communications between patient and therapist is equivalent to study of a stress-producing interper-

2. Laing (1967).

sonal communication system, and that internalized reference groups in both patient and therapist affect what transpires in therapy. In this sense, all therapy is group therapy.

The treatment setting includes an office or clinic in which therapy lasts for at most an hour or so several times a week, day hospitals or half-way houses in which patients spend an appreciable portion of their lives, and mental hospitals in which they are immersed for twenty-four hours a day. A residential setting creates the possibility for milieu therapy, or the creation of a therapeutic community. That is, some of the therapeutic benefit is presumed to lie in the organizational rules and value system of the institution itself and the types of activities it fosters, independent of particular patients or staff members.

These categories are, of course, not mutually exclusive. Ideally, patients should be able to move freely back and forth between different settings, depending on how much environmental protection and support they require. Moreover, most hospitals include some individual or group treatment, and outpatient family therapy may be viewed as a kind of intermittent milieu therapy.

Despite their differences, all settings provide a relatively protected environment where the patient can feel free to express forbidden thoughts, release his pent-up emotions, or experiment with new ways of behaving without fear of consequences, because the setting is clearly distinguished from real life. That is, what the patient does in therapy does not commit him to doing the same outside. Because of this, the ultimate test of the success of any form of treatment depends on whether the patient can sustain the changes it has accomplished in his everyday life, either because he has achieved greater inner strength, enabling him to resist pressures to revert to earlier patterns, or because his new behavior elicits responses from others that reinforce it. This is one of many reasons for trying to involve those closest to the patient in his treatment.

All psychotherapeutic procedures involve cognitive, emotional, and behavioral components of the patient's personality. They differ, however, in relative emphasis. From a cognitive standpoint, psychotherapy provides the patient with new information about himself and a new way of conceptualizing his experiences, which clarify his symptoms and problems and help him to form a more workable self-image and assumptive world. Therapies aimed primarily at fostering self-understanding or insight represent this emphasis.

Successful psychotherapy is always an emotionally charged experience, and the emotions are more often unpleasant than pleasant. To be sure, there are interludes of hope, optimism, even elation; but episodes of unpleasant feelings such as fear, anger, despair, and guilt are apt to be more frequent and more prolonged. Since these states are often precipitated by the therapist, one can ask why the patient continues in treatment with him. The main psychological reason is, of course, that these emotions occur in a context of expectation of benefit, just as a patient will take a bitter medicine if the bitterness is linked in his mind with its curative effect.

In any case, emotional reactions accompany significant attitudinal shifts and an optimal level of arousal facilitates learning of all sorts. In addition, as considered in the next chapter, massive, intense emotional reactions sometimes seem to be followed by marked relief of certain forms of distress. To this end, some therapies focus on eliciting strong emotional reactions related to past or present sources of psychological pain.

Since all mental illnesses have behavioral manifestations and a major criterion of therapeutic success is change in these, many forms of psychotherapy focus on helping the patient change his troublesome behavior. These are included under the generic term of behavior modification.

Finally, certain therapies move on all fronts at once with equal vigor, trying to elicit new behaviors, emotional discharges, and conceptualizations. These responses are often evoked virtually simultaneously or in rapid succession. Psychodrama is the prototype of this approach.

The emotional, cognitive, and behavioral changes that psychotherapy seeks to effect are closely intertwined. If all goes well, each reinforces the others. A more workable assumptive world leads to behavior that is more successful and less frustrating. This reduces the patient's anxiety, heightens his self-confidence, and fosters positive emotions that increase the flexibility of his thinking and behavior. This in turn leads to new behavior which, if successful, further strengthens the new assumptive systems. This happy state of affairs is rarely, if ever, fully achieved, but it affords a useful model for thinking about the methods and goals of different forms of treatment.

For purposes of exposition, it is convenient to make a rough distinction among different forms of therapy according to whether they leave the therapeutic process essentially unstructured or actively guide it. The first category, which may be termed "evocative,"[3] aims to promote the patient's total personality development and is exemplified by psychoanalysis and Rogerian "client-centered therapy."[4] The second, which we shall term "directive," covers a wide range of goals and procedures and is characterized by the therapist's openly exerting control over the treatment process. It includes procedures as diverse as meditation exercises, hypnosis, emotional flooding, and techniques of behavioral modification.

Evocative therapies are based on the more or less explicit assumption that all humans are utilizing only a small part of their potentials for self-actualization, joy, and harmonious relationships with others. The reason is that in the course of their upbringings they have suffered painful or frightening experiences, leading them to develop self-protective or avoidance maneuvers to guard against further hurts. Patients differ from "normal" people only in degree—that is, they are more crippled and their self-protective maneuvers more blatant. These are the symptoms for which they seek help.

The essence of evocative therapy, then, is the provision of experiences with the therapist or group that will enable the person to overcome his fears, abandon his defenses, and so become free to resume his personality growth. Evocative therapies try to help the patient to become generally more mature, creative, and spontane-

---

3. Terms like "permissive" or "passive" are more commonly used to contrast these approaches with directive ones. Such terms imply that the therapist exerts less influence on the patient which, as appears later in this chapter, is probably not the case. (See Ehrenwald [1966].) DeGrazia (1952) offers a brilliant, if polemical, account of the therapist's influencing power in all "permissive" therapies. The term "evocative," which I believe comes closest to describing what occurs, was suggested by Whitehorn (1959).

4. C. R. Rogers (1951). C. R. Rogers (1942) contains a verbatim protocol.

ous so that he will be able to gain more success and satisfaction from all aspects of living. To this end they aim to evoke as wide a range as possible of his strengths, weaknesses, helpful and hurtful emotions, so that he gains greater self-knowledge and with it a sense of increased inner freedom. Concomitantly, symptoms, which are simply manifestations of his faulty ways of coping with life, will automatically fall away. The therapist views himself as facilitative and permissive, making no attempt to influence the patient toward any particular way of solving his problems.

Since the goals of evocative treatment are open-ended and criteria of personal maturation are essentially subjective, progress cannot be adequately evaluated by objective tests. Since there is no clear stopping place, patients often continue in this form of treatment as long as they find it rewarding and can afford it. Proponents of these approaches, consistent with their position that everyone is crippled in his personality development to some extent, maintain that everyone can benefit from them.

Directive therapies, in contrast with evocative ones, involve a defined set of activities through which the therapist guides the patient. He actively tries to produce beneficial changes in the patient's feelings, thinking, and behavior and remains firmly in charge at all times. We shall consider some examples of directive therapies in Chapter 9.

In the remainder of this chapter and those that follow we shall examine one or two exemplars of individual, group, and milieu therapy occupying different spots on the evocative-directive continuum, with special attention both to the influencing and healing components they share and to the features that are unique to each.

EVOCATIVE INDIVIDUAL THERAPIES
AND PSYCHOANALYSIS

Before plunging into a description of evocative individual therapies, we should pause a moment to place them in cultural perspective. They all spring from Freudian psychoanalysis, which reflected certain cultural attitudes of its time and place, and subsequent modifications can also be related to changes in the surrounding culture.

Freud developed psychoanalysis within a competitive society which placed a high value on individual integrity and achievement. Its ideal person would be an inner-directed one, guided by high moral principles, striving for success, and resistant to social pressures that might lead him to violate his principles and ideals. Such a person would be fearful of too much openness. For one thing, it might give others knowledge of his weaknesses which they could then exploit to their own advantage. Furthermore, if he allowed himself to become too concerned with the welfare of others, this might hamper him in achieving his own goals, which necessarily involved hindering others from reaching theirs.

His success depended on his maintaining a righteous, self-confident façade, which required denying or suppressing inner impulses that, if admitted to consciousness, could create self-doubts. Freud postulated that self-deception and repression of unacceptable impulses and feelings were major sources of psychic distress, disturbances in intimate relationships, and poor work performance. Therefore the goal of therapy was to enable the patient to admit repressed material to consciousness. Removal of inner barriers, by increasing the patient's personal integration and his self-confidence, would presumably enable him to dare to be more honest and more loving with others, as well as more effective in his work.

Freudian theories of the causes of repressions and how analysis resolves them need not detain us, but one important feature of the technique is relevant to our purposes in that it seems clearly related to the nineteenth-century European family. Family matters were strictly private and the family structure was authoritarian—father knew best. Furthermore, children were expected to have no secrets from their parents, but the reverse emphatically did not hold. The psychoanalytic session mirrors this pattern in that it is conducted in the strictest privacy. The analyst holds all the authority, although he elects not to exert it directly, and all the confiding is done by the patient.

Psychoanalysis also accorded well with the nineteenth-century faith in science as holding the solution to all problems, a belief which Freud, as a medical scientist, fully shared. He insisted that the information about the patient's past revealed by psychoanalysis had the status of scientific fact because it was elicited by an impartial, trained observer, the psychoanalyst. We now know, of course, that this was to some extent erroneous, because the patient's productions are so strongly influenced by the analyst's expectations. But the scientific method is not the only path to truth, and there is no doubt that, with all its sources of error, psychoanalysis has greatly increased our knowledge of human nature.

As a cultural offshoot of Europe, with more stress on competition and a greater faith in science, America was highly sympathetic to both the goals and scientific pretensions of psychoanalysis, so that it was readily transplanted to American soil. Evocative therapies in the United States, however, have come to diverge from the original psychoanalytic model in two directions that seem related to cultural differences between twentieth-century America and nineteenth-century Europe. Reflecting the more relaxed, less hierarchical organization of the American family, the American therapist has descended from his pedestal. American psychotherapeutic literature places much stress on the therapeutic interview as an encounter in which both participants are engaged and in which the therapist should reveal something of himself, especially the feelings the patient elicits in him. He should also feel free to be supportive. In short, the American therapist has ceased to be an aloof European parent and become a comradely American one.

The second influence of American culture on psychoanalysis derives from its pragmatic orientation, which receives full expression in directive therapies. Americans are action-oriented and are impatient for results. This may be connected with the shift in evocative therapies from leisurely exploration of the historical origins of the patient's symptoms to exploration of the forces perpetuating them in his current life. By focusing on these forces, American psychotherapists think it may be possible to correct the symptoms more promptly.

In reading the description of evocative therapies that follows, the reader should keep in mind that, from a sociological standpoint, the place of these therapies is limited because they put considerable emphasis on the patient's ability to describe his inner states. Requiring verbal skill, they have little appeal to the poorly educated. Furthermore, since evocative approaches may unearth upsetting memories or feelings with which the patient is unable to cope, except in skillful hands they are not suitable for patients so disorganized that they require hospitalization.

The essence of evocative methods lies in the fostering of a particular type of relationship between patient and therapist that promotes enlargement of the former's self-knowledge, thereby enabling him to discover and achieve the type of change that is best suited to his own particular personality and circumstances. To facilitate this process, the therapist encourages the patient to express himself with complete freedom. No matter how humiliating or unpleasant the patient's revelations, the therapist maintains an attitude of serious, consistent, impartial interest. His attitude is one of attempting to understand the patient, to follow his leads, and to talk about what is on the patient's mind rather than on his own. He not only accepts, but may encourage, opposition. He makes no claim to omniscience or infallibility and, in fact, may explicity disclaim any such powers and openly admit his ignorance or his failure to comprehend. In these ways he seeks to prevent the patient from developing an unrealistic dependence and to strengthen his sense of autonomy.

Feeling himself accepted by someone he admires, and to whom he feels increasingly close by virtue of the intimacy of his revelations, the patient, it is claimed, dares to reveal more and more of the shameful or frightening aspects of himself that he has pushed out of awareness. These include the feelings that cause his distress. As, through this process, his self-understanding increases and his self-esteem becomes stronger, he is able to become more spontaneous and his interactions with persons important to him become successful and satisfying. This further enhances his self-confidence, and so he continues to progress. In short, through psychotherapy the patient learns progressively to trust his therapist, and this may be the first step to the development of greater faith in his fellow man and in himself.

While fully recognizing that much of this process, and perhaps its most important part, occurs as the patient tries out his new insights in his relations with persons in his daily life, evocative therapists, in accordance with their philosophy, seldom explicitly instigate changes in the patient's behavior. They reason that as he becomes inwardly more free such changes will occur automatically.

The patient's communication of his feelings and thoughts as freely and honestly as possible leads to an ever-widening exploration of his psychic life. To facilitate this process Freud devised the method of free association, in which the patient is instructed to report everything that comes into his mind without exercising any selection. To minimize distractions introduced by the reactions of the analyst, and also to encourage relaxation, which fosters the free flow of thought, he had the patient lie on a couch and sat out of his line of vision. Many current practitioners of evocative therapy believe these arrangements to be unnecessary and simply conduct a face-to-face conversation.

Practitioners of client-centered evocative therapy believe that the therapist's entire function is to maintain an attitude of "unconditional positive regard," while encouraging the patient with simple signs of interest. This is deemed sufficient to enable the patient to discover, reveal, and reintegrate ever more deeply hidden or rejected aspects of himself. Analytical schools, while concurring about the importance of the analyst's impartial attitude, believe that he can facilitate the therapeutic process by interpretations of the patient's productions, as discussed below.

Analytic schools differ somewhat in the areas of the patient's mental life that receive the chief scrutiny. Some make much use of dreams, others deemphasize them. Initially great emphasis was placed on the recovery of upsetting experiences with the patient's immediate family in infancy and early childhood, thought to have been the sources of the anxieties and distorted assumptive systems responsible for his current difficulties. Many modern schools focus more sharply on the patient's contemporary problems, delving into the past chiefly to elucidate these. All agree that in an intimate, prolonged relationship with the therapist, the patient eventually shows feelings and behavior toward him similar to those making trouble for him outside of therapy. Some evocative therapies put great weight on the mutual exploration by patient and therapist of these "transference reactions," as the major route to increased self-knowledge.

Evocative therapies may bring about beneficial changes in patients in a variety of ways, all of which cannot be fully encompassed in this essay. We shall consider only those features that seem analogous to those encountered in other forms of interpersonal influence, while recognizing that this may be but a small part of the story.

EVOCATIVE THERAPIES AS METHODS OF PERSUASION

Evocative therapies may influence patients as much as directive ones. The powerful influencing effects of psychoanalysis and other "permissive" therapeutic methods have long been noted,[5] and experimental evidence has been presented in the discussion of experiments on the transmission of influence and in the chapter on the psychotherapist-patient relationship. To recapitulate, the contents of the patient's utterances in nondirective therapy follow the therapist's unwitting leads, and the patient's values shift toward those of the therapist in the course of successful treatment.

We may now add that it has long been known that dreams may be "produced in a form that will best please the analyst."[6] The dream the therapist hears is, of course, not necessarily the one the patient dreamed, since considerable time has usually elapsed between the dream and its report. One study, by comparing reports of dreams told immediately on awakening with those told to a psychiatrist in a subsequent interview, showed that material the dreamer anticipated would not be approved was not recalled.[7] Another noted considerable differences in spontaneous reports of the same dream which the patient told to a number of different people.[8] These findings are reminiscent of the effect of an anticipated audience on recall, and a reminder that a patient's utterances, whether labeled memories or not, are influenced by his attitudes toward the listener.

---

5. Macalpine (1950) and Nunberg (1951) discuss how transference reactions give the analyst power over the patient. See also Strupp (1972).
6. W. Stekel, quoted in Wolff (1954).
7. Whitman et al. (1963).
8. Winick and Holt (1962).

Along the same lines, the kind of improvement reported by patients in evocative therapy also tends to confirm the therapist's theory. Patients in psychoanalysis, which relates mental health to the extent of the patient's self-knowledge, express increasing amounts of hitherto unconscious material as therapy progresses. Those who improve in client-centered therapy show on suitable tests that the discrepancy between their perceived self and ideal self has been reduced, which is the change the theory underlying this form of treatment equates with improvement.[9] Therapists who view ability to sense and express one's feelings directly as a sign of progress find that their patients are better able to do this as therapy progresses.[10]

It is unnecessary to belabor the point further that evocative therapies influence patients' productions. Indeed, in view of the experimental studies showing that a major source of responsiveness to the experimenter's expectations is evaluation apprehension—and this is, almost by definition, high in all patients in psychotherapy—it would be surprising were this not so. Let us, therefore, proceed to a consideration of some of the features of evocative therapies that form the sources and modes of their persuasive and healing powers.

Modeling or Identification

A major source of the therapist's influence is not specific to evocative therapies, but operates in any long-term relationship in which one person feels dependent on another. This has been termed "identification" or, to avoid unnecessary theoretical implications, simply imitation or modeling. It has been shown to be a powerful mechanism of learning, especially in children.[11]

Long-term evocative psychotherapies resemble parent-child relationships in that the patient enters into emotionally charged interactions with someone on whom he feels dependent. As children learn adult roles through identification with the parents, so pa-

9. Rogers and Dymond (1954).
10. Murray (1956).
11. Bandura (1971).

tients to some extent model themselves on their therapists. At the most superficial level, they mimic their therapists' mannerisms, but the identification is often broader and deeper. The patient may imitate the therapist's way of approaching problems or adopt aspects of his value systems. The therapist's ability to be tolerant and flexible may influence the patient to become more so; his willingness to accept and openly admit his limitations without becoming insecure may help the patient to accept his own short-comings. Since the therapist serves as a model, it behooves him to have his own emotional house in order—a major reason for the requirement of psychoanalytic schools that the therapist himself undergo psychotherapy.

The "Neutrality" of the Therapist

One of the more specific persuasive and therapeutic features of evocative psychotherapies is the conceptual scheme, which insists that the therapist is strictly neutral and does not influence the patient's productions. All of us try to gain support for our assumptive systems by getting others to confirm them, and confirmation that appears to be arrived at independently is, of course, more convincing than that obtained by a request or overt persuasion. Hence the therapist's belief that he does not influence his patients may strongly motivate him to get them to produce material confirming his ideas, especially since his theory enables him to conceal from himself that he is doing so.

The claim to objectivity of evocative treatment methods may heighten their influencing power with some patients because this implies that they are scientific, and science has high prestige. Many patients have more confidence in a therapist who appears to be scientifically open-minded than in one who is dogmatic, and therefore they are more susceptible to his influence.

Although the theories underlying evocative therapies do not claim infallibility, they seem to have retained certain characteristics of the self-consistent, irrefutable conceptual schemes underlying other forms of psychic healing and influence. Many psychotherapists recognize that their concepts are tentative and preserve a detached, critical attitude toward them in theoretical discussions. For the purposes of therapy, however, the concepts are not open to question. In the actual therapeutic situation the patient's feelings and behavior are interpreted in terms of the psychiatrist's particular view of human functioning, and treatment is expected to continue until the patient somehow acknowledges the correctness of the interpretation. The theory may assume that the patient's troubles are due primarily to repressed intrapsychic conflicts or to an unrealistic self-image, to take two examples. Therapy is not complete until the patient produces data confirming this assumption and, presumably as a result, modifies his behavior in the direction deemed to represent improvement. The possibilities that his psychic life does not contain the phenomena in question or that they may be irrelevant to his illness are not entertained.

The therapist's activities in evocative therapies have strong persuasive components. In accord with the emphasis of these methods on objectivity, the psychiatrist is apt to conclude his initial interview by offering the patient an opportunity to explore his problems further, but to refrain from any explicit claims that this will be helpful. That the patient nevertheless maintains his expectancy of help, which contributes to his susceptibility to influence, is indicated by his willingness to persist in treatment, even at the cost of considerable time, effort, and sometimes emotional distress. Mere curiosity about his inner life would scarcely supply sufficient motivation for this. As Karl Menninger, a leading psychoanalyst, writes: " . . . the essence of psychoanalytic treatment is intellectual honesty, and no one in honesty can predict with definiteness what the future will bring. Yet if the analyst did not *expect* to see improvement, he would not start—and so taking the case *is* an implied prediction." "The patient who submits himself for psychoanalytic therapy begins with a certain blind faith in the psychoanalyst, regardless of the disclaimers he may profess. He begins, too, with various hopes and expectations, regardless of the skepticism he may express. . . . "[12]

In the initial phases, his expectancy of help is probably maintained by the culturally induced expectations discussed in Chapter 7. If, as often occurs, the therapist takes a history not too dissimilar from a medical one, concluding with a formulation of the

12. Menninger (1958). Quotes are from pp. 31 and 42. Author's italics.

patient's problems, this links him in the patient's eyes with other physicians. If he does not, the patient's hopes may be sustained by the symptomatic improvement that so often occurs early in treatment, or perhaps by signs emitted by the therapist, such as evidence of deep and continuing interest, which belie his overt reluctance to claim therapeutic power. In any case, there is no reason to think that evocative techniques are less successful in mobilizing the hope of recovery in patients who accept them than are other healing methods.

As therapy progresses, the therapist's behavior may be at variance with the patient's expectations, and this may contribute to both his influencing and healing effects. He differs from the usual physician in offering no prescriptions or advice and in his willingness to admit uncertainty or even error. At the same time he differs from persons familiar to the patient by failing to respond to his provocations. He does not react to criticism by either anger or contrition, to complaints by sympathy or impatience, or to seductive behavior by amorousness, embarrassment, or rebuff. He thus disconfirms aspects of the patient's assumptive world, tending to cause the patient to modify them. This therapeutically important process is usually accompanied and facilitated by emotional reactions as indicated earlier, leading to the use of the term "corrective emotional experience" for it.[13]

The very subtlety and unobtrusivenss of the therapist's influencing maneuvers, coupled with his explicit disclaimer that he is exerting an influence, may increase his influencing power.[14] For how can a person fight influences that he does not know exist? He has no target against which to direct his resistance. Furthermore, common sense, as well as the experiments cited earlier,[15] suggest that a person is more likely to adopt ideas he believes he has thought of himself than those he believes are imposed upon him.

The therapist's steadfast refusal to assume active leadership tends to create an ambiguous situation for the patient, who has only a vague idea of what he is supposed to do, how long he is to keep it up, and how he will know when he is finished. In response

13. Alexander and French (1946).
14. Haley (1959).
15. King and Janis (1956), described on pp. 110–11 above.

to the patient's attempts to gain clarification, the therapist does nothing at all or may make noncommittal encouraging sounds or ask noncommittal questions. The resulting unclarity of the situation may enhance its influencing power. As pointed out in Chapter 2, everyone constantly tries to form stabilized and clear assumptions by which to guide his behavior. Therefore a person in an ambiguous situation is impelled to try to clarify it, that is, to assume the initiative in trying to find out what is expected of him and then do it. In therapy this leads him actively to participate in the treatment process. Thus participation is as important in evocative therapies as in other forms of healing and influences.

To the extent that a person cannot unaided construct a clear set of expectations in a situation, he tends to look to others for direction.[16] This may explain the finding that confusion increases suggestibility.[17] In evocative therapy, the patient's tendency to scrutinize the therapist for clues of what is expected of him may be heightened by his belief that relief from his suffering depends on his doing or saying the right thing. Therefore he is likely to be acutely aware of the therapist, even when he sits out of sight, as in psychoanalysis, and subtle signs such as the analyst's shifting in his chair, and so on, may serve as cues that affect his productions.

Ambiguity or unclarity tends to arouse unpleasant emotions such as anxiety and resentment, which heighten the patient's desire for relief, thereby increasing his influencibility. The relation of ambiguity to anxiety is obvious. Nothing is harder to stand than uncertainty as to how to proceed, especially when making the correct choice seems vital. Resentment may be aroused by the patient's mounting feelings of frustration as the therapist consistently refuses to satisfy his implicit or explicit demand for help. This occurs particularly in classical psychoanalysis, in which the therapist may remain virtually silent for long periods. As Karl Menninger puts it:

The patient's sense of frustration affords a continuing provocation to resentment. For, as the days go by, there develops in the patient a growing suspicion that there exists between him and his therapist what an economist would call "an unfavorable trade balance." The patient has "cooperated," he has

16. Sherif and Harvey (1952).
17. Cantril (1941).

obeyed instructions, he has given himself. He has contributed information, exposing his very heart, and in addition to all this he has paid money for the sessions in which he did it. And what return has he gotten from the physician? Attention, audience, toleration, yes—but no response. No "reaction." No advice. No explanation. No solution. No help. No love.[18]

The analyst's refusal to come to the patient's rescue may serve many valuable functions. The state of mind it produces, although unpleasant, may facilitate attitude change, not only by arousing the patient emotionally, but by helping him to recognize his unrealistic expectations of the therapist and so achieve a more objective attitude toward others.

One of the direct or indirect effects of all successful psychotherapy, whatever its form, is the heightening of the patient's sense of mastery or control over himself and his environment. At first glance, evocative therapies do not seem to offer many opportunities for success experiences, from which the sense of mastery is derived. The therapist offers no overt encouragement, and treatment lacks a clear structure and definite end-point; so the patient has no easy way of judging his progress. Thus the therapeutic "task" is difficult, which may be one reason why patients have to have considerable ego-strength or frustration tolerance in order to profit from it.

By the same token, however, evocative therapies are congenial to persons who are skilled at verbalizing and conceptualizing their feelings and who have derived success experiences in the past from this type of activity. Moreover, increased self-awareness—a goal of evocative therapy—in itself enhances a person's sense of self-control. Freud, in one of his brilliant metaphors, pictured the conscious self, the Ego, as a rider on a powerful and fractious horse, his Unconscious or Id. So the psychoanalytic dictum "Where Id was there shall Ego be" implies that the goal of treatment is increased self-mastery.

Along the same lines, one of the goals of all evocative therapies is to "evoke an awareness of self-initiated thinking and action,"[19]

18. Menninger (1958), p. 55. He adds: "This is not quite right, of course, because there have been some responses . . . on the part of the therapist. But they have not been what the patient expected."
19. Bruch (1961), p. 54.

and to this end the therapist maintains the attitude that any gains the patient makes are due to his own efforts, which fosters his sense of self-direction and self-mastery.

Finally, although the ultimate criterion of success—completion of therapy—may be long delayed in such a procedure as psychoanalysis, when it does come it implies entry into the highly select group of the successfully analyzed, which enhances the patient's sense of achievement.

Exploration of the Past

Returning to the influencing properties of evocative thera物ies, we may note that those in the analytic tradition place considerable weight on detailed exploration and interpretation of the patient's psychic life, with emphasis on his past history. That this may be an influencing process is suggested by its similarity to procedures in thought reform and primitive healing rites,[20] in which the same historical material is reviewed repeatedly in the presence of someone who maintains a consistent attitude toward it, and this repetition seems important for learning new patterns of response.

Exploration of the patient's past is much more than a fact-finding expedition—an effort to help him gain insight into his current maladjustments by uncovering their historical sources. From a cognitive standpoint, even in prolonged therapy a patient recalls only a minute fraction of all his past experiences, so the question arises as to what principle of selectivity he employs and the extent to which his choice may be influenced by the psychiatrist's expectations. Man is a time-binding creature whose self-image includes expectations about his future and is supported by his picture of his past. To change a person's image of himself today, it is necessary to change his view of his future. But the future is not yet here, so his view of it can only be changed by a reinterpretation of his past.

A social psychologist has suggested that a patient's account of his life might be appropriately termed an apologia, "an image of [a

20. Cf. pp. 64–66 and 96–99 above.

person's] life course, past, present and future—which selects, abstracts, and distorts in such a way as to provide him with a view of himself that he can usefully expound in current situations."[21] This view gains support from a quantitative study that compared information mothers gave about their children and their own feelings when the children were one-year old with information given retrospectively when the children were six. The researchers found considerable discrepancies between the two sets of data and concluded that "the anamnestic material did not reflect their earlier experiences so much as their current picture of the past."[22]

The selectivity of memory is influenced by many factors. One is the patient's current state of feeling; this becomes clear by comparing the histories given by a depressed patient before and after his mood has lifted. Unhappy past experiences and overwhelming, insoluble problems that seemed to compose his whole life when he is depressed may shrink to minor episodes when he is feeling well and are replaced by new, more optimistic memories or more optimistic reevaluations of those reported earlier.

Another important factor influencing memories is the patient's feelings toward the person to whom he is reporting them, including his anticipation of this person's reactions, as noted with reports of dreams. One may produce quite different life histories, all true, for a prospective employer, a sweetheart, or a therapist.

The effect of present context on recall of past experiences was dramatically illustrated by a study in which childhood memories about experiences with parents, siblings, or childhood sexual experiences reported by twelve patients in early group therapy sessions were transcribed on cards and the whole pack, including an average of twenty-five memories from each, given to each patient three months to four years later. Each was asked to sort them into three piles—his own statements, not his own memories but generally true about his past life, and false or inapplicable. Not one patient was able to identify all of his previously reported memories—the average correctly recalled was about half. Moreover, the change in recall reflected changed relations with the interviewer, who had been the therapist.

21. Goffman (1959), p. 133.
22. Haggard et al. (1961). The quote is from p. 318.

For both sexes, memories involved in the initial effort to impress the therapist disappeared during the retesting. These included memories of exhibitionistic sex play for the women and memories of rejecting or paragon-like fathers for the men. The author concludes: "It is systematically impossible to reconstruct the childhood life space from retrospective reports by adults . . . geared to the requirements of the situations in which the retrospection is made."[23]

From the therapeutic standpoint, detailed review of the past is a way of helping the patient to construct a new self-image less burdened with guilt and, in general, supporting a happier, more successful pattern of life. He comes to treatment with an apologia that justifies and supports an unsound picture of himself. To this end, he has blotted certain experiences out of his memory and overemphasized others. Supported and implicitly guided by the therapist, he recalls some of the forgotten material and reinterprets some of it.

In this way he gradually constructs a new apologia that gives him a more favorable view of the future and sustains a new and better self-image. Thus, from the cognitive standpoint, "insight" can be viewed as the result of the reworking of the past that leads not only to the discovery of new facts and of new relationships between previously known ones but also to reevaluation of their significance.

From the standpoint of emotion, review of the past inevitably mobilizes feelings of guilt. In the absence of overt direction from the therapist, the patient is tempted to become ever more self-revealing, partly in the hope of producing something that will gain a supportive response. Since he knows he is supposed to bring up troublesome and painful experiences, he does so, and many of these may make him feel guilty, as described in the following quotation, which incidentally clearly suggests an analogy between this process in psychotherapy and in thought reform.

"Sooner or later . . . the confessions and confidings . . . begin to include material which the patient had not been aware of any need to confess. . . . he soon gets into the position of 'betraying' himself

23. Bach (1952). The quote is from p. 97.

and implicating others. He finds himself telling tales out of school and admitting things which he had previously denied—perhaps even to himself. So, whereas at first he had been relieved by the diminished pressure of his confessions, now new pressures develop because of them. . . . "[24]

The therapist's continued, impartial interest in the face of guilt-arousing material tends to be experienced as a kind of implicit forgiveness. Since the therapist in some sense represents society, this may help to counteract the patient's sense of isolation and enable him to feel more closely integrated with his group. Thus the phenomena of guilt, confession, and absolution, which play such an important part in religious healing, conversion, and thought reform, have analogies in evocative psychotherapy.

Interpretations

In most forms of evocative therapy, the therapist from time to time offers interpretations of the patient's productions aimed to foster self-revelation and insight, and the patient is expected to draw his own implications for his conduct from them. Though many interpretations may have a purely evocative function, they are probably the chief means whereby the therapist influences the patient. As Aldous Huxley has written in another context: " 'A mere matter of words' we say contemptuously, forgetting that words have the power to mold men's thinking, to canalize their feeling, to direct their willing and acting. Conduct and character are largely determined by the words we currently use to discuss ourselves and the world around us."[25]

The simplest form of interpretation consists of repeating something the patient has said, perhaps with some change in emphasis, so that he becomes more clearly aware of it. In a roughly ascending scale of degree of inference and amount of complexity, other forms of interpretation are summarizing, in order to coordinate and emphasize certain aspects, verbalizing the feelings that seem to lie behind the patient's utterances, and confronting him sharply

24. Menninger (1958), pp. 100–101.
25. Huxley (1962). The quote is from p. 2.

with attitudes implied by his statements that he had not recognized. Complex interpretations may indicate similarities between a patient's feelings toward significant persons in his past and toward important contemporaries, including the therapist. They may also suggest symbolic meanings of his statements or link them to a theoretical scheme.

Interpretation of the attitudes and feelings of the patient toward the therapist, so-called "transference reactions," have received increasing emphasis in recent years. They color the patient's reports about all aspects of his life. At a simple level he may exaggerate his suffering if he believes the therapist can be won over by arousing his sympathy, hide material that he thinks will arouse the therapist's contempt, and so on. Therefore his productions can be properly evaluated only in the light of his attitudes toward the therapist and the treatment situation.

The major significance of transference reactions lies in the fact that they afford valuable clues to the patient's feelings and behavior toward persons important to him outside of therapy. If the patient can be brought to see how his reactions to the therapist are caused by a confusion of the therapist with other persons, this highlights the inappropriateness of the responses and also increases his ability to detect the inappropriateness of similar reactions outside treatment. If he discovers that in some respects he is reacting to the therapist as if he were his childhood image of his father, for example, he then may find that he is doing the same to other "father figures," such as employers. By identifying his maladaptive behavior and feelings, he becomes more able to modify them.

As mentioned earlier, the possibility that interpretations might directly influence the patient's productions has long been recognized. Psychoanalysts in keeping with their emphasis on therapeutic objectivity have sought to deny that interpretations can operate as suggestions in this sense.[26] Evidence from psychoanalysis itself casts considerable doubt on this contention. Freud's well-known statement that "we are not in a position to force anything on the patient about the things of which he is ostensibly ignorant or to influence the products of the analysis by arousing an expec-

26. For example, Kubie (1936), chap. 7.

tation"[27] was made before his discovery that patients fabricated infantile memories in accord with his theories. A leading analyst once went to some lengths to draw a distinction between correct and incorrect interpretations, agreeing that the latter might operate by suggestion but offering elaborate reasons why the former did not. That he did not entirely convince himself is suggested by the following quotation, from an article written some twenty years later: ". . . despite all dogmatic and puristic assertions to the contrary, we cannot exclude or have not yet excluded the transference effect of suggestion through interpretation."[28]

The central function of interpretations, however simple or complex, is to change a patient's cognitions in a direction believed to be therapeutic. Thus they have healing, as well as persuasive, functions. At the simplest level, an interpretation gives a name or label to a patient's experience; at the most complex, it relates the experience not only to other experiences in the patient's life but to a body of doctrine. Since the verbal apparatus is the chief tool for analysing and reorganizing experience, interpretation, by making sense out of experiences that had seemed haphazard, confusing, or inexplicable, increases the patient's sense of control. This has been termed the principle of Rumpelstiltskin after the fairy tale in which the queen broke the wicked dwarf's power over her by guessing his name.[29]

To have this effect, an interpretation need not necessarily be correct, but merely plausible.[30] One therapist demonstrated this by offering six "all-purpose" interpretations to four patients in intensive psychotherapy. An example is: "You seem to live your life as though you are apologizing all the time." The same series of interpretations, spaced about a month apart, was given to all four patients. In twenty of these twenty-four instances, the patients responded with a drop in anxiety level (two interpretations were rejected and two simply ignored). All patients experienced this move from the "pre-interpreted" to the "post-interpreted" state at least once.[31]

27. Breuer and Freud (1957), p. 295.
28. Glover (1931, 1952). The quote is from the second paper, p. 405.
29. Torrey (1972).
30. Reid and Finesinger (1952).
31. Mendel (1964a).

As the chief means whereby the therapist demonstrates his understanding of the patient and his command of technique and theory, skillful interpretations arouse and maintain the patient's confidence in him as a master of a special healing art, thereby enhancing the patient's hopes for help. Incidentally, the ability to make interpretations also reassures the therapist about his own competence; thus young and inexperienced practitioners are often tempted to offer too many interpretations.

Interpretations influence the patient in what the therapist believes to be a therapeutic direction by subtly conveying his acceptance or rejection of the patient's productions. By simply labeling a patient's feeling, for example, the therapist implies that he is not afraid of it, that it is familiar to him, and that he will continue to accept the patient in spite of it. Such an interpretation has an enabling function—it encourages the patient to continue further in the same direction. Other interpretations, especially those that point out some inappropriateness in the patient's feelings or behavior are implicit criticisms. By indicating that an aspect of the patient's psychic life is maladaptive, the therapist implicitly suggests that he do something else. Such an interpretation differs from a conventional suggestion in that it does not tell the patient how he should change, but only that change would be desirable. Thus its effect is to inhibit certain lines of feelings or conduct and encourage the patient to develop more acceptable ones.

Interpretations may affect the general level of the patient's emotional tension and also arouse specific emotions. Tension tends to be reduced by any interpretation that heightens the patient's sense of mastery or increases his faith in the therapist. Interpretations indicating the therapist's acceptance of the patient's feeling may induce a feeling of relief and relaxation in the patient on the one hand, or encourage the patient to let himself feel and express the emotion more fully on the other. Interpretations that confront the patient with fantasies, feelings, or behavior he has repressed because they are inconsistent with his self-image may heighten his tension.

The same type of interpretation may enhance the self-esteem of one type of patient and weaken that of another. Thus a patient who is overwhelmed with feelings of guilt may gain considerable support from interpretations that imply that these feelings were inevitable reactions to the actions of others and he is not to blame. Such a formulation might aggravate the condition of patients who are already too prone to transfer responsibility for their difficulties to the shoulders of others. They often feel a powerless resentment, as if they were pawns at the mercy of a malignant fate, and so may gain support from interpretations that highlight their own contributions to their predicaments. By implying that the patient brought his troubles on himself, this type of interpretation suggests that he has the power to resolve them, and thus is indirectly reassuring.[32] Such an interpretation strengthens his sense of mastery.

In addition to these general and indirect effects, an interpretation can directly alter a patient's emotions. This would be expected from the finding that the experience of an emotion is a fusion between awareness of an internal state and what the person believes to be its cause,[33] based on his own past experiences and clues in the immediate environment. In patients, this frequently creates a vicious circle. A patient attributes a pounding heart to incipient heart disease, or difficulty in concentrating to impending insanity. This makes him anxious, and the anxiety increases his symptoms. Simple reassurance—that is, supplying the patient with a convincing, less ominous alternative explanation of his symptoms—may produce a marked improvement.

A more complex example of the same phenomenon in which the reassurance consisted of a reconceptualization of the historical cause of the patient's symptoms is afforded by a patient who seems to have been relieved of recurrent bouts of severe depression, preoccupation, and irritability in a single interview.[34] These had occurred at one- or two-week intervals since shortly before her marriage, which was of some five years' duration. Following the birth of a daughter a few months before coming to treatment, she was determined to be a perfect mother, and developed extreme irritability, often culminating in violent outbreaks connected with

32. The example of Mr. Angelo (pp. 284–85 below), although taken from group therapy, illustrates this point.
33. See pp. 108–9 above.
34. The example is slightly modified from Frank (1962).

fears that she was not handling the child exactly right. She feared she would fail the child as her mother had failed her. The intensity of her feelings played into her fear of impending insanity. She came to see me reluctantly, at the insistence of her husband, in whose eyes I had high prestige.

A review of her past history revealed that her mother was away much of the time during her infancy and then had vanished completely when she was about three. Her few memories of her mother were scenes of tender care. The father soon remarried and shortly thereafter went overseas in the armed forces for a year and a half. During this period the patient described herself as a crybaby. After the father's return, she became apparently happy and carefree until at the age of fourteen she discovered some of her mother's letters and a newspaper clipping in the attic which seemed to imply that she had been mentally ill and had committed suicide. This precipitated a new period of brooding and irritability. She was afraid to tell her father of her discovery lest she hurt his feelings. She angrily withdrew from him and began to fantasize about whether her mother had committed suicide, whether her father was somehow responsible through his insensitivity, and whether she, too, would commit suicide. Again these feelings lifted, apparently spontaneously, after a year or so, and she became her former self until late in her courtship. Since she was Jewish and her fiancé Protestant, both families opposed the marriage, and this led to tension between the engaged couple, which seemed to contribute to the recurrence of her depression. A final bit of information was that in the interview she showed obvious conflict about whether to confide in me.

My interpretation was that, having been twice abandoned by people on whom she felt dependent, her mother and her father, she was afraid to put her trust in anyone, including her husband, and that she was showing this by her reluctance to see me and her behavior in the interview itself. The earlier periods of depression I attributed to the original desertions by her mother and father, and their reactivation by discovery of the letter.

As she said in the next interview, the interpretation went off like a gong. She confirmed her acceptance of it by spontaneously attributing the recurrence of her depression and irritability during the courtship to her fiancé's periodic threats to terminate the engagement because of family opposition, which had reactivated the feelings of desertion by her mother and father. In the three months that I was able to follow her, during which she was seen only twice, she continued essentially symptom-free. For the first time she fully accepted the fact that her mother had committed suicide. Previously she had always toyed with possible alternative explanations. She felt more friendly to her father, and he seemed less reserved toward her. She no longer tried to be a perfect housewife and mother. For example, she had been able to admit to her husband sometimes that she was too tired to cook. Above all, she began to confide her feelings to him and realized, to her astonishment, that in her brooding periods she thought she was speaking her feelings aloud but was actually reciting them to herself.

A plausible explanation of what happened runs as follows. The patient's feelings were inexplicable to her. Insofar as she had an explanation for them, namely that she was going crazy and would commit suicide like her mother, this aggravated them. Because they were so frightening, she could not share these feelings with anyone and grew isolated. An additional source of stress was her perfectionism, which could be viewed as an effort to reassure herself that she was not incompetent like her mother and did not have to depend on anyone.

On the basis of the history she gave, plus her behavior in the interview, I offered an explanation of her feelings which was plausible and which was the more acceptable because of my high prestige in her eyes. Before my explanation, she had labeled her feelings as "abnormal" signs of impending insanity.[35] My interpretation enabled her to relabel her feelings as "normal" expressions of a fear of again being abandoned by someone on whom she depended, her husband. This in itself sharply reduced her anxiety. Furthermore, the explanation strongly implied that she should change her behavior. That is, instead of trying to banish her fears by proving to herself that she did not need her husband, she should seek his reassurance by telling him about them. Instead of not confiding in him and trying to do everything herself, she

35. Valins and Nisbett (1971).

should take him into her confidence. Fortunately he was able to respond by offering support and encouragement, dissolving the barrier between them and reinforcing the new behavior.

In the example, the interpretation made sense of the patient's current feelings in terms of her past experience, and this is consistent with the view of neuroses as caused by experiences in early life. It would follow from this hypothesis that the core of therapy is confrontation of the person's adult self with the distortions he has unconsciously carried over from childhood. Once he clearly sees their inappropriateness to his current situation, he may be better able to modify them. Interpretations that stress the past also enable the patient to construct a more satisfactory "apologia."

While there is little doubt that maladaptive neurotic patterns have their roots in the past, they are perpetuated by forces in the present. That is, the cause of a symptom should not be confused with its current meanings, which often can be changed regardless of their cause.[36] To return to our patient, the interpretation changed the meaning of her symptoms to her, leading to beneficial changes in her self-image and her behavior toward her husband and her father, without in any way affecting their historical causes.

This line of thinking leads to a somewhat different conceptualization of neurotic symptoms which has promising therapeutic implications. It starts with the assumption that everyone tries to control his social environment in the sense of eliciting such responses as affection, attention, and respect from others. Note that "control" in this sense is not the same as dominance. A dependent wife controls her husband's behavior in that he has to make all decisions for her. A neurotic symptom, according to this view, is an oblique effort to control other persons without taking responsibility for it. That is, the symptom conceals from the patient and others what he is really trying to do. If one does not know what end one is trying to gain, one never can be sure one has succeeded, and so the neurotic symptom becomes self-perpetuating.[37] Presumably the patient has to resort to oblique tactics because he is

36. Whitehorn (1947).
37. Haley (1963).

too insecure to use direct ones. The aim of therapy then becomes to support the patient until he gets the courage to face what he is up to. This may then enable him to modify his goals in a healthier direction or change his behavior in such a way that he gains them more effectively.[38]

Occasionally this approach will work with patients with deep-seated and complex symptoms. An example was a young married secretary with crippling obsessions of several years duration, among them fears of running over elderly people.[39] The obsessions had started at her first meeting with her future mother-in-law, who, she felt, disapproved of her. She had undergone a very traumatic childhood, as the result of which she was filled with impotent resentments toward her own family and had a strong feeling of self-hatred coupled with a fear of rejection by others. Her husband, himself a rather obsessional lawyer, was angered by his wife's efforts to change him and had demanded that she leave her first therapist because he felt that the therapist was trying to change him through his wife. He told her he could not see why a wife should ever be angry at her husband. The patient was consciously angry at her husband for his "indifference" and not showing her enough tenderness, but was unable to tell him so directly because of fear of her own destructiveness and of rejection by him.

She was a heavy smoker, against her husband's wishes, and on one occasion he became angry when she lit a cigarette despite his protests. She said nothing but instantly had a flare-up of obsessive fears that she had run over an old lady while driving home from work the day before.

The next day, while out for a drive with her husband, she meant to ask him to stop at the place to make sure nothing had happened, but forgot to mention it. After he drove past, she demanded that he turn around and go back. Quite naturally he refused. Then she flew into a violent rage at him for refusing. Her symptoms enabled her to express her anger at her husband, which had a legitimate basis, but only on grounds that were obviously

38. Frank (1966).
39. *Ibid.*

absurd, so that neither he nor she took the anger seriously. At the same time he could not respond appropriately because he did not know what she was really angry about.

After some months of treatment she announced that she had discovered that she could "trust" her husband—that is, that his feelings for her were genuine and that his apparent indifference was often simply preoccupation with other matters. This enabled her to talk more openly with him about her feeling of neglect, and he was able to respond with affection. Thereupon her obsessions sharply diminished and she lost her fear of pregnancy.

There was, of course, more to her treatment than the one feature that has been singled out for comment. An important aim of therapy, however, was to bring into her awareness the connection between flare-ups of her irrational fears and occasions for legitimate anger at her husband. That is, their "unconscious" purpose was to elicit more consideration from her husband for her as a person. They did, to be sure, gain his consideration for her as a *patient*, but this was of little help because it was given on the basis that she was sick, not that her demands were legitimate. It also further undermined her self-esteem. She remained greatly improved over a follow-up period of several years.

The view of a symptom as a miscarried communication implies that others are also always involved, so that if the patient gives up the symptom they must change also. This has led to emphasis on the inclusion of the patient's "social atom" in treatment, as considered in the chapter on group therapies. Here it suffices to note the implication that if a patient recovers, someone else may get "sick," which occurred in the case just described.

The husband, who had been outwardly loving and tolerant of his wife while she had her obsessions, came to see me in great distress about fourteen months after their subsidence. He said that he had lost all interest in his wife, had abdominal pains, had lost about ten pounds, felt very restless, and could not concentrate. He quickly recognized that when his wife was psychically crippled, he could maintain a protective attitude toward her. This fulfilled his need to dominate the marriage and helped to counteract his anger at her exasperating behavior. Her recovery made his dominance less certain and also deprived him of his defenses against his anger at her. His wife, in turn, aggravated his condition through trying to "help" him by analysing his feelings—that is, she placed herself in the superior position by casting him in the role of patient. His symptoms subsided and his affection for his wife returned rapidly after a joint session in which all this came out into the open and the wife agreed to stop "treating" him and give his spontaneous recuperative powers a chance.

It must be added that the patient at the follow-up interview three years later did not remember my interpretations. She attributed her improvement to the fact that I had made her "feel like a real person," suggesting again that a major therapeutic effect of all maneuvers may lie in their indirect ability to heighten a patient's sense of self-worth by conveying that the therapist values him.

This brings us to a final component of interpretations, which is that they convey, implicitly or explicitly, a conceptual scheme that can be helpful in many ways. The therapist's ability to link the patient's personal troubles to an established set of concepts in itself implies that he is not unique, thereby diminishing his sense of isolation, especially when the same concepts are applied to normal persons. Such interpretations enable him to reconceptualize his problems in terms that simultaneously make him feel closer to his fellow man and his society. Moreover, some conceptual schemes, notably those in the Freudian or Jungian tradition, have a highly dramatic quality. The patient is no longer an insignificant creature but becomes a battleground of titanic forces or a storehouse of the accumulated myths and wisdom of the ages. There may be a slight echo here of the linkage of the individual to suprapersonal forces, which seemed to be important in thought reform, conversion, and religious healing. In any case, such interpretations heighten a patient's sense of importance and thus may bolster his morale.

Paradoxically, interpretations based on existentialist philosophies, which view individual existence as objectively meaningless, can also strengthen morale. For the goal of such interpretations is to enable the patient to withstand the realization that life is meaningless by convincing him that he can, nevertheless, make it meaningful. As one existential psychotherapist has put it, the goal of therapy is to show the person that he can choose and make his world instead of succumbing to reality.[40] While he cannot escape his ultimate fate or control many external events that affect his welfare, he is free to determine what position he will take toward them. Thus he can preserve his sense of inner freedom and find meaning in suffering and despair, even as an inmate of a Nazi death camp.[41]

SUMMARY

Psychotherapy may be viewed as a morale-enhancing influencing process that has emotional, cognitive, and behavioral facets. Emotionally it tries to produce and maintain a degree of arousal optimal for learning, to foster hope, self-confidence, and trust, and to combat despair, insecurity, and suspicion. Cognitively psychotherapy helps the patient to achieve clarification of his problems and ways of dealing with them. From the behavioral standpoint, it requires that the patient participate repetitively in some form of activity that leads to behavioral changes outside the therapeutic situation.

Psychotherapies can be classified according to whether they deal primarily with the individual patient alone, with the patient as a member of a group or, in residential settings, with the patient's total milieu. They can also be roughly classified as directive or evocative. In the former, the therapist tries openly to alleviate specific symptoms or to bring about limited changes in the patient's behavior. In the latter, he tries to evoke and explore a wide range of the patient's feelings and attitudes as a means of promoting personality growth, with the expectation that as he becomes better able to function in general, his symptoms will be resolved.

This chapter has focused on evocative individual therapy and has examined the sources of its persuasive and healing properties, using psychoanalysis as the chief example. The therapist is a model with whom the patient can identify. His refusal to offer overt guidance leads the patient to become increasingly dependent on him on the one hand and, on the other, to attribute progress to his

40. Mendel (1964b).
41. Frankl (1959).

own efforts, thereby increasing his sense of mastery. The detailed review of the patient's past life mobilizes guilt feelings with confession and implicit forgiveness, conveyed by the therapist's steady interest. It also helps the patient to reconstruct his history in order to support a better self-image. Interpretations implicitly convey approval or disapproval and reduce the patient's cognitive confusion by naming his inchoate feelings and ordering them within a conceptual framework. They may stir the patient up by confronting him with disowned aspects of himself or alleviate distressing emotions by changing his perception of their causes. Interpretations of symptoms as oblique efforts to control others may lead to beneficial changes in behavior. Finally, they implicitly convey the therapist's theory of human nature and philosophy of existence, which may help the patient to bear his suffering or actually reduce it by placing it in a broader context that gives it significance.

IX

DIRECTIVE FORMS OF INDIVIDUAL PSYCHOTHERAPIES

"Where do you come from?" said the Red Queen.
"And where are you going?
Look up, speak nicely,
and don't twiddle your fingers all the time."

Through the Looking Glass

INTRODUCTION

The aim of all forms of psychotherapy is to help a person change his troublesome attitudes and behavior. As we have seen, evocative therapies try to achieve this indirectly by creating favorable conditions for change but leaving the actual change up to the patient. They seek to promote his emotional growth by placing him in an unstructured, permissive situation that leaves him free to modify and extend his habitual ways of feeling, thinking, and behaving, but at the same time challenges him to do so. Directive therapies, by contrast, seek to structure the therapeutic situation as much as possible and to reduce ambiguity to a minimum.

The directive therapist does not hesitate to use any of the familiar forms of persuasion—including exhortation, advice, instruction, and providing a good example. Directive therapies also encompass a variety of specialized techniques. All are grounded on conceptual schemes, many of which require that the procedures be applied in a highly systematic, precise way. As will be seen, the conceptualizations and methods vary widely, but they have certain common features that justify considering them together.

Central to almost all directive therapies is emphasis on the fact that the symptoms of persons seeking psychotherapy are expressions of loss of control or ineffective efforts to gain control over certain thoughts, feelings, or behaviors. As a result, the patients are both distressed and unable to function at the level of their full potential. An experimental study has confirmed, as Freud long ago recognized, that anxiety, the most common complaint of the mentally ill, or its somatic manifestations are expressions of a feeling of helplessness.[1] In more positive terms, perhaps the primary human need is to have a sense of control or mastery over oneself and one's environment.[2] In any case, all directive approaches seek to help the patient gain or regain his sense of control.

The specific goals of directive therapy vary widely. Some, such as reality therapy,[3] seek to improve the patient's general adaptation by confronting him with his self-deceptions and, in general, teaching him how to live right. Others train patients to use self-administered exercises that enable him to overcome his symptoms and to function better in general by gaining control of his muscular and visceral reactions. Notable examples in the West are progressive relaxation[4] and autogenic training.[5] The latter resembles yoga in some ways. These methods, while they have much to offer, lie outside the scope of this book, so we shall turn to methods focusing on alleviation of the patient's complaint. Presumably, if the patient learns to conquer it, not only will his immediate distress be relieved but he will gain increased self-confidence, enabling him to tackle and master situations that he had previously avoided. This "ripple effect" may show itself in areas far removed from the initial complaint, as in a patient who on regaining his sexual potency through hypnosis was able for the first time to protect himself from exploitation by business partners and to discharge dishonest employees.[6]

1. Luborsky (1970).
2. Strupp (1970).
3. Glasser (1965).
4. Jacobson (1957).
5. Schultz and Luthe (1959).
6. Spiegel and Linn (1969).

In short, the directive therapies we shall consider use a strategy opposite to that of evocative ones. They assume that personality development will take care of itself if the symptoms that block it are alleviated. Since the goals of these therapies are circumscribed and clearly defined, therapeutic progress can be objectively measured and treatment is characteristically briefer than that for evocative therapy.

Although directive therapies vary widely in their methods, the relationship between patient and therapist is always conceived as one of guidance and cooperation rather than of collaboration. The therapist uses the patient's dependence on him—his "transference"—as a means to gain the necessary leverage, rather than as a potential source of increased self-understanding. From the start, the therapist demonstrates his skill in the use of a particular technique, thereby enhancing the patient's faith in his ability to be helpful. The patient's active participation is assured by the requirement that he follow the therapist's instructions not only during the sessions but, in many cases, between them as well.

Directive therapies can be roughly classified as emphasizing the patient's cognitions, his behavior, or his emotions, although, of course, each inevitably involves all of them. In this chapter we shall examine one or two samples of each approach, singling out their persuasive and healing features while leaving open the still unanswerable question of how much of their success results from the unique features of each method and how much from their common characteristics.

COGNITIVE APPROACHES

A form of directive therapy that focuses on cognitions assumes that distressing emotions or inhibitions of behavior are caused by intervening thoughts of which the patient is more or less unaware. To take a specific example, a patient who felt anxious every time he saw a dog, even a chained one or a puppy, had the fleeting thought "He is going to bite me." This "intervening variable" caused him to feel anxious. By bringing it to the forefront of consciousness so that he could recognize its absurdity with respect to most dogs, he was able to overcome his fear.[7]

7. Beck (1970).

A complete system of therapy based on the assumption that neurotic distress and crippled behavior is caused by such "internalized sentences" is "rational emotive therapy."[8] The sentences are more general than in the above example and in a sense represent a pervasive attitude toward life. An example would be that in order to survive one must be loved at all times. The therapist unearths these hidden postulates, of which he assumes there are only a limited number, and then proceeds to try to get the patient to recognize their illogicality and to act on his new-found understanding: "to un*do* (as well as to un*think*) his self-defeating indoctrinations."

To achieve this end, the therapist uses any appropriate means of persuasion—including exhortation, argument, browbeating, insistence that the patient indulge in behaviors that would expose the falsity of his assumptions, and instruction on how to do so. An example of successful treatment of a subjective symptom and a behavioral difficulty by rational emotive psychotherapy follows.[9] The unusually favorable outcome of this case should not be regarded as typical. Of those homosexuals who wish to change their object choice, many do not respond to this or any other form of psychotherapy.

The patient was a thirty-five-year-old man who was exclusively homosexual and also had periodic attacks of chest pain and palpitation. His homosexual activities had been going on for sixteen years. He also was emotionally overdependent on his parents, which was related to his having reluctantly and resentfully abandoned his teaching career to take over his father's business after the latter had suffered a stroke. The therapist first attacked his homosexuality, since this concerned the patient most. He made clear that his goal was not to cause the patient to surrender his homosexual desires, but to overcome his irrational block against heterosexual behavior. After determining that the patient never once made the initial homosexual advance, the therapist told him that his outstanding motive for remaining homosexual was fear of rejection, springing from his illogical belief that being rejected, especially by a girl, was a terrible thing. "His fear of rejection, of losing approval, of having others laugh at and criticize him was

8. Ellis (1962). The quote is from p. 123. Author's italics.
9. Ellis (1959). The quotes are from pp. 341 and 342. Author's italics.

examined in scores of its aspects, and revealed to him again and again . . . [and] scornfully, forcefully *attacked* by the therapist."

Concomitantly the patient was encouraged to date girls so that he could overcome his fears by actual experiences with them. The therapist instructed him how to behave with a girl, what to expect, how to avoid being discouraged by rebuffs, and when to make sexual advances. After seven weekly sessions the patient had heterosexual relations that were mutually satisfying. By the twelfth week he was "virtually a hundred percent heterosexual. All his walking and sleeping fantasies became heterosexually oriented and he was almost never interested in homosexual outlets."

The patient's psychosomatic symptoms and vocational problems were attacked and overcome in a similar manner, as a result of which he was able to resume his interrupted academic career. It should be noted that some basic issues in the patient's life, such as his resentful overattachment to his mother, and his probable jealousy of his father's hold over his mother, were virtually never discussed during the entire therapeutic procedure.

The patient discontinued treatment after nineteen sessions. A letter from him three years later revealed he was married, was completely uninterested in homosexual activity, held a university teaching post, and was free of the heart symptoms with which he came to therapy.

As this example illustrates, the directive psychotherapist operates within a clear and definite conceptual framework. He takes enough of the patient's history to formulate a diagnosis of the maladaptive attitudes and behavior patterns responsible for the patient's distress and sets the goals of treatment on the basis of his understanding of these. The goals are more or less circumscribed and characteristically involve resolution of current interpersonal difficulties. To achieve this, the therapist guides the patient to new ways of behaving, typically involving more direct expression of aggressive and affiliative drives, and improvement in communication skills.

BEHAVIOR THERAPIES

The last decade has witnessed an explosive growth of therapies whose primary aim is stated as the modification of behavior. Their chief proponents and practitioners have been psychologists, for reasons that are not far to seek. Behavior therapies are backed by a large body of psychological experimentation on human and animal learning which supplies a scientifically respectable rationale. Thus, they hold out the hope, which has some justification, of at last grounding psychotherapeutic methods on truly scientific principles. Behavior therapists are called upon to state their goals and means of achieving them in explicit, objectively verifiable terms, check whether the method has, in fact, achieved the goal, and be willing to try something else if it has not.

This experimental attitude not only encourages innovativeness and flexibility, but leads to gains in knowledge, even if many prove to be negative—that is, the disproving of hypotheses rather than their verification. It is through investigation of behavior therapies themselves that the limitations and the inadequacies of their conceptualizations are being exposed, leading to the development of progressively more adequate theories and procedures. This is a real advance over many evocative therapies, whose rationales are so constructed that their validity cannot be tested.

Practitioners of behavior therapies make the same enthusiastic claims as do practitioners of all other methods, but these methods are convincingly superior to interview therapies only in curing circumscribed phobias, symptoms seen in less than 3 percent of persons seeking psychotherapy.[10] Whatever their ultimate therapeutic value proves to be, however, their demonstration that the therapy of mental illness can be experimentally studied is a permanent contribution.[11]

Behavior modification techniques fall into three main groups: reinforcement, modeling,[12] and counterconditioning. Positive and negative reinforcements are technical terms for reward and punishment. As we have seen,[13] subtle reinforcements such as small signs of approval or disapproval can shape verbal behavior even when the reinforcer is not aware of what he is doing and believes himself to be completely neutral, as in client-centered therapy. Systematic

10. Marks (1969), p. 77.
11. Goldiamond and Dyrud (1968).
12. Bandura (1967) offers a concise overview. Research to date on counterconditioning is reviewed in detail by Eysenck and Beech (1971); on reinforcement by Krasner (1971); on modeling, by Mowrer (1966) and Bandura (1971).
13. See p. 129 above.

manipulation of reinforcements through token economies in mental hospitals, institutions for the mentally retarded, and the like have proved effective in improving the behavior of certain severely handicapped persons. The procedure consists of rewarding certain behaviors by tokens, which can then be exchanged for candy or increased priveleges. Although these programs often seem to be quite mechanical, actually their success depends on close relations between patients and staff, and additional reinforcement of the desired behaviors by praise.

Modeling means demonstrating the desired behavior. Imitation may be a much more rapid means of inducing learning than reward and punishment. Often a single demonstration will teach behavior that might take months to teach by reinforcement. Modeling has been used with great success to overcome strongly established, abnormal behavior such as avoidance of dogs or snakes. Simply witnessing someone else showing pleasure while patting a dog or fondling a snake may quickly enable a person to follow suit.

Counterconditioning, the third major form of behavior therapy, can be either positive or negative. Positive counterconditioning consists in associating an anxiety-provoking event with a pleasant stimulus of sufficient strength to neutralize the anxiety. Negative or aversive conditioning associates a satisfying but undesirable behavior with an unpleasant stimulus. An example would be trying to cure alcoholics by making them vomit repeatedly after taking a drink, or eliminating the sexual response to homosexual stimuli or fetish objects by coupling their presentation with a painful shock.

Systematic Desensitization

Systematic desensitization was conceptualized by its originator as a particular form of positive counterconditioning, based on the notion, which has some support from animal experiments, that if anxiety is evoked simultaneously with a response physiologically incompatible with it, the anxiety will be extinguished.[14] It in-

14. Wolpe and Lazarus (1966). The original theoretical basis for systematic desensitization has been shown to be an inadequate explanation for its effects (Locke, 1971; Wilkins, 1971). This illustrates the point that the validity of a therapy's rationale may be unrelated to its effectiveness.

volves three steps: training in deep muscle relaxation by the method of progressive relaxation, construction of anxiety hierarchies, and counterposing relaxation with anxiety stimuli from the hierarchies. For example, if the patient is afraid of snakes, the lowest level of the hierarchy may be catching a glimpse of a snake across the field, the highest letting the snake wrap itself around his neck. The patient relaxes, then repeatedly imagines the lowest level of the hierarchy, alternating the visualization with relaxation, until he can stay relaxed while visualizing it. He then moves to the next step in the hierarchy until eventually he can imagine the most anxiety-arousing scene without fear. Throughout, the therapist is at his side, helping him to relax and encouraging him in general.

Since the discussion that follows draws heavily on experimental studies of systematic desensitization, some cautions about the findings must be mentioned. Many of the studies use volunteer college students whose fears are unearthed by surveys. From the standpoint of the research therapists, they are an ideal population—relatively plentiful (which facilitates setting up control groups), cooperative, and intelligent. Since they are not seriously handicapped, they can be assigned to different experimental conditions without concern that one prove less effective than another. Most are induced to volunteer by, for example, being excused from a course examination or by pay. That is, their motivation for participation may be as much to please the teacher or get the reward as to gain relief from their symptoms. Since students are highly motivated to please instructors, their reports and behavior are especially subject to contamination by compliance with the experimenter's expectations and other demand characteristics of the situation. These characteristics raise questions as to how far one can generalize and apply findings obtained with students to *bona fide* patients, whose motivation is to seek relief not to gain extraneous rewards and who, by and large, are considerably more distressed or handicapped. In this connection, reexamination of a group of patients with chronic phobias an average of four years after their desensitization treatment revealed that the phobias of almost half were undiminished.[15]

15. Marks (1971).

Keeping these cautions in mind, we shall consider four features of systematic desensitization, not incorporated in its rationale, that account for an indeterminate part of its success. These features have been selected because of their relevance to the concerns of this book. They are the patient's confidence in his therapist, his expectation of help, his belief that he is improving, and the strengthening of his sense of mastery through belief that his improvement is due to his own efforts.

The patient's trust in his therapist is no less important in behavior therapies than in all other forms. A leading clinical practitioner and researcher has concluded that "the single factor which seems most relevant to the outcome of behaviour therapy is the [therapist-patient] relationship. . . . symptoms often increased when the patient felt annoyed with or rejected by the therapist."[16]

Another therapist reports that two homosexual patients who had been responding well to aversive conditioning suffered serious relapses immediately after becoming angry at him. One, who had been free not only from homosexual contacts but even from homosexual urges, relapsed when he became angry because he believed that the therapist had violated his confidence. He immediately sought a homosexual partner to see "how really good" the treatment was and, thereafter, never again was completely free of homosexual urges and activities despite much more treatment. The other indulged in a series of homosexual acts immediately after expressing his irritation at the physician, whom he accused of being more interested in the results than in him as a person.[17]

Experimental evidence concerning the significance of the therapeutic relationship is provided by a carefully designed experiment on systematic desensitization with students in a speech course who reported performance anxiety while anticipating speaking or actually doing so. Four matched groups were used, one receiving systematic desensitization, another an "attention-placebo" procedure resembling the first in that the subjects had to perform a supposedly therapeutic systematic activity in the presence of the therapist, the third conventional interview therapy, and the fourth

16. Meyer and Gelder (1963), p. 26.
17. Marmor (1971).

no treatment. The first group obtained 100 percent relief in five sessions over six weeks; the next two, 50 percent; and the control group, 17 percent. That is, all the improvement obtained with insight therapy could be accounted for by the attention-placebo effect and desensitization clearly added something more. The point for our purposes, however, is that patients in the first three groups, who were equal with respect to the therapeutic relationship, showed significant improvement in comparison with the fourth group, who had no relationship. A follow-up two years later found that improvement had endured.[18]

Pursuing the therapist-patient relationship, the experimenter ascertained that subjects' ratings of the therapists' competence correlated with their improvement reported on a self-rating scale. Moreover, the therapists' ratings of their own comfort in using the technique correlated not only with the patients' observed improvement while making a speech, but also with reduction of two physiological measures of anxiety, palmar sweat and pulse rate.

The therapeutic relationship and the demand characteristics of the situation might be expected to have different effects on internal bodily states, overt behavior, and subjective reports of anxiety. The findings of several studies are consistent with this possibility. One study found, for example, that heart rate did not vary in any consistent fashion with changes in avoidance behavior during therapy. Another found that several subjective measures of fear correlated only weakly, if at all, with each other and with actual avoidance of snakes.[19] Along the same lines, another investigator found that many subjects who looked relaxed, and reported that they were when undergoing successful desensitization, actually showed considerable muscle tension as measured by an electromyograph. He explained this awkward finding by attributing the favorable results to a subjective state of calmness induced by the relaxation technique.[20]

As with other forms of psychotherapy, the patients' expectations partially account for the favorable outcome. That behavior therapists recognize this is suggested by the effort they make to

18. Paul (1966, 1967).
19. For the first study, see Leitenberg et al. (1971); for the second, see Lang (1968).
20. Rachman (1968).

indoctrinate patients before starting the procedure.[21] A controlled experiment similar to the one on the role induction interview reported earlier[22] found that students with snake phobias who received instruction in reinforcement theory and information about how they and the therapist would behave during therapy showed a significantly greater degree of desensitization after treatment, as measured by willingness to touch the snake, than a control group receiving no advance information. The importance of expectations was further revealed by the interesting finding that the advance information led nine of the twenty-four students to touch the snake before desensitization began (as compared with only one of the control groups).[23] Along the same lines, groups of students with snake phobias who were told in advance that the procedure was therapeutic showed significantly more improvement than those who were told it was an experiment in imagery.[24] In both studies the uninformed or misinformed groups also showed some improvement, indicating that the method itself had some effect. But this leaves unanswered the question of what proportion of the improvement is accounted for by the various components of systematic desensitization.

Efforts to partial out the relative effects of the hierarchy of fear-producing stimuli and relaxation have yielded conflicting results and, because of the methodological problems mentioned earlier, none is conclusive. Thus, one study compared four groups of snake-phobic students. One received the full treatment; one was asked to imagine an irrelevant hierarchy while relaxing; one went through the graded set of fear-producing scenes without relaxing; and a fourth had no treatment. Only the first group showed substantial gains in ability to approach a snake.[25]

On the other hand, a variety of studies have cast doubt on the necessity of either the hierarchy or relaxation or both.[26] That relaxation may be irrelevant to behavioral improvement is suggested by the findings of a study which divided systematic desensi-

21. See p. 162 above.
22. See pp. 163–64 above.
23. Parrino (1971); Leitenberg et al. (1969).
24. Oliveau et al. (1969).
25. Davison (1968).
26. These studies are summarized in Murray and Jacobson (1971).

tization of patients into three phases of equal length. In the first and third, the patients, deeply relaxed, imagined steps in the fear hierarchy; in the second, the procedure was identical except that they were placed in hard, straight-backed chairs and told it was important not to relax. Although the patients made less progress on subjective measures during the nonrelaxation phase, behavioral progress continued at the same rate as in the relaxation phases. The authors conclude that "expectation is the overriding therapeutic variable in desensitization."[27]

The findings of another study cast serious doubt on the assumption that for anxiety to be extinguished it must be paired with a response incompatible with it.[28] Patients, who were instructed not to stop visualizing a scene in the hierarchy when they felt anxious and to concentrate on the bodily feelings it aroused, experienced a sharp rise in anxiety, followed by disappearance of all affect associated with the experience. The finding that enhancement of anxiety under certain conditions may rapidly extinguish it is consistent with the results of emotional flooding, considered in the next section.

Just as systematic desensitization may relieve anxiety in the absence of relaxation, so studies of aversive conditioning to reduce drinking or smoking have cast doubts on the importance of actually delivering the punishment. One example may suffice. One group of smokers received an electric shock when they smoked; another was shown irrelevant slides connected with the shock; and a third was told that they were receiving subliminal shocks, but actually got none. All reduced their smoking equally.[29] Along the same lines, it has been shown that aversive conditioning can be conducted entirely in fantasy—that is, by having the subject imagine, for example, taking a drink and promptly vomiting all over himself.[30]

An important therapeutic ingredient of both systematic desensitization and aversive conditioning is that they are structured. This enables the patient to ascertain his own progress at all times. The

27. Agras et al. (1971), p. 513.
28. Gendlin (1962) summarized by Weitzman (1967).
29. Carlin and Armstrong (1968).
30. Cautela (1971).

significance of structure is suggested by the results of a bogus treatment which resembled conventional desensitization only in having the same configuration.[31] Two groups of snake-phobic students were used, one assigned to conventional desensitization and the other to something labeled "t-scope therapy." In this treatment the subjects constructed the usual fear hierarchy but no relaxation was used. Instead they were told that the items would be presented to them by means of a tachistoscope so rapidly that they could not be seen, but would register subliminally. These presentations would occasionally be accompanied by a mild electric shock which, so the plausible rationale went, would extinguish their anxiety by aversive conditioning. They then went through eight twenty-minute sessions (the same number as the desensitization group) in which blank cards were flashed on the tachistoscope, occasionally accompanied by a mild shock, and certain physiological responses were supposedly recorded. At the end of each session a technician produced a printout of these measures indicating that the subject's anxiety was diminishing. At the end of the treatment, subjects receiving t-scope therapy showed as much improvement in ability to approach snakes as those receiving desensitization.

All counterconditioning procedures encourage the subject to attribute his progress to his own efforts, thereby heightening his sense of mastery. This suggests that the effectiveness of desensitization might be enhanced by permitting the patient to administer it to himself, which has indeed proved to be true. The hierarchy of fear-inducing stimuli, followed at each level by instructions to relax, is put on a tape recorder which the patient controls.[32]

Along the same lines, in desensitization if the patient is given a drug and told it will relax him, it seems to be ineffective in reducing his fears; but it works if he is first trained in relaxation exercises and then told that the drug will help him to relax further but that he must "work along with it."[33]

Perhaps heightening of the patient's sense of mastery explains why apparently irrelevant success experiences may be thera-

31. Marcia et al. (1969).
32. Migler and Wolpe (1967).
33. Brady (1967), p. 259.

peutic.[34] This is suggested by the results of a study comparing the relative effectiveness of three procedures for reducing anxiety in patients suffering from chronic anxiety. The patients were divided into three groups, each receiving twelve treatment sessions. One group received whatever combination of behavioral methods seemed indicated, including systematic desensitization. The second received insight therapy. The third underwent "graded structure therapy." In this group the treatment was divided into four blocks of three weeks each.

What went on in the four blocks was not specifically related to the patient's complaints. In the first he was asked to examine salient life experiences. In the second the therapist discussed with him the significance of some of his responses to an incomplete-sentence test. In the third block he read aloud some writings of Maslow and discussed the concept of self-actualization. The final three weeks were devoted to a series of simple exercises termed visual training, auditory training, and awareness training. At the end of each block the patient was given an examination to determine whether he had mastered the material in it sufficiently to be qualified to move on to the next. Of course, he always passed; that is, he was given an experience of success.

According to their subjective reports, all patients improved, regardless of the group they were in, again raising the specter of the demand character of the situation. On a behavioral test, however, only two of the ten receiving psychotherapy improved, as compared with seven who received behavior therapy and six who had received graded structure therapy. That is, nonspecific success experiences were as effective in overcoming the patient's behavioral inhibitions as behavior methods tailored to their specific symptoms.

This review justifies the conclusion that symbolic processes play an important role in behavior therapies. This is not to minimize the importance of real events, particularly in conditioning of the autonomic nervous system. For example, it has been shown that the mere threat of a shock produces as intense physiological fear responses as threat followed by actual shock. Fear responses

34. Lazarus (1968).

produced by the threat alone, however, instantly subsided when the subject was told that no shock would be given; those produced by actual shock required a period of extinction by repeated presentation of the threat without the shock.[35]

To take a clinical example, it would be hard to explain on the basis of symbolic processes alone the finding that pairing a shock with a specific fetish object extinguishes sexual responses, as measured by penile erection, to that object alone and not to others.[36] Similarly, while cognitive rehearsal of an anticipated fearful situation may effectively reduce anxiety on subsequent exposure to it,[37] actually entering a feared situation with proper encouragement and support is more effective. Thus systematic desensitization to fear of water, while it extinguished anxiety aroused by fantasied scenes, had no effect on the subjects' ability to enter the water, while graded exposure to the pool itself, with encouragement, was highly effective.[38]

A well-designed, similar study compared the effect of two forms of desensitization on snake phobias; watching a film of persons handling snakes (symbolic modeling) and live modeling with participation, in which the experimenter handled the snake more and more intimately while encouraging and guiding the patient to do likewise. Live modeling with participation overcame the phobia in every subject, including those who had previously failed to reach maximum improvement with either of the other methods.[39] Similarly, all of a series of phobic patients improved when given prolonged exposure in practice to the situations they feared.[40]

EMOTIONAL AROUSAL AND THERAPY

All forms of psychotherapy reviewed so far assume implicitly or explicitly that there is an optimal range of emotional arousal for promoting attitude change and try to keep the patient within this range. It is self-evident that certain moderately intense emotions

35. Bridger and Mandel (1964).
36. Marks and Gelder (1967).
37. Folkins *et al.* (1968). Cf. Janis (1958).
38. Sherman (1969).
39. Bandura (1971).
40. Watson, Gaind, and Marks (1971).

promote mental alertness and interaction with the environment, thereby enhancing a person's ability to profit from new experiences, such as those provided in therapy.

The positive relationship between therapists' enthusiasm and their therapeutic success may be partly due to the emotional response their attitude evokes in their patients. Directive therapists stir patients emotionally by urging them to enter situations or attempt activities they fear. Some openly criticize patients. Evocative therapists do the same indirectly through interpretations that are implicitly critical or that force patients to face unacceptable aspects of themselves. They also arouse patients by not responding as the patient expects, sometimes giving no response.

Very intense emotional states, which may be lumped under the term "emotional flooding," also are able to facilitate changes in attitude and behavior. These states may be conceived as forms of *kairos*—moments at which a person is ripe for profound personality change.[41] Their adequate conceptualization requires considerably more knowledge about brain functioning than is now available. One feature is temporary disorganization of the person's psychic structure, sometimes enabling him to achieve a new and better integration with relief of symptoms.[42] In any case, the production of emotional flooding is a component of many forms of healing and persuasion.[43]

Emotionally shocking procedures have always been used in the treatment of the mentally ill. In the first century A.D., Celsus wrote of certain patients showing abnormal behavior: "When he has said or done anything wrong, he must be chastised by hunger, chains and fetters. . . . It is also beneficial in this malady, to make use of sudden fright, for a change may be effected by withdrawing the mind from the state in which it has been."[44] Brutal treatment of the mentally ill continued during the intervening centuries, often in the guise of exorcising demons. In the nineteenth century, even the great humanitarian Pinel, who struck the chains from the insane, believed that fright was an effective remedy, and "scien-

41. Kelman (1969).
42. Sargant (1968).
43. Cf. examples of primitive healing (p. 61 above), religious revivalism (pp. 81–82 above), and thought reform (pp. 91–93 above).
44. Quoted in Zilboorg (1941), p. 70.

tific" treatments to restore the patient to his rational senses included submerging him until he was almost drowned or spinning him in a chair until he lost consciousness. Pinel's American contemporary Benjamin Rush asserted: "Terror acts powerfully on the body through the medium of the mind and should be employed in the cure of madness."[45]

Such measures as insulin shock and electroconvulsive therapy, whatever their other therapeutic effects may be, are modern equivalents of beatings and duckings as means of producing intense states of emotional arousal. A modern exponent of Zen draws an explicit parallel between Western shock treatments and "the inducement of shock by blows with a stick or a thundering cry. . . . We can see a good example in the case of a student who attempted suicide several times and was awakened and cured by a thundering cry of a master."[46]

Since the days of Mesmer, certain forms of psychotherapy in the West have also mobilized intense emotions. In mesmeric sessions, the female patients sat about the baquet (a container filled with "magnetized" water) holding hands and pressing their knees together to facilitate the flow of magnetic fluid, and touching the diseased parts of their bodies from time to time with iron rods that had been dipped into the baquet. Then the assistant magnetizers entered, strong handsome young men who massaged the ladies in various ways and stared intently into their eyes, to the accompaniment of "a few wild notes on the harmonica . . . or the piano-forte, or the melodious voice of a hidden opera singer. . . . Gradually the cheeks of the ladies began to glow, their imaginations became inflamed; and off they went, one after the other, in convulsive fits."[47] Some of the convulsions lasted more than three hours. Then Mesmer, dressed in an elegant silk robe, would solemnly enter and touch each patient with his magnetic white wand, quickly restoring them "to sensibility and sometimes to health."

While disdaining such dramatic methods, Freud initially strove to produce similarly intense arousal states by encouraging the

45. Blain (1970). The quote is from p. 80.
46. Sato (1958). The quote is from p. 214.
47. Mackay (1962), quoted by Schwitzgebel and Traugott (1968). The quote is from p. 268.

patient, with the aid of hypnosis, to "abreact" early traumatic experiences in their full intensity.[48] While this "cathartic" technique produced dramatic improvement, the results often proved to be transitory, and Freud soon abandoned it for free association and interpretation. Catharsis in one form or another, however, has remained a therapeutic component of certain modifications of Freudian techniques such as that of Wilhelm Reich, as well as of hypnotherapy.[49]

In each war, abreaction creates a new flurry of interest because it produces such rapid relief in many soldiers with acute anxiety caused by traumatic battle episodes; yet interest diminishes again because abreaction proves much less effective in resolving emotional disturbances of civil life. One reason for its greater effectiveness in relieving battle reactions may be that the soldier does not return to the traumatic situation, which is safely in the past, while the civilian remains caught in it. For him, enduring benefit from abreaction may depend on his ability to find new and better ways of coping with his problems, which presents a different therapeutic task.

Recently therapies centered on the production of abreactions have again come into prominence. Before we consider some examples, it may be well to mention that abreactions represent one of many altered states of consciousness, which include states as diverse as extreme fatigue, hypnotic trance, and mystical experiences. Each shares the characteristic of shaking up existing psychic structures in such a way that the person becomes hypersuggestible. This arises from reduction of his critical faculties, coupled with feelings of loss of control over his mental functions, leading him to seek support and clarification from some authoritative source— typically an authority figure, sometimes a religious or political dogma, or even an inner voice. He feels himself to be in the power of this strong force and accepts ideas proceeding from it as ultimate truth. As discussed in Chapter 4, an altered state of consciousness characteristically precedes religious conversions.

Consciousness-altering drugs, of which LSD has become the prototype in the United States, are receiving considerable atten-

48. Breuer and Freud (1957).
49. Rosen (1952).

tion as adjuncts to psychotherapy. They can be used to produce either "psychedelic" or "psycholytic" experiences, depending on the treatment setting and the goals of the therapist.[50] The former closely resemble ecstatic states accompanying religious conversions. The subject experiences an intense feeling of unity with a benevolent universe, and a conviction that his personal life has significance. This can help restore to useful life some alcoholics and drug addicts[51] and has been used to ease the despair of dying patients.[52] As psycholytic agents, the same drugs dissolve ego boundaries, allowing emotionally laden memories of early experiences to emerge into consciousness, thus facilitating abreaction and reintegration of these experiences into the patient's conscious life. While these methods may hold great promise for certain sufferers, their pharmacological aspects lie outside the scope of this discussion. Their psychological features will be considered in the discussion of psychological ways of producing emotional flooding.

Experiments on Emotional Arousal and Attitude Change

Before we discuss contemporary psychotherapies based on emotional flooding, it seems appropriate to describe an experimental approach to the relation of emotional arousal and attitude change in psychiatric outpatients, using ether inhalation to produce emotional arousal. Ether was the agent chosen because in doses smaller than those producing unconsciousness it causes excitement in most persons. In these doses it is essentially safe, and because it is rapidly exhaled, the dose level is easily regulated. It should be added that when in the excitatory state the patient's consciousness is somewhat clouded. The Semantic Differential[53] was used as a measure of attitude change.

We conducted two experiments, the first a preliminary one and the second more rigorous. In the first,[54] patients received conventional interview therapy for several sessions, during which the ther-

50. Abramson (1967).
51. Kurland et al. (1971).
52. Kurland et al. (1969).
53. Osgood et al. (1957).
54. Hoehn-Saric et al. (1968).

apist, in consultation with the research staff, selected a focal concept that he would try to shift and other concepts, selected by criteria that need not concern us here, that he would not try to change. The focal concept was chosen to be one related to the patient's major problems but not so central that it could not be shifted in a few interviews, nor so linked to events in the patient's current life that it might change from day to day. That is, we tried to choose one related to the patient's internal conflicts. Examples of focal concepts were "my mother's influence on me," "my tolerance of imperfections in persons close to me."

The patient was asked to rate the focal concept and other concepts on the Semantic Differential before and after one regular therapy session without ether, then before and after three sessions a week apart, lasting about one and a half hours, in which sufficient ether was given by open drip inhalation to bring the patient to the excitatory stage of anesthesia. The patient's therapist guided the interview toward emotionally charged experiences in the patient's life and gave the suggestion concerning the focal concept whenever the patient seemed emotionally aroused. He tried to embed the suggestion in a dynamic interpretation that offered an explanation of the origin of the attitude he was trying to change, indicated its inappropriateness to the patient's present life situation, and suggested a more constructive alternative.

We found that the focal concept showed significantly more variability—that is, shifts in either direction—than the other ones. The crucial question was whether, on the average, the shift in the focal concept was in the direction in which the therapist tried to move it. (Directional shifts in the other concepts were irrelevant, because the therapist did not try to shift them.)

As can be seen from Figure 4, the focal concept did undergo a cumulative shift which reached statistical significance as compared with shift during the pre-ether session, by the third arousal session. Between sessions it drifted back toward its initial level, but the gains were partially preserved.

Since the preparation for the ether sessions involved considerable fuss, such as going without breakfast, wearing no wool and the like, and the sessions themselves were dramatic procedures, and since, furthermore, the researchers knew the purpose of the

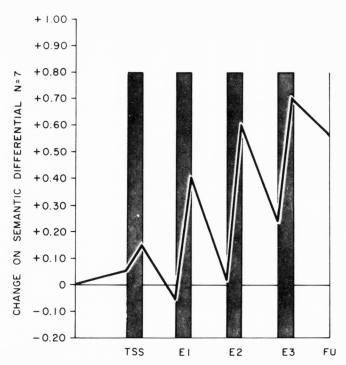

TSS, therapy session with suggestion; E1, 2, 3, ether-arousal sessions with suggestion; FU, follow-up session.

Fig. 4   Change of the Focal Concept during and between Ether Arousal Sessions

study, these findings could be explained by a combination of the placebo effect, compliance with the demand character of the situation, and unwitting transmission of the researchers' expectations.

To rule out these alternatives, we repeated the experiment with the most rigorous controls we could devise.[55] A low-arousal control group was used who received a tranquilizing pill before the experimental sessions and no ether during them. Patients in the high-arousal condition received a blank pill before the sessions and ether during them. The therapists, who conducted regular therapeutic interviews before the experimental sessions and selected the focal concepts, did not know to which group their patients were

55. Hoehn-Saric *et al.* (1972).

assigned. The suggestions during the experimental sessions were given by outside consultants who did not know the design or purpose of the study. A strong ether odor pervaded the experimental room for all patients, so the consultants thought all were receiving ether.

As might be expected, the findings of the controlled study were not as striking as those of the preliminary one, but they did confirm it. The focal concepts showed more lability and shifted more in the desired direction in the high-arousal than in the low-arousal condition. As before, the changes in the focal concept were transient.

Like most experiments, these studies have raised more questions than they answered. Ether both clouds consciousness and produces emotional arousal. Since perceptual confusion is known to increase influencibility, to what extent this accounts for the increased suggestibility of the group receiving ether remains undetermined. In neither study could the timing of the suggestion be sharply controlled, so that it might be given at times when the patient was maximally aroused and at others when he was in a state of relaxation or exhaustion after arousal. Since methods like systematic desensitization and hypnosis rely on relaxation to heighten suggestibility, it may be that the suggestions given during periods when the patient was relaxed may account for the positive findings. In this connection, abreactions can occur spontaneously in states of relaxation,[56] and emotional excitation may be followed by a state of exhaustion resembling relaxation, suggesting that these superficially different states of consciousness may have more in common than appears at first glance.

Despite their limitations, the two experimental studies in conjunction give support to three clinical impressions concerning emotional arousal. The first is that it shakes the psychic structure, as shown by increased lability of the focal concepts in the aroused condition. The second is that it heightens the patient's susceptibility to the therapist's influence, as shown by significant shift in the focal concept in the desired direction under arousal, and the third is that typically the change is transient.

56. Schultz and Luthe (1959).

The last finding confirms the importance of distinguishing between aspects of psychotherapy that cause attitude change and those that maintain it. It may also help to explain the puzzling fact that methods like hypnosis and abreaction wax and wane in popularity. Perhaps their ability to produce change is continually being rediscovered to be followed by disillusionment when the change does not persist. In any case, a form of treatment should not be lightly discarded simply because its benefits are not maintained. The first task is to produce change—the problem of maintaining it is methodologically and conceptually distinct.

Emotional Flooding Therapies

In the clinical field, at least three therapies based on emotional flooding are currently in vogue—implosive therapy, reevaluation counseling, and primal therapy.[57] While each has its own rationale, all are modifications, with embellishments, of Freud's initial conceptualization. In general, their practitioners maintain that traumatic experiences in early life which arouse intensely painful or threatening emotions lead to banishment of the original trauma from consciousness and avoidance of stimuli that are reminiscent of it. Cues closely linked with the event are avoided first, then progressively more distant cues that become associated with them. If the patient cannot avoid the stimulus, he responds to it by reexperiencing the original painful feeling in an attenuated form and develops defensive maneuvers to escape it. These in turn adversely affect his personal relationships, so he becomes progressively more crippled in his activities and more subject to emotions of fear, anger, depression, and the like. At the same time, repression, avoidance, and defensive maneuvers prevent him from correcting his initial distortions or discovering that the original trauma no longer contains anything to frighten or enrage him.

The aim of treatment is that the patient experience the past or present stimuli he fears and avoids at peak vividness, accompanied by maximal emotional discharge, continued to the point of exhaustion. This process of emotional release followed by relaxation

57. Hogan (1968), Jackins (1965), Janov (1970), respectively.

may be beneficial in itself and may also facilitate changes in the patient's attitudes by disorganizing his habitual ways of responding. In addition, as the patient discovers that he can survive the avoided stimulus at full intensity, it and all the cues which have become linked to it lose their power to elicit anxiety, anger, or depression, and he no longer has to avoid them or defend himself against their impact. Thus he is freed from his crippling inhibitions, his sphere of action is widened, and he is better able to enjoy life.

Emotional abreaction or flooding can be accomplished in a variety of ways, but all require a highly supportive setting, a therapist who takes full charge, and various methods of encouraging the patient to remember or fantasy upsetting situations. One, called implosive therapy, has been used for relief of phobias. It involves helping the patient to fantasy encounters with the feared object or situation in ever more exaggerated form until he is emotionally exhausted. The therapist guides the fantasies and gradually pushes them to preposterous extremes. For example, a person with a fear of snakes is asked, after he has fantasied less frightening scenes, to imagine the snake biting his tongue, crawling into his stomach and laying eggs there which hatch into thousands of slimy little snakes which shred his lungs, swim in the blood in his stomach, and so on.

One study compared the effects of a single session of implosive therapy with an equal period of time spent relaxing with neutral imagery in two groups of college girls who feared rats and refused to pick them up. Of twenty-one who received implosive therapy, fourteen picked up the rat, as compared to only two of twenty-two of the girls who relaxed. That the implosive session was, in fact, emotionally arousing was suggested by the finding that it produced marked changes in pulse rate, which did not occur in the control group.[58] This finding is open to many of the reservations concerning student subjects mentioned earlier, but it gains credibility from a clinical study that compared implosive therapy and desensitization with patients suffering from single or multiple phobias. A crossover design was used in which each patient re-

58. Hogan and Kirchner (1967).

ceived six sessions of each form of treatment in sequence, the order being varied from one to another. Patients with multiple phobias responded better to the implosive technique, those with single phobias to desensitization.[59]

While emotional flooding for certain disorders may well have specific healing effects not as readily attainable by other methods, our interest is in the therapeutic features abreactive techniques share with other approaches. Three stand out—enhancement of the therapist's influence, arousal of the patient's expectations, and heightening of the patient's sense of mastery.

Certain altered states of consciousness create hypersuggestibility in their own right. This is enhanced by the fact that a therapist's ability to alter a subject's subjective state by any method is an impressive demonstration of his power and so heightens his credibility and the patient's dependence on him. One abreactive method, primal therapy, deliberately enhances the patient's dependency on the therapist by demanding that he first undergo one or two days of self-imposed isolation, in this resembling Morita therapy.[60] As a result, he develops hunger for stimuli, especially those provided by human contact, and the therapist is the only one to whom he can turn. Prolonged isolation in itself also forces the patient into self-examination, often to the accompaniment of considerable psychic distress, so that even before the therapist starts to work on him, he is emotionally aroused.

Any strong emotion, whether pleasant or unpleasant, may strengthen affectional bonds. Children are often devoted to cruel, brutal parents as are prisoners to harsh jailers. Nor is this phenomenon confined to humans. Puppies develop as strong an attachment to a punitive as to a kind master, and baby monkeys cling tenaciously to manikins that emit frightening noises and blast them with air.[61] Thus it is scarcely surprising that emotional flooding heightens the patient's dependence on his therapist.

That these methods create a strong expectation of benefit hardly needs elaboration. This expectation is fostered by the patient's dependence on his therapist, the therapist's working

59. Boulougouris *et al.* (1971).
60. Kora (1965).
61. Scott (1962).

intensively with him for a long period, and the highly dramatic nature of the procedures. All in all, flooding therapies must appear to the patient as powerful remedies.

Emotional flooding techniques particularly excel in their ability quickly to change the patient's vision of himself from a person who is at the mercy of his emotions to one who can control them. This sense of heightened mastery is fostered by the patient's discovery that he can survive the fantasied, feared situation in a much more intensive form than could possibly occur in real life, as in the example of treatment of snake phobia.

The example also illustrates another way in which the patient's sense of mastery is increased, namely by convincing him that his fears are ridiculous. A technique for achieving this is so-called paradoxical intention, in which the patient is encouraged to try to intensify a feared symptom instead of combating it. For example, a person with cardiac palpitations who was afraid of collapsing was told when he felt an attack coming on, to try to make his heart beat still faster and to make himself collapse. Another person, who was afraid of sweating in public, was advised to show persons how much he could *really* sweat. The next time he felt anticipatory anxiety he told himself: "I only sweated a quart before—this time I'm going to sweat 10 quarts. Of course, the patient finds that he cannot produce the symptom voluntarily, and he soon comes to perceive his fears to be absurd. As a result, in the words of the originator of paradoxical intention, the patient detaches himself from the symptom or puts himself above them. The writer adds: "Such a procedure must make use of the unique potentiality for self-detachment inherent in a sense of humor."[62]

SUMMARY

Directive therapies seem at least as effective as evocative ones for many types of patients, and for some produce improvement more rapidly. Behavior therapies in particular may be much more efficient in combating specific fears such as performance anxiety or phobias of animals, or in extinguishing certain cravings and behav-

62. Frankl (1960). The quote is from p. 523.

ior linked to them. However, these account for only a small proportion of patients seeking help. That techniques of emotional
flooding may be especially therapeutic for some patients is suggested by their recurrent popularity, but, by the same token, their
repeated fall into relative neglect raises questions concerning their
ultimate value. Perhaps it will be proved that they only induce
changes in feelings and attitudes, while other methods may be
required to enable these changes to persist.

Whatever their therapeutic benefits ultimately prove to be, all
directive therapies encourage the therapist to be flexible and
willing to try new approaches, while at the same time requiring
him to evaluate the success of his maneuvers by objective criteria.
This has a salutary effect on the whole field of psychotherapy, and
may be their most enduring contribution.

With respect to their healing features, directive therapies share
with evocative therapies the dependence of success on the therapist's ability to win the patient's trust and inspire his hopes, and to
enlist his active participation in the therapeutic process. Moreover,
despite their conceptualizations, most behavioral therapies rely as
much as evocative treatments on symbolic processes.

Directive therapies differ from evocative ones primarily in
attempting to eliminate all ambiguity instead of fostering it. In all
directive therapies the therapist takes full charge, acts as if he
knows what he is doing at all times, and structures therapy so that
the immediate goals are always clear and the patient can judge his
progress toward them. He also accepts the patient's dependence
and deliberately encourages it instead of subjecting it to analytic
scrutiny, and puts more explicit emphasis on encouraging the
patient to try out in real life what he has learned in therapy. In
contrast with evocative therapies, which strive for a moderate
degree of emotional arousal, flooding techniques try to push it to
maximal intensity.

By focusing on the conquest of specific symptoms, all directive
methods may be more effective than evocative ones in heightening
the patient's sense of mastery, resulting in a general increase in his
self-confidence. As a result, he confronts situations and inner
feelings previously avoided, thereby opening up renewed opportunities for learning and leading to progressive gains.

X GROUP PSYCHOTHERAPIES

"I'm glad they've come without waiting to be asked," she
thought; "I should never have known who were the
right people to invite!"

Through the Looking Glass

INTRODUCTION

As noted in Chapter 2, personalities of individuals are
largely formed by the groups into which they are born
or which they join. Each person constructs his assumptive world through interactions with others and has a
strong need to check the validity of his perceptions and
feelings against theirs. At first, the child is mainly influenced by parents and other elders whom he perceives as
possessing superior power and knowledge. In many
societies, as he grows older and becomes aware of the
split between generations, he becomes increasingly influenced by his age mates, whom he perceives as being
more like himself and as having more experiences in
common with him than he has with his elders.

As life goes on, he acquires some group memberships
by virtue of his position in society and others by voluntary adherence. Both become sources of validation of
his own feelings and perceptions and of his self-esteem.
A person dreads ostracism by groups to which he hun-
gers to belong and experiences a powerful surge of relief
and joy when they accept him. The standards, expecta-

tions, and emotional contagion of such groups can sometimes produce striking and permanent shifts of values and behavior, as in religious conversions, and these same forces can inspire members to extraordinary acts of heroism, self-sacrifice, or villainy of which they would be incapable acting alone. One thinks of the atrocities perpetrated by the staffs of the Nazi extermination camps, for example, or the martyrdom of the early Christians. Indeed, as the second example suggests, in extreme cases, group standards override even such powerful personal needs as self-preservation, as shown by followers of Gandhi and Martin Luther King, who held themselves to nonviolent action even in the face of threats to their lives.

Largely, highly structured organizations formed to represent certain common interests or goals of their members may strongly influence members' attitudes relevant to these interests. The National Rifle Association, for example, influences the views of its members toward gun control laws, and the American Medical Association affects physicians' attitudes toward health maintenance programs, but in both cases the influence is limited primarily to certain issues. Small face-to-face groups like the family, by contrast, exert a powerful pervasive influence on many aspects of the assumptive worlds of their members, and therapy groups share this quality.

Group therapies have flourished particularly in the United States. At first glance, one might be inclined to attribute their popularity to the proverbial gregariousness of Americans, who have always been great joiners of social, fraternal, and political groups; therapy groups might be simply the latest addition to the list. On further reflection, however, the subject appears more complex. A look at our history suggests that our gregariousness is far from being an uncomplicated expression of desire for the company of our fellows. Another, probably more important, motivation may be the need to counteract or dispel feelings of competitiveness and suspicion.

Historically the American continent was settled by people who rejected, or were rejected by, their own societies. Many came to escape economic hardship or political oppression unrelated to their personalities, but many were aggressive, adventurous individualists and rebels. One may speculate that their relations with their fellow men were characterized by considerable antagonism and mistrust. Many moved to frontier areas where the nearest neighbor might be several days' journey away.

Group needs, however, cannot be completely denied, and even frontiersmen needed support from their fellows. Group activities helped them obtain release from emotional tensions produced by the rigors of frontier life. Prominent among such activities were periodic religious revival meetings characterized by intense emotional outbursts, public confession of sins and, for some participants, intimate sexual activities. Such features characterize some contemporary encounter groups. So it may be that to some extent the American hunger for group activities is an effort to compensate for feelings of isolation and suspicion. At any rate, we have always tried to maintain our own masks while being consumed with curiosity about what lies behind the other fellow's.

Popular literature "exposing" the private feuds, treacheries, and lusts behind the bland façade of daily life has always pandered to this need, as has the literature of self-confession. In recent times, motion picutures, radio, and television, which have a more vivid impact and reach much larger audiences than the written word, have added new dimensions to the exploitation of curiosity about others' private lives, reaching a sort of climax in the broadcasting of live group therapy sessions over national television networks.

PERSONAL GROWTH CENTERS AND THE ENCOUNTER GROUP MOVEMENT

The historical American fondness for group activities, whatever its sources, is insufficient to explain the recent explosive proliferation of "personal growth centers" (to use a generic term) that offer all sorts of group activities aimed at promoting spontaneity, joy, feelings of intimacy, and general enrichment of the lives of the participants. Although they cannot be adequately encompassed by one label, for purposes of exposition I shall call them all encounter groups. Possible explanations for their sudden popularity lie in certain special features of contemporary life, which foster "utopian" communities, with which these groups share many fea-tures.[1]

Political scientists have noted that small, face-to-face groups flourish whenever a society is in transition, as in pre-revolutionary France, America, and Russia. At such junctures, they perform at least three functions relevant to psychotherapy. They form oases of the like-minded against the buffetings of the outside world, forums in which members feel that they have some power to influence each other, and nuclei of a counterculture which ham-mers out the new values and political forms that eventually super-sede the old ones. Perhaps the current popularity of encounter groups implies that we are in a pre-revolutionary stage. In any case, Carl Rogers has characterized these new group activities as "the most significant social invention of the century,"[2] and indeed they may prove to be the most promising means of coun-teracting certain damaging features of contemporary life, espe-cially alienation from the past and from one's fellow man.

Our alienation from the past follows from extensive, rapid, and unprecedented changes in the conditions of life. No one can pre-dict how instantaneous, worldwide mass communication, nuclear weapons, ecological damage, or trips to the moon and planets will ultimately affect our habits and values, but certainly they will force changes in many time-hallowed rules of conduct, including those governing human relations. In the 1920s, the philosopher Alfred North Whitehead remarked to his students that they were the first generation in human history that could not rely on the precepts of its grandfathers. Since then, the pace of change has accelerated to the point that a youth today can scarcely rely on the precepts of his older brother. Projections of the future depend on the assumption that past conditions will continue to hold, so disconnection from the past implies disconnection from the future. As a result, to a greater extent than ever before, we live in an uncertain present, unable to make plans and plagued by feelings of insecurity.

1. Jacobs (1971).
2. Rogers (1968), p. 268.

The mobility of many Americans and other features of American society, furthermore, have deprived us of the emotional security formerly provided by the extended family, enduring marriages, and small, stable work groups. The shallow and shifting sociability of the residential development, the office, the committee, and the club, being tainted with undercover competition for popularity, power and prestige, offers no adequate substitute.

James Thurber summed up the prevailing state of mind in one of his "Fables for Our Time," which tells of a "fairly intelligent" fly who wisely refused to land on a spider web because there were no other flies in it, but lit on a piece of fly paper crowded with flies because he assumed they were dancing. His moral is: "There's no safety in numbers, or in anything else."[3]

One way in which persons seek to counter this uncertainty is to experience the timeless verities through the mystical experience. Another, the route of some encounter groups, is to seek reassurance through intense, sharply timebound interactions with other persons. Encounter groups provide experiences through which members can drop their masks and enter into open, emotionally intense, honest interactions with one another. In this way, each gains a more complete and accurate awareness of the effects of his own behavior on others and of theirs on him. Concomitantly, he becomes more accessible and accepting of his own inner feelings. To this extent, encounter groups resemble the therapy groups to be discussed below. Some go beyond therapy groups in seeking to produce peak experiences, not unlike those of religious revivalism or the psychedelic experience sometimes produced by consciousness-altering drugs. Both types of groups, however, are alike in seeking to enable their members to achieve greater self-acceptance and acceptance of others, with a resulting increase in spontaneity and happiness.[4]

It has been suggested that all humans must struggle against three basic fears—fear of loss of health, fear of alienation from others, and fear that life is meaningless.[5] Since feelings of cosmic despair and social alienation are often two sides of the same coin, methods

3. Thurber (1939), p. 13.
4. Rogers (1971).
5. Masserman (1971).

which seek primarily to relieve one also affect the other. Religious revivals foster a strong sense of fellowship, and persons may emerge from mystical experiences feeling a greater sense of unity not only with the Universe, but with their fellow men. Similarly, the intense, intimate interactions fostered by encounter groups may enhance or restore faith that existence has meaning and that life is good. As a result, many members come away from a successful encounter group with a sense of having had a rewarding experience and some may be able to function better socially. There is little evidence, however, that encounter groups produce any deep changes in the personalities of most participants.[6] On the other hand, these groups can seriously upset some members, and the bad effects may endure for some time.[7] A common source of difficulty is the "reentry problem" created by collisions between the new attitudes fostered by the counterculture of the group and the expectations of family and friends.

Reflecting the competitiveness and commercialism of American culture, leaders of encounter groups compete frantically to devise new, sensational procedures to maintain the appeal of novelty. We shall resist the temptation to explore the colorful and often bizarre world of nude marathons, sensory awareness exercises, Gestalt confrontations, and the like,[8] although we recognize that many of them contain some admixture of promising innovations.

Since our interest is primarily in therapy groups, we may conclude this hasty glance at encounter groups with a brief consideration of features distinguishing them from therapy groups and mention of some of their procedures that seem to be therapeutic advances. The differences between therapy and encounter groups spring primarily from differences in their target populations. Members of therapy groups seek relief from distressing and disabling symptoms. Members of encounter groups are presumably seeking, not relief from specific symptoms, but enhancement of experience. This is not to deny that many candidates for therapy groups also seek out encounter groups, nor that many can derive

6. Parloff (1970).
7. Yalom and Lieberman (1971).
8. See Howard (1970) for a readable, perceptive survey and Back (1972) for a comprehensive description and theoretical analysis.

benefits from them. But by and large the major difference between the two target populations is that those of therapy groups have more to unlearn and, being more anxious, are less able to respond positively to new experiences.

Whether this is a tenable distinction remains to be seen. It does imply certain differences, however, in the two types of groups, especially with respect to responsibility for what transpires in them. Since the participants in an encounter group have not come to be healed, the trainer can deny responsibility for their reactions during the experience or after it is over. Moreover, he can participate on an essentially equal footing with the other members and can behave as one. Because their members are ostensibly not trying to solve personal problems, encounter groups can be of brief duration and all members can stop at the same time.

Participants in a therapy group look to the therapist to relive their sufferings, so they may need to continue for differing periods to achieve maximum benefit. Nor can or should the therapist divest himself of his role as healer. How much this affects the nature of his own participation, including revelation of his own reactions, is a matter of debate, but most would agree that he must keep his role distinct from that of the members, and his responsibility for their welfare is not limited to the group sessions.

Two features introduced by encounter groups, which may well represent therapeutic advances, are filtering into the armamentarium of group therapists. The first is the use of "marathon" sessions to speed up group formation and facilitate emotional arousal.[9] The second is the rediscovery of the body. They have reminded us that full communication involves more than talk, that mental states are reflected in bodily postures so that reduction of bodily tensions may reduce psychic ones, and especially that touching and caressing need not always have sexual connotations and can be powerfully consoling.[10] Along the same lines, the value system of encounter groups,, which affirms that the pleasures of sensuous experience are legitimate and valuable, helps to overcome the alienation from one's own body or rejection of it characteristics of certain overinhibited psychiatric patients.

9. Stoller (1968). Sohl (1967) has written a fictionalized but essentially accurate account of a weekend marathon.
10. Schutz (1967).

DIRECTIVE AND EVOCATIVE
GROUP THERAPIES

Therapy groups in the narrower sense can be divided into those composed of pre-existing groups such as families and those consisting of strangers. Since many of the ills deemed amenable to psychotherapy are caused or maintained in part by self-perpetuating distortions of communication involving the patient and his family, it makes sense to include the family in the therapeutic purview. Today, in contrast with the early days of psychoanalysis in which family members were rigidly excluded, many psychotherapists include the patient's family in therapy to some degree.

Family therapy in the narrower sense treats all members of the family simultaneously, with a view to exposing and correcting their mutual misunderstandings and aggravating behaviors. It has developed into a flourishing field,[11] and one innovator even includes members of the patient's social network—including employers, colleagues, friends, and neighbors—in the therapy group.[12]

Although naturally occurring groups require some differences in procedure from those composed of strangers, the therapeutic forces mobilized by both seem essentially similar, so we shall consider only therapy groups composed of strangers.[13] This chapter concerns outpatient groups. In the next chapter, groups of hospitalized patients will be considered as components of the total therapeutic program of the hospital. The principles and methods of group therapy that are identical with those of individual approaches will not be considered again. Rather, we shall concentrate on the differences between individual treatment and group therapy introduced by the participation of fellow sufferers.

Like individual forms of psychotherapy, group therapies can be roughly characterized as directive and evocative. Group forms of directive therapy can be applied to groups consisting of as many as fifty or more members, although the groups are usually smaller. All firmly guide the transactions of the members, either through the direct leadership of the therapist or through the group code

---

11. Ackerman (1970); Satir (1967).
12. Speck and Rueveni (1969).
13. An excellent overview of the field is Yalom (1970).

that he has established. Thus these groups offer members certain selected ways of relating to others that combat their perceptual distortions, lift their spirits, and help them develop and practice social skills. Many forms explicitly cultivate a strong sense of group cohesiveness through rituals, testimonials, and formal group-recognition of members' progress.

Peer self-help psychotherapy groups[14] typically use directive approaches. Alcoholics Anonymous, a prominent example, is said to help about three-fourths of those who join.[15] This movement is run solely by and for alcoholics. Group meetings are devoted almost entirely to inspirational testimonials by members who describe the horrors of life as an alcoholic and tell how much better things are since they stopped drinking. As alcoholics are comfortable only with each other, they tend to congregate in bars, where their drinking habits are reinforced. The groups of Alcoholics Anonymous afford them the same type of companionship in a group whose standards support total abstinence.

Another health-promoting standard, which combats the alcoholic's unrealistic feelings of omnipotence, is the insistence that he admit the craving for alcohol to be stronger than himself so that he must rely on forces greater than himself to conquer it. He is also required to make restitution to those he has harmed, which counteracts demoralizing feelings of guilt and remorse and helps to restore his self-respect. Members reinforce their good resolves by seeking out and trying to help other alcoholics, not only strengthening their self-esteem but also reminding themselves vividly of the fate in store for them if they resume drinking.

A similar type of directive group conducted by the members themselves is Recovery Incorporated.[16] Originally members of this movement were ex-patients from mental hospitals, and the groups were conducted by the late Dr. Abraham Low. After his death, the movement has continued autonomously, using his writings as its guide. Membership has come to include all types of mental patients capable of functioning in the community. Meetings start with a reading from Dr. Low's book, followed by testimonials in

14. See Hurvitz (1970) and Scheff (1972).
15. Alcoholics Anonymous (1953).
16. Wechsler (1960).

which members describe how the principles of Recovery Incorporated have helped them to handle certain problems more effectively. These testimonials and the subsequent discussion follow a
prescribed form and make much use of slogans. This type of group
gives direct guidance and fosters group solidarity through repeated
affirmation of common values and the use of a common language.
Like Alcoholics Anonymous, the use of testimonials encourages a
hopeful outlook.

These two programs differ, however, in one crucial respect.
Alcoholics Anonymous insists that the alcoholic admit that he is
powerless to control his drinking; the cornerstone of Recovery
Incorporated is that the patient can overcome his symptoms by
will power. As its founder put it: "The first step in psychotherapeutic management is to convince [patients] that the sensation
can be endured, the impulse controlled, the obsession checked."[17]

This difference in philosophy may be justified by the fact that
the alcoholic has tried and failed innumerable times to master his
inner distress alone, whereas the neurotic typically has never tried
because he has assumed the effort to be futile. To encourage the
alcoholic to believe that he can control his symptoms is simply to
reinforce his habit of failing; to encourage the neurotic to do so
may open new possibilities for success.

A highly elaborated set of group therapeutic methods that
combine directive and evocative techniques is known by the term
"psychodrama." In these methods, originated by Dr. J. L. Moreno,
the patient acts out, or watches others act out, a personal
problem.[18] Other patients and therapists serve as both actors and
audience, and the patient's therapist is the stage director. To a
varying degree he helps the patient choose the problem, selects the
other players, suggests the dialogue and action, and guides the
discussion in which the audience participates.

With institutionalized patients, psychodrama tends to be highly
structured, as described in the next chapter. With outpatients, the
psychodrama often has an evocative component. A patient is
encouraged to improvise the acting out of a personal problem

17. Low (1950), p. 19.
18. Moreno (1971).

involving persons emotionally close to him such as parents or spouse. He calls on others to help him and tells them how to play the roles that he assigns them. As the playlet proceeds, the actors become increasingly spontaneous and emotionally involved. Frequently members of the audience participate vicariously so that the situation may develop an intense emotional impact for many of the participants, which forms the basis for the discussion following the psychodrama. Incidentally, many features of encounter groups, including role playing, body contact, and bodily modes of expression, can be traced to psychodrama.

Evocative group therapies strive to promote members' self-knowledge through free discussion and honest self-revelation.[19] This requires small, face-to-face groups, consisting of not more than eight members, in which free interaction is encouraged. Through mutual examination of their transactions with important persons in their lives, with each other, and with the group leader in a supportive emotional atmosphere, patients gain insights that help them to correct aspects of their assumptive worlds. The absence of formal structure coupled with pressure toward candid self-expression creates many occasions for arousing members emotionally. At the same time it allows considerable latitude for experimentation. Thus members learn how they appear to each other, and are motivated to make suitable modifications in their behavior.

An example of the kind of therapeutic experience that can happen in a free-interaction group occurred in a group of six housewives with neurotic difficulties.[20] The meetings were very lively, with much interaction among the members and free expression of feelings toward each other and the male psychiatrist who conducted the group.

Mrs. Smith, the central patient of this episode, was a thirty-two-year-old housewife who complained of nervousness, gagging, and fullness in the stomach. She connected her symptoms directly with her mother, a demanding, complaining woman who, the patient felt, favored her younger sister. The mother brought all her complaints to the patient, asked her advice, then rejected it. She

19. Descriptions of representative types of free-interaction groups are given by Foulkes (1964); Frank and Powdermaker (1959); and Yalom (1970).
20. The example is modified from Frank and Ascher (1956).

expressed strongly ambivalent feelings toward her mother: "I love her so much, I resent what she is doing." She could not tell her mother how she felt and was ashamed of her attitude. Her stomach cramps and jittery feelings came on when she felt anger at her mother and was unable to express it. She often had anxiety attacks when her mother criticized her. Her general attitude seemed to be that "you must not show your feelings or people will take advantage of you."

In the group she participated actively from the start, at first in a superficial way. She frequently spoke of problems with her mother and gradually came to identify Mrs. Jones, an older woman, with her. As the result of certain experiences in the group, she came to resent Mrs. Jones for not appreciating her, but could mention this only when Mrs. Jones was not present. At the same time she wanted to help her, thus practically duplicating her attitudes toward her mother.

In the course of months Mrs. Smith's symptoms improved. Her feelings toward her mother had eased to the extent that "I don't get sick when she makes the same old nuisance of herself," yet she still could not express her resentment. She took the lead in focusing the group discussion on sexual difficulties, over the protests of Mrs. Jones.

The day before the seventy-second meeting (in the nineteenth month of treatment), Mrs. Jones called Mrs. Smith and told her she wasn't coming to the group because Mrs. Smith talked about sex all the time. In reporting this to the group, Mrs. Smith said that Mrs. Jones was acting exactly like her mother and that she had felt frightened and resentful after the telephone conversation. She added that she still felt extremely guilty and could talk this way only because Mrs. Jones was absent. Scarcely had these words left her lips when Mrs. Jones walked in, looking deeply distressed. She wore no make-up, her hair was stringy, and, as she collapsed in her chair, she seemed about to weep. Mrs. Smith's tension visibly mounted until suddenly she burst into tears and began screaming hysterically: "I caused it, I know it's my fault! I caused it, I caused it! I know it's my fault!"

To reduce the almost unbearable tension, the doctor asked Mrs. Smith to explain her outburst. Mrs. Smith said: "It's the way I feel

about my mother. I know I caused her to feel the way she does."
Mrs. Jones listened carefully and then said calmly: "What makes
you think you upset me? It's something entirely different." She
then described some recent temper outbursts against her husband
and son, then resentment at her husband for his indifference.
While she spoke, Mrs. Smith brightened up more and more as she
came to see that her assumption of responsibility for Mrs. Jones'
upset was baseless. At the following meeting, Mrs. Smith said she
felt a good deal better after having discovered that Mrs. Jones had
not been mad at her but was upset at something else. The next
week she indicated that she no longer felt obligated to listen to her
mother's complaints or give in to her demands.

It was not until two months later that Mrs. Smith was able to
criticize Mrs. Jones to her face. She did so by laughingly telling
Mrs. Jones, who was complaining, that she was just trying to make
everyone feel bad because she was feeling bad. Some weeks later
the therapist noted: "Mrs. Smith can take Mrs. Jones much better
and there is a good deal of warm exchange between the two."

In this example, Mrs. Smith, under the impact of her group
experiences, gradually became less fearful of and guilty toward
Mrs. Jones, who represented her mother, until finally she was able
to defy her openly by continuing to discuss details of her sexual
difficulties. Mrs. Jones' emotional upset seemed to confirm her
worst fears, but this was immediately followed by the startling
discovery that Mrs. Jones was really disturbed about something
quite unconnected with Mrs. Smith. This experience, which helped
Mrs. Smith to see that her feelings were not as destructive to
others as she had feared, was followed by her increasingly direct
criticism of Mrs. Jones, leading to a much better relationship between them. Concomitantly, she gained increased emotional
independence from her mother.

Therapeutic Features of Evocative
Group Therapies

Let us now examine more closely certain features of evocative
groups related to their therapeutic efficacy, using the conventional
free-interactive type as representative. Since most patients who

benefit from free-interaction groups have already participated in a wide range of groups based on school, work, common interest, social activites, and the like without losing their symptoms, evocative therapy groups must have features not present in those of daily life. Three properties can be distinguished.

The first, shared by all forms of therapy groups, is that they place no weight on success or achievement.[21] In fact, the ticket of admission is precisely that one has failed to meet certain problems of living. When persons first enter a therapy group, they tend to evaluate each other according to the standards prevailing in the wider society. While these standards never completely vanish, as a group continues, members gain status less on the basis of outside accomplishments than on their sincerity and ability to discuss their own and each other's problems constructively. Acceptance by their fellows is based more on what they are than on what they have accomplished. The therapy group, like Robert Frost's "home," is "something you somehow haven't to deserve."[22]

The two other characteristics distinguishing therapy groups from other group activities apply to evocative groups only. Both are ground rules. The first encourages "uninhibited conversation."[23] Members are expected to drop their façades and reveal, as honestly as possible, feelings about themselves and each other. Openness inevitably leads to emotionally arousing confrontation and conflict, so a second ground rule of these groups requires members to continue communicating in the face of antagonism. As will be considered more fully below, these characteristics enhance opportunities for learning.

In accepting members without regard to failures and other imperfections and in provoking and permitting free expression of feeling, therapy groups resemble families, but differ from them in affording opportunities, incentives, and means for identifying and breaking up patterns of distorted communications. In families these interactions are characteristically self-aggravating because each party responds to the other in ways that reinforce the other's

21. Dreikurs (1951).
22. Frost (1915).
23. The phrase is used by C. A. Mace in his introduction to Foulkes and Anthony (1957).

behavior. Therapy groups enable members to identify and sometimes escape from such traps.

Free-interaction groups have certain therapeutic potentials not present at all, or not present to the same degree, in individual therapies. They also have certain drawbacks, which will be considered presently.

In general, interactions among members and between members and the group provide members with new information, combat their demoralization, support their self-esteem, arouse them emotionally, confront them sharply with discrepancies between their assumptive systems and social reality, and facilitate transfer of gains into daily life.

In individual therapy, the only source of information is the therapist; in the group, other members also serve as sources of feedback, as models, and as guides. The therapist's ability to serve as a model is limited by the patient's view of him as very different from himself. In the group, the patient is more likely to find models he can use. Each can learn from observing how others handle contingencies arising in the group and hearing how they have coped with living problems resembling his own. Although seeing other group members improve may make some members discouraged or envious, more typically it inspires emulation and raises hopes.

Feedback from others concerning their impressions of one's own behavior and their reactions to it can aid self-understanding and provide a powerful incentive for change. In daily life persons can seldom afford to be strictly honest with one another. In fact, the social system could probably not survive if everyone always said exactly what he felt. Persons conceal or distort their true feelings about each other out of diverse motives such as, for example, desire to avoid hurting the other person, fear of his retaliation, or wish to manipulate him. Persons who come to psychotherapy characteristically behave in ways that bother other people, often without knowing it, and have also come to distrust their responses.

As the ground rule that feelings be honestly expressed takes effect, however, group members increasingly trust one another. As they come to accept one anothers' statements as true reflections of underlying attitudes, they profit increasingly from feedback concerning the impression they are making.

As sources of feedback, group members may be less useful than the therapist because their perceptions are more apt to be biased by their own problems and preconceptions, and, especially in initial meetings, their tolerance for each other may be relatively low. Since they lack the therapist's authority, however, any advice or interpretation that is not helpful can be more easily rejected than can similar statements from the therapist.

On the other hand, a patient may be able to sense another's feelings and express them more comprehensibly than the therapist because he is more like his fellow group members or has had similar experiences. For the same reasons, patients can sometimes transmit the therapist's views to each other better than he himself can do it.

Along the same lines, acceptance by patients may be more effective than acceptance by the therapist because the therapist is seen as having no choice—his professional role demands that he be accepting. This was vividly illustrated by a nineteen-year-old Catholic man who was overwhelmed with guilt over masturbation. After several individual sessions in which I tried in vain to reassure him, I placed him in a group of older men. He remained mute for a few sessions until finally, with the encouragement of other members, he "confessed" his secret. The other members, some of whom were also Catholics, showed no shock or surprise. At the same time they did not minimize the importance of the problem or the justification for his guilt feelings but discussed the problem seriously with him. His depression had vanished by the next session and he soon stopped coming. A follow-up interview a year later revealed that he had maintained his improvement. He attributed his cure to the group session and remembered an identifying feature of each member. When asked why my reassurance had been ineffective he replied: "It is good to have things come from a bunch of guys. The therapist lives in his own little world."

Support can also be conveyed by criticism or even anger. Many mental patients are accustomed to being pitied, scorned, or ignored. Such a patient may feel an angry blast from a group member as supportive because it shows that he is taken seriously enough to arouse anger. Moreover, criticism can be supportive if it implies that the critic knows the person he criticizes is capable of doing better.

The similarities of group patients to one another create a power-ful therapeutic component of group therapy that has been termed "universality."[24] The demoralization of many patients is aggra-vated by feelings of isolation and the belief that their problems are unique. Practically all members of therapy groups. including those who are outwardly very successful, characteristically report that one of the main values of the group experience is hearing from other members' own lips that they have similar problems or weak-nesses. It is as if everyone, while suspecting that others see through his own façade of competence and poise, take others' masks at face value. Thus the mutual self-revelation that occurs in therapy groups, after the first shock, can bring enormous relief.

A morale-enchancing feature unique to therapy groups is the incentive and opportunity they afford for members to help one another. Altruism combats morbid self-centeredness, enhances the individual's feelings of kinship with others, and strengthens his sense of personal worth and power. As noted earlier, many forms of primitive healing require that the patient do something for others, and shrines like Lourdes encourage pilgrims to pray not for themselves but for one another.

Everybody needs to feel that he is needed. Mental patients have characteristically felt, or been made to feel, that they are a burden to others. Individual therapy offers little opportunity to dispel this feeling, since help flows only from the therapist to the patient. The relationship is complementary, not reciprocal. All the patient can do for the therapist is pay his bills promptly, gratify him by reporting improvement, and recommend him to friends. Rarely, the therapist may be willing to accept a present.

In group therapy, each member can give as well as receive help. Participants find they can help each other by comparing experi-ences or giving useful insights or advice. This discovery is often a great aid to regaining a sense of personal worth.

Groups not only provide opportunities for altruism, they also provide many occasions for conflict.[25] In addition to being emo-tionally arousing, conflicts can provide important learning experi-

24. Yalom (1970), pp. 10-11.
25. Frank (1957b).

ences. They confront members with distortions in their assumptive systems and increase their self-assurance by teaching them how to assert themselves and how to withstand antagonisms.

Before considering some causes and functions of group conflicts in more detail, we may pause to note that merely attending a group is apt to be more tension-arousing than seeing a therapist privately, because it is a public acknowledgement of the need for psychotherapy. In addition to this source of discomfort, initial group sessions are characterized by the tension strangers feel when thrown together for the first time. This is heightened by members' knowledge that they are expected to reveal intimate details of their lives to other persons whom they derogate. For to the extent that each feels contemptuous of himself he is likely to have the same feeling for others perceived to be like himself.

In general, conflicts in therapy groups are generated by disparities in the outlooks of group members based on their different positions in society, on rivalries generated by aspects of the group situation itself, and on distortions arising from individual life experiences. Examples of sources of conflict grounded in social realities would be differences in viewpoint between a southern white and a northern black or between an employer and a worker. Conflicts arising from the properties of the group itself would be rivalries for such group roles as the sickest, the therapist's favorite, or the group leader, especially when, as in these examples, the prize is a position that only one member can hold at a time.

The most important conflicts arise from distortions based on members' personal life histories. Two common categories are so-called mirror and transference reactions.[26] The first term refers to a person's tendency to detect and disapprove a trait in someone else that he dislikes in himself, before he recognizes it as his own. An example was the mutual antagonism of two Jewish members of a group. One ostensibly gloried in his background and the other tried to deny it. After bitterly criticizing each other for months, each recognized that he secretly entertained the same feelings he was attacking in his antagonist.

26. The examples of mirror and transference reactions are described and discussed more fully in Powdermaker and Frank (1953), pp. 237–39 and 245–48.

By transference is meant the tendency to transfer to an inappropriate object those feelings that once were or still are appropriate to persons important in one's life, usually members of the family. Members may experience the same emotional reactions to other group members and the therapist in the group as they do their counterparts outside.

The example of Mrs. Jones cited earlier illustrates this phenomenon. Another example was an interchange between two group members, one of whom described his pleasure in fantasying different roles, especially after he had had a few drinks. The other became furious at him for "living in a dream world." It soon turned out that the angry man had an alcoholic mother who lived in a dream world and whom he had been vainly trying to reform for years. She was the real target of his feelings.

In contrast with individual therapy, in which only the therapist can evoke transference and mirror reactions, the group affords multiple stimuli for them. Since only repsonses that are operative in a situation can be changed by it, provision of the opportunities for the members to experience such reactions in a context encouraging change represents one of the therapy group's major therapeutic potentials.

As the central figure of the group, the therapist arouses transference reactions at least as strong as those in individual therapy, and these may be especially helpful in illuminating attitudes toward authority figures or help-givers.

The context of a free-interaction group seems to enable patients to experience and express angry or fearful feelings toward the therapist more promptly than in individual treatment. This is probably because they feel both protected and supported by the other patients. A member who attacks the therapist may be a spokesman for others as well, and the public character of the proceedings is a good guarantee against the therapist's feared retaliation.

In two different groups, for example, a patient whose parents had been brutal and unpredictable never sat next to the therapist. He always made sure that at least one other patient intervened. When asked about this, both patients said they did it to preclude the therapist's striking them. One added that he thought the therapist kept a loaded revolver in his desk drawer! Neither had dared to mention these feelings in individual sessions.

In short, evocative therapy groups provide multiple occasions to confront members with discrepancies between their assumptive worlds and objective reality. The ground rules that members should express their feelings without holding back and that they must continue communicating despite conflict maximize the likelihood that they will learn something from these confrontations, unlike similar situations in real life. Ordinarily antagonists break off communication. This prevents discovery of distortions that might have contributed to their hostility, or of ways of resolving it.[27]

In the group, the presence of the therapist and other members helps antagonists to obey the ground rules by implicitly guaranteeing that matters will not get out of hand. Furthermore, those not involved in the conflict can support both antagonists or, if need be, support the weaker one. As the conflict continues, each protagonist brings up more and more material to bolster his position and displays his characteristic ways of conducting conflict. Through this process each learns more about himself as well as about his opponent. Finally, through prolonged group conflicts each antagonist may learn to express himself more effectively. At the same time each gains self-confidence from the realization that he can maintain his ground in the face of opposition. This may help both to develop more effective ways of resolving disagreements or conducting interpersonal conflicts outside of therapy.

Patients are apt to react especially strongly to issues about which they have inner conflicts, and so become embroiled with others over them. Individual therapy helps the patient to develop more harmonious relations with his fellows by resolving his internal tensions. Group therapy offers an opportunity to reduce inner tensions by working through their externalized manifestations. Although this may sound like a reversal of cause and effect, it need not be so, because the feelings of anger and frustration produced by chronic unresolved conflicts with others may be the chief impediments to resolving the corresponding internal ones.

27. Newcomb (1947).

In short, free-interaction groups engender crises—discoveries that one's habitual ways of coping are inadequate to the occasion—accompanied by strong emotional arousal. Such an event sometimes disrupts the patient's habitual patterns and provides the impetus for a new solution;[28] that is, it can be one form of *kairos*—the auspicious moment which, if seized, can result in sharp changes in attitudes and behavior.[29]

Under favorable circumstances all the phenomena described contribute to a final therapeutic property of all types of therapy groups, which may be the one most essential to their success. This is group cohesiveness, a property that individual therapy cannot possess.[30] Group cohesiveness develops out of a shared history of supportive and tension-arousing experiences such as those just outlined, and makes members increasingly able to tolerate the more disturbing ones.

The more cohesive a group is the more its standards influence its members, not only during group sessions but between them, and the more effectively it combats demoralization. Hence it is not surprising that deliberate efforts by the therapist to speed the development of group cohesiveness have been shown to accelerate both symptomatic improvement and desired personality change in the group's members.[31]

Since therapy groups are composed of emotionally ill persons, the questions arise as to why evocative types do not become cohesive on the basis of unhealthy group standards. It has been surmised that "the deepest reason why [group] patients can reinforce each other's normal reactions and wear down and correct each other's neurotic reactions is that *collectively they constitute the very Norm*, from which, individually they deviate."[32]

Less speculative is the probability that a group can become really cohesive only by accepting and incorporating the standards of the therapist. Conceivably members could develop cohesiveness by using him as a common enemy and this may, indeed, be a phase of group information. Since they depend on him for help, how-

28. Whitaker and Lieberman (1964), especially pp. 143-85.
29. Kelman (1969).
30. Frank (1957a); Yalom (1970), pp. 36-59.
31. Liberman (1971).
32. Foulkes (1948), p. 29. (Author's italics and capitalization.)

ever, they cannot afford to demolish him. A therapy group cannot remain unanimously hostile to its leader for long, and he soon will find members coming to his defense.

Another puzzling question is why evocative therapy groups become cohesive at all. Since psychiatric patients typically derogate themselves, it is hard to understand why they should want to belong to a group consisting of other patients, much less gain enhanced morale from membership in such a group. Some may achieve self-esteem by maintaining that joining a therapy group shows them to be superior to other patients who lack the good sense to do the same. In addition, membership in a cohesive group enhances each member's feeling of personal power, for the group in some way represents an extension of himself. Each exerts an influence on its functioning, if only by the fact that his absence makes a difference. The sense of shared responsibility for the group's activities enhances feelings of competence and may account for the fact that dependence on a therapy group does not seem to be as demoralizing to patients as a similar degree of dependence on the therapist would be.

In any case, as compared with individual therapy, a therapy group increases the likelihood that the changes it produces in its members will endure, because persons tend to internalize the standards of the groups with which they identify themselves. Even when a member is away from the group, he carries it around inside himself, as it were, and when the need to make decisions related to the group's standards arises, these are apt to influence his choice. This may occur without his awareness, or he may be consciously influenced by a desire not to let his fellow members down, and this may be reinforced by his anticipation of having to confess his deviation at the next meeting.

This consideration brings us to the reentry problem. As already suggested, psychiatric symptoms are interpersonal tactics, and by the time a patient comes to therapy his patterns of interpersonal behavior have been built into the family equilibrium. If he changes, others must change also, so his improvement may pose a threat to their own adjustment.[33] As a result, family members may more or less unwittingly oppose a patient's gains, and his

33. For an example, see pp. 231–32 above.

ability to maintain them may depend on the extent to which he has internalized the group's standards and has learned, through his group experiences, how to conduct conflict.

In this connection, the therapy group more closely resembles daily life than does individual treatment. Other members are more like persons the patient meets in the community than is the therapist, and their responses may be better guides of what he can expect outside the group. In many respects the group is Society in miniature. This makes it a good testing ground and enables its members more readily to transfer to daily life behavior that was successful in it.

The superior power of a group to produce enduring change is shown most clearly by patients who make permanent shifts in their assumptive systems and behavior following group discussions after individual sessions had had no effect. The young man with masturbation guilt is an example. Another, which may serve to conclude this section, because it ties together many therapeutic aspects of groups, is afforded by Mr. Angelo, a thirty-year-old married man who had had individual treatment for about three years before entering a group. His major complaint was that he had "no urge to live" because he knew that he suffered from progressive familial loss of hearing. Several members of his family were already severely affected. It soon appeared that the main source of his distress lay not in the disability itself but in his family's attitude toward it, which he shared. All of them regarded it as a disgrace, to be concealed from others. As a result they were often teased or scorned for their seeming inattentiveness, and they misinterpreted these reactions as confirming their conviction that their affliction was disgraceful.

Although Mr. Angelo learned a lot about himself in individual treatment, and this particular problem was discussed repeatedly, his chronic depression did not lift, and he continued to try to conceal his handicap. In the group his reticence very gradually diminished, and finally in the thirty-sixth meeting he finally overcame his fears sufficiently to reveal the whole story. In the process he mentioned a new fear that had never come up in individual sessions, namely that when he became completely deaf he would be helpless and his wife would abandon him. As he spoke, he burst into tears. Of course no one in the group mocked him, and no one saw his affliction as disgraceful. Instead they were supportive and reassuring. The next day he left on vacation (the imminence of a break in treatment may have precipitated his self-revelation), and in sharp contrast to previous occasions he immediately told some new-found acquaintances about his disability. He enjoyed his vacation as never before. Thereafter he gained ground steadily as he accepted the idea of dealing with his deafness like any other handicap. His long-standing depression lifted almost completely in spite of the fact that his hearing was obviously deteriorating, and he soon terminated therapy. Except for infrequent transient flurries of depression, each relieved by one or two interviews, his improvement has been maintained for many years.

Apparently the attitudes of the group convinced Mr. Angelo, as his psychiatrist could not, that his conviction that others regarded his loss of hearing as a disgrace was unfounded. On the basis of this, he experimented outside the group and the experiment was successful, leading to his progressive recovery.

This example illustrates several other points. Mr. Angelo was aided to speak out by his knowledge that the group did not derogate admissions of weakness and difficulties and by the group code, which stressed honest revelation of feelings. This also helped him to trust the responses of his fellow members and since they represented the larger society, he could easily generalize this experience to other situations. The aspect of confession of a guilty secret followed by reaffirmation of the group's acceptance, which plays such a large part in religious healing, was also implicitly present. The result was a major beneficial change in the patient's assumptive world.

This example also illustrates a point relevant to all psychotherapy, namely that an interpretation which shows the patient his contribution to an interpersonal problem that he had attributed exclusively to a malign fate may increase his sense of power to do something about it.

Drawbacks and Disadvantages of Evocative Groups

One disadvantage of free-interaction groups compared with individual therapy—invasion of privacy—has not proved to be important, at least in the United States. To be sure, members initially often hesitate to reveal feelings or experiences of which they are ashamed, but so do they in individual therapy; and many patients may find a confession to their fellow group members easier to contemplate than one to the therapist in the privacy of his office. In any case, in a mature group, no topic is too "hot" to handle.

A more serious potential drawback of free-interaction groups is that they may fail to develop the necessary degree of cohesiveness. Directive groups actively foster the development of cohesiveness through structured activities, insistence on members giving only favorable reports, and the like. Free-interaction groups lack these safeguards, so the therapist may sometimes be unable to prevent disruptive and discouraging activities. Within the free-interaction framework, he cannot always establish group standards early enough to inhibit members' complaining or counteract the censorious judgmental reactions sometimes characteristic of the "peer court" of early meetings.[34] Since cohesiveness takes awhile to develop, the group may never get off the ground and the drop-out rate in early meetings of a group is usually high.[35]

The most important potential drawback of free-interaction groups is the same as one of their strongest potential assets—their ability to engender crises. A crisis does not always inspire the patient to rise to a new solution. It may cause him to get worse or to flee. Unless anxiety, resentment, guilt, and similar feelings aroused by the group experience are counteracted by group support, the situation may become so unpleasant for a member that he quits. Since in directive groups the leader actively guides and protects members, severely uneasy or disturbed patients may tolerate them better than evocative ones.

In short, one of the hazards of evocative groups for certain patients, is that stress may outrun support, causing the patient to drop out, and perhaps even harming him. An example is afforded by a middle-age spinster who had devoted her life to caring for other family members, at considerable emotional cost to herself. She dealt with her resentment and frustrations by complaining constantly about her health. Her complaints made life tolerable by

34. Bach (1954).
35. Nash et al. (1957); Sethna and Harrington (1971).

eliciting some attention and affection from her relatives and enabling her to express her anger indirectly. This martyr-like behavior, however, was unacceptable to the group members, who persistently ignored or criticized her. At the same time group discussions stimulated her repressed hostile and sexual feelings. Her anger at her mother reached the point that she struck the senile old lady on two occasions, creating intense guilt, which the group did not assuage. At this point she needed an operation, which enabled her to stop group treatment without loss of face. Her group experience, which stimulated her unacceptable feelings without offering the emotional support necessary to enable her to deal with them, could scarcely be considered helpful.

Finally, a major difference between individual and group forms of treatment should be mentioned, the significance of which is as yet unclear. In therapy groups, each patient must continuously cope with the real or anticipated reactions of others. When he speaks, he is aware that others want the floor, and he must be prepared for a variety of responses to whatever he says. Moreover, the group has little patience with private worlds; members prefer to discuss topics in which all have an interest. The therapy group is not a suitable place for the detailed examination of an individual member's past history or his fantasies.

In individual treatment, the patient is assured of the undivided, attention of the therapist for the duration of the treatment session. He can take his time, relax, let himself go in describing dreams or fantasies, secure in the knowledge that nothing he says will stimulate someone else to interrupt with his own preoccupations.

Thus group therapies may be unduly strenuous for patients who are easily hurt by criticism or have difficulty holding their own in a competitive atmosphere, and may impede the progress of patients who need to retreat from others and solve their problems by unhurried meditation or indulgence in fantasy in the presence of an understanding listener.

It may be that the ideal form of psychotherapy would utilize both individual and group methods. Group and individual sessions may interfere with each other under some circumstances, for example, by leading patients to withhold material in one setting, knowing that they can bring it up in the other. On the other hand, they can usefully supplement each other. For this reason, when time and resources are available, many group therapists also see group members individually from time to time.[36]

In this connection it may be relevant that primitive healing rituals often include a private session between patient and shaman, and thought reform combines both individual and group methods of influence.

SUMMARY

After a glance at the encounter group movement and examples of directive group therapies, this chapter focuses on the dynamics of free-interaction groups comprised of strangers. The persuasive power of these groups probably resides in the tendency of each person to look to others for validation of his feelings and attitudes. Therapy groups differ from individual therapy in that other patients are present. They differ from ordinary social groups by encouraging honest expression of feeling, requiring members to continue communicating despite conflict, and in granting status for reasons other than achievement.

This combination of factors helps patients to discover unsuspected similarities, which counteracts their sense of isolation. Therapy groups arouse patients emotionally through pressure to self-revelation, through members' differences in outlook, through rivalries arising from differences in life experiences, and through members' distorted perceptions of one another based on mirror and transference reactions. They increase members' hopes, combat their demoralization, and heighten their self-confidence by offering mutual support, giving members opportunities to help each other, and fostering group cohesiveness. They promote cognitive and behavioral change through the provision of multiple models in the form of group members.

Psychopathological responses can be corrected by a therapeutic situation only to the extent that they achieve full expression in it. Therapy groups provide a variety of occasions for evoking dis-

36. Bieber (1971); Bach (1954), especially pp. 50–66.

torted feelings, perceptions, and behavior, as well as incentives to change them. These changes are stabilized by the members' internalization of group standards, which characteristically are healthier in some respects than those of the individuals composing the group.

Like any powerful remedy, therapy groups can produce harm as well as benefit. Their greatest potential drawback is the failure to supply sufficient support, especially in early meetings, to enable members to cope with the stresses they generate. They also afford no opportunity for unhurried examination of personal experiences and fantasies in the presence of an understanding listener whose attention is exclusively devoted to the patient. These disadvantages may often be counteracted by suitable combinations of group and individual sessions.

THE TRADITIONAL MENTAL HOSPITAL AND THE THERAPEUTIC XI COMMUNITY

"We're all mad here. I'm mad. You're mad."
"How do you know I'm mad?" said Alice.
"You must be," said the Cat, "or you wouldn't have come here."
Alice didn't think that proved it at all.

Alice's Adventures in Wonderland

With the exception of thought reform and certain types of religious healing, this book has focused on forms of healing and persuasion that are brought to bear on patients intermittently, in the setting of their daily lives. It now remains to glance briefly at the healing and influencing forces operating on patients who are placed in a special environment around the clock. The hospitalized patient is separated from all his usual contacts and immersed in a new culture, all aspects of which may affect him. The effects of the social structure of hospitals, of their routines, and of personal contacts of staff with patients, staff with staff, and patients with patients have been extensively studied in recent years, leading to progressive changes in their organization.[1] Adequate consideration of these matters lies beyond the scope of this book. We shall be concerned only with those aspects of the treatment of hospitalized patients that involve principles operative in the forms of healing and persuasion already considered. Of particular interest is the contrast

1. See Caudill (1958); Stanton and Schwartz (1954); Goffman (1962); Rubenstein and Lasswell (1966).

290

between the old-fashioned mental hospital and the concept of the "therapeutic community."

THE TRADITIONAL STATE MENTAL HOSPITAL

Over the past few decades, in response to changing concepts of mental illness, the traditional mental hospitals have been evolving toward therapeutic communities, as described below. Hence the following account is something of a caricature. It attempts to describe the traditional mental hospital in pure form, recognizing that few fit the model exactly, in order to highlight how its basic assumptions, structure, and procedures shape the behavior and attitudes of those committed to its care.

The traditional mental hospital reflects an outmoded view of mental illness, according to which the "insane" were victims of mysterious brain diseases that made them irresponsible and prone to violence. Moreover, these diseases were apt to be chronic, even lifelong. As a result, the insane, for their own protection and the safety of their fellow citizens, had to be shielded from harm in institutions geared to long-term care. Eventually, it was hoped, the underlying brain diseases could be identified and successfully treated, but in the meanwhile, the best that could be done was to provide the mentally ill with a protective, humane environment.

These assumptions led to the building of mental hospitals in isolated settings, far from the communities they served, in which patients were cared for as economically as possible behind locked doors. Since most patients committed to a mental hospital stayed there, the institutional populations gradually accumulated, forming large, self-contained communities with thousands of members. Many hospitals had farms and grew their own food; some even wove their own linens and made the patients' clothes. No provisions existed for helping patients back into the community, and contact with the outside world was limited to visits from relatives and friends. Since visitors had to overcome geographical barriers and conform to strict visiting hours, the frequency of visits inevitably decreased the longer the patient was hospitalized.

Reflecting the concept that mental illnesses are analogous to medical illnesses, the social structure of the mental hospital resembles that of the general hospital. The treatment staff forms a complex hierarchy, with physicians at the apex, aided by clinical psychologists. Beneath them are professionally trained ancillary personnel such as nurses and social workers, and aides or attendants are at the bottom.[2] The patient's role is to submit to treatment and take orders without question. Since he is presumed to be irresponsible, he does not know what is in his own best interest and must, therefore, accept the judgment of the staff. Patients are treated as objects rather than as persons. Their communications with treatment personnel are strictly limited, and the nature of these communications is chiefly determined by the staff.

Because of the very small ratio of therapists to patients, the therapists spend most of their time with those newly admitted patients who seem most likely to respond to treatment. Others who appear to be poor treatment prospects, such as senile patients, are placed immediately in custodial wards, to be joined by those who, failing to respond promptly to therapy, must make room for newcomers. Thus the hospital becomes an end station for most of its inmates, where they are expected to spend the rest of their lives. It shelters, feeds, clothes, and protects them; but they are no longer regarded as able to profit from treatment or as candidates for return to the community, and they receive minimal attention from the treatment personnel. Virtually abandoned by their families, they pass their lives in an atmosphere of apathy and despair.

Any environment that engulfs a person completely is bound to influence him, for better or worse, and the traditional mental hospital is no exception. At the risk of stretching an analogy, its basic assumptions, social structure, and activities exert on patients emotional, cognitive, and behavioral effects which may be conveniently compared with those operative in thought reform.[3]

The similarities between hospitalization for a mental illness and thought reform are already present in the prodromal phase. The path to the mental hospital is often at least as emotionally unset-

2. Administrative problems created by the "multiple subordination" principle of hospital organization are excellently discussed by Henry (1954).
3. The comparison of the traditional mental hospital with thought reform leans heavily on Goffman (1962) and the quoted phrases are his.

tling as that to prison. The patient may go through a period of progressively more severe embroilment with or alienation from his work associates, friends, and family before he is hospitalized. Before this climax, he may be subjected to such humiliations as arrest, court appearance, and some time in jail. Although these experiences are fortunately not typical, hospitalization always requires some sort of formal procedure which emphasizes the importance of the step and the patient's abdication of control over himself to others, thereby reinforcing his feelings of powerlessness.

Involuntary procedures, known as certification or commitment, are based on the assumption that the patient is incapable of making rational decisions about his own welfare and so must relinquish his responsibility to legally constituted authorities. Though commitment procedures differ widely among states, physicians participate in all.

The actual admission to the hospital may evoke various emotional reactions. At best the patient welcomes it as the first step toward his recovery. At worst, the family may have deceived him about his destination in order to get him to go quietly, or he may be put to sleep with sedatives and wake up among strangers in the unfamiliar environment of the hospital. Even if everything has been explained to him, he may dread the loss of personal freedom and share the popular image of the mental hospital as a "snake pit" peopled by maniacs and brutal guards. Thus, even more than the prisoner in thought reform, he may enter the hospital badly frightened and demoralized, feeling abandoned and betrayed by his loved ones. This emotional state, if used by the treatment staff as a means of leverage, may facilitate his progress, but it can be very damaging, perhaps even lethal, as suggested earlier.[4]

The implicit assumption of irrationality is absent from voluntary admission procedures, which are being used increasingly. Under these, the patient formally requests hospitalization in writing and promises to give the hospital authorities several days advance notice of his intention to leave. Although voluntary admission involves no legal coercion, the patient often seeks it only in response to strong family pressure, and the procedure empha-

4. See p. 54 above.

sizes the staff's control over him while he is hospitalized. Nevertheless, properly conducted, the interview culminating in voluntary admission can heighten the patient's hope of benefit from his
stay and his confidence in the hospital's staff. Involuntary com-
mitments ordinarily do not have this effect.

As with thought reform, the patient must meet the desires of
the treatment staff in order to gain release from the hospital.
Although this statement is not strictly true in that there are legal
means by which a patient may attempt to force his release and his
family can remove him without the staff's consent, most patients
feel themselves to be in the power of the hospital staff. Even in
voluntary hospitals, the three-days'-notice stipulation enables the
authorities to hold over the patient's head the implicit or explicit
threat of arranging involuntary commitment at another institution
if he continues to insist on leaving.

In the traditional mental hospital, as in thought reform, the
patient may be subjected to a "mortification of the self," which
strips him of the usual supports of his personal identity. He may
have to ask permission to carry out the simples activities, such as
smoking. He must be deferential to the staff, including the lower
echelons, whom he may feel to be beneath him. In addition, channels of communication with his former world are severely restricted through limitation of visiting hours and censorship of outgoing mail. These measures intensify his feelings of dependence on
the treatment staff and his awareness that he must meet their
requirements to gain release. Yet often he has no clear idea what
these requirements are, other than that he cause no trouble. His
situation is often uncomfortably reminiscent of the predicament
of the hero of Kafka's *The Trial*.

If the patient is confused, the staff are not. Its members are
guided by an irrefutable conceptual scheme that views any non-
conforming behavior as evidence of mental illness and everything
the staff does as therapeutic, even though the patient may rightly
perceive it as done for the staff's convenience, or as a form of
punishment for misbehavior.

As in thought reform, nothing the patient says or does can
shake the staff's assumptive world, especially since they view him
as irresponsible. If he protests, he is met with the "institutional

smirk," which implies that the staff knows better than he does what is good for him. If this drives him to covert or open rebellion—becoming mute, refusing to eat, tearing up his clothes, or attacking the furniture—this simply confirms that he is mentally ill and belongs where he is. Patients who persist in rebelling are transferred to ever more simplified and restrictive quarters, forcing them to resort to ever more primitive ways of revolting. If one is thrown naked into a bare, locked room, among the few remaining means of protest are urinating on the floor and smearing feces on the walls. Such behavior, of course, serves only to reassure the staff that its decision to put the patient in a seclusion room was correct.

Ironically, kindly treatment of patients also reinforces their feelings of incompetence:

> . . . when [the patient] fails to obey instructions—for example, to take off his clothes—it is done for him gently and with hardly any criticism. If he resists or strikes out, no one strikes back; he is simply held firmly while the necessary steps are taken. No one expresses surprise at his behavior; in fact, everyone acts as though he is unable to do anything for himself. . . . He is called "sick" and told that he must be cared for. He is morally relieved of responsibility for his own failures at the price of being identified as one suffering from a condition which makes his own impulses, thoughts and speech largely irrelevant to any practical activities of daily life.[5]

That the staff may "train" patients to show crazy behavior is suggested by a fascinating finding obtained from time samples of patients' behavior in the presence of staff members. The researcher found that patients' behavior under such circumstances could be reliably classified into unusual and common forms; the former included unusual verbal or physical acts (for example, yelling incoherently and ritualistic motions) and performing a private gesture in public such as making a sexual advance; the latter, expressing distress, complaining about living conditions, being negligent toward property, and threatening to attack someone. In a large public hospital the amounts of unusual and common behavior were about the same and did not vary from weekdays to evenings and weekends. In a private teaching hospital, by contrast, unusual dis-

5. Gruenberg (1967), p. 1484.

turbances, especially verbalizations, were almost ten times as common on weekdays as on weekends and evenings. During weekdays they were almost twice as frequent as in the public hospital. Common disturbances in the private hospital showed no variation according to the timetable, and were at the same level as in the public hospital.

Staff members of the private teaching hospital included residents in training and medical students, many more of whom were on the wards during weekdays than in the evenings or on weekends. Students and psychiatrists in training are on the lookout for "unusual" behavior because it is a sign of psychopathology. They expect patients to show such behavior, and it makes their time on the wards interesting. Apparently patients responded to these expectations, possibly because they found that crazy behavior gained them more attention. When students and trainees were absent, this behavior was no longer reinforced and dropped off. If this explanation is correct, one would have expected less unusual behavior in the state hospital because the staff was more blasé. In addition, the difference in numbers of staff on the ward during weekdays and weekends would not be so great, a condition consistent with less fluctuation of unusual behavior according to the timetable.[6]

Thus far I have stressed the psycho-noxious influences exerted by the traditional state mental hospital, but some of its features can also be beneficial. For example, it encourages behavior that both the staff and society at large consider to be healthy. It exerts pressure in this direction indirectly through supervised, organized, goal-directed activities, including housekeeping or maintenance chores, occasional social and recreational functions, and, often, some occupational therapy. Direct guidance is afforded by a systematic scale of privileges and penalties, meted out in accordance with the patient's behavior. In large state hospitals the essential criterion for the granting or withdrawal of privileges is whether or not the patient conforms to regulations. In private hospitals, the criterion of conformity tends to be tempered by recognition that a given form of behavior may represent progress for one patient

6. Melbin (1969).

and retrogression for another, so that a patient's behavior is evaluated not only from the standpoint of its effect on hospital discipline, but also with respect to whether or not it represents a move in the direction of health for him. In any case, the privilege system serves to mold the patients' verbalizations and behavior along lines deemed desirable by the staff.

Nor is the mental hospital's isolation from the community harmful to patients. It is unfortunate that the word "asylum" has fallen into disuse, since providing a person with an asylum from the buffetings of life, when they are overwhelming, may be the first step toward restoring his capacity to function. The mental hospital's geographical isolation; authoritarian organization; simple, structured environment; and absence of challenges or problems requiring decisions may help a very anxious or confused patient to recover his psychological balance. While it lacks sources of helpful stimulation, the traditional mental hospital is unlikely to expose patients to problems that might overtax their capacities and cause them to have demoralizing failure experiences. By sheltering the patients, it gives spontaneous recuperative forces a chance to operate and it interferes minimally with them. Its unpleasantness may bolster a patient's motivation to "pull himself together" and gain release. It is not rare for patients to improve promptly on transfer from a private hospital to a state institution, suggesting that what these particular ones needed most was to be left alone. If a patient has not progressed under such a regime in a few months, however, to continue it is self-defeating, since it leads to progressive loss of his sense of personal identity and to demoralization, through separation from his former contacts and activities.

MENTAL ILLNESS AS SOCIAL DEVIANCE OR BREAKDOWN

Since World War II, mental hospitals have been undergoing a massive transformation from essentially custodial institutions into active treatment centers. The process involves progressive breakdown of the barrier between the mental hospital and the community and a redefinition of roles of patients and treatment staff within the hospital walls. These trends were initiated by programs for rehabilitating repatriated British prisoners of war who were emotionally disturbed,[7] and received conceptual support by the emergence of a sociological conception of mental illness that challenged the medical one.[8]

According to this view, mental illness is not analogous to medical illness, but rather a label applied by society to certain offensive forms of behavior. Society demands that its members conform to two types of rules—explicit ones, or laws, and residual ones, or canons of acceptable behavior. A person who deliberately breaks a law is labeled a criminal and sent to a prison for punishment; one who persistently violates residual rules, thereby frightening or offending those about him, is called mentally ill and sent to a hospital for treatment. Examples of residual rule violations that are called signs of mental illness would be claiming to get messages from Mars, accusing others of persecutory intent, ceasing to speak, or wandering about the house at night aimlessly turning on lights. The sociological view makes the further assumption that much of the deviant behavior of the mentally ill is a response to social oppression emanating from a family or a social system that will not tolerate deviance, and that much of their distress is created by the rejecting attitudes of others.

In short, according to these views, the mental patient, like everyone else, tries to cope with certain stresses produced by his interaction with social forces that emanate from his immediate circle or from society at large. What differentiates his means of coping from those of the "sane" person is that other people find them unacceptable.

Most students of mental illness, while recognizing some truth in this formulation, cannot accept it in its extreme forms. Many persons called mentally ill have biological vulnerabilities, sometimes genetically based, and respond to medications with improvement in their psychic states and social behavior.

A formulation that takes account of both medical and sociological perspectives and fits especially well with modern concepts of the roles of hospitals in psychiatric treatment considers "mental

7. Bion and Rickman (1943).
8. Scheff (1966).

illness" to be both a cause and a manifestation of the "social breakdown syndrome."[9] The social breakdown begins when a discrepancy appears between what a person can do and what he is expected to do, and the environment blames him for being unable to meet its demands. This shakes his self-confidence and increases his suggestibility. His uncertainty about himself leads him to explore new ways of thinking and behaving and increases his sensitivity to his environment. Such a state of mind facilitates change and, under favorable circumstances, enables the person to find a solution through which he regains his equilibrium. There are also various possibilities for escape, such as denying the justification of the environmental demands. If the person accepts the validity of the demands he can maintain that they are being asked of the wrong kind of person—that he is too old or too ill medically to meet them.

If he cannot improve his performance or find an exculpating explanation for his failures to meet the demands placed on him, he becomes increasingly demoralized. As a result, his behavior deteriorates further. He may become impulsive, apathetic, sleepless, and any neurotic or psychotic symptoms become worse, leading his family to become increasingly worried. A vicious circle results in which their anxious concern or anger and his failure to meet their demands aggravate each other. Finally the family takes him to a physician who diagnoses him as "mentally ill" and recommends hospitalization. This step requires the concurrence of the family. The fact that those closest to him join with officialdom in labeling him as incompetent carries great psychological weight and further undermines his confidence in himself.

When he is in the hospital, everything conspires to strengthen the impression that he is mentally ill and is therefore not responsible for his behavior. Typically he struggles against these influences for awhile, but all too often comes to accept the staff's definition of him, and then is well down the road to permanent hospitalization.

To prevent or interrupt this unfortunate sequence requires, first of all, close collaboration between treatment personnel and the

9. Gruenberg (1967).

patient's family, with an eye to breaking the vicious circle. If the patient nevertheless decompensates to the point of requiring hospitalization, the hospital program should be directed to restoring his sense of personal responsibility, rather than further undermining it, and toward getting him back into the community as rapidly as possible. This requires, finally, close ties between the hospital and community agencies and, above all, that comprehensive responsibility for helping the patient to be assigned to the same team in the hospital and in the community. Implementation of a program based on these principles in one New York State county has cut to one-half the annual incidence of social breakdown syndromes lasting four years or more.[10]

The dominant current conception of mental illnesses, then, views them as expressions of a patient's failure to cope with certain stresses of life, usually in the interpersonal sphere, leading to certain types of subjective distress and deviant behavior. His failure may have many interrelated causes including genetic vulnerabilities, past life experiences, and stressful interactions with his present social environment. He becomes a candidate for hospitalization if he becomes a threat to himself or if others cannot tolerate his behavior, a factor which depends on their attitudes as well as his own. In any case, he is not a helpless victim of obscure, impersonal, pathological processes that can be treated only by physical and chemical agents but a person capable of exerting some degree of self-control and participating responsibly in decisions about his welfare.

The purpose of hospitalization, in addition to affording the patient and others protection, should be to provide experiences that will help to rebuild his self-confidence and to correct some of his distorted perceptions and maladaptive behavior. Providing these experiences requires that the hospital be changed from a storage warehouse for humans to a therapeutic community in which patients share with the staff the responsibility for the therapeutic effectiveness of the community. This includes sharing in decisions concerning their privileges and responsibilities and dealing with community problems through open discussions with staff members.

10. Gruenberg *et al.* (1969).

THE THERAPEUTIC COMMUNITY

Although the transformation of mental hospitals from custodial institutions to therapeutic communities was well under way before the advent of antipsychotic drugs, they facilitated the transition. Their role illustrates how closely knit the social system of a mental hospital is, so that change in any one aspect of it creates changes in all the rest. Antipsychotic drugs, by diminishing patients' combativeness or suicidal behavior, made them less frightening to the treatment staff and to one another, and demonstrated that patients formerly considered hopeless could improve. As a result, the drugs rekindled therapeutic optimism in the staff and increased their interest in psychotherapeutic approaches, with the consequence that they began to take more interest in patients as individuals. Patients responded to these changed expectations by behaving less crazily, further reinforcing the new attitudes in both patients and staff.

It has been said that the main initial effect of antipsychotic drugs was to treat the staff; that is, to produce therapeutically beneficial changes in their attitudes. That this statement is not entirely facetious is suggested by the observation that their effects seem to be more striking in public than in private mental hospitals. Presumably this was because the staffs of private hospitals had more of a therapeutic orientation than the staffs of public hospitals before the drugs were introduced.

The defining trait of the therapeutic community is extensive use of groups of patients, patients and staff, and staff alone to create therapeutic group standards and to provide therapeutic experiences for the patients as individuals.[11] The power of group standards of a hospital ward to shape patients' behavior is illustrated by the transformation of an admission ward of a naval hospital, where patients admitted in an excited state had been controlled by heavy sedation, seclusion, and physical restraints. These measures implicitly encouraged the patients to abandon all self-control by intoxicating and terrifying them and by conveying the staff's expectations that they could not control themselves. A new ward administrator was determined to establish powerful group expectations,

---

11. Good descriptions of therapeutic communities are given by Baker *et al.* (1953); Jones (1953); and Wilmer (1958). See also Greenblatt *et al.* (1955).

shared by patients and staff, that patients could exert self-control and that restraints would not be needed. He achieved this through daily community meetings of patients and staff followed by a meeting of the staff alone. In the course of ten months, during which nearly a thousand patients were admitted to the service, he did not have to put one in restraint or seclusion.[12]

The principles of group therapy in the narrower sense are essentially the same with hospitalized patients and outpatients, but differences in types of patients and in the setting have led to certain modifications in technique. For maximal value, groups within the hospital are tailored to the degree of illness of the patients and also are closely integrated with the general program of the hospital. In general, since inpatients tend to be sicker than outpatients, their groups for the most part use directive methods which make less demand on the participant than evocative ones.[13]

The most withdrawn patients may benefit from simple group activities such as rhythm bands, which break the monotony of their lives and enhance their capacity for sensory discrimination and ability to cooperate with others. Patients who are in better contact may respond well to didactic groups in which the therapist assumes major responsibility for the group's functioning. The therapist assigns topics for reading at a level of difficulty within the limits of the patients' capabilities and actively guides the discussion. The material affords intellectual stimulation and, because it is emotionally neutral, enables the patients to discuss it without more emotional involvement than they are able to handle.[14]

Free-interaction groups are useful for convalescent patients and even for ones who are quite sick, though for the latter they may be overstimulating. Schizophrenics have difficulty communicating with others, and groups which do not offer them direct guidance may become quite stormy. The introduction of a group therapy program using free interaction methods into one ward of a hospital led to an increase in combative and destructive behavior on the ward, as compared with a similar ward in which patients did not receive group therapy. These and other signs of disturbance, how-

12. Wilmer (1958).
13. See Frank (1963).
14. Klapman (1959), chap. 12.

ever, fell off more sharply in the therapy than in the control ward with the passage of time. More importantly, they were accompanied by a drop in nighttime sedation to about half the previous level, suggesting that patients may have gained increased inner calmness through expressing their feelings more freely. The group patients also showed a prompt and striking improvement in control of bladder functions, which seems to be related to an increase in self-respect.[15]

Psychodramatic methods in hospitals can be used in a wide variety of ways, from helping patients to solve deep-seated personal problems to simple behavioral training. At one extreme they have been used, for example, to free a schizophrenic patient from her attachment to an imaginary lover, by having a therapist play the role of an intimate friend of the lover in such a way as to bring about a resolution of the relationship.[16] At the other end of the spectrum, psychodramatic techniques have been found especially helpful in enabling chronic institutionalized patients whose coping skills have atrophied to confront and master practical problems they will meet on return to community life, such as how to shop and how to answer questions about where they have been.[17] Reentry into the community can also be facilitated by therapeutic social clubs, conducted by the patients under staff supervision. These clubs elect their own officers and plan social and recreational activities. Through these activities, members strengthen their capacities to handle themselves in social situations.[18]

Another kind of inpatient group allows patients to share some responsibility for the hospital program, within the limits set by their disability. One ward administrator, for example, held weekly group meetings of his most disturbed patients. Under his guidance they elected officers, ran the sessions along parliamentary lines, and held to an agenda consisting of administrative problems of the ward that they wished to consider. On the basis of their discussion they made recommendations that he always took seriously, ac-

15. Frank (1952). Stanton and Schwartz (1954, chap. 16) offer an interesting discussion of the psychological and social meanings of incontinence in hospitalized mental patients.
16. Moreno (1944).
17. Overholser and Enneis (1959).
18. Blair (1955).

cepting some and explaining to the group why he could not accept others. In addition to helping the patients by giving them a sense of responsibility for their own care, this type of group enabled the psychiatrist to learn of conditions requiring modification that would otherwise have escaped his attention.[19]

In one private hospital the least disturbed patients assumed responsibility for organizing their own activities and making suggestions for the overall hospital program. It is reported that patients in these groups lost their originally indifferent attitude about the hospital. Instead, "They had begun to think of the hospital as something in which they had a share, and they tried to make it something of which they could be proud."[20]

An ingenious example of coordination of group therapy with the overall hospital program is "round table psychotherapy."[21] Six patients, initially elected by an entire ward, form the round table, which meets at most for an hour three times a week. The rest of the ward is the audience. For the first half hour the round table listens to a recording of the last meeting—an effective means of stressing to each patient how he sounds to others. As already suggested, this type of confrontation between a person's self-image and the actual impact of his behavior can supply a powerful incentive toward change of attitudes. During the next half hour the group members discuss one another's symptoms and try to help each person to find better solutions to their difficulties in living. Before each meeting the therapist, who, with the patient's knowledge, listens to the meetings behind a one-way screen, has a ten-minute interview with each member. This includes a friendly critique of what he did at the last group session, an opportunity for him to explain what he would do at the next session, and encouragement to take an active interest in the other patients. Each patient is told that when he is considered for parole, the advice he has given others will be used as evidence in determining the soundness of his judgment.

The round table is responsible for maintaining order during the meeting. It is empowered to eject unruly members of the audience

19. Cruvant (1953).
20. Wender and Stein (1953). The quote is from p. 213.
21. McCann (1953).

and can also, by majority vote, expel those of its own members who are not ready for it and elect replacements. Its most important administrative function is to recommend its members for parole. This recommendation is usually followed, but if not, the reasons are fully explained to the round table. Thus, the round table technique seeks to modify patients' behavior by encouraging them to overcome their self-centeredness and to strengthen their self-esteem by permitting them to assume responsibilities.

In short, an important overall beneficial effect of group methods with inpatients, as with outpatients, is to restore to patients a sense of individuality and of some control over their own destinies. The expectation that they are capable of self-control and of assuming some degree of responsibility for themselves and others, which is implicit in all forms of group therapy, bolsters their self-respect, stimulates their hopes, and in general helps to restore their morale.

Since patients cannot collaborate in their own treatment without actively involving the staff, it follows naturally that both should meet together to discuss issues of common concern. Thus the program of the therapeutic community includes groups attended by patients and treatment staff. Usually regular patient-staff group meetings are confined to hospital units, such as wards. In an English hospital that has been a trailbreaker in developing the therapeutic community, all the patients and staff meet together daily to discuss personal problems of patients and disciplinary questions.[22] The procedure is highly informal, staff members as well as patients being addressed by their first names, and most decisions on policy matters or how to deal with patients' infractions of rules are made by the entire group.

The introduction of a group therapy program inevitably changes the whole social structure of the hospital. Patients participating in these groups can no longer be expected to follow the staff's orders blindly. They expect to have a say in planning hospital programs, demand explanations, and, with the support of the group, may talk back. This change in the patients requires corresponding changes in the attitudes of the staff. They do not in any sense

22. Baker *et al.* (1953).

abdicate their authority or responsibility, but they must discharge their functions in a democratic rather than an authoritarian manner. This may arouse considerable anxiety in those who were trained to perform in the traditional way. As the patients become persons instead of objects, the staff members must become persons instead of functionaries.

The concept of treatment as the responsibility of everyone on the ward has also led to increasing participation of lower-echelon personnel such as music aides and to changes in roles of the professional staff. Since emerging roles often cannot be clearly defined, the transition period is characterized by role blurring, which can create considerable tension among staff members as they jostle for position.[23]

Both patients and staff are under continual temptation to relapse into the older, more comfortable arrangement in which the staff assumed virtually total responsibility for the patients' welfare. This is what patients expect when they come to the hospital, so maintaining a therapeutic community requires a continuing effort by the staff. They must be supported by a training program that makes full use of group methods in which staff members have a chance to express and discuss their own feelings. The program also creates and maintains group standards supporting them in their new roles.

To maintain a therapeutic group structure, moreover, the community's leaders must be familiar with principles of group dynamics, leadership, and administration—topics not ordinarily part of the training or experience of psychotherapists. These are best taught through seminar training programs that include both experiential and didactic features.[24]

In short, the introduction of group methods tends to improve the entire communication network of the hospital. Patients come to communicate more successfully with one another and the staff as they discover that their opinions and feelings count. Patients also become a major means of conveying the group standards of the hospital to one another. In the conventional hospital, patients also strongly affect each other, but their communications occur

23. Rubenstein and Lasswell (1966).
24. Artiss and Schiff (1968); Sherman and Hildreth (1970).

largely outside of the staff's awareness and control. Through group methods, the staff is able to impart their standards effectively and also to keep better informed of the patient's attitudes toward the hospital program. Group methods increase the actual amount of therapeutically oriented contact between patients and staff and make it easier for patients to express their true feelings. These methods also enable patients and staff to discuss common institutional problems and to participate jointly in decisionmaking. Staff members are impelled to communicate more fully with each other as they seek to modify their own behavior along lines required by the new program and to help each other work through the feelings aroused by their changing role relationships and more personalized contacts with patients.

INTEGRATION OF THE HOSPITAL
WITH THE COMMUNITY

As patients demonstrate their capacities for responsibility and self-control, the barriers between the mental hospital and the surrounding community are less justifiable, so changes within the hospitals have been paralleled by their increasing integration with the world outside. This has been signalized by the unlocking of doors, which now open in both directions for patients. It is becoming easier both to enter mental hospitals and to leave them.

Gains made by patients within the hospital must be reinforced by changes in the attitudes of the community toward the mentally ill, or many patients will promptly relapse. For example, a study of patients who had been hospitalized three years on the average compared a rehabilitation program centering on autonomous, patient-led, task-oriented groups with routine hospital care.[25] Patients in the rehabilitation programs left the hospital after a considerably shorter stay than their controls, but the recidivism rate was about the same.

Such findings have stimulated the development of community mental health programs based on the concept of bringing certain therapeutic consultative services out of isolated institutions into more central spots. These facilities include units for mental pa-

25. Fairweather (1964).

tients within general hospitals, community facilities for brief hospitalization, day care centers, and follow-up clinics where patients can receive medications. As aspects of the same trend, programs have been developed which use psychiatric treatment teams that visit patients in their homes to forestall hospitalization.[26]

From the community's side, growing understanding and support is reflected in increased budgets for mental health as well as active participation by women's clubs, churches, and other community groups in planning and conducting programs for patients both inside and outside the hospitals. Women's auxiliaries conduct a variety of programs inside hospitals, and volunteers take patients to meals, chaperon them on shopping trips, and help them organize socialization and work-experience programs in the community.[27] The growth of publicly and privately financed health insurance policies that include psychiatric hospitalization is another sign of favorable changes in community attitudes. More and more patients rely on insurance to pay their hospital bills, and coverage is usually limited to thirty days. This has become a powerful incentive to private hospitals to discharge patients within this time.

As a result of the development of therapeutic communities inside and changing community attitudes outside, hospitals are coming to be links in a therapeutic chain, rather than end stations. This is tangibly demonstrated by rising admission and discharge rates. Especially gratifying is that, despite increasing admissions, the resident populations have shown steady, progressive decline, indicating that hospitals are, indeed, functioning as active treatment centers geared to returning patients to the community as rapidly as possible.

SYNANON

Striking examples of the maximization of healing forces in a residential institution through both its internal structure and its therapeutic integration with the community are afforded by residential programs for drug addicts, of which Synanon, the pioneer, may

26. Friedman *et al.* (1960).
27. Michelson (1964).

serve as a prototype.[28] Starting as a specific rehabilitation modality for addicts, it has expanded into a type of communal living arrangement that also appeals to nonaddicts searching for a more satisfying life. With this has come relaxation of its original admission procedures and modifications of its programs, including, especially, the development of its own system of education, not only for members but for their children.

In its original form, however, Synanon shows striking parallels with medieval monasteries, evidence that the principles on which it is based have stood the test of time. Like the postulant who seeks acceptance by a monastic order, the applicant to Synanon must convince the group of the sincerity of his desire to join. To enter the monastic order he must prove that he feels himself to be a sinner in search of salvation; to enter Synanon he must convince its members that he is a drug addict who truly seeks to "kick the habit." To this end he may have to undergo a rigorous initiation. Once in, he must submit himself completely to the code of the organization.

Although the organization's members differ in responsibilities and authority, all are completely dedicated to serving its ends. To the novitiate, the older members serve as models who, through their dedication, have freed themselves from personal desires felt to be evil and have come closer to achieving a sense of inner peace and personal integration.

On becoming members of the organization, novitiates surrender to it all their assets, as well as any earnings if they continue to work in the larger community. In return they receive food, shelter, and clothing. Synanon, bowing to the American ethos, also provides a little cash, but the highest salary is fifty dollars a month. Novitiates are first assigned menial tasks with minimal responsibilities, gradually rising to greater responsibilities and privileges as they continue to demonstrate their loyalty to the organization's principles and dedication to its welfare.

The organization's philosophy is reinforced by rituals occupying a considerable portion of each day—religious rites in the monastery, the "game" and the "search" in Synanon. In the "game,"

28. Deissler (1970).

members ruthlessly expose each other's self-deceptions and manipulative attempts, much as in certain encounter groups; in the "search," which is oriented toward intellectual rather than emotional experiences, they discuss matters of common interest. Both types of groups are viewed as fostering members' personality development and ability to cope with life.

Integration of Synanon with the surrounding community is achieved in several ways. Community members may attend its groups and they do, by the hundreds. Many members hold jobs, and Synanon itself runs several industries. From the psychological standpoint, however, the most powerful integrating force may be that Synanon depends upon the community for financial support. Like many monastic orders, it is mendicant—75 percent of its assets of over $7 million come from private contributions and government grants. Just as the medieval community's support of the monastery represented a powerful stamp of approval, so there can be little doubt that this tangible evidence of community endorsement increases the morale of Synanon's members and strengthens them in their resolve to be useful citizens.

SUMMARY

Traditional mental hospital programs are based on the assumption that mental patients have been rendered irresponsible and potentially dangerous to themselves and others by obscure brain diseases. Hence they must be removed from the community into protective custody where all decisions regarding their care must be made by the treatment staff. These hospitals exert pressures on patients in many ways analogous to those used by thought reform. Experiences culminating in admission often frighten and demoralize the patient. In the hospital he perceives himself as entirely dependent on the treatment staff for release. He is completely immersed in the hospital world, his communication with the outside world is severely restricted, and his sense of personal identity is weakened through the hospital routines. These routines are based on an unshakable assumptive system according to which the patient is incompetent and everything that happens to him is treatment. His behavior is guided primarily by the hospital privilege system, which rewards conformity and passivity. The isolation, highly simplified life, authoritarian atmosphere, and impersonality of the hospital enable certain patients to mobilize their recuperative forces, but for many who do not respond promptly, these features may retard recovery.

Recognition of the antitherapeutic group influences of the conventional mental hospital, coupled with a changed conceptualization of reasons for hospitalization, has led to the increasing transformation of these hospitals into therapeutic communities. These are based on the assumption that patients are hospitalized as the final stage of a social breakdown syndrome, characterized by the persistence of frightening or otherwise unacceptable behavior which they can be encouraged to control. This end is achieved through participation of both patients and staff in a variety of group activities, aimed at restoring patients' self respect and encouraging them to assume responsibility for their own welfare and that of the total group. The resulting democratization of the hospital creates tensions in the staff resulting from the blurring of their traditional roles, so the maintenance of the therapeutic community requires staff training programs and continuing group support.

Changes within the hospital are paralleled by progressive breakdown of the barriers between it and the community, signalized by unlocked doors, community mental health centers, and participation of community members in hospital programs. The gratifying result has been increasing utilization and greater efficacy of the hospitals, as shown by rising admissions coupled with a steadily declining resident population. Synanon is described as a prototype of the mobilization of therapeutic group expectations within an institution and its integration with the wider community.

XII AMERICAN PSYCHOTHERAPY IN PERSPECTIVE

"Impenetrability! That's what I say!"
"Would you tell me, please," said Alice, "what that means?"
"I meant by 'impenetrability,' " said Humpty Dumpty,
"that we've had enough of that subject and it would be just
as well if you'd mention what you mean to do next, as
I suppose you don't mean to stop here all the rest of your life."

Through the Looking Glass

Human beings spend most of their lives interacting with each other. In the process they influence one another powerfully for good or ill. This book has singled out for study one particular class of influencing procedures—the psychotherapy of adults. This is a help-giving process in which a professionally trained person, sometimes with the aid of a group, tries to relieve certain types of distress by facilitating changes in attitudes. As a relationship in which one person tries to induce changes in another, psychotherapy has much in common with child-rearing, education, and various forms of leadership. Its closest affinities, however, are with time-limited interactions between a sufferer and specially trained persons that stress either healing or attitude change. The former include therapeutic rituals in primitive societies and healing religious shrines in our own; the latter include religious revivalism and Communist thought reform. This chapter considers the nature of psychotherapy in the light of our survey and then proceeds to review certain implications for psychotherapy in America today.

312

DEMORALIZATION—THE COMMON CHARACTERISTIC OF PERSONS IN PSYCHOTHERAPY

At this point it becomes necessary to ask in what sense it is legitimate to refer to psychotherapy as a single entity, rather than to different psychotherapies. At first glance the question seems to answer itself. The number of schools of psychotherapy exceeds the tens and continues to increase. The conditions which psychotherapies purport to treat also cover an enormous range. They include the whole gamut of neurotic and psychotic reactions, personality disorders, disturbances of sexual functions, addiction, school phobias, marital discord—the list could be continued indefinitely.

On closer inspection, however, certain aspects of the psychotherapeutic scene strongly suggest that the features shared by psychotherapies far outweigh their differences. Practitioners of all schools claim to be able to treat persons with a wide variety of diagnostic labels, and each can report success with patients who had failed to respond to the methods of another. Since all can do this, however, the claims cancel each other. That is, therapists using method A cure some patients whom method B failed to help, but method B also succeeds after method A has failed.

In view of this state of affairs, it is not surprising that all therapeutic schools persist. Despite vigorous and prolonged polemics, no school has yet succeeded in driving a rival from the field. The obvious conclusion is that all must do some good but that none has produced results clearly superior to the results of any other.

There is one exception to this statement. Phobias seem to respond more promptly to brief behavioral techniques than to evocative interview therapies, and emotional flooding may prove superior to systematic desensitization in the treatment of agoraphobics. Findings such as these justify continued searching for differential effects of different procedures for different conditions. Since phobic patients comprise less than 3 percent of persons seeking psychotherapy, however, this may be the exception that proves the rule.

To put the issue in terms of an analogy, two apparently very different psychotherapies, such as psychoanalysis and systematic desensitization, might be analogous to penicillin and digitalis—

totally different pharmacological agents suitable for completely different conditions. On the other hand, the active ingredient of both may be the same, analogous to two compounds, marketed under different names, both of which contain aspirin. I believe the second alternative is closer to the mark. In this connection, it is intriguing that the company that initially put aspirin on the market now advertises that its product is "pure" aspirin, implying that other agents reduce its effectiveness. This is uncannily similar to Freud's comment about diluting the "pure gold" of psychoanalysis with the dross of suggestion.

To forestall misunderstanding, let me remind the reader that aspirin is not a placebo. It has powerful pharmacological effects, among them inhibition of the synthesis of prostaglandins. These substances play a part in inflammation. By reason of its pharmacological action, aspirin reduces fever and alleviates aches and pains almost regardless of the specific illness with which they are associated.

Pursuing the analogy one step further, we must ask: is there a state common to all persons seeking psychotherapy that this treatment alleviates, just as aspirin relieves aches and pains? I believe that there is such a state, which may be termed "demoralization."

Dictionaries define "to demoralize" as "to deprive a person of spirit, courage, to dishearten, bewilder, to throw him into disorder or confusion." These terms well describe the state of candidates for psychotherapy, whatever their diagnostic label. They are conscious of having failed to meet their own expectations or those of others, or of being unable to cope with some pressing problem. They feel powerless to change the situation or themselves. In severe cases they fear that they cannot even control their own feelings, giving rise to the fear of going crazy which is so characteristic of those seeking psychotherapeutic help. Their life space is constricted both in space and time. Thus they cling to a small round of habitual activities, avoid novelty and challenge, and are reluctant to make long-term plans. It is as if psychologically they are cowering in a spatio-temporal corner. In other terms, to various degrees the demoralized person feels isolated, hopeless, and helpless, and is preoccupied with merely trying to survive.

Having lost confidence in his ability to defend himself against a threatening world, the demoralized person is prey to anxiety and depression (the two most common complaints of persons seeking psychotherapy) as well as to resentment, anger, and other dysphoric emotions. Persons with certain personality structures manage to use symptoms to conceal these feelings. Their presence just under the surface is shown by the fact that the feelings erupt into consciousness if the symptom is removed while the patient is still demoralized. The hypnotic removal of a hysterical paralysis, for example, has been known to precipitate suicidal depression.

Although some demoralized patients fight help-givers because they are so mistrustful, most actively seek help and respond readily to a helper; that is, they are in a state of heightened suggestibility. Usually they find help in their own circle. The psychotherapist sees only those who have failed in this attempt.[1]

At their first meeting the therapist examines the patient and gives him a diagnostic label. The patient abets him in this by presenting a specific complaint as his reason for coming. More often than not, however, this is merely his admission ticket—the basis for his claim on the therapist's attention. It may be a direct expression of his demoralization such as depression, an unsuccessful attempt to overcome it such as excessive drinking, or even be irrelevant such as a circumscribed phobia. The psychotherapist's orientation leads him to accept the complaint presented as the real reason the patient has come to him and proceeds to make its relief the object of treatment.

But most persons do not seek therapy because they hallucinate or fear snakes or enjoy a few drinks too many, much less because they have obsessional, hysterical, or passive-aggressive personalities. The community is full of people with these and other psychopathological conditions going about their daily business. In fact, most persons who are entitled to psychiatric diagnoses probably never come to the psychotherapist's attention. University researchers on psychotherapy, for example, by giving a class a fear survey schedule, can always unearth sufficient numbers of students with phobias who never thought of seeking treatment until the researcher offered it.

Morale can be restored by removal of crippling symptoms, and different psychotherapeutic procedures may be differentially ef-

1. Kadushin (1969).

fective for some of these. Conversely, insofar as the patient's symptoms are expressions of his demoralized state, restoration of his self-esteem by whatever means causes them to subside. Not infrequently, successful psychotherapy enables a patient to function more successfully in the face of persisting symptoms.[2] Examples are the paranoid patient whose delusions are unchanged but who has become able to keep them to himself, or the patient who no longer avoids the phobic situation although he still has the same physiological symptoms of anxiety in its presence.

In most general terms, a person becomes demoralized when he finds that he cannot meet the demands placed on him by his environment, and cannot extricate himself from his predicament. This situation has been conceptualized as "crisis" if acute and "the social breakdown syndrome" if chronic.[3] Although demoralization depends on the interaction between factors in the person and in the environment, it is convenient to consider them separately.

Environmental stresses may overtax a person's adaptive capacities for reasons beyond his control. As wartime experiences have shown, everyone has a breaking point. In peace, as in war, environmental stress sets limits to what psychotherapy can accomplish. No amount of treatment will abolish stresses created by a brutal, unpredictable alcoholic parent, a spouse with a slowly fatal illness, or those impinging on a child whose parents are a militant atheist and a devout Catholic. Limits to psychotherapeutic benefit are also set by poverty, unemployment, and other forms of social oppression. Since a person's attitudes and behavior affect his environment, however, demoralization may aggravate crisis. Psychotherapy, by bolstering the patient's morale and enabling him to modify his perceptions and behavior, can sometimes help to break the resulting vicious circle.

From the standpoint of the person, adaptive capacity can be limited by constitutional defects or vulnerabilities. By "constitutional" is meant that they are built into his structure, either be-

2. Sifneos (1972).
3. For the first term, see Caplan (1964) and Rusk (1971); for the second term, see Gruenberg (1967).

cause they are genetic or because they are the after-effects of trauma occurring early enough to affect the subsequent development of his nervous system. Sometimes constitutional factors wax and wane periodically—and with them the patient's capacity to cope—as in manic depressive disorders. Problems which seem overwhelming to a patient when he is depressed shrink to trivialities when his mood brightens. Constitutional sources of weakness in coping capacity cannot be directly treated by psychotherapy, but some may be helped by drugs. Psychotherapy, however, can help such persons to maintain their morale despite their handicaps.

Two other personal sources of demoralization do respond to psychotherapy. One may be termed "learned incapacity." That is, through unfortunate past experiences, a person may have learned faulty ways of perceiving and dealing with life's stresses. As a result, he may fall short in his ability to perform and to develop satisfying relationships with others, leading to feelings of failure and alienation. His symptoms are self-defeating, self-perpetuating maneuvers to deal with these feelings. Most American schools of psychotherapy subscribe to this view of the cause of psychopathological symptoms insofar as they are not based on constitutional flaws. Psychoanalytically-oriented interview therapies try to overcome these symptoms by unearthing their initial causes. Behavioral therapies seek the same end by teaching the patient to identify and combat features of his present environment that perpetuate his inappropriate responses.

The other personal source of demoralization has been characterized by such terms as ontological anxiety or existential despair. The philosopher Santayana characterized life as a predicament. We have many defenses against recognizing this demoralizing fact, such as religious faith or membership in organized groups with high morale. Both these sources of support are weak in today's society, which may partly account for the large numbers of persons, especially among the young, who seek psychotherapy for what is best described by the German word "Weltschmerz"—world pain. Existentialist and mystical therapies strive to combat this source of psychopathology.

Later in this chapter we shall review features shared by all forms of psychotherapy which combat demoralization. First, however, let us attempt to place mental illness and psychotherapy in their cultural perspective.

MENTAL ILLNESS, PSYCHOTHERAPY, AND SOCIETY

Mental illnesses are results or expressions of disharmonies within a person and between him and his society. Because a person's patterns of perceiving and relating to others reflect his internal psychic state, and affect it in turn, these are two sides of the same coin. Moreover, the cause-effect sequence runs both ways. A person's internal harmony or conflict affects his relationships with others, and his interpersonal experiences influence his internal state. They may disorganize him, as seen in the primitive who dies from a witch's curse, or help him to reintegrate himself, as in religious conversion.

Cultural factors determine to a large extent which conditions are singled out as targets of psychotherapy and how they manifest themselves. The same phenomena may be viewed as signs of mental illness in one society, of demoniacal possession in another, and as eccentricities to be ignored in a third. Moreover, the behavior of the afflicted person is greatly influenced by culturally determined expectations of how persons so defined should behave.

It has been suggested that psychotherapies flourish in eras such as ours when cultural values and social norms break down. At such times, organized religion and other traditional institutions for maintaining a sense of ontological security and of community lose their effectiveness and psychotherapy seems to be one substitute for them.[4] In complex societies, the difficulties leading a person to seek or be offered psychotherapy, and the type he receives, depend to some extent on his geographical location and class position. Psychotherapists and their patients congregate in cities, perhaps because city dwellers suffer especially from alienation and insecurity. Furthermore, knowledge of the availability of psychotherapy is related to educational level, and the density of city populations assures sufficient numbers of the well-educated. Educated, middle- or upper-class urbanites seek or are brought to psychotherapy for less severe or vaguer complaints than poorly

4. May (1968); Masserman (1971).

educated, lower-class farmers, and are more apt to receive evocative individual or group therapies, as contrasted with directive approaches or those that rely heavily on medication.

Since the therapist's power over the patient rests in part on his role and function as a mediator between the patient and the larger society and may even extend to power to incarcerate the patient if his behavior is socially unacceptable, he inevitably functions as an agent of social integration. This is explicit in pre-industrialized societies, in which illness is thought to be punishment for transgression and recovery involves atonement and reacceptance by the group under the guidance of the shaman.[5] In the past the democratic ethos has obscured this aspect of the psychotherapist's function in the West. Recently, it has surfaced with a vengeance.

The issue of the psychotherapist as an agent of social control directly concerns psychiatrists because of their power to lock people up in mental hospitals, "for care and treatment." It is not always clear whether a patient is committed for his own benefit or to relieve others of his irritating, frightening, or embarrassing presence.[6]

Although this issue presents itself in more subtle form to nonmedical psychotherapists, they too cannot escape it. Symptoms and behavior hitherto regarded as signs of mental illness, we are told, may be appropriate responses to oppression by society or the patient's family. Should the psychotherapist use his power to help the patient submit more gracefully or to encourage him to resist? If the therapist throws his weight on the side of conformity, is he helping to perpetuate social evil?

Consistent with this line of thought, black militants are abjured to avoid psychotherapy, lest it destroy their revolutionary zeal by convincing them that their distress is caused by internal conflicts rather than social oppression. Some writers even suggest that to be truly effective the psychotherapist must be a revolutionary himself.[7]

Most therapists would regard this position as extreme, for it is clear that the psychotherapist lacks power to correct culturally induced stresses. The best he can do is strengthen the patient's

5. Cawte (forthcoming).
6. Szasz (1963).
7. Halleck (1971).

ability to deal with them; their correction lies in the hands of the political and economic elite. Sometimes the psychotherapist may have a marginal ameliorating effect on social oppression by offering insights that help shape the aims and guide the activities of a society's leaders, but this is prevention, not treatment.[8]

Since the distress and disability for which persons seek psychotherapy, however, is almost always related to friction with their surroundings, past or present, and since improvement therefore necessarily involves achieving greater harmony with the larger group or finding the courage to rebel more effectively against it, the issue of the political implications of psychotherapy is a real and important one. It is also complex and controversial, and to pursue it further would lead too far afield.

In any case, American psychotherapy is colored by certain interrelated features of American society, notably its diversity, the high value it places on democracy and science, and the methods of training psychotherapists. The diversity of American society permits the coexistence of various therapies based on differing conceptual schemes representing the value systems of different subcultures. This may have certain virtues. A patient whose outlook is at variance with one group may find acceptance in another. If after therapy he can no longer find support from his former group, he may be able to get it from a new one. Group support need not be expressed as liking. What really counts is whether the patient's new self or behavior achieves recognition and respect. Psychotherapy may help him to gain increased group support by enabling him to embody the group's values more successfully, or, in line with our democratic values, by becoming able to think and act more independently. In any case, he can more readily maintain changes induced by therapy to the extent that they enable him to feel less derogated and isolated.

Moreover, the pluralism of American society enables the psychotherapist to represent attitudes and values differing from those of the patient. If the differences are not too great, this may help him to gain some new and useful perspectives on his problems. On the other hand, differences in world view of psychothera-

8. Examples are Group for the Advancement of Psychiatry (1957); Frank (1967).

pist and patient, based on differences in their backgrounds, may impede communication between them. In addition, the absence of a single, all-embracing world view shared by the patient, the therapist, and the larger society limits the amount of pressure the therapist can mobilize to help the patient change his attitudes. No form of American psychotherapy can approximate the influencing power of primitive healing or thought reform in this respect, though perhaps an ideal therapeutic community, which completely immersed the patient in a culture expressing a self-consistent assumptive world, could approach it.

Almost all segments of American society place a high value on democracy and science. The democratic ideal assigns high worth to individual self-fulfillment. It regards behavior that is apparently self-directed as more admirable than behavior apparently caused by external pressures. Thus it values independence of thought and action within limits, and the rebel or deviate, if not too extreme, may continue to count on group tolerance and even respect. The concept of the therapeutic community, with its view of the hospital inmate as a responsible person entitled to kindness, understanding, and respect, is an expression of the democratic world view.

The scientific ideal reinforces the democratic one by valuing lack of dogmatism. In addition, its emphasis on objectivity and experimentation provides a congenial intellectual atmosphere for behavior therapies and is also a powerful source of their appeal in the West. Being ostensibly based on rigorous animal experimentation, these therapies have impeccable scientific credentials, and they follow scientific canons in claiming to be concerned only with objectively measurable behavior. They also conceptualize therapy in terms of the formulation of hypotheses whose validity is determined by verification of predictions based on them. To be sure, they may achieve conceptual rigor by excluding much of what goes on in psychotherapy, and in actuality many behavior therapies deal primarily with fantasy rather than behavior, but they can more plausibly assume the mantle of science than can interview therapies.

Scientific values of objectivity and intellectual comprehension are not entirely unmixed blessings. Even in interview therapy, they tend to foster an overvaluation of the cognitive aspects of the treatment. "Insight" in the sense of ability to verbalize self-understanding may be mistaken for genuine attitude change, and the therapist may place undue stress on interpretations. The scientific attitude also justifies avoidance of "unscientific," emotion-arousing procedures such as group rituals and dramatic activities, even though there is universal agreement that in order to succeed, psychotherapy must involve the patient's emotions.

Both democratic and scientific ideals tend to cause many American therapists to underestimate the extent to which psychotherapy is a process of persuasion. Members of a democracy do not like to see themselves as exercising power over someone else, and the scientist observes—he does not influence. In this connection, evocative therapies are often termed permissive, reflecting the reluctance of practitioners of these methods to recognize the extent of their influence on patients. Even many behavior therapists formulate their activities in terms of placing themselves under the patient's control rather than manipulating him. That is, their role, as they see it, is to help the patient to discover the environmental contingencies that are sustaining his maladaptive behavior and then to help him change them. In short, reflecting this cultural setting, most psychotherapies in America claim to be both scientific and democratic, although in many respects they are neither.

In concluding this consideration of psychotherapy in relation to its cultural setting, it may be useful briefly to consider how different forms of psychotherapy resemble and differ from medical healing. The medical model is defined by the role and function of the physician, the prototype of the healer in Western society. He embodies the scientific world view in that he seeks to apply scientific principles and methods to the diagnosis and treatment of diseases, which are disorders of the body. This conceptualization implies a relationship between patient and physician that is authoritarian, in this respect being an exception to the democratic ethos. Furthermore, since illness lies entirely within the patient, the physician's obligation is exclusively to him and the physician-patient relationship is strictly private. In the examining room the physician takes full charge. He asks questions, performs examinations, makes a diagnosis, and prescribes a remedy. The patient plays the reciprocal role of passivity and dependency; he answers the physician's questions, submits to his examinations, and follows treatment instructions. Treatment of chronic disabilities is a partial exception to this in that the patient must voluntarily carry out the activities necessary to promote his rehabilitation. Since these may be difficult and require perseverance, the success of treatment largely depends on its ability to strengthen the patient's motivation and morale. In this respect, rehabilitation resembles psychotherapy.

The psychotherapeutic conceptualization of illness differs in a fundamental respect from the medical one and this difference has important consequences. Insofar as psychopathological processes are amenable to psychotherapy, they are conceptualized as expressing disorders of communication resulting from past experiences and the major psychotherapeutic tools are communicative symbols—that is, words. This view implies that the patient's illness does not exist solely within himself but is an expression of a disturbed communication system as well. The member of a family who comes for help is labeled the patient by this act, but the major locus of disturbance may lie in a relative. Hence the purview of psychotherapy cannot stop with the patient but must include his past and present relations to the persons close to him.

Nonmedical psychotherapists have stressed the point that this conceptualization implies that psychotherapy is a form of learning rather than treatment. While the position has considerable validity, it can be overdone, with unfortunate consequences for the field. Patients do not come to psychotherapy to learn something but to be relieved of distress and disability. In the process, to be sure, they may learn a great deal, but this is a by-product of treatment not its aim. It therefore seems closer to the truth to consider psychotherapy to be a healing art, like medicine, which uses methods derived from principles of learning rather than anatomy, physiology, and biochemistry.

Exaggeration of the distinctions between psychotherapy and medical treatment has contributed to the relative neglect of bodily factors and medications by psychologically oriented psychotherapists and to their overemphasis by those adhering to the medical model. Presumably this split will be resolved by advances in neurophysiology and psychopharmacology, which should eventually make it possible to trace out in some detail the interplay between bodily and mental states.

Although psychotherapies conceptualize the conditions they treat in terms of symbolic processes rather than bodily ones, to varying degrees many continue to exemplify three aspects of the medical model: the focus primarily on the patient, the ascendant role of the therapist, and adherence to the scientific world view. Directive therapies are closest to the medical model in all three respects. They apply scientific methods to the diagnosis and treatment of patients, explore the patient's difficulties entirely through his own eyes, and grant the therapist full charge of the treatment situation.

Evocative individual therapies also focus on the patient, but cover a wide range with respect to claiming to base their methods on science. Psychoanalytic therapies are at one end of this spectrum; existential ones at the other. All, however, while forced to recognize the therapist's ascendancy, abjure the authoritarian model, try to combat the patient's feelings of dependency, and set a high value on autonomy, self-realization, and other goals that are of no concern to medicine. They emphasize such qualities in the therapist as empathy–qualities which differ sharply from the cognitive processes involved in acquiring scientific knowledge.

Group therapies cover a similar range. In some the leader functions authoritatively, and many focus primarily on individual members. Some, however, carry the view of mental illness as a disturbance in communcation to its logical conclusion and focus on helping patients to bring to light and correct distorted perceptions and communications as manifested in interactions within the group. In this respect, they are furthest removed from the medical model.

All these therapies function within the mainstream of the dominant American world view. Healing cults do not, but, by making unashamed efforts to mobilize the uncritical faith of their adherents, they succeed in helping many persons whom more conventional therapies do not reach. The cult leader glories in his claimed healing powers, exerts them without self-doubt, and his ministrations are supported by a group of believers in his powers. These healing approaches prize emotion above intellect, subjective certainty above objective analysis, and seek to foster belief and dependence rather than insight and autonomy. Those based on a religious doctrine add another powerful ingredient to the therapeutic brew by claiming to bring supernatural healing forces to the sufferer's aid. For persons who can abandon skepticism, these cults obviously mobilize strong psychological forces for the production and maintenance of therapeutic change.

COMMON FEATURES OF PSYCHOTHERAPY

At this point, let us return to our main quest, which is to tease out features of psychotherapy common to all societies and cultures as they have emerged in our survey of the field. In approaching this topic, one should keep in mind that demoralization, the common property of the conditions that psychotherapy attempts to relieve, involves all aspects of personal functioning. Although the locus of the major disturbance may differ considerably in the different types of distress with which we have been concerned, biological, psychological, and social components are always involved to some degree. Thus successful psychotherapy, whatever its major focus, affects all three.

Four shared features of all psychotherapies seem distinguishable. The first is a particular type of relationship between the patient and a help-giver, sometimes in the context of a group. The essential ingredient of this relationship is that the patient has confidence in the therapist's competence and in his desire to be of help. That is, the patient must feel that the therapist genuinely cares about his welfare.

Caring in this sense does not necessarily imply approval, but rather a determination to persist in trying to help no matter how desperate the patient's condition or how outrageous his behavior. Thus the therapeutic relationship always implies genuine acceptance of the sufferer, if not for what he is, then for what he can become, as well as the therapist's belief that the patient can master his problems.

The therapist's acceptance, based on empathic understanding, validates the patient's personal outlook on life. The patient's sense that he is understood and accepted by someone he respects is a strong antidote to feelings of alienation and is a potent enhancer of morale. Caring and empathy imply some emotional investment by the therapist, which, as already indicated, can be conveyed by such qualities as active participation, warmth, empathy, and enthusiasm. Some stern and harsh therapists, however, also succeed in conveying that they care. In any case, the patient's discovery that someone has enough faith in him to make a big effort to help is in itself a powerful boost to morale, especially since most patients reach the psychotherapist only after they have failed to gain help from others.

The patient's faith in the therapist's competence is enhanced by the latter's socially sanctioned role as a help-giver, evidenced by the fact that he has had special training and, in therapy, by his mastery of a special technique. The success of relatively untrained therapists, however, is evidence that this is not always necessary.

A second common feature of all psychotherapies is that their locales are designated by society as places of healing. Thus the setting itself arouses the patient's expectation of help. Furthermore, it is a temporary refuge from the demands and distractions of daily life. It also is sanctioned by the value system of its society. Thus, in pre-industrialized societies, healing rituals are typically conducted in sacred buildings such as temples. If the setting is the sufferer's home, this is transformed into a sacred place by purification rituals. Some personal growth centers, newcomers to the American scene, also have an ambience with religious overtones. In industrialized societies, however, therapy is typically conducted in the therapist's office, a hospital, or a university health clinic, all of which have the aura of scientific healing.

In any case, the setting is sharply distinguished from the rest of the patient's environment by its special qualities, including clearly delineated temporal and spatial boundaries. Protected by the setting, the patient can concentrate on the prescribed therapeutic activities. He can participate in complex, emotionally charged rituals, suspend his critical faculties, freely express his emotions, indulge in leisurely self-exploration, daydream, or do whatever else the therapy prescribes, secure in the knowledge that no harm will come to him during the session and that he will not be held accountable in his daily life for whatever he says or does during it. By thus freeing him to experiment, the combination of healer and setting create favorable conditions for change.

Third, all psychotherapies are based on a rationale or myth which includes an explanation of illness and health, deviancy, and normality. If the rationale is to combat the patient's demoralization, it must obviously imply an optimistic philosophy of human nature. This is clearly true of the rationales underlying most American psychotherapies, which assume that aggression, cruelty, and other unattractive forms of human behavior result from past hurts and frustrations and that, as the person progressively frees himself from these and achieves fuller self-awareness, leading him to feel more secure, he will become kinder, more loving, more open to others, and more able to reach his full potential.

Those psychotherapies imported from Europe, notably psychoanalysis and the existential psychotherapies, while more pessimistic about human nature, still place their therapies in an optimistic context. The Freudian view of human nature, which sees the human psyche as a battleground between the instincts of Life and Death, with the latter winning in the end, could hardly be called cheerful, but it is redeemed by the faith that, to use a religious phrase, the truth shall make you free. Truth was Freud's god, and psychoanalysis, as the scientific search for it, enabled humans, by gaining control of the base impulses of the Unconscious, to free more energy for the life-instinctual goals of love and work.

The most pessimistic of the philosophies on which psychotherapies are based are those existentialist ones that stress the essential meaninglessness of human existence. They manage to give this outlook a heroic twist, however, by maintaining that the human, although he cannot control his fate, does have the potential ability to wrest a sense of meaning and purpose out of life.

Within a broad often not fully articulated philosophy of life, the rationale of each school of psychotherapy explains the cause of the sufferer's distress, specifies desirable goals for him, and prescribes procedures for attaining them. To be effective, the therapeutic myth must be compatible with the cultural world view shared by patient and therapist. The hypothesis that all mental illnesses, insofar as they respond to psychological treatment are products of damaging early life experiences, underlies almost all Western psychotherapies, including behavioral approaches. Psychotherapies based on it, however, may be ineffective for patients in cultures that attribute mental illness to, for example, spirit possession.

The provocative word "myth" has been used to emphasize that, although the rationales of many Western psychotherapies do not invoke supernatural forces, they resemble the myths of primitive ones in that they cannot be shaken by therapeutic failures. That is, they are not subject to disproof. The infallibility of the rationale protects the therapist's self-esteem, thereby strengthening the patient's confidence in him. In addition, for both patient and therapist, it provides the powerful emotional support of a like-minded group, whose members may gain further ego-support by viewing themselves as a select few, superior in some respects to ordinary mortals. Thus the conceptual scheme combats the patient's sense of alienation.

The therapeutic rationale, finally, enables the patient to make sense of his symptoms. Since he often views them as inexplicable, which increases their ominousness, being able to name and explain them in terms of an overarching conceptual scheme is in itself powerfully reassuring. The first step in gaining control of any phenomenon is to give it a name.

The fourth ingredient of all forms of psychotherapy is the task or procedure prescribed by the theory. Some therapeutic procedures closely guide the sufferer's activities, others impel him to take the initiative; but all share certain characteristics. The procedure is the means by which the sufferer is brought to see the error of his ways and correct them, thereby gaining relief. It also affords the patients a face-saving device for relinquishing his symptoms when he is prepared to do so. The procedure demands some effort or sacrifice on the patient's part, ranging all the way from collaborating in hypnosis to undergoing repeated painful shocks. Since it requires active participation of both patient and therapist and is typically repetitive, it serves as the vehicle for maintaining the therapeutic relationship and transmitting the therapist's influence. It also enhances the therapist's self-confidence by enabling him to demonstrate mastery of a special set of skills. Procedures such as hypnosis, relaxation, or emotional flooding in which the therapist alters the patient's subjective state are especially convincing demonstrations of the therapist's competence. Any procedure that can alter one's state of consciousness must be powerful indeed.

The central point is that the therapeutic efficacy of rationales and techniques may lie not in their specific contents, which differ, but in their functions, which are the same. The therapeutic relationship, setting, rationale, and task in conjunction influence patients in five interrelated ways which seem necessary to produce attitude change and therapeutic benefit. First, they provide him with new opportunities for learning at both cognitive and experiential levels. Cognitively the therapist may help the patient to clarify sources of his difficulties in his past life, or the contingencies in his environment that maintain his distress. The therapist and other members of a group in group therapy also serve as models of alternative ways of handling problems. But the most important learning in therapy is probably experiential and is provided by confronting the patient with discrepancies or contradictions between his assumptive world and actuality. Insight-oriented therapies confront him with discrepancies between his self-image and his own hidden feelings; group methods face him with discrepancies between his assumptions about others and their actual feelings or between the impression he thinks he is making and his actual effect. Awareness of these dissonances creates a powerful incentive to change in directions suggested by the cognitive insights the patient is gaining simultaneously.

Second, all therapies enhance the patient's hope of relief. This hope rests in part on the patient's faith in the therapist and the treatment method. Experienced therapists in early interviews explicitly try to strengthen the patient's favorable expectations and to tailor them to the therapeutic procedure.

A more enduring source of hope deserves a heading of its own because it includes other components. This is, third, the provision of success experiences which enhance the sufferer's sense of mastery, interpersonal competence, or capability. The detailed structure of behavior therapies, the objective measures of progress, and the emphasis on the patient's active participation virtually assure that he will experience successes as treatment progresses.

Unstructured, open-ended procedures like psychoanalysis also provide success experiences. These therapies seem ideally suited for intelligent, verbally adept patients who rely heavily on words to cope with life's problems. The patient experiences a feeling of mastery when he gains a new insight or becomes aware of a hitherto unconscious thought or feeling. The therapist enhances the patient's sense of achievement by maintaining that all progress is due to the patient's own efforts. Thus all successful therapies implicitly or explicitly change the patient's image of himself as a person who is overwhelmed by his symptoms and problems to that of one who can master them.

Fourth, all forms of psychotherapy help the patient to overcome his demoralizing sense of alienation from his fellows. Through his interactions with the therapist and the group (if there is one) within the framework of a shared conceptual scheme, he discovers that his problems are not unique and that others can understand him and do care about his welfare.

Finally, all forms of psychotherapy, when successful, arouse the patient emotionally. The role of emotional arousal in facilitating or causing psychotherapeutic change is unclear. One can only note that it seems to be a prerequisite to all attitudinal and behavioral change. It accompanies all confrontations and success experiences, and production of intense arousal is the central aim of emotional flooding techniques.

In short, when successful, all forms of psychotherapy relieve dysphoric feelings, rekindle the patient's hopes, increase his sense of mastery over himself and his environment, and in general restore his morale. As a result, he becomes able to tackle the problems he had been avoiding and to experiment with new, better ways of handling them. These new capabilities decrease the chance that he will become demoralized again and, with good fortune, enable him to continue to make gains after psychotherapy has ended.

IMPLICATIONS FOR RESEARCH

As this book has made evident, though there is an abundance of clinical lore, the amount of experimentally verified knowledge about psychotherapeutic processes is meager, though not through want of trying. Psychotherapy has absorbed the attention of many able investigators,[9] and while this is not the place for detailed consideration of research aspects of psychotherapy, a brief attempt to make explicit some of the major areas of difficulty and the most promising directions of progress seems appropriate.

One set of problems arises from the fact that psychotherapists have a vested interest in their methods. Each has become expert in a particular mode of psychotherapy as the result of long and arduous training. His self-esteem, status, and financial security are linked to its effectiveness. Under these circumstances he can hardly be expected to be an impartial student of his own method, and any data he reports cannot escape the suspicion of bias. Theoretically there is an easy solution to this dilemma, which is to separate the roles of researcher and therapist. The therapist would permit himself to be observed by trained researchers through a one-way vision screen or by means of sound films and tape recordings of interviews. Psychiatrists have resisted this on the ostensible grounds that it infringes on the confidentiality of the patient-physician relationship, but they have been progressively yielding to the blandishments of researchers and the good example set by their psychologist colleagues. Since the self-esteem of psychologists rests on research ability as well as therapeutic skill, most psychotherapy that has been the object of research has been conducted by them.

There is no denying that research poses threats to the therapist. He may discover that what he actually does differs considerably from what he thinks he does, that changes in patients are not caused by the maneuvers he thinks causes them, and that his results are no better than those obtained by practitioners of other methods. All in all, he can hardly be blamed for subscribing to a bit of wisdom attributed to Confucius: "A wise man does not examine the source of his well-being." This understandable prudence, however, has forced researchers to rely too often on therapists in training, especially graduate students in psychology,

9. For recent reviews of the experimental literature on psychotherapy see Meltzoff and Kornreich (1970); Bergin and Garfield (1971).

in which case the results obtained are open to criticism on the grounds of the therapists' lack of experience.

Furthermore, human beings can be disciplined only to a certain point, so unless the subjects of research are students whose grades depend on their participation, carrying through a research design in psychotherapy is far from easy. Therapists chafe at the restrictions imposed by research requirements and are tempted to circumvent them on the grounds that they interfere with treatment. Captive patients in hospitals can be fairly easily controlled. In contrast with them, outpatients break appointments, drop out of treatment without warning, and take vacations at the wrong times.

Research in psychotherapy bears a painfully close resemblance to the nightmarish game of croquet in *Alice in Wonderland*, in which the mallets were flamingos, the balls hedgehogs, and the wickets soldiers. Since the flamingo would not keep its head down, the hedgehogs kept unrolling themselves, and the soldiers were always wandering to other parts of the field, "Alice soon came to the conclusion that it was a very difficult game indeed."

If the subjects of psychotherapy create special problems, so does its subject matter. Being concerned with all levels of human functioning from the biological to the social, psychotherapy raises all the issues concerned with human nature and the communication process. The range and complexity of this material create difficulties of conceptualization. Some formulations try to encompass all its aspects. Many of these have been immensely insightful and stimulating and have illuminated many fields of knowledge. To achieve all-inclusiveness, however, they have resorted to metaphor, have left major ambiguities unresolved, and have formulated their hypotheses in terms that cannot be subjected to experimental test.

The opposite approach has been to try to conceptualize small segments of the field with sufficient precision to permit experimental test of the hypotheses, but these formulations run the risk of achieving rigor at the expense of significance. The researcher is faced with the problem of delimiting an aspect of psychotherapy that is amenable to experimental study and at the same time includes the major determinants of the problem under consideration. He finds himself in the predicament of the Norse god Thor who tried to drain a small goblet only to discover that it was connected with the sea. Under these circumstances there is an inevitable tendency to guide the choice of research problems more by the case with which they can be investigated than by their importance. One is reminded of the familiar story of the drunkard who lost his keys in a dark alley but looked for them under the lamp post because the light was better there.

A persistent, nontrivial research problem is that of definition and measurement of improvement.[10] Patients seek psychotherapy for a wide variety of complaints, ranging from something as vague as spiritual malaise to a specific disability like stage fright. Since only the patient knows how badly he feels, measures of improvement must include self-reports, but these may be distorted by the impression the patient wishes to make on the interviewer as well as by other extraneous factors.

The measurement of change in a circumscribed symptom presents little problem, especially if it involves a specific bit of behavior that can be observed, but the complaints of most patients include multiple miseries. One way of dealing with this diversity, which, while not completely satisfactory, has led to research progress, is to devise scales that include the major types of unpleasant feelings and use changes in average scores as measures of improvement; another is to use a great number of measures and define improvement in terms of positive change in most of them.

Evaluations of social behavior can be more objective but they must also include a subjective component, since what is improvement for one patient may represent a worsening for another, depending on his attitudes toward the situation. A good example would be divorce, which may be a healthy step or a tragedy for different people. As the research reviewed in this book shows, however, scales of subjective distress and social behavior have been devised that yield usable results.

A more difficult problem with respect to improvement is determining how much of it is actually due to therapy. The psycho-

10. Parloff *et al.* (1954); Group for the Advancement of Psychiatry (1966); Frank (1968).

therapeutic session represents only a tiny fraction of the patient's encounters with others, so results attributed to psychotherapy may really be due to concurrent life events, including the patient's seeking help from someone other than the therapist.[11] Therapy may be given credit for improvement really due to a change in the patient's living pattern such as getting married, or its potentially beneficial effects may be wiped out by a personal catastrophe. To complicate matters further, improvement in the patient started by therapy may lead him to enter into new personal transactions which he had been avoiding. Because of the reciprocal nature of social behavior, this may produce favorable changes in the attitudes of others. Therapy may have given him the courage to ask his girl to marry him, affording her the opportunity to accept him. Questions of this type loom especially large with respect to the evaluation of long-term treatment, which requires some way of determining whether the patient handles stress subsequent to undergoing therapy more confortably and effectively than before.

In any case, it is important to distinguish conceptually between influences that produce therapeutic benefit and those that maintain it. If a therapeutic method does not produce any beneficial change, then it is of no interest. If therapy does produce some benefit, whether it is maintained or not may depend primarily on factors that are beyond the control of the therapist.

Every experienced psychotherapist has treated cases in which therapy seemed to have far-reaching and permanent effects, enabling the patient to reach a level of comfort and effectiveness that he would have been most unlikely to attain without treatment. By and large, however, the effect of successful psychotherapy seems to be to accelerate or facilitate healing processes that would have gone on more slowly in its absence. This is, of course, the function of most medical treatment. If psychotherapists did no more than reduce duration of suffering and disability, this would be well worth their efforts.

It seems that many patients come to psychotherapy when they are under internal or external pressures to modify their feelings and behavior, and the psychotherapist assists in the process much

11. See discussion of "spontaneous" improvement in Bergin (1971), pp. 239–46.

as a midwife might at the birth of a baby. What he does may make a lot of difference in how smoothly or rapidly the process occurs, but the extent to which he causes it is uncertain.

Among the therapeutic features of all psychotherapies, four that seem to afford especially promising areas for research have beem emphasized in this book. The first concerns determinants and transmitters of the therapist's influence. The other three are the determinants of the patient's emotional states, his expectation of help, and his sense of mastery.

Especially pertinent to psychotherapy has been the experimental demonstration that evaluation apprehension, as experienced by most patients, makes them highly sensitive to the therapist's influence, which can be transmitted through cues so subtle that the therapist may not notice them. In fact, it seems plausible that one mode of transmission of the therapist's influence may be telepathy. Research into this phenomenon presents many inherent difficulties, as indicated earlier, but the major obstacle is probably that it lacks scientific respectability. In any case, recent studies have shown that rigorous research into telepathy is possible.

Studies of transmission of the terapist's influence, in addition to illuminating an important aspect of psychotherapy, are reminders of the need for caution in evaluating patients' productions. If the therapist has an hypothesis in mind—and he could not do research without one—he may unwittingly convey it to the patient, who may oblige by producing supportive material. Obviously, this type of confirmation is of dubious value. Until the personal and situation conditions determining the influence of the therapist's expectancies on the patient's productions, and the kinds of material most susceptible and most resistant to this type of influence are better understood, hypotheses about human nature supported solely by patients' productions in psychotherapy must be regarded as unproven.

Improved methods of monitoring, evoking, and modifying emotional states are opening up new vistas for research.[12] These methods may help to define the personal and situational factors arousing patients' anxieties on the one hand and hopes on the

12. Lang (1971).

other, as well as personal differences in emotional responsivity, which have formed the basis of personality classifications since the days of Hippocrates. Some patients are too phlegmatic, others too excitable, and the optimal degrees of therapeutically useful tension for them may be quite different.

Monitoring emotional states during psychotherapy can also cast light on the difficult question of the relationship between a patient's self-reports and his actual emotional state. Thus it has been found that a patient's report that he feels relaxed may not be confirmed by actual reduction of autonomic tension. Modern advances in telemetry now make possible unobtrusive, continuous monitoring of a person's autonomic functions as he goes about his daily affairs, overcoming a serious obstacle to the evaluation of therapeutic improvement.

Of more potential therapeutic significance is the experimental production of emotional arousal to facilitate therapeutic change. The use of agents such as ether, adrenalin, and especially LSD, which can be brought under some degree of experimental control, represents a potentially important research advance. The most exciting prospect, however, has been created by the demonstration that through operant conditioning techniques patients can be taught to control their own visceral functions.[13] This opens up new vistas for the study and treatment of bodily symptoms of anxiety and depression, as well as psychosomatic disorders such as high blood pressure, peptic ulcer, and asthma.

A third promising research area deals with the determinants and effects of the patient's favorable expectations. An experimental approach to this problem has been investigation of conditions determining responses of psychiatric patients to inert medications whose therapeutic properties lie in their symbolization of the physician's role. The placebo response proves to be quite a complex matter involving the interaction of personality characteristics, attitudes toward physicians and medication, and properties of the therapeutic situation. A simple experimental approach which deserves further exploration has been the mobilization and intensification of patients' positive expectations through preparatory interviews.

13. Barber *et al.* (1971).

The fourth promising research area, an unexpected by-product of experiments in behavior therapy, lies in investigation of ways of heightening the patient's sense of mastery over his symptoms and his environment through providing him with success experiences in therapy, an area that has barely been tapped.

In conclusion, mention should be made of features of therapy which may actually be the most important determinants of outcome but which have received practically no research attention because they seem to defy conceptualization in terms of the scientific world view. One is the therapist's healing power. This seems to transcend such qualities as warmth, acceptance, enthusiasm, and the like, and may depend in part on telepathy.

Nor do we understand nearly enough about the determinants of *kairos*, the auspicious moment.[14] A great variety of psychological states in combination with certain external circumstances may be followed by abrupt, large, enduring changes in a person's outlook, values, and behavior. Examples of *kairos* range from an alcoholic's "hitting bottom" and other experiences of extreme demoralization, to ecstatic peak experiences. Sometimes it occurs in psychotherapy—every experienced psychotherapist has seen profound changes in a patient following a single interview.[15] Perhaps *kairos* can be commanded by drugs like LSD or the production of emotional flooding. Perhaps the resulting changes involve the same principles as the gradual ones occurring typically in psychotherapy; perhaps they are quite different. It may be that all the principles of psychotherapy we have explored produce only minor changes in patients' personalities; major ones may always depend on *kairos*. Unfortunately, the research genius who can encompass such phenomena as healing power and *kairos* has not yet revealed himself.

IMPLICATIONS FOR PRACTICE

Psychotherapeutic practice today is experiencing changes that are revolutionary in their extent and the speed with which they are happening. The professional practitioners of psychotherapy—

14. Kelman (1969).
15. For a case report, see pp. 226–28 above.

psychiatrists, psychologists, social workers, and some clergymen—
bid fair to be swamped by housewives, ex-drug addicts, and other
laymen who are graduating in large numbers from brief mental
health career programs that are being financed on a vast scale by
public and private agencies.[16] At this writing at least 150 such
programs are known to exist. Nonprofessionals conduct psychotherapy in conventional settings such as clinics, hospitals, and
social agencies, as well as in mental health community centers,
crisis clinics, drug abuse centers, and other facilities that have
emerged to meet the increasing demands for psychotherapeutic
help. Although not ostensibly offering psychotherapy, a variety of
groups conducted in homes, churches, personal growth centers,
and other seetings attract many persons who in the past would
have sought more conventional forms of psychotherapy.

These developments can be traced to several factors. One of the
most important is economic—the demand for psychotherapy hopelessly exceeds the supply of professional psychotherapists, so
others have rushed in to fill the vacuum. This imbalance has been
created by public education, which has convinced countless persons that what they had regarded as distress caused by the ordinary vicissitudes of life was treatable by something called psychotherapy. It was a great gain when the manifestations of mental
illnesses came to be seen as signs of personal malfunctioning rather
than as manifestations of demoniacal possession or mysterious
brain diseases. But this makes it impossible to draw a clear line
between abnormal and normal distress, so that many persons suffering from essentially normal responses to the wear and tear of
life now see themselves—and are seen by others—as suitable candidates for psychotherapy.

The inability of professionals to meet this increased demand has
been aggravated by the warped distribution of their activities. Too
many of the ablest, most experienced psychotherapists spend most
of their time with patients who have the least need of their highly
developed skills. Medically trained psychotherapists, especially if
their training has been along psychoanalytic lines, have the highest
prestige; hence they attract the affluent, who can afford to seek

16. Simon (1971).

their services for relatively minor troubles. Psychoanalytic types of training also appeal to many of the ablest young psychiatrists. Having completed this expensive undertaking, they settle down in cities to recoup their depleted coffers by devoting themselves to the long-term treatment of upper-middle and upper-class patients. They would have to be superhuman to resist this opportunity. They cannot very well turn away persons who come to them for help, especially when they are congenial (that is, of the same intellectual and social level as themselves), pay their bills, are seldom worrisome during the course of treatment, and show a gratifying response.

Most psychologically trained psychotherapists are immured in universities, where they spend most of their time with another intelligent, attractive group whose members are seldom very ill—students with academic problems, often related to the vicissitudes of adolescence. Although most psychiatric social workers work in community agencies, they, too, have been trained in interview therapies that are most appropriate for the verbal, intelligent, middle-class client.

As a result, there are not nearly enough trained psychotherapists to meet the demands of those who could be helped by interview therapies, much less the nonverbal, lower-class patients whom many professionals find unattractive. These crowd state hospitals and outpatient clinics and, from both a therapeutic and a social standpoint, often present a greater challenge. Simple supportive individual and group approaches, with emphasis on behavior rather than talk, are more appropriate for these patients than psychotherapies relying mainly on verbal interchanges.

A second major reason for the growth of nonprofessional therapists follows from the change in the conceptualization of mental illness. It is increasingly recognized that all the manifestations lumped under this term can be responses to crises—predicaments in which environmental stress exceeds the person's adaptive capacities. Whatever their underlying psychopathology, great numbers of people seek psychotherapeutic help because they are demoralized by such experiences. As mentioned earlier, crisis may create incentives and opportunities for achieving new levels of personal integration, but most people who have become demoralized are content to regain their previous level of functioning. Helping them to regain self-confidence and emotional balance usually requires only simple supportive measures which can be offered on an individual or group basis by nonprofessionals.

The nonprofessional lacks the healing aura conveyed by the professional's training and status, but this is in part carried by the settings in which nonprofessionals work and, in any case, is less important than personal qualities of the therapist. Leaving out such attributes as telepathic ability and healing power, which, if they exist, would be as widely distributed in nonprofessionals as professionals, laymen can fully utilize the common ingredients of psychotherapy listed earlier. Those who resemble the patient may be better able to convey concern and understanding than professionals. Housewives and widows can be very effective with their counterparts, and it is well established that ex-addicts and alcoholics are more helpful to many of those still enslaved to these substances than professionals who have never experienced the horrors of addiction.

The ability to inspire hope does not depend solely on professional training and is conveyed to some extent by the setting, which also gives the patient an opportunity to experiment without penalty, whether or not the therapist is a professional. Emotional arousal is an aspect of the crisis response by definition, and restoration of a person's sense of mastery under such circumstances seldom requires more than steady support and reassurance. Finally, the nonprofessional, like his professional counterpart, requires some sort of conceptual scheme linked to a therapeutic task, but this scheme does not have to be elaborate and can be easily taught.

If, as seems certain, the great bulk of psychotherapy will be conducted by nonprofessionals, where does this leave the professional therapist? At this juncture no one can predict his ultimate roles, but certain trends are discernible. Many persons for whom psychotherapy is part of the treatment regime will still require the help of trained professionals. Among them are psychotics, whose difficulties include a significant biological component best managed by pharmaceutical agents. Increasing knowledge of the neurophysiological and biochemical bases of behavior will almost certainly enlarge the range of disturbances of personal functioning in which biological disturbances are found to play a part. For example, intravenous infusion of lactate produces anxiety attacks in anxiety neurotics, but not in normal subjects,[17] and it is hard to believe that severe obsessions or compulsions and hysterical amnesias or paralyses do not have biological underpinning.

Insofar as biological abnormalities contribute to an illness, its proper treatment may require the use of drugs. Today we know that phenothiazines and related compounds help certain schizophrenics, that other drugs aid depressed persons, and that perturbations of the central nervous system produced by LSD and similar drugs may facilitate psychotherapy. There is no reason to believe that there will not be further developments along these lines, and treatment involving drugs will probably always be supervised, if not directly conducted, by trained professionals.

It also seems likely that some mental illnesses represent the end results of specific early life experiences, and that these will respond best to specific forms of therapy, whether of the interview or the behavioral type. To conduct such therapies effectively requires specialized training.

Interview therapies that seek to facilitate major beneficial changes in personality, characterized by such terms as personality growth, self-actualization, and the like, may also demand considerable professional skill. Examples of these therapies are Rogerian client-centered therapy, psychoanalysis and its offshoots, gestalt therapy, and existential therapies. Since each of them directly or indirectly espouses a philosophy of human nature and an articulated value system, they may well meet the needs of some sufferers from existential despair more effectively than organized religions and other traditional sources of consolation.

If the role of the professional in directly treating patients may shrink, his work with paraprofessionals will almost certainly expand. For society continues to hold him ultimately responsible for the outcome of treatment, even though he does not personally conduct it. Therefore, he must exercise supervisory functions over agencies staffed by laymen, including assumption of responsibility

17. Pitts (1969).

for the overall program, for screening applicants to detect those who may require more specialized help than the nonprofessional can offer, and for backstopping him if he finds himself out of his depth. The professional will also continue to have the task of training lay therapists, much of it on the job.

An obvious implication of these developments is that professionals by and large will devote less time to working directly with patients and more to supervising the work of others. As a result, perhaps training programs for professionals may eventually differentiate into those placing more emphasis on direct care and those emphasizing development of organizational and leadership skills. In any case, all such programs will probably devote increasing time to teaching about organizations and institutions.

In concluding our survey, let us abandon the crystal ball and turn to some implications of the contemporary scene for professional psychotherapists. The fact that much of the effectiveness of different forms of psychotherapy may be due to features that all have in common rather than to those that distinguish them from one another does not necessarily mean that all therapies are interchangeable. It seems probable that certain approaches are better for some types of patients or problems than for others. Until this question is clarified, the advance of both knowledge and practice is probably better served by members of different schools defending their own positions, while being tolerant of other schools, than by being uncritical eclectics. For the therapist's ability to help his patient depends partly on his self-confidence, and this in turn depends on mastery of a particular conceptual scheme and its accompanying techniques. Since the leading theories of psychotherapy represent alternative rather than incompatible formulations, it is unlikely that any one of them is completely wrong. As an eminent philosopher has wisely said: "A clash of doctrines is not a disaster—it is an opportunity."[18] The activity stimulated by the clash of psychotherapeutic doctrines will eventually yield sufficient information either to prove that they are all practical purposes identical or to clarify and substantiate differences between them.[19]

18. Whitehead (1925), p. 266.
19. Dreikurs (1960).

Since mobilization of the patient's expectancy of help is a powerful therapeutic agent, the psychotherapist should be prepared to modify his approach, within limits possible for him, to meet his patient's conceptions of therapy, insofar as he can discern them. For patients who cannot conceive of a treatment that does not involve getting a pill or injection, it may be advisable to offer a prescription as a means of establishing and solidifying a therapeutic relationship. Once this has occurred, it is often possible to help the patient modify his expectations and the medication is dispensed with.

The question of how far a therapist should go to meet a patient's expectations is a thorny one. Obviously he cannot use methods in which he himself does not believe. Moreover, reliance on the healing powers of faith, if it led to neglect of proper diagnostic or treatment procedures, would clearly be irresponsible. On the other hand, faith may be a specific antidote for certain emotions such as fear or discouragement, which may constitute the essence of a patient's illness. For such patients, the mobilization of expectant trust by whatever means may be as much an etiological remedy as penicillin for pneumonia.

Finally, this review emphasizes the desirability of exploiting group forces more fully to produce and sustain therapeutic change. This means not only the use of group therapeutic methods, but the inclusion of persons important to the patient in his treatment. For hospitalized patients it means full use of the potentialities of the "therapeutic community." For outpatients it implies involvement of families and more attention to the resources in the patient's environment that might be mobilized to facilitate and perpetuate his improvement. "No man is an island," and the degree and permanence of change in any individual will depend in part on corresponding changes in those close to him and on support from his wider milieu.

SUMMARY

This chapter first explores the psychotherapeutic implications of the hypothesis that demoralization characterizes all persons seeking psychotherapy and is the main reason they come to treat-

ment. It is suggested that the effectiveness of all forms of psychotherapy depends on features they share that combat this state of
mind. After consideration of the cultural components of mental
illness and their implications for psychotherapy, features common
to all forms of treatment that have emerged from our survey are
reviewed, followed by brief consideration of implications for research and practice.

BIBLIOGRAPHY

Abramson, H. A. 1967. *The use of LSD in psychotherapy and alcoholism.* Indianapolis: Bobbs-Merrill.

Ackerknecht, E. H. 1942. Problems of primitive medicine. *Bull. History Med.* 11:503-21.

Ackerman, N. W., ed. 1970. *Family therapy in transition* (International Psychiatry Clinics, vol. 7, no. 4). Boston: Little, Brown.

Adland, M. L. 1947. Review, case studies, therapy and interpretation of the acute exhaustive psychoses. *Psychiat. Quart.* 21:38-69.

Agras, W. S.; Leitenberg, H.; Barlow, D. H.; Curtis, N. A.; Edwards, J.; and Wright, D. 1971. Relaxation in systematic desensitization. *Arch. Gen. Psychiat.* 25:511-14.

Alcoholics Anonymous: Twelve steps and twelve traditions. 1953. New York: Alcoholics Anonymous Publishing Co.

Aldrich, C. K. 1968. Brief psychotherapy: A reappraisal of some theoretical assumptions. *Amer. J. Psychiat.* 125:587-92.

Alexander, F., and French, T. M. 1946. *Psychoanalytic therapy; principles and application.* New York: Ronald Press.

Argyle, M. 1958. *Religious behaviour.* London: Routledge & Kegan Paul.

Artiss, K. L., and Schiff, S. B. 1968. Education for practice in the therapeutic community. In *Current psychiatric therapies,* ed. J. H. Masserman, 8:233-47. New York: Grune & Stratton.

Asch, S. E. 1952. *Social psychology.* New York: Prentice-Hall.

Bach, G. 1952. Some diadic functions of childhood memories. *J. Psychol.* 33:87-98.

———. 1954. *Intensive group psychotherapy.* New York: Ronald Press.

Back, K. W. 1972. *Beyond words: The story of sensitivity training and the encounter movement.* New York: Russell Sage Foundation.

Baker, A. A.; Jones, M.; Merry, J.; and Pomryn, B. A. 1953. A community method of psychotherapy. *Brit. J. Med. Psychol.* 26:222-44.

345

Bandura, A. 1956. Psychotherapists' anxiety level, self-insight, and psychotherapeutic competence. *J. Abnorm. Soc. Psychol.* 52:333-37.

――. 1967. Behavioral psychotherapy. *Scientific American* 216:78-86.

――. 1969. *Principles of behavior modification.* New York: Holt, Rinehart & Winston.

――. 1971. Psychotherapy based upon modeling principles. In *Handbook of psychotherapy and behavior change: An empirical analysis*, ed. A. E. Bergin and S. L. Garfield, pp. 653-708. New York: John Wiley & Sons.

――; Lipsher, D. H.; and Miller, Paula E. 1960. Psychotherapists' approach-avoidance reactions to patients' expressions of hostility. *J. Consult. Psychol.* 24:1-8.

Barber, T. X. 1961a. Physiological effects of "hypnosis." *Psychol. Bull.* 58: 390-419.

――. 1961b. Death by suggestion: A critical note. *Psychosom. Med.* 23: 153-55.

――; DiCara, L. V.; Kamiya, J.; Miller, N. E.; Shapiro, D.; and Stoyva, J., eds. 1971. *Biofeedback and self-control 1970.* Chicago: Aldine-Atherton.

Barron, F. 1953a. Some test correlates of response to psychotherapy. *J. Consult. Psychol.* 17:235-41.

――. 1953b. An ego-strength scale which predicts response to psychotherapy. *J. Consult. Psychol.* 17:327-33.

Bateson, G.; Jackson, D. D.; Haley, J.; and Weakland, J. 1956. Toward a theory of schizophrenia. *Beh. Sci.* 1:251-64.

Bauer, R. A. 1958. The communicator and the audience. *J. Conflict Resolution* 2:67-77.

Beck, A. T. 1970. Cognitive therapy: nature and relation to behavior therapy. *Behavior Therapy* 1:184-200.

Beck, F., and Godin, W. 1951. *Russian purge and the extraction of confessions.* New York: Viking Press.

Beecher, H. K. 1955. The powerful placebo. *J. Amer. Med. Assoc.* 159:1602-6.

Begbie, H. 1909. *Twice-born men: A study in regeneration.* New York: Fleming H. Revell.

Bergin, A. E. 1971. The evaluation of therapeutic outcomes. In *Handbook of psychotherapy and behavior change: An empirical analysis*, ed. A. E. Bergin and S. L. Garfield, pp. 217-70. New York: John Wiley & Sons.

――, and Garfield, S. L., eds. 1971. *Handbook of psychotherapy and behavior change: An empirical analysis.* New York: John Wiley & Sons.

Bernstein, B. 1964. Social class, speech systems and psychotherapy. In *Mental health of the poor: New treatment approaches for low income people*, ed. F. Riessman, J. Cohen, and A. Pearl, pp. 194-204. New York: Free Press of Glencoe.

Bettelheim, Bruno. 1943. Individual and mass behavior in extreme situations. *J. Abnorm. Soc. Psychol.* 38:417-52.

――. 1952. Remarks on the psychological appeal of totalitarianism. *Amer. J. Econ. and Soc.* 12:89-96.

Betz, B. J. 1963. Differential success rates of psychotherapists with "process" and "non-process" schizophrenic patients. *Amer. J. Psychiat.* 119:1090-91.

Biderman, A. D. 1963. *March to calumny: The story of American POW's in the Korean War.* New York: Macmillan.

Bieber, T. B. 1971. Combined individual and group psychotherapy. In *Comprehensive group psychotherapy*, ed. H. I. Kaplan and B. J. Sadock, pp. 153-69. Baltimore: Williams & Wilkins.

Binder, A.; McConnell, D.; and Sjoholm, Nancy A. 1957. Verbal conditioning as a function of experimenter characteristics. *J. Abnorm. Soc. Psychol.* 55:309-14.

Binswanger, L. 1956. Existential analysis and psychotherapy. In *Progress in psychotherapy*, ed. Frieda Fromm-Reichmann and J. L. Moreno, pp. 144-48. New York: Grune & Stratton.

Bion, W. R., and Rickman, J. 1943. Intra-group tensions in therapy: Their study as the task of the group. *Lancet* 245:678-81.

Blain, D. 1970. Benjamin Rush, M.D.—1970. *Transactions & Studies of the College of Physicians of Philadelphia* 38:61-98.

Blaine, G. B., and McArthur, C. C. 1958. What happened in therapy as seen by the patient and his psychiatrist. *J. Nerv. Ment. Dis.* 127:344-50.

Blair, D. A. S. 1955. The therapeutic social club. *Ment. Hyg.* 39:54-62.

Board, F. A. 1959. Patients' and physicians' judgments of outcome of psychotherapy in an outpatient clinic. *Arch. Gen. Psychiat.* 1:185-96.

Boslow, H. M., and Manne, S. H. 1966. Mental health in action; Treating adult offenders at Patuxent Institution. *Crime and Delinquency* (Jan. 1966), pp. 22-28.

Boulougouris, J. C.; Marks, I. M.; and Marset, P. 1971. Superiority of flooding (implosion to desensitization for reducing pathological fear. *Behav. Res. and Therapy* 9:7-16.

Bowden, C. L.; Endicott, J.; and Spitzer, R. L. 1972. A-B therapist variable and psychotherapeutic outcome. *J. Nerv. Ment. Dis.* 154:276-88.

Brady, J. P. 1967. Comments on methohexitone-aided systematic desensitization. *Behav. Res. and Therapy* 5:259-60.

Brenner, C. 1955. *An elementary textbook of psychoanalysis.* New York: International Universities Press. Paperback edition, New York: Doubleday, Anchor Books, 1957.

Breuer, J., and Freud, S. 1957. *Studies on hysteria.* New York: Basic Books.

Bridger, W. H., and Mandel, I. J. 1964. A comparison of GSR fear responses produced by threat and electric shock. *J. Psychiat. Res.* 2:31-40.

Bruch, H. 1961. Conceptual confusion in eating disorders. *J. Nerv. Ment. Dis.* 133:51-67.

Bruner, J. 1956. Freud and the image of man. *Amer. Psychol.* 11:463-66.

Cameron, D. E. 1950. *General psychotherapy: Dynamics and procedures.* New York: Grune & Stratton.

Cannon, W. B. 1957. "Voodoo" death. *Psychosom. Med.* 19:182-90.

Cantril, H. 1941. *The psychology of social movements.* New York: John Wiley & Sons. Also published in paperback.

———. 1950. *The "why" of man's experience.* New York: Macmillan.

———. 1957. Perception and interpersonal relations. *Amer. J. Psychiat.* 114:119-26.

Caplan, G. 1964. *Principles of preventive psychiatry.* New York: Basic Books.

Carkhuff, R. R. 1969. *Helping and human relations: A primer for lay and professional helpers.* Boston: Houghton, Mifflin.

Carlin, A. S., and Armstrong, H. E. 1968. Aversive conditioning: Learning or dissonance reduction. *J. Consult. Clin. Psychol.* 32:674-78.

Caudill, W. A. 1957. Problems of leadership in the overt and covert social structure of psychiatric hospitals. In *Symposium on preventive and social psychiatry*, pp. 345-63. Washington, D.C.: Walter Reed Army Institute of Research.

———. 1958. *The psychiatric hospital as a small society.* Cambridge, Mass.: Harvard University Press.

Cautela, J. R. 1971. Covert conditioning. In *The Psychology of Private Events*, ed. A. Jacobs and L. B. Sachs, pp. 109-30. New York: Academic Press.

Cawte, J. E. Forthcoming. *Medicine is the law: Studies in psychiatric anthropology in Australian tribal societies.* Honolulu: University of Hawaii Press.

Chappell, M. N.; Stefano, J. J.; Rogerson, J. S.; and Pike, F. H. 1936. The value of group psychological procedures in the treatment of peptic ulcer. *Amer. J. Diges. Dis. Nutrition* 3:813-17.

Christensen, C. W. 1963. Religious conversion. *J. Nerv. Ment. Dis.* 9:207-23.

Clark, E. T. 1929. *The psychology of religious awakening.* New York: Macmillan.

Clausen, J. A. 1959. The sociology of mental illness. In *Sociology Today*, ed. R. K. Merton, L. Broom, L. S. Cottrell, Jr., pp. 485-508. New York: Basic Books.

Conn, J. H. 1953. Hypnosynthesis III: Hypnotherapy of chronic war neuroses with a discussion of the value of abreaction, regression, and revivication. *J. Clin. Exp. Hypnosis* 1:29-43.

Cranston, Ruth. 1955. *The miracle of Lourdes.* New York: McGraw-Hill. Paperback edition, New York: Popular Library, 1957.

Cruvant, B. A. 1953. The function of the "administrative group" in a mental hospital group therapy program. *Amer. J. Psychiat.* 110:342-46.

Davis, J. 1971. *The interview as arena.* Stanford, California: Stanford University Press.

Davison, G. C. 1968. Systematic desensitization as a counterconditioning process. *J. Abnorm. Psychol.* 73:91-99.

DeGrazia, S. 1952. *Errors of psychotherapy.* New York: Doubleday, pp. 66-102.

Deissler, K. J. 1970. Synanon—its concepts and methods. *Drug Dependence* 5:28-35.

Deren, Maya. 1953. *Divine horsemen: The living gods of Haiti.* London: Thames & Hudson.

Dreikurs, R. 1951. The unique social climate experiences in group psychotherapy. *Group Psychother.* 3:292-99.

———. 1960. Are psychological schools of thought outdated? *J. Ind. Psychol.* 16:3-10.

Duncan, S., Jr.; Rosenberg, M. J.; and Finkelstein, J. 1969. The paralanguage of experimenter bias. *Sociometry* 32:207-19.

Ehrenwald, J. 1966. *Psychotherapy: Myth and method.* New York: Grune & Stratton.

Eisenbud, J. 1970. *PSI and psychoanalysis.* New York: Grune & Stratton.

Ellis, A. 1957. Outcome of employing three techniques of psychotherapy. *J. Clin. Psychol.* 13:344-50.

———. 1959. A homosexual treated with rational psychotherapy. *J. Clin. Psychol.* 15:338-43.

———. 1962. *Reason and emotion in psychotherapy.* New York: Lyle Stuart.

Everson, T. C., and Cole, W. H. 1966. *Spontaneous regression of cancer.* Philadelphia: W. B. Saunders.

Eysenck, H. J. 1960. What's the truth about psychoanalysis? *Reader's Digest* 76:38-43.

———. 1965. The effects of psychotherapy. *Int. J. Psychiat.* 1:97-142.

———, and Beech, R. 1971. Counterconditioning and related methods. In *Handbook of psychotherapy and behavior change: An empirical analysis,* ed. A. E. Bergin and S. L. Garfield, pp. 543-611. New York: John Wiley & Sons.

Ezriel, H. 1956. Experimentation within the psychoanalytic session. *Brit. J. Phil. Sci.* 7:29-48.

Fairweather, G. W., ed. 1964. *Social psychology in treating mental illness: An experimental approach.* New York: John Wiley & Sons.

Festinger, L. 1954. A theory of social comparison processes. *Hum. Relat.* 7:117-40.

———. 1957. *A theory of cognitive dissonance.* Evanston, Ill.: Row, Peterson & Company.

———; Riecken, H. W.; and Schachter, S. 1956. *When prophecy fails.* Minneapolis: University of Minnesota Press. Paperback edition, New York: Harper and Row, Torch Books.

Fiedler, F. E. 1953. Quantitative studies on the role of therapists' feelings toward their patients. In *Psychotherapy: Theory and research,* ed. O. H. Mowrer, pp. 296-315. New York: Ronald Press Co.

Field, M. J. 1955. Witchcraft as a primitive interpretation of mental disorder. *J. Ment. Science* 101:826-33.

Folkins, C. H.; Lawson, K. D.; Opton, E. M., Jr.; and Lazarus, R. S. 1968. Desensitization and the experimental reduction of threat. *J. Abnorm. Psychol.* 73:100-113.

Ford, E. S. C. 1963. Being and becoming: The search for identity. *Amer. J. Orthopsychiat.* 17:472–82.

Fortin, J. N., and Abse, D. W. 1956. Group psychotherapy with peptic ulcer. *Int. J. Group Psychother.* 6:383–91.

Foulkes, S. H. 1948. *Introduction to group analytic psychotherapy.* London: Heinemann.

———. 1964. *Therapeutic group analysis.* New York: International Universities Press.

———, and Anthony, E. J. 1957. *Group psychotherapy: The psycho-analytic approach.* Paperback edition, Baltimore: Penguin Books.

Fox, J. R. 1964. Witchcraft and clanship in Cochiti therapy. In *Magic, faith and healing*, ed. A. Kiev, pp. 174–200. New York: Macmillan.

Frank, J. D. 1946. Emotional reactions of American soldiers to an unfamiliar disease. *Amer. J. Psychiat.* 102:631–40.

———. 1952. Group therapy with schizophrenics. In *Psychotherapy with schizophrenics*, ed. E. B. Brody and F. C. Redlich, pp. 216–30. New York: International Universities Press.

———. 1957a. Some determinants, manifestations, and effects of cohesiveness in therapy groups. *Int. J. Group Psychother.* 7:53–63.

———. 1957b. Some aspects of cohesiveness and conflict in psychiatric outpatient groups. *Bull. Johns Hopkins Hospital* 101:224–31.

———. 1959. Problems of controls in psychotherapy as exemplified by the Psychotherapy Research Project of the Phipps Psychiatric Clinic. In *Research in psychotherapy*, ed. E. A. Rubinstein and M. B. Parloff, 2:10–26. Washington, D.C.: American Psychological Assoc. Reprinted in *The investigation of psychotherapy: Commentaries and readings*, ed. A. P. Goldstein and S. J. Dean, pp. 79–91. New York: John Wiley & Sons, 1966.

———. 1962. The role of cognitions in illness and healing. In *Research in psychotherapy* 11:3–12. Washington, D.C.: American Psychological Assoc.

———. 1963. Group therapy in the mental hospital. In *Group psychotherapy and group function*, ed. M. Rosenbaum and M. Berger, pp. 453–68. New York: Basic Books.

———. 1966. Treatment of the focal symptom: An adaptational approach. *Amer. J. Psychother.* 20:564–75.

———. 1967. *Sanity and survival: Psychological aspects of war and peace.* New York: Random House. Paperback edition, Vintage Books.

———. 1968. Methods of assessing the results of psychotherapy. In *Ciba Foundation Symposium on the Role of Learning in Psychotherapy*, ed. R. Porter, pp. 38–55. London: J. & A. Churchill.

———. 1971. Therapeutic factors in psychotherapy. *Amer. J. Psychother.* 25:350–61.

———, and Ascher, E. 1956. Therapeutic emotional interactions in group treatment. *Postgrad. Med.* 19:36–40.

———; Gliedman, L. H.; Imber, S. D.; Nash, E. H., Jr.; and Stone, A. R. 1957. Why patients leave psychotherapy. *Arch. Neurol. and Psychiat.* 77:283-99.

———; Gliedman, L. H.; Imber, S. D.; Stone, A. R.; and Nash, E. H. 1959. Patients' expectancies and relearning as factors determining improvement in psychotherapy. *Amer. J. Psychiat.* 115:961-68.

———; Nash, E. H.; Stone, A. R.; and Imber, S. D. 1963. Immediate and long-term symptomatic course of psychiatric outpatients. *Amer. J. Psychiat.* 120:429-39.

———, and Powdermaker, F. B. 1959. Group psychotherapy. In *American Handbook of Psychiatry*, ed. S. Arieti, pp. 1362-74. New York: Basic Books.

Frankl, V. E. 1959. *From death camp to existentialism: A psychiatrist's path to a new therapy.* Boston: Beacon Press.

———. 1960. Paradoxical intention, a logotherapeutic technique. *Amer. J. Psychother.* 14:520-35.

———. 1965. *The doctor and the soul: From psychotherapy to logotherapy.* New York: Knopf. Paperback edition, New York: Bantam Books.

Freedman, L. Z., and Hollingshead, A. B. 1957. Neurosis and social class: I. Social interaction. *Amer. J. Psychiat.* 113:769-75.

Freedman, N.; Cutler, R.; Engelhardt, D.; and Margolis, R. 1967. On the modification of paranoid symptomatology. *J. Nerv. Ment. Dis.* 144:29-36.

Freud, S. 1920. *A general introduction to psychoanalysis.* New York: Liveright. Paperback edition, New York: Simon and Schuster.

———. 1953. *The complete psychological works of Sigmund Freud.* Edited and translated by J. Strachey. Vol. 7. London: Hogarth Press & Institute of Psychoanalysis.

Friedman, H. J. 1963. Patient expectancy and symptom reduction. *Arch. Gen. Psychiat.* 8:61-67.

Friedman, T. T.; Rolfe, Phyllis; and Stewart, S. E. 1960. Home treatment of psychiatric patients. *Amer. J. Psychiat.* 116:807-9.

Frost, R. 1915. *North of Boston.* New York: Henry Holt.

Garfield, S. L. 1971. Research on client variables in psychotherapy. In *Handbook of psychotherapy and behavior change: An empirical analysis,* ed. A. E. Bergin and S. L. Garfield, pp. 271-89. New York: John Wiley & Sons.

———, and Bergin, A. E. 1971. Therapeutic conditions and outcome. *J. Abnorm. Psychol.* 77:108-14.

Gelder, M. G. 1968. Verbal conditioning as a measure of interpersonal influence in psychiatric interviews. *Brit. J. Soc. Clin. Psychol.* 7:194-209.

Gendlin, E. T. 1962. *Experiencing and the creation of meaning.* New York: Free Press of Glencoe.

Gillin, J. 1948. Magical fright. *Psychiatry* 11:387-400.

Ginsburg, S. W. 1950. Values and the psychiatrist. *Amer. J. Orthopsychiat.* 20:466–78.

Glass, A. J. 1957. Observations upon the epidemiology of mental illness in troops during warfare. In *Symposium on preventive and social psychiatry*, pp. 185–98. Washington, D.C.: Walter Reed Army Institute of Research.

Glasser, W. 1965. *Reality therapy: A new approach to psychiatry.* New York: Harper.

Gliedman, L. H.; Nash, E. H., Jr.; Imber, S. D.; Stone, A. R.; and Frank, J. D. 1958. Reduction of symptoms by pharmacologically inert substances and by short-term psychotherapy. *Arch. Neurol. and Psychiat.* 79:345–51.

Glover, E. 1931. The therapeutic effect of inexact interpretation: a contribution to the theory of suggestion. *Int. J. Psychoanal.* 12:397–411.

———. 1952. Research methods in psychoanalysis. *Int. J. Psychoanal.* 33:403–9.

Goffman, E. 1959. The moral career of the mental patient. *Psychiat.* 22:123–42.

———. 1962. *Asylums: Essays on the social situations of mental patients and other inmates.* Chicago: Aldine. Paperback edition, New York: Doubleday, Anchor Books.

Goldiamond, I., and Dyrud, J. E. 1968. Some applications and implications of behavioral analysis for psychotherapy. In *Research in psychotherapy*, ed. J. M. Schlien, 3:54–89. Washington, D.C.: American Psychol. Assoc.

Goldstein, A. P. 1962. *Therapist-patient expectancies in psychotherapy.* New York: Pergamon Press.

———; Heller, K.; and Sechrest, L. B. 1966. *Psychotherapy and the psychology of behavior change.* New York: Wiley.

Greenblatt, M.; York, R. H.; and Brown, Esther L. 1955. *From custodial to therapeutic patient care in mental hospitals.* New York: Russell Sage Foundation.

Greenspoon, Joel. 1954. The effect of two nonverbal stimuli on the frequency of members of two verbal response classes. *Amer. Psychol.* 9:384.

———. 1955. The reinforcing effect of two spoken sounds on the frequency of two responses. *Amer. J. Psychol.* 68:409–16.

Group for the Advancement of Psychiatry. 1957. *Psychiatric aspects of school desegregation.* Report No. 37. New York: Group for the Advancement of Psychiatry.

———. 1966. *Psychiatric research and the assessment of change.* Report No. 63. New York: Group for the Advancement of Psychiatry.

Gruenberg, E. M. 1967. The social breakdown syndrome—some origins. *Amer. J. Psychiat.* 123:1481–89.

———; Snow, H. B.; and Bennett, C. L. 1969. Preventing the social breakdown syndrome. In *Association for Research in Nervous and Mental Disease, Social psychiatry.* Research Publication, 57:179–95. Baltimore: Williams & Wilkins.

Haggard, E. A.; Brekstad, A.; and Skard, A. G. 1961. On the reliability of the anamestic interview. *J. Abnorm. Soc. Psychol.* 61:311-18.

Haley, J. 1959. Control in psychoanalytic psychotherapy. In *Progress in Psychotherapy*, ed. J. L. Moreno and J. Masserman, 4:48-65. New York: Grune & Stratton.

———. 1963. *Strategies of psychotherapy*. New York: Grune & Stratton.

Halleck, S. L. 1971. *The politics of therapy*. New York: Science House.

Hankoff, L. D.; Freedman, N.; and Engelhardt, D. M. 1958. The prognostic value of placebo response. *Amer. J. Psychiat.* 115:549-50.

Hardy, K. R. 1957. Determinants of conformity and attitude change. *J. Abnorm. Soc. Psychol.* 54:289-94.

Harlow, H. F., and Harlow, M. K. 1965. The affectional systems. In *Behavior of nonhuman primates*, ed. A. M. Schrier, H. F. Harlow, and F. Stollnitz, 2:287-334. New York: Academic Press.

Health resources statistics. 1969. Rockville, Md.: U.S. National Center for Health Statistics.

Heine, R. W. 1953. A comparison of patients' reports on psychotherapeutic experience with psychoanalytic, nondirective and Alderian therapists. *Amer. J. Psychother.* 7:16-23.

———, ed. 1962. *The student physician as psychotherapist*. Chicago: University of Chicago Press.

Helson, H.; Blake, R. R.; Mouton, Jane S.; and Olmstead, J. A. 1956. Attitudes as adjustments to stimulus, background and residual factors. *J. Abnorm. Soc. Psychol.* 52:314-22.

Henry, J. 1954. The formal structure of a psychiatric hospital. *Psychiat.* 17:139-51.

Henry, W. E. 1966. Some observations on the lives of healers. *Human Development* 9:47-56.

———; Sims, J. H.; and Spray, S. L. 1971. *The fifth profession*. San Francisco: Jossey-Bass.

Hildum, D. C., and Brown, R. W. 1956. Verbal reinforcement and interviewer bias. *J. Abnorm. Soc. Psychol.* 53:108-11.

Hinkle, L. E. 1961. Ecological observations of the relation of physical illness, mental illness, and the social environment. *Psychosom. Med.* 23:289-96.

———, and Wolff, H. G. 1956. Communist interrogation and indoctrination of "enemies of the state." *Arch. Neurol. and Psychiat.*, 76:115-74.

Hjelle, L. A., and Clouser, R. 1970. Susceptibility to attitude change as a function of internal-external control. *Psychol. Record.* 20:305-10.

Hoehn-Saric, R.; Frank, J. D.; Imber, S. D.; Nash, E. H., Jr.; Stone, A. R.; and Battle, C. C. 1964. Systematic preparation of patients for psychotherapy: I. Effects on therapy behavior and outcome. *J. Psychiat. Res.* 2:267-81.

———; Frank, J. D.; and Gurland, B. J. 1968. Focused attitude change in neurotic patients. *J. Nerv. Ment. Dis.* 147:124-33.

———; Liberman, B.; Imber, S. D.; Stone, A. R.; Pande, S. K.; and Frank, J. D. 1972. Arousal and attitude change in neurotic patients. *Arch. Gen. Psychiat.* 26:51–56.

Hoffer, E. 1958. *The true believer.* New York: New American Library of World Literature. Paperback edition, New York: Harper and Row.

Hogan, R. A., and Kirchner, J. H. 1967. Preliminary report of the extinction of learned fears via short-term implosion therapy. *J. Abnorm. Psychol.* 72:106–9.

———. 1968. The implosive technique. *Behav. Res. and Therapy* 6:423–32.

Hollingshead, A. B., and Redlich, F. C. 1958. *Social class and mental illness.* New York: John Wiley & Sons. Also published in paperback.

Holt, R. R., and Luborsky, L. 1958. *Personality patterns of psychiatrists,* vol. 1. New York: Basic Books.

Housman, A. E. 1922. *Last poems.* London: Richards Press.

Hovland, C. I.; Janis, I. L.; and Kelley, H. H. 1953. *Communication and persuasion: Psychological studies of opinion change.* New Haven: Yale University Press. Also published in paperback.

Howard, J. 1970. *Please touch: A guided tour of the human potential movement.* New York: McGraw-Hill. Paperback edition, New York: Dell.

Hurvitz, N. 1970. Peer self-help psychotherapy groups and their implications for psychotherapy. *Psychotherapy: Theory, Research and Practice* 7:41–49.

Huxley, A. 1959. *Heaven and hell.* Paperback edition, Baltimore: Penguin Books, 1959.

———. 1962. Words and their meanings. In *The importance of language,* ed. M. Black, pp. 1–12. Englewood Cliffs, N.J.: Prentice-Hall, Spectrum Books.

Huxley, Elspeth. 1959. Science, psychiatry—or witchery? *New York Times Magazine,* May 31, pp. 17–19.

Imber, S. D.; Frank, J. D.; Nash, E. H.; Jr.; Stone, A. R.; Gliedman, L. H. 1957. Improvement and amount of therapeutic contact; an alternative to the use of no-treatment controls in psychotherapy. *J. Consult. Psychol.* 21:309–15.

Imboden, J. B. 1957. Brunswik's theory of perception: A note on its applicability to normal and neurotic personality functioning. *Arch. Neurol. and Psychiat.* 77:187–92.

———; Canter, A.; and Cluff, L. E. 1961. Convalescence from influenza. *Arch. Int. Med.* 103:393–99.

———; Canter, A.; Cluff, L. E.; and Trevor, R. W. 1959. Brucellosis, Ill: psychological aspects of delayed convalescence. *Arch. Int. Med.* 103:406–14.

Inglis, B. 1965. *The case for unorthodox medicine.* New York: G. P. Putnam's Sons.

Jackins, H. 1965. *The human side of human beings.* Seattle: Rational Island Publishers.

Jacob, Ruth H. 1971. Emotive and control groups as mutated new American communities. *J. Appl. Behav. Sc.* 7:234–51.

Jacobson, E. 1957. *You must relax.* 4th ed. New York: McGraw-Hill. Also published in paperback.

Jacobson, G. 1968. The briefest psychiatric encounter. *Arch. Gen. Psychiat.* 18:718–24.

Jahoda, G. 1961. Traditional healers and other institutions concerned with mental illness in Ghana. *Int. J. Soc. Psychiat.* 7:245–68.

James, W. 1936. *The varieties of religious experience.* New York: Modern Library. Paperback edition, New York: Macmillan.

Janet, P. 1925. Miraculous healing. In *Psychological healing*, vol. 1, chap. 1. New York: Macmillan.

Janis, I. 1953–54. Personality correlates of susceptibility to persuasion. *J. Personality* 22:504–18.

———. 1958. *Psychological stress.* New York: John Wiley & Sons.

———, and King, B. T. 1954. The influence of role-playing on opinion change. *J. Abnorm. Soc. Psychol.* 49:211–18.

———, and Field, P. B. 1956. A behavioral assessment of persuasibility: Consistency of individual differences. *Sociometry* 19:241–59.

———, and Mann, L. 1965. Effectiveness of emotional role-playing in modifying smoking habits and attitudes. *J. Exp. Res. Pers.* 1:84–90.

Janov, A. 1970. *The primal scream—primal therapy: The cure for neurosis.* New York: G. P. Putnam's Sons.

Jaspers, K. 1964. *The nature of psychotherapy: A critical appraisal.* Translated by J. Hoenig and M. W. Hamilton. Chicago: University of Chicago Press, Phoenix Books.

Jones, M. 1953. *The therapeutic community.* New York: Basic Books.

Kadushin, C. 1969. *Why people go to psychiatrists.* New York: Atherton.

Kardiner, A.; Linton, R.; DuBois, C.; and West, J. 1945. *The psychological frontiers of society.* New York: Columbia University Press. Also published in paperback.

Kaufman, M. R., and Beaton, L. E. 1947. A psychiatric treatment program in combat. *Bull. Menninger Clinic* 11:1–14.

Kelley, H. H. 1967. Attribution theory in social psychology. In *Nebraska symposium on motivation 1967*, ed. D. Levine, pp. 192–238. Lincoln, Nebraska: University of Nebraska Press.

Kelly, G. A. 1955. *The psychology of personal constructs*, Vol. 2, *Clinical diagnosis and psychotherapy.* New York: W. W. Norton.

Kelman, H. 1969. Kairos: The auspicious moment. *Amer. J. Psychoanal.* 29:59–83.

Kelman, H. C. 1958. Compliance, identification and internalization: Three processes of attitude change. *J. Conflict Resolution* 2:51–60.

Kiesler, D. J. 1971. Experimental design in psychotherapy research. In *Handbook of psychotherapy and behavior change: An empirical analysis*, ed. A. E. Bergin and S. L. Garfield, pp. 36–74. New York: John Wiley & Sons.

Kiev, A., ed. 1964. *Magic, faith and healing.* New York: Macmillan.

King, B. T., and Janis, I. L. 1956. Comparison of the effectiveness of impro-
vised versus non-improvised role-playing in producing opinion changes.
Hum. Relat. 9:177–86.

Kinkead, E. 1959. *In every war but one.* New York: W. W. Norton.

Kirtner, W. L., and Cartwright, D. S. 1958. Success and failure in client-
centered therapy as a function of in-therapy behavior. *J. Consult. Psychol.*
22:329–33.

Klapman, J. W. 1959. *Group psychotherapy: Theory and practice.* New
York: Grune & Stratton.

Klein, M. H.; Dittman, A. T.; Parloff, M. R.; and Gill, M. W. 1969. Behavior
therapy: Observations and reflections. *J. Consult. Clin. Psychol.* 33:259–66.

Kluckhohn, C.; Murray, H. A.; and Schneider, D. M. 1953. *Personality in
nature, society and culture.* New York: Knopf.

Knupfer, Genevieve; Jackson, D. D.; and Kireger, G. 1959. Personality differences between more and less competent psychotherapists as a function of
criteria of competence. *J. Nerv. Ment. Dis.* 129:375–84.

Kora, T. 1965. Morita therapy. *Int. J. Psychiat.* 1:611–40.

Korner, I. N. 1970. Hope as a method of coping. *J. Consult. Clin. Psychol.*
34:134–39.

Kraines, S. H. 1943. *The therapy of neuroses and psychoses.* Philadelphia:
Lea & Febiger.

Krasner, L. 1971. The operant approach in behavior therapy. In *Handbook of
psychotherapy and behavior change: An empirical analysis,* ed. A. E. Bergin and S. L. Garfield, pp. 612–52. New York: John Wiley & Sons.

Krause, M. S. 1966. A cognitive theory of motivation for treatment. *J. Gen.
Psychol.* 75:9–19.

Krippner, S., and Ullman, M. 1970. Telepathy and dreams: A controlled
experiment with electroencephalogram-electro-oculogram monitoring.
J. Nerv. Ment. Dis. 151:394–403.

Kubie, L. 1936. *Practical aspects of psychoanalysis.* New York: W. W. Norton. Paperback edition, New York: International Universities Press.

Kurland, A. A.; Goodman, L. E.; Richards, W. A.; and Pahnke, W. N. 1969.
LSD-assisted psychotherapy with terminal cancer patients. In *Psychedelic
Drugs,* ed. R. E. Hicks and P. J. Fink, pp. 33–42. New York: Grune &
Stratton.

————; Savage, C.; Pahnke, W. N.; Grof, S.; Olsson, J. E. 1971. LSD in the
treatment of alcoholics. *Pharmakopsychiatrie Neuro-Psychopharmakologie*
4:83–94.

LaBarre, W. 1964. Confession as cathartic therapy in American Indian tribes.
In *Magic, faith and healing,* ed. A. Kiev, pp. 36–49. New York: Macmillan.

Laing, R. D. 1967. *The politics of experience.* New York: Pantheon Books.
Paperback edition, New York: Ballantine Books.

Lang, P. J. 1968. Fear reduction and fear behavior: Problems in treating a
construct. In *Research in Psychotherapy,* ed. J. M. Shlien, H. F. Hunt,

J. D. Matarazzo, and C. Savage, 3:90-102. Washington, D.C.: American Psychological Assoc.

———. 1971. The application of psychophysiological methods to the study of psychotherapy and behavior modification. In *Handbook of psychotherapy and behavior change: An empirical analysis*, ed. A. E. Bergin and S. L. Garfield, pp. 75-125. New York: John Wiley & Sons.

Lasagna, L.; Mosteller, F.; von Felsinger, J. M.; and Beecher, H. K. 1954. A study of the placebo response. *Amer. J. Med.* 16:770-79.

Lazarus, A. A. 1968. Behaviour therapy and graded structure. In *The role of learning in psychotherapy*, ed. R. Porter, pp. 134-42. London: J. & A. Church.

Leary, T. F. 1957. *Interpersonal diagnosis of personality*. New York: Ronald Press.

Lederer, W. 1959. Primitive psychotherapy. *Psychiat.* 22:255-63.

Leighton, A. H. 1968. Contribution to the therapeutic process in cross-cultural perspective—a symposium. *Amer. J. Psychiat.* 124:1176-78.

Leitenberg, H.; Agras, W. S.; Barlow, D. H.; and Oliveau, D. C. 1969. Contribution of selective positive reinforcement and therapeutic instructions to systematic desensitization therapy. *J. Abnorm. Psychol.* 74:113-18.

———; Agras, S.; Butz, R.; and Wincze, J. 1971. Relationship between heart rate and behavioral change during the treatment of phobias. *J. Abnorm. Psychol.* 78:59-68.

Lennard, H. L., and Bernstein, A. 1960. *The anatomy of psychotherapy: Systems of communication and expectation*. New York: Columbia University Press.

———, and Bernstein, A. 1967. Role learning in psychotherapy. *Psychotherapy: Theory research and practice* 4:1-6.

Lesse, S. 1958. Psychodynamic relationships between the degree of anxiety and other clinical symptoms. *J. Nerv. Ment. Dis.* 127:125-30.

Lévi-Strauss 1958. *Anthropologie structurale*. Paris: Librairie Plon.

Liberman, R. 1964. An experimental study of the placebo response under three different situations of pain. *J. Psychiat. Res.* 2:233-46.

———. 1971. Behavioural group therapy: A controlled study. *Brit. J. Psychiat.* 119:535-44.

Lifton, R. J. 1956. "Thought reform" of western civilians in Chinese communist prisons. *Psychiat.* 19:173-95.

———. 1957. Thought reform of Chinese intellectuals: A psychiatric evaluation. *J. Soc. Issues* 13:5-20.

———. 1961. *Thought reform and the psychology of totalism: A study of "brainwashing" in China*. New York: W. W. Norton. Also published in paperback.

Linn, L., and Schwarz, L. W. 1958. *Psychiatry and religious experience*. New York: Random House.

Locke, E. A. 1971. Is "behavior therapy" behavioristic? An analysis of Wolpe's psychotherapeutic methods. *Psychol. Bull.* 76:318-27.

London, P. 1964. The modes and morals of psychotherapy. New York: Holt, Rinehart & Winston.

Lorr, M.; McNair, D. M.; and Weinstein, G. H. 1962. Early effects of chlordiazepoxide (librium) used with psychotherapy. *J. Psychiat. Res.* 1:257–70.

_____; McNair, D. M.; Michaux, W. W.; and Raskin, A. 1962. Frequency of treatment and change in psychotherapy. *J. Abnorm. Soc. Psychol.* 64:281–92.

_____, and McNair, D. M. 1964. The interview relationship in therapy. *J. Nerv. Ment. Dis.* 139:328–31.

Low, A. 1950. *Mental health through will-training.* Boston: Christopher Publishing House.

Lowinger, P., and Dobie, S. 1969. What makes the placebo work? A study of placebo response rates. *Arch. Gen. Psychiat.* 20:84–88.

Luborsky, L. 1970. New directions in research on neurotic and psychosomatic symptoms. *Amer. Scientist* 58:661–68.

_____; Auerbach, A. H.; Chandler, M.; Cohen, J.; and Bachrach, H. M. 1971. Factors influencing the outcome of psychotherapy. *Psychol. Bull.* 73:145–85.

Macalpine, Ida. 1950. The development of the transference. *Psychoanal. Quart.* 19:501–39.

McCann, W. H. 1953. The round-table technique in group psychotherapy. *Group Psychother.* 5:233–39.

McClelland, D. C. 1951. *Personality*, pp. 538–42. New York: Henry Holt & Co., Holt-Dryden Book.

Mackay, C. 1962. *Extraordinary popular delusions and the madness of crowds.* Originally pub. in London, 1841. New York: Farrar, Straus & Cudahy.

McNair, D. M.; Callahan, D. M.; and Lorr, M. 1967. Therapist "type" and patient response to psychotherapy. *J. Consult. Psychol.* 26:425–29.

Malan, D. H. 1963. *A study of brief psychotherapy.* Springfield, Mass.: Charles C. Thomas.

Mann, L., and Janis, I. 1968. A follow-up study on the long-term effects of emotional role playing. *J. Person. Soc. Psychol.* 8:339–42.

Marcia, J. E.; Rubin, B. M.; and Efran, J. S. 1969. Systematic desensitization: Expectancy change or counterconditioning. *J. Abnorm. Psychol.* 74:382–95.

Marks, I. M. 1969. *Fear and Phobias*, pp. 203–23. New York: Academic Press.

_____. 1971. Phobic disorders four years after treatment: A prospective follow-up. *Brit. J. Psychiat.* 118:683–88.

_____, and Gelder, M. G. 1967. Transvestism and fetishism: Clinical and psychological changes during faradic aversion. *Brit. J. Psychiat.* 113:711–29.

Marlowe, D. 1962. Need for social approval and the operant conditioning of meaningful verbal behavior. *J. Consult. Psychol.* 26:79–83.

Marmor, J. 1971. Dynamic psychotherapy and behavior therapy—are they irreconcilable? *Arch. Gen. Psychiat.* 24:22–28.

Mason, R. C.; Clark, G.; Reeves, R. B.; and Wagner, B. 1969. Acceptance and healing. *J. Religion and Health* 8:123-30.

Masserman, J. H. 1971. *A psychiatric odyssey*. New York: Science House.

May, P. R. A. 1969. The hospital treatment of the schizophrenic patient. *Int. J. Psychiat.* 8:699-722.

———. 1971. For better or worse? Psychotherapy and variance change: A critical review of the literature. *J. Nerv. Ment. Dis.* 152:184-92.

May, R. 1968. Contribution to the therapeutic process in cross-cultural perspective—a symposium. *Amer. J. Psychiat.* 124:1179-83.

Mayer, M. W. W. 1956. The evaluation of the American soldier in combat. Paper presented to the Conference of Air Science, Maxwell Air Force Base, November 27, 1956 (unpublished).

Medvedev, Z., and Medvedev, R. 1971. *A question of madness*. New York: Knopf.

Meehl, P. 1965. Discussion of Eysenck, The effects of psychotherapy. *Int. J. Psychiat.* 1:156-57.

Melbin, M. 1969. Behavior rhythms in mental hospitals. *Amer. J. Soc.* 74:650-65.

Meltzoff, J., and Kornreich, M. 1970. *Research in psychotherapy*. New York: Atherton Press.

Mendel, W. M. 1964a. The phenomenon of interpretation. *Amer. J. Psychoanal.* 24:184-89.

———. 1964b. Introduction to existential psychiatry. *Psychiat. Dig.* 25:23-34.

Menninger, K. 1958. *Theory of psychoanalytic technique*. New York: Basic Books. Paperback edition, New York: Harper and Row.

Merton, R. K. 1957. *Social theory and social structure*. Glencoe, Ill.: Free Press.

Meyer, V., and Gelder, M. G. 1963. Behaviour therapy and phobic disorders. *Brit. J. Psychiat.* 109:19-28.

Michelson, Elaine. 1964. Volunteer work aids mental patients. *J. Rehabil.* 30:14-16.

Migler, B., and Wolpe, J. 1967. Automated self-desensitization, a case report. *Behav. Res. and Therapy* 5:133-35.

Molling, P. A.; Lochner, A. W.; Sauls, R. J.; and Eisenberg, L. 1962. Committed delinquent boys, the impact of perphenazine and of placebo. *Arch. Gen. Psychiat.* 7:70-76.

Moos, R. H., and MacIntosh, S. C. 1970. Multivariate study of the patient-therapist system: A replication and extension. *J. Consult. Clin. Psychol.* 35:298-307.

Moreno, J. L. 1944. A case of paranoia treated through psychodrama. *Sociometry* 7:312-27.

———. 1971. Psychodrama. In *Comprehensive group psychotherapy*, ed. H. I. Kaplin and B. J. Sadock, pp. 460-500. Baltimore: Williams & Wilkins.

Mouton, Jane S.; Blake, R.; and Olmstead, J. A. 1955-56. The relationship between frequency of yielding and the disclosure of personal identity. *J. Personality* 24:339-47.

Mowrer, O. H. 1966. The behavior therapies with special reference to modelling and imitation. *Amer. J. Psychother.* 20:439-61.

Murray, E. J. 1956. A content-analysis method for studying psychotherapy. *Psychol. Monographs.* 70:420.

———, and Jacobson, L. I. 1971. The nature of learning in traditional and behavioral psychotherapy. In *Handbook of psychotherapy and behavior change: An empirical analysis,* ed. A. E. Bergin and S. L. Garfield, pp. 909-50. New York: John Wiley & Sons.

Nardini, J. E. 1952. Survival factors in American prisoners of war of the Japanese. *Amer. J. Psychiat.* 109:241-47.

Nash, E. H., Jr.; Frank, J. D.; Gliedman, L. H.; Imber, S. D.; and Stone, A. R. 1957. Some factors related to patients' remaining in group psychotherapy. *Int. J. Group Psychother.* 7:264-74.

———; Hoehn-Saric, R.; Battle, C. C.; Stone, A. R.; Imber, S. D.; and Frank, J. D. 1965. Systematic preparation of patients for short-term psychotherapy: II. Relation to characteristics of patient, therapist and the psychotherapeutic process. *J. Nerv. Ment. Dis.* 140:375-83.

Newcomb, T. M. 1947. Autistic hostility and social reality. *Hum. Relat.* 1:69-86.

———. 1963. Persistence and regression of changed attitudes: Long-range studies. *J. Soc. Issues* 19:3-14.

Nunberg, H. 1951. Transference and reality. *Int. J. Psychoanal.* 32:1-9.

Oliveau, D. C.; Agras, W. S.; Leitenberg, H.; Moore, R. C.; and Wright, D. E. 1969. Systematic desensitization, therapeutically oriented instructions and selective positive reinforcement. *Behav. Res. and Therapy* 7:27-33.

Opler, M. E. 1936. Some points of comparison and contrast between the treatment of functional disorders by Apache shamans and modern psychiatric practice. *Amer. J. Psychiat.* 92:1371-87.

Orne, M. T. 1969. Demand characteristics and the concept of quasi-controls. In *Artifacts in behavioral research,* ed. R. Rosenthal and R. L. Rosnow, pp. 143-79. New York: Academic Press.

———. 1970. Hypnosis, motivation, and the ecological validity of the psychological experiment. In *Nebraska Symposium on Motivation,* ed. W. J. Arnold and M. M. Page, pp. 187-265. Lincoln, Nebr.: University of Nebraska Press.

———, and Wender, P. H. 1968. Anticipatory socialization for psychotherapy: Method and rationale. *Amer. J. Psychiat.* 124:1202-11.

Osgood, C. H.; Suci, G. J.; and Tannenbaum, P. H. 1957. *The measurement of meaning.* Urbana, Ill: University of Illinois Press.

Oursler, W. 1957. *The healing power of faith.* New York: Hawthorne Books.

Overall, B., and Aronson, H. 1964. Expectations of psychotherapy in patients of lower socioeconomic class. In *Mental health of the poor: New treat-*

ment approaches for low income people, ed. F. Riessman, J. Cohen, and A. Pearl, pp. 76–87. New York: Free Press of Glencoe.

Overholser, Winfred, and Enneis, J. M. 1959. Twenty years of psychodrama at Saint Elizabeths Hospital. *Group Psychother.* 12:283–92.

Pande, S. K. 1968. The mystique of "Western" psychotherapy: An Eastern interpretation. *J. Nerv. Ment. Dis.* 146:425–32.

———, and Gart, J. J. 1968. A method to quantify reciprocal influence between therapist and patient in psychotherapy. In *Research in psychotherapy*, ed. J. Schlien, H. F. Hunt, J. D. Matarazzo, and C. Savage, 3:395–415. Washington, D.C.: American Psychological Association.

Park, L. C., and Covi, L. 1965. Non-blind placebo trial: An exploration of neurotic patients' responses to placebo when its inert content is disclosed. *Arch. Gen. Psychiat.* 12:336–45.

———, and Imboden, J. B. 1970. Clinical and heuristic value of clinical drug research. *J. Nerv. Ment. Dis.* 151:322–40.

Parloff, M. B. 1956. Some factors affecting the quality of therapeutic relationships. *J. Abnorm. Soc. Psychol.* 52:5–10.

———. 1970. Group therapy and the small group field: An encounter. *Int. J. Group Psychother.* 20:267–304.

———; Kelman, H. C.; and Frank, J. D. 1954. Comfort, effectiveness, and self-awareness as criteria of improvement in psychotherapy. *Amer. J. Psychiat.* 3:343–51.

Parrino, J. J. 1971. Effect of pretherapy information on learning in psychotherapy. *J. Abnorm. Psychol.* 77:17–24.

Pattison, E. M. 1965. Social and psychological aspects of religion in psychotherapy. *J. Nerv. Ment. Dis.* 141:586–97.

Paul, G. L. 1966. *Insight vs. desensitization in psychotherapy.* Stanford, Calif.: Stanford University Press.

———. 1967. Insight vs. desensitization in psychotherapy two years after termination. *J. Consult. Psychol.* 31:333–48.

Pitts, F. N., Jr. 1969. The biochemistry of anxiety. *Sci. American* 220:69–75.

Platonov, K. 1959. *The word as a physiological and therapeutic factor: The theory and practice of psychotherapy according to I. P. Pavlov.* Moscow, U.S.S.R.: Foreign Languages Publishing House.

Potter, H. W.; Klein, H. R.; and Goodenough, D. R. 1957. Problems related to the personal costs of psychiatric and psychoanalytic training. *Amer. J. Psychiat.* 113:1013–19.

Powdermaker, Florence B., and Frank, J. D. 1953. *Group psychotherapy.* Cambridge, Mass.: Harvard University Press.

Prince, R. 1968. Contribution to the therapeutic process in cross-cultural perspective—a symposium. *Amer. J. Psychiat.* 124:1171–76.

Rabiner, E. L.; Reiser, M. F.; Barr, H. L.; and Gralnick, A. 1971. Therapists' attitudes and patients' clinical status. *Arch. Gen. Psychiat.* 25:55–69.

Rachman, S. 1968. The role of muscular relaxation in desensitization therapy. *Behav. Res. and Therapy* 6:159–66.

Rado, S. 1956. *Psychoanalysis of behavior.* New York: Grune & Stratton.

The Random House dictionary of the English language. 1966. New York: Random House.

Rashkis, H. A. 1960. Cognitive restructuring: Why research is therapy. *Arch. Gen. Psychiat.* 2:612-21.

Rasmussen, K. 1929. An Eskimo shaman purifies a sick person. In *Report of the Fifth Thule Expedition (1921-24): Intellectual culture of the Igluik Eskimos,* 7:133-41. Copenhagen: Gyldendalske Boghandel, Nordisk Forlag.

Reed, L. S. 1932. *The healing cults: A study of sectarian medical practice—its extent, causes and control.* Chicago: University of Chicago Press.

Rehder, H. 1955. Wunderheilungen, ein Experiment. *Hippokrates* 26:577-80.

Reid, J. R., and Finesinger, J. E. 1952. The role of insight in psychotherapy. *Amer. J. Psychiat.* 108:726-34.

Reider, N. 1953. A type of transference to institutions. *J. Hillside Hosp.* 2:23-29.

Richter, C. P. 1957. On the phenomenon of sudden death in animals and man. *Psychosom. Med.* 19:191-98.

Rickels, K. 1967. Anti-anxiety drugs in neurotic outpatients. In *Current psychiatric therapies,* ed. J. H. Masserman, 7:121. New York: Grune & Stratton.

——, and Downing, R. W. 1967. Drug- and placebo-treated neurotic outpatients: Pretreatment levels of manifest anxiety, clinical improvement, and side reactions. *Arch. Gen. Psychiat.* 16:369-72.

Rickett, Allyn, and Rickett, Adele. 1957. *Prisoners of liberation.* New York: Cameron Associates.

Riessman, F.; Cohen, J.; and Pearl, A., eds. 1964. *Mental health of the poor: New treatment approaches for low income people.* New York: Free Press of Glencoe.

Rigney, H. W. 1956. *Four years in a red hell.* Chicago: Henry Regnery & Co.

Rioch, M. J. 1967. Pilot projects in training mental health counselors. In *Emergent approaches to mental health problems,* ed. E. L. Cowen, E. A. Gardner, and M. Zax, pp. 110-27. New York: Appleton-Century-Crofts.

Rogers, C. R. 1942. *Counseling and psychotherapy.* New York: Houghton Mifflin.

——. 1951. *Client-centered therapy: Its current practice, implications and theory.* Boston: Houghton Mifflin. Also published in paperback.

——. 1968. Interpersonal relationships: Year 2000. *J. Appl. Behav. Sci.* 4:265-80.

——. 1971. The process of the basic encounter group. In *The proper study of man: Perspectives on the social sciences,* ed. J. Fadiman, pp. 211-27. New York: Macmillan.

——, and Dymond, R., eds. 1954. *Psychotherapy and personality change.* Chicago: University of Chicago Press.

Rogers, J. M. 1960. Operant conditioning in a quasi-therapy setting. *J. Abnorm. Soc. Psychol.* 60:247-52.

Rogers, M.; Lilienfeld, A. M.; and Pasamanick, B. 1955. Prenatal and para-natal factors in the development of childhood behavior disorders. *Acta Psychiatrica & Neurologica*, Supplement No. 102.

Rogow, A. A. 1970. *The psychiatrists*. New York: G. P. Putnam's Sons. Paperback edition, New York: Dell.

Rokeach, M. 1968. *Beliefs, attitudes and values*. San Francisco: Jossey-Bass, Inc.

Rosen, H. 1952. The hypnotic and hypnotherapeutic unmasking intensifica-tion and recognition of an emotion. *Amer. J. Psychiat.* 109:120-27.

Rosen, J. N. 1946. A method of resolving acute catatonic excitement. *Psychiat. Quart.* 20:183-98.

Rosenberg, M. J. 1969. The conditions and consequences of evaluation appre-hension. In *Artifact in behavioral research*, ed. R. Rosenthal and R. L. Rosnow, pp. 280-350. New York: Academic Press.

Rosenthal, D. 1955. Changes in some moral values following psychotherapy. *J. Consult. Psychol.* 19:431-36.

———, and Frank, J. D. 1956. Psychotherapy and the placebo effect. *Psychol. Bull.* 53:294-302.

Rosenthal, R. 1969. Interpersonal expectations: Effects of the experimenter's hypothesis. In *Artifact in behavioral research*, ed. R. Rosenthal and R. L. Rosnow, pp. 181-277. New York: Academic Press.

Rotter, J. B. 1966. Generalized expectancies for internal versus external con-trol of reinforcement. *Psychol. Monographs*, vol. 80, no. 1.

Rubenstein, R., and Lasswell, H. D. 1966. *The sharing of power in a psychi-atric hospital*. New Haven: Yale University Press.

Rubinstein, E. A., and Lorr, M. 1956. A comparison of terminators and remainers in outpatient psychotherapy. *J. Clin. Psychol.* 13:295-98.

Ruesch, J. 1953. Social factors in therapy. In *Association for Research in Nervous and Mental Disease, Psychiatric treatment*. Research publication 31, pp. 59-92. Baltimore: Williams & Wilkins.

Rusk, T. N. 1971. Opportunity and technique in crisis psychiatry. *Compre-hensive Psychiat.* 12:249-63.

Ryan, W. 1966. *Distress in the city: A summary report of the Boston Mental Health Survey*. Jointly published by the Massachusetts Association for Mental Health, Inc., Massachusetts Department of Mental Health, and United Community Services of Metropolitan Boston, Inc.

Sachs. W. 1947. *Black anger*. New York: Grove Press. Also published in paperback.

Salzman, L. 1953. The psychology of religious and ideological conversion. *Psychiatry* 16:177-87.

Sapolsky, A. 1965. Relationship between patient-doctor compatibility, mu-tual perception and outcome of treatment. *J. Abnorm. Psychol.* 70:70-76.

Sarason, I. G. 1958. Inter-relationships among individual difference variables, behavior in psychotherapy, and verbal conditioning. *J. Abnorm. Soc. Psychol.* 56:339-44.

Sarbin, T. R. 1964. Role theoretical interpretation of psychological change. In *Personality change*, ed. P. Worchel and D. Byrne, pp. 176–219. New York: John Wiley & Sons.

Sargant, W. 1957. *Battle for the mind: A physiology of conversion and brainwashing*. Garden City, New York: Doubleday & Co. Paperback ed., New York: Harper and Row.

———. 1968. The physiology of faith. *Brit. J. Psychiat.* 115:505–18.

Satir, Virginia. 1967. *Conjoint family therapy*. Rev. ed. Palo Alto, Calif.: Science and Behavior Books. Also published in paperback.

Sato, Koji. 1958. Psychotherapeutic implications of Zen. *Psychologia* 1:213–18.

Schachter, S. 1959. *The psychology of affiliation: Experimental studies of the sources of gregariousness*. Stanford, Calif.: Stanford University Press.

———. 1965. The interaction of cognitive and physiological determinants of emotional state. In *Psychobiological approaches to social behavior*, ed. P. H. Leiderman and D. Shapiro, pp. 138–73. London: Tavistock Publications.

Scheff, T. J. 1966. *Being mentally ill: A sociological theory*. Chicago: Aldine.

———. 1972. Reevaluation counselling: Social implications. *J. Humanistic Psychol.* 12:58–71.

Schein, E. H. 1956. The Chinese indoctrination program for prisoners of war. *Psychiat.* 19:149–72.

———. 1957. Reaction patterns to severe chronic stress in American Army prisoners of war of the Chinese. *J. Soc. Issues* 13:21–30.

Schmale, A. H. 1958. Relationship of separation and depression to disease. *Psychosomat. Med.* 20:259–77.

Schofield, W. 1964. *Psychotherapy, the purchase of friendship*. Paperback edition, Engelwood Cliffs, N.J.: Prentice-Hall, Spectrum Books.

Schramm, W., and Danielson, W. 1958. Anticipated audiences as determinants of recall. *J. Abnorm. Soc. Psychol.* 56:282–83.

Schultz, J. H., and Luthe, W. 1959. *Autogenic training, a psychophysiologic approach in psychotherapy*. New York: Grune & Stratton.

Schutz, W. C. 1967. *Joy: Expanding human awareness*. New York: Grove Press.

Schwitzgebel, R. K., and Traugott, M. 1968. Initial note on the placebo effect of machines. *Beh. Sci.* 13:267–73.

Scott, J. P. 1962. Critical periods in behavioral development. *Science* 138:949–57.

Sears, R. R. 1950. Ordinal position in the family as a psychological variable. *Amer. Soc. Rev.* 15:397–401.

Segal, B. 1970. A-B distinction and therapeutic interaction. *J. Consult. Clin. Psychol.* 34:442–46.

Segal, J. 1957. Correlates of collaboration and resistance behavior among U.S. Army POW's in Korea. *J. Soc. Issues* 13:31–40.

Sethna, E. R., and Harrington, J. A. 1971. A study of patients who lapsed from group psychotherapy. *Brit. J. Psychiat.* 119:59–69.

Shapiro, A. K. 1959. The placebo effect in the history of medical treatment:

Implications for psychiatry. *Amer. J. Psychiat.* 116:298-304.

Sherif, M., and Harvey, O. J. 1952. A study in ego functioning: Elimination of stable anchorages in individual and group situations. *Sociometry* 15:272-305.

Sherman, A. R. 1969. Therapeutic factors in the behavioral treatment of anxiety. Doctoral thesis, Yale University.

Sherman, R. W., and Hildreth, A. M. 1970. A resident group process training seminar. *Amer. J. Psychiat.* 127:372-75.

Shlien, J. M.; Mosak, H. H.; and Dreikurs, R. 1962. Effect of time limits: A comparison of two psychotherapies. *J. Couns. Psychol.* 31:24.

Sifneos, P. E. 1972. *Short-term psychotherapy and emotional crisis.* Cambridge, Mass.: Harvard University Press.

Simon, R. 1971. The paraprofessionals are coming! The paraprofessionals are coming! *Clin. Psychologist* 3:3-6.

Singer, Margaret, and Schein, E. H. 1958. Projective test responses of prisoners of war following repatriation. *Psychiat.* 21:375-85.

Skinner, B. F. 1953. *Science and human behavior.* New York: Macmillan Co. Paperback edition, New York: Free Press, 1965.

Sloane, R. B.; Cristol, A. H.; Pepernik, M. C.; and Staples, F. R. 1970. Role preparation and expectation of improvement in psychotherapy. *J. Nerv. Ment. Dis.* 150:18-26.

Sohl, J. 1967. *The lemon eaters.* New York: Simon & Schuster.

Speck, R. V., and Rueveni, U. 1969. Network therapy—a developing concept. *Family Process* 8:182.

Spiegel, H., and Linn, L. 1969. The "ripple effect" following adjunct hypnosis in analytic psychotherapy. *Amer. J. Psychiat.* 126:53-58.

Spiro, M. G. 1967. *Burmese supernaturalism: A study in the explanation and reduction of suffering.* Englewood Cliffs, N. J.: Prentice-Hall.

Spitz, R. 1954. Unhappy and fatal outcomes of emotional deprivation and stress in infancy. In *Beyond the germ theory*, ed. I. Galdston, chap. 8. New York: New York Academy of Sciences, Health Education Council.

Stanton, A. H., and Schwartz, M. 1954. *The mental hospital.* New York: Basic Books.

Steiner, L. 1945. *Where do people take their troubles?* New York: International Universities Press.

Stoller, F. H. 1968. Marathon group therapy. In *Innovations to group psychotherapy*, ed. G. M. Gazda, pp. 42-95. Springfield, Ill.: Charles C. Thomas.

Stone, A. R.; Imber, S. D.; and Frank, J. D. 1966. The role of nonspecific factors in short-term psychotherapy. *Austral. J. Psychol.* 18:210-17.

Storms, M. D., and Nisbett, R. E. 1970. Insomnia and the attribution process. *J. Person. Soc. Psychol.* 16:319-28.

Stotland, E. 1969. *The psychology of hope.* San Francisco: Jossey-Bass.

Strassman, H. D.; Thaler, M. B.; and Schein, E. H. 1956. A prisoner of war syndrome: Apathy as a reaction to severe stress. *Amer. J. Psychiat.* 112: 998-1003.

Strupp, H. H. 1958. The psychotherapists' contribution to the treatment process. *Beh. Sci.* 3:34-67.

_____. 1970. Specific vs. non-specific factors in psychotherapy and the problem of control. *Arch. Gen. Psychiat.* 23:393–401.

_____. 1972. On the technology of psychotherapy. *Arch. Gen. Psychiat.* 26:270–78.

_____; Fox, R. E.; and Lessler, K. 1969. *Patients view their psychotherapy.* Baltimore: Johns Hopkins Press.

_____; Wallach, M. S.; Wogan, M.; and Jenkins, J. W. 1963. Psychotherapists' assessments of former patients. *J. Nerv. Ment. Dis.* 137:222–30.

Stunkard, A. 1951. Some interpersonal aspects of an Oriental religion. *Psychiat.* 14:419–31.

_____. 1961. Motivation for treatment: Antecedents of the therapeutic process in different cultural settings. *Comprehen. Psychiat.* 2:140–48.

Sullivan, H. S. 1953. *The interpersonal theory of psychiatry.* New York: W. W. Norton. Also published in paperback.

Szasz, T. S. 1963. *Law, liberty, and psychiatry: An inquiry into the social uses of mental health practices.* New York: Macmillan. Also published in paperback.

Taffel, C. 1955. Anxiety and the conditioning of verbal behavior. *J. Abnorm. Soc. Psychol.* 51:496–501.

Thelen, M. H. 1969. Repression-sensitization: Its relation to adjustment and seeking therapy among college students. *J. Consult. Clin. Psychol.* 33:161–65.

Thompson, Clara. 1950. *Psychoanalysis: Evolution and development.* New York: Hermitage House.

Thurber, J. 1939. *Fables for our time.* New York: Harpers.

Torrey, E. F. 1972. *The mind game: Witchdoctors and psychiatrists.* New York: Emerson Hall.

Truax, C. B.; Wargo, D. G.; Frank, J. D.; Imber, S. D.; Battle, C. C.; Hoehn-Saric, R.; Nash, E. H.; and Stone, A. R. 1966. Therapist empathy, genuineness and warmth and patient therapeutic outcome. *J. Consult. Psychol.* 30:395–401.

_____, and Carkhuff, R. R. 1967. *Toward effective counseling and psychotherapy: Training and practice.* Chicago: Aldine.

Tyhurst, J. S. 1957. The role of transition states—including disasters—in mental illness. In *Symposium on preventive and social psychiatry,* pp. 149–72. Washington, D.C.: Walter Reed Army Institute of Research.

Uhlenhuth, E. H.; Canter, A.; Neustadt, J. O.; and Payson, H. E. 1959. The symptomatic relief of anxiety with meprobamate, phenobarbitol and placebo. *Amer. J. Psychiat.* 115:905–10.

_____, and Duncan, D. B. 1968a. Subjective change with medical student therapists: Course of relief in psychoneurotic outpatients. *Arch. Gen. Psychiat.* 18:428–38.

_____, and _____. 1968b. Subjective change with medical student therapists: II. Some determinants of change in psychoneurotic outpatients. *Arch. Gen. Psychiat.* 18:532–40.

Ullman, M., and Krippner, S. 1970. An experimental approach to dreams and telepathy: II. Report of three studies. *Amer. J. Psychiat.* 126:1282–89.

Valins, S., and Nisbett, R. E. 1971. *Attribution process in the development and treatment of emotional disorders.* New York: General Learning Corporation.

Volgyesi, F. A. 1954. "School for patients" hypnosis-therapy and psychoprophylaxis. *Brit. J. Med. Hypno.* 5:8–17.

Warner, W. L. 1941. *A black civilization: A social study of an Australian tribe.* New York: Harpers.

Watson, J. P.; Gaind, R.; and Marks, I. M. 1971. Prolonged exposure: A rapid treatment for phobias. *Brit. Med. J.* 1:13–15.

Watts, W. 1967. Relative persistence of opinion change induced by active compared to passive participation. *J. Person. Soc. Psychol.* 5:4–15.

Weatherhead, L. D. 1951. *Psychology, religion and healing.* New York: Abingdon-Cokesbury Press.

Webster, H. 1942. *Taboo, a sociological study.* Stanford, Calif.: Stanford University Press.

Wechsler, H. 1960. The self-help organization in the mental health field: Recovery, Inc., a case study. *J. Nerv. Ment. Dis.* 130:297–314.

Weininger, B. 1955. The interpersonal factor in the religious experience. *Psychoanal.* 3:27–44.

Weinstein, W. K., and Lawson, R. 1963. The effect of experimentally induced "awareness" upon performance in free-operant verbal conditioning and on subsequent tests of "awareness." *J. Psychol.* 56:203–11.

Weiss, R. L.; Krasner, L.; and Ulman, L. P. 1960. Responsivity to verbal conditioning as a function of emotional atmosphere and patterns of reinforcement. *Psychol. Rep.* 6:415–26.

Weitzman, B. 1967. Behavior therapy and psychotherapy. *Psychol. Rev.* 74:300–317.

Welkowitz, J.; Cohen, J.; and Ortmeyer, D. 1967. Value system similarity: Investigation of patient-therapist dyads. *J. Consult. Psychol.* 31:48–55.

Wender, L., and Stein, A. 1953. Utilization of group psychotherapy in the social integration of patients: An extension of the method to self-governing patient groups. *Int. J. Group Psychother.* 3:210–18.

Wheelis, A. 1958. *The quest for identity.* New York: W. W. Norton. Also published in paperback.

Whitaker, D. S., and Lieberman, M. A. 1964. *Psychotherapy through the group process.* New York: Atherton Press (Prentice-Hall).

Whitehead, A. N. 1925. *Science and the modern world.* New York: Macmillan. Paperback edition, New York: Free Press.

Whitehorn, J. C. 1947. The concepts of "meaning" and "cause" in psychodynamics. *Amer. J. Psychiat.* 104:289–92.

———. 1959. Goals of psychotherapy. In *Research in Psychotherapy*, ed. E. A. Rubinstein and M. B. Parloff, pp. 1–9. Washington, D.C.: American Psychological Association.

————, and Betz, B. J. 1954. A study of psychotherapeutic relationships between physicians and schizophrenic patients. *Amer. J. Psychiat.* 111: 321–31.

————, and————. 1960. Further studies of the doctor as a crucial variable in the outcome of treatment with schizophrenic patients. *Amer. J. Psychiat.* 117:215–23.

Whitman, R. M.; Kramer, M.; and Baldridge, B. 1963. Which dream does the patient tell? *Arch. Gen. Psychiat.* 8:277–82.

Wilkins, W. 1971. Desensitization: Social and cognitive factors underlying the effectiveness of Wolpe's procedure. *Psychol. Bull.* 76:311–17.

Will, O. A. 1959. Human relatedness and the schizophrenic reaction. *Psychiat.* 22:205–23.

Wilmer, H. 1958. *Social psychiatry in action: A therapeutic community.* Springfield, Ill.: C. C. Thomas.

————. 1962. Transference to a medical center. *California Med.* 96:173–80.

Winick, C., and Holt, H. 1962. Differential recall of the dream as a function of audience perception. *Psychoanal. and Psychoanal. Rev.* 49:53–62.

Winokur, G. 1955. "Brainwashing"—a social phenomenon of our time. *Hum. Organiz.* 13:16–18.

Wolberg, L. R. 1967. *The technique of psychotherapy.* 2d ed. New York: Grune & Stratton.

Wolf, S. 1950. Effects of suggestion and conditioning on the action of chemical agents in human subjects—the pharmacology of placebos. *J. Clin. Invest.* 29:100–109.

————, and Pinsky, R. H. 1954. Effects of placebo administration and occurrence of toxic reactions. *J. Amer. Med. Assoc.* 155:339–41.

Wolff, W. 1954. Fact and value in psychotherapy. *Amer. J. Psychother.* 8: 466–86.

Wolpe, J., and Lazarus, A. A. 1966. *Behavior therapy techniques: A guide to the treatment of neuroses.* New York: Pergamon Press.

Wyatt, F. 1956. Climate of opinion and methods of readjustment. *Amer. Psychologist* 11:537–42.

Wyler, A. R.; Masuda, M.; and Holmes, T. H. 1971. Magnitude of life events and seriousness of illness. *Psychosom. Med.* 33:115–22.

Yalom, I. D. 1970. *The theory and practice of group psychotherapy.* New York: Basic Books.

————; Houts, P. S.; Newell, G.; and Rand, K. H. 1967. Preparation of patients for group therapy. *Arch. Gen. Psychiat.* 17:416–27.

————, and Lieberman, M. A. 1971. A study of encounter group casualties. *Arch. Gen. Psychiat.* 25:16–30.

Yamamoto, J., and Goin, M. K. 1965. On the treatment of the poor. *Amer. J. Psychiat.* 122:267–71.

Zilboorg, G. 1941. *A history of medical psychology.* New York: W. W. Norton. Also published in paperback.

INDEX

Thorndike, E. L., 5

Thought reform: and changes in attitudes, 86; and emotional arousal, 92–94; and evocative therapies, 219; goals of, 78–79; interrogation in, 89–91; physical maltreatment in, 92; and prisoners of war, 90–103; and psychoanalytic training, 171; and psychotherapy, 86–88, 103–5, 221–22; and religious conversion, 100

Thurber, James, 266

Tou-cheng, 96–97

Tranquilizers, 144–45

Transference: defined, 44, 174, 279–80; in directive therapy, 237; example of, 272–74; and interpretations, 223, 226; in thought reform, 90

Treatment. *See* Psychotherapy

T-scope therapy, 247

Ulcers, peptic, 140, 158–59

Value judgments. *See* Therapists, values of

Vocational counselors, 16

Voodoo, 82, 84–85

Watson, J. B., 5

"Weltschmerz," 317

Wesley, John, 82–83

Whitehead, Alfred North, 265

Witchcraft. *See* Supernatural forces

Witch doctor. *See* Shaman

Withdrawal, 47, 53

World pain, 317

World view: and American society, 321–22; and collaboration, 88–89; and healing rituals, 56; and Lourdes, 67; and mental illness, 11; of pre-literate societies, 179; and proselytizers, 89; and psychotherapy, 105, 324; and religious healing, 67; similarity of, of patient and therapist, 320–21, 327–28; and thought reform, 86, 91, 94, 100–101, 103; of Wesley, 83. *See also* Assumptive systems; Assumptive world; Conceptual scheme

Zen Buddhism, 81, 99n, 251

Zuni of New Mexico, 88–89

Library of Congress Cataloging in Publication Data

Frank, Jerome David, 1909–
Persuasion and healing.

Bibliography: p.
1. Psychotherapy. I. Title.
RC480.F67 1973   616.8'914   72-4015
ISBN 0-8018-1443-X